2

WAITING FOR THE MAN

BY HARRY SHAPIRO

Harry Shapiro has worked in the drugs field for twenty years. His previous books include *Jimi Hendrix: Electric Gypsy*; *Eric Clapton: Lost in the Blues*; *Graham Bond: the Mighty Shadow* and *Alexis Korner: the biography*

This edition published in 1999 by Helter Skelter Publishing
4 Denmark Street, London WC2H 8LL

Copyright 1999 © Harry Shapiro

First published 1988 by Quartet Books Ltd.

All rights reserved. International copyright secured. Reprinted by permission.

Cover design by SAF Publishing Typesetting by Caroline Walker
Printed in Great Britain by Redwood Books, Trowbridge

A CIP record for this book is available from the British Library

ISBN 1-900924-08-0

Harry Shapiro

WAITING FOR THE MAN

THE STORY OF DRUGS AND POPULAR MUSIC

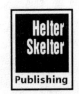

Helter Skelter Publishing, London

THIS BOOK IS DEDICATED TO MY FAMILY, SOURCE OF ALL THE INNER
QUIETNESS AND RAGING FIRES.

Contents

PREFACE TO THE NEW EDITION

When this book was first written between 1985-87, both Britain and America were in the grip of fervent anti-drug rhetoric. Nancy Reagan's 'Just Say No' message still held the public imagination while in Britain a new wave of heroin use sparked off our first government anti-drug campaigns under the slogan 'Heroin Screws You Up'.

From the point of view of the history of drugs and popular music, the book was itself almost a historical piece. Punk was finished and most of what passed for mainstream music in the mid-eighties is best forgotten. There were no new high profile heroes, no vibrantly new trends and no new casualties for the media to drool over. Meanwhile the old heroes were cleaning up their act in a serious way and telling everybody about it. Pete Townshend in particular with his Double O charity was at the forefront of anti-drug campaigns. What happened during the first part of the 1980s is covered in the introduction to a new Part Three.

However, while there was plenty of gung-ho anti-heroin sentiment, there was also more than a sneaking suspicion that no such similar antipathy existed within the music business towards the old Bolivian marching powder. And indeed, as it turned out, if the 1980s was the time of the post-heroin angst, in the 1990s, the great and the greedy 'fessed up to coke habits of cosmic proportions. As Chris Maund of *Melody Maker* noted, 'If most of those groups at Live Aid had donated their cocaine bills for the year, it would have saved as many lives'. Confirmation came straight out of the horse's nose; Francis Rossi told *Q Magazine* of Status Quo at Live Aid in 1985,

'We were the first band on and we were already high as kites by midday. After we finished we spent most of the time doing loads of cocaine in the toilets. We didn't spend much time thinking about the starving in Ethiopia.'

Back out in the real world, while Britain was coming to terms with smokable heroin, the streets of America were blighted by a cocaine habit of a very different stripe. This was crack and it coincided with a new form of urban black music, rap, many of whose artists were both participants in the drug scene and chroniclers of the damage it caused.

The predicted crack epidemic never hit Britain, although the drug has caused enough problems on the streets of some of our major cities. Instead, we pioneered our own drug/music revolution – ecstasy, the dance culture and the indie band scene. Enter the Happy Mondays, Stone Roses and Oasis – the 24 hour party people.

And over in the chill-out area, ever present and reshaped for the nineties – the all purpose weed. The issue of cannabis law reform is now being hotly debated. Many American musicians such as the Black Crowes and a host of rap artists all support the call for legalisation. In Britain, both Sting and Noel Gallagher have been quoted as being in favour of law reform.

It is unlikely that any of the current debate about drugs would have been taking place without the astonishing growth of drug use among young people across Europe which has occured against the marching 4/4 beat of dance music. Unfortunately, with the rise in drug use has come the inevitable casualties and fatalities. Over seventy young people have died in the UK in ecstasy-related incidents – and we have also seen the return of the wasted rock star. Some like David Gahan of Depeche Mode and Shaun Ryder have survived, others like Kurt Cobain and Michael Hutchence did not. Although neither died from drug overdoses, during their lives, they both dealt with their pain and frustrations in a mode all too common in the music business.

Except for purposes of comparison, this book excludes any detailed consideration of alcohol. This is not to suggest that alcohol is not a drug; whatever other drugs have been in fashion among musicians, alcohol has never been out of favour. In health terms, it has caused more problems than all the other drugs put together and claimed lives across the spectrum of popular music from Bix Beiderbecke to John Bonham. However, alcohol is an accepted legal drug in Western society. Its use is not surrounded by the excitement, fear and ignorance which attends the use of other drugs like heroin, cocaine and marijuana – a phenomenon central to the narrative which follows.

For this very reason, there are some people whose valuable assistance I have promised not to acknowledge publicly. Instead I nod gratefully but silently in their direction. Reticence to openly discuss drugs and the music business was not surprising in the mid eighties, but in some quarters still exists today.

I can, however, restate my thanks to: Roy Carr, Andy Cornwell, Paul Du Noyer, Pete Frame, John Gribbens, John Glover, Lee Harris, Dick Heckstall-Smith, Graham Langley, Ken Leech, Tony Levene, Dennis Muirhead, Paul Oliver, John Platt, John Tobler and Andrew Tyler. Thanks also to Al Bloomfield, Buddy Arnold of the Musicians' Assistance Program in Los Angeles, Steve Abrams and Sean Body of Helter Skelter.

I owe a debt to the staff of *Billboard* and *Variety* magazines for allowing me access to back copies and to take up office space looking through them all; the National Sound Archive; Officers of the District Court of Macon, Georgia; the Middle Georgia Regional Library, and the library of the University of Pennsylvania.

Extract from *On the Road* (Andre Deutsch, US edition, 1980) reproduced by kind permission of the publisher; extract from *High Times* interview with Peter Tosh (November 1981) reproduced by kind permission of the Trans High Corporation, 211 East 43rd Stn NY 10017. Lyrics of 'Tea for Two' (Caesar/ Youmans) reproduced by kind permission of Chappel Music Ltd. 129 Park St, London WAY 3FA; of 'Wacky Dust' (Adams/Levant 1938) reproduced by kind permission of SBK United Partnership, 3-5 Rathbone Place, London W1P IDA; of 'Reefer Man' (by 1932) and 'Light Up' (by 1938) reproduced by kind permission of J.R. Lafleur and Son Ltd. 295 Regent St, London W1A 1BR; of 'Cocaine Habit Blues' (id) 1930) and 'Pipe Dream Blues' (© 1924) reproduced by kind permission of Southern Music, 8 Denmark St, London WC2 8LT; and of 'Minnie the Moocher' (Calloway/Mills) reproduced by kind permission of EMI Publishing Ltd. 138-40 Charing Cross Rd. London WC2H OLD. Attempts to contact copyright holders of some other lyrics reproduced have not proved successful at the time of going to press; the author apologises for any resultant inadvertent breach of copyright.

INTRODUCTION

Society has undergone the most remarkable changes since the turn of the century. Projected into the future, an inhabitant of the 1920s would find the late 1990s a strange, fantasy world straight from the science-fiction pulps. He would feel more at home, however, if he read the current media coverage of the drugs scene. Here he would find the same words and images with which William Randolph Hearst, role model for Rupert Murdoch, filled his dailies: dark enticing tales of dope pedlars, playground pushers, opium dens and teeny addicts.

Serious discussion has been allowed on most social and political issues of today – gay rights, censorship, abortion, racial discrimination and the position of women in society. But although high on the political agenda for action, actual discussion of the drugs issue remains at the level of base propaganda. Any attempt at raising the level of debate is swamped by allegations of being 'soft on drugs' or condoning their use. The press retains an invidious grip on providing drug 'information' for public consumption.

Since the enactment of the Harrison Narcotics Act in 1914, America has led the way in the global war against drugs. Under American instigation, international treaties have theoretically obliged nations to combat drug use in their own countries and American-influenced international agencies have been at work in third-world producer countries, attempting to channel agricultural activities away from the production of opium, marijuana and cocaine. America has also used its economic and political influence abroad to coerce producer nations and often accuses those hostile to American influence of being centres or transit points for illegal drugs.

Since the mid-1980s, a new tactic in the war has been to seize the money and property of convicted drug smugglers. Given the extent to which drug money passes through the world's legitimate banking systems, much depends on the extent to which the time-honoured secrecy of these systems can be overcome. However, taken together with the breaking of insider-dealing rackets, enforcement agencies are making previously unheard-of inroads into the heartlands of international finance.

These global efforts have been stepped up dramatically since the early sixties when drugs 'came out of the ghetto', and frightened WASP America to its foundations. In practice, these 'wars' have amounted to just yet another reorganisation of the drug enforcement agencies and further millions being thrown at the problem.

The statistics of today's drug scene are both mind-boggling and meaningless. Nobody knows how many people use any particular drug, what the illicit drug market is worth or how much of it is seized by police and customs. Millions of dollars of government money chase a business worth billions, which supplies the drug demands of yet more unquantified millions. In magic there is an ancient saying that 'to know a devil's real name is to be its master', so too with drug statistics: a belief exists that quantification – however inaccurate – puts you on the road to taming the beast.

One small story from the recent past illustrates the scale of the illicit drug market. In 1985, a trafficker was sentenced to fifty years' imprisonment in Florida. In six years of dealing, he had sold 1.5 million pounds of Colombian marijuana, amassing in the process a personal fortune of $750 million. The problem was that he could not find a bank that could 'launder' such a huge amount – so he bought one.[1] His was one case among thousands going through the American courts every day.

Widespread public concern about drugs in Britain was also born in the sixties. Then as now, heroin, the staple drug of all drug scares, was the focus of attention. In fact, in contrast to marijuana and amphetamine users, this sector of the illegal drug-using population numbered only a few hundred in the London area. There was virtually no black market in imported heroin; most of the heroin sold on the streets came from a handful of doctors, some greedy, some misguided, who over-prescribed. Policies devised to head off the development of a black market in imported heroin failed and in the eighties, with addict figures at record highs, media and government attention reached unprecedented levels. In 1985, a drugs advisory service in Liverpool reported that during the first few months of its operation, for every call received from a drug user three came from journalists. Earlier in the year, a delegation of British politicians from the Home Affairs Committee was shown around New York as part of a fact-finding mission on drug problems. Haunted by the spectre of Christmas to Come, they returned home to recommend using the army and navy in Britain's own war against drugs.

When sending in the gunboats was an integral part of British foreign policy in Victorian times, the drug scene here and in the States was very different; large sectors of the population consumed opiate drugs, cocaine and marijuana provided by a patent-medicine industry run by a handful of men who became exceedingly rich. And it was all legitimate. Drugs now feared and reviled were then standard entries in the medical pharmacopoeias, and far from using military might to keep drugs out of Britain, the Navy protected British exports of opium to China. We were the first international drug traffickers, fighting not only against the Chinese to protect our market, but against increasing pressure from the international community to end the trade.

Civil actions against tobacco companies and the increasing moves against smoking in public places and offices albeit only in the West, indicate that the tobacco multinationals are no longer having it all their own way. Even so, the attitude of most governments to alcohol and tobacco is both contradictory and ironic. Huge revenues accrue from the tax on products that unequivocally cause thousands of premature deaths every year. Willing to attribute devastating side-effects to some drugs on the flimsiest of evidence (e.g. the chromosome damage attributed to LSD), governments fudge the effects of cigarettes with 'warnings' on labels, while no warning at all appears on a bottle of whisky. Such is the power of the alcohol and tobacco lobbies. Replicated the world over, these contradictions demonstrate that the formulation of drug policies has very little to do with the pharmacological reality of the substances under review.

In their book *Drug Control in a Free Society*, James Bakalar and Lester Grinspoon state:

Looked at as a series of incidents, the history of the social and legal responses to drug use, especially in the last century and in the United States, sometimes seems melancholy and haphazard. It is easy to find inadequate pharmacology, inconsistent *ad hoc* responses based on poor information, indulgence of passions and prejudices, including racism, in response to drug scares, institutional self-aggrandisement by narcotics police and a fair amount of hypocrisy and corruption.[2]

The social history of drugs is replete with examples of the importance of symbolism. In other words the effects of any drug have always been overshadowed by who is using it and for what purposes. Some users and purposes are socially and morally acceptable, others are not, and laws are enacted to set the parameters, to determine social deviancy, to establish what is beyond the pale. This is important for the history of drugs and music, because by very dint of their occupation musicians have often been regarded as 'beyond the pale', associating with other fringe elements such as prostitutes and criminals, in areas of predominantly immigrant or ethnic minority population. With little political status or influence, groups within this sector have tended to suffer most from the implementation of laws against drugs that were previously in legitimate use.

As each new drug has been introduced, it has passed through various status positions dictated by political, moral and economic expediency. Celebration is the first stage. From England to China, tobacco was heralded as a cure for everything from headache to malaria, cholera, venereal disease and worms. Approbation followed as the upper classes and the clergy began to use it recreationally although the problems of dependence became apparent. Inevitably, use of tobacco began to percolate through society and the authorities became anxious that it was diverting the working man away from his labours and damaging his capacities as a unit of production. In addition, it was considered that relaxing with a pipe or a cup of coffee or even a drink was tantamount to plotting against the State. Pubs and coffee houses were branded as 'dens of iniquity'. The banning of youngsters from pubs was originally to protect them against the corrupting influence of political intrigue not against the evils of drinking. James I's *Counterblaste to Tobacco* (1604) was a blueprint for future attitudes regarding recreational drug use by the working class whereby certain drugs became vilified and/or legislated against:

> Whereas tobacco ... was used and taken by the better sort, both then and now only as physic to preserve health, it is now at this day through evil custom and the toleration thereof, excessively taken by a number of riotous and disordered persons of mean and base condition who contrary to the use which persons of good calling and quality make thereof, do spend most of their time in that idle vanity to the evil example and corrupting of others... by which great and immoderate taking of tobacco, the health of a great number of people is impaired and their bodies weakened and made unfit for labour.

The oldest documented drug is alcohol, so that by the sixteenth and seventeenth centuries, when the first attempts were made around Europe and the Middle East to curb smoking and coffee drinking, alcohol was firmly established as an acceptable recreational diversion. What laws existed were against drunkenness rather than drinking itself. Would-be smokers and coffee drinkers, however, were subject to the most vicious punishments. In Turkey, a sly puff was likely to result in your having a pipe shoved through your nose and a free ride backwards round town on a donkey. Amurath the Cruel, the aptly named Sultan of Turkey from 1623-40, later decided that the pipe through the nose was being 'soft on drugs'. He had a neat line in entrapment: tracking down a tobacco dealer, the Sultan, in disguise, offered him a huge sum of money and total secrecy if he sold him a pound of tobacco. The hapless dealer produced the goods, whereupon Amurath produced a scimitar and sliced his head off. Elsewhere, limb crushing, beheading and quartering were decreed. Selling tobacco in seventeenth-century Russia earned you the right to be flogged to death. Smoking in China was deemed to be 'against the national interest', and heads rolled. Even as late as 1832, smoking in public in the streets of Prussia was regarded as a demonstration against the government.

Despite such horrific retribution successive rulers discovered that they could not stop people enjoying themselves so they decided that instead of making people pay with their lives, they should pay with their money. So drugs such as tobacco and coffee moved into the assimilation phase, as the revenues derived from each became vital to royal coffers everywhere. Attempts at prohibiting alcohol, especially in America, continued into this century, but the era of Prohibition demonstrated the impossibility of a nationwide ban on a drug that had earned such universal acceptability.

The period 1820-1920 saw opium, its derivatives morphine and heroin, and cocaine and marijuana pass through the integration pattern to vilification and legislation, where they remain over sixty years later. Those with a libertarian view on drugs can draw little comfort from the response of governments since the days of 'flower power'. The political and economic interdependence of nations, modern communications systems and sophisticated intelligence networks bind Marshall McLuhan's 'Global Village' tighter than ever. The political and social tensions of many Western nations, caused by urban decay and unemployment, are kept in check by law-and-order administrations steeped in the rhetoric of a non-existent golden age – even if in the UK, the below stairs Nanny of Conservative Party 'Victorian Values' has now been allowed free run of the house.

There seems little evidence that the policies of the 'caring' nineties, has done much to improve the lot of people over the 'get-stuffed' eighties. However, regarding drug policy and after a decade of ecstasy, there appears to be a new mood of pragmatism across the governments of Europe. While every administration remains implacably committed to reducing the levels of drug use and refuses to contemplate radical changes in the law, nevertheless, the battle armour of drug war rhetoric is showing some chinks. Not only Holland, but Italy, Spain and part of Germany have relaxed some controls on personal use. France has become more open to the idea of methadone treatment for addiction and there is even ministerial support for medical use of cannabis. The United Kingdom is more cautious, but has been prepared to adopt harm reduction measures in relation to drug use by young people and now eschews the crassness of the Just Say No approach albeit only because it doesn't work.

However none of this counts for much at an international level where the American-dominated agencies such as the United Nations and World Health Organisation refuse to countenance anything other than the *status quo*. A recent WHO research report on cannabis omitted one paper which concluded that for the most part cannabis was no worse for health than tobacco or alcohol.

But if modern technology, especially the Internet, has finally realised the Global Village, then no less has the international drug scene become all of a piece. Traditionally, the producer countries, often located in the developing world, have been accused by the West, especially America, of not doing enough to stem the tide of heroin, cocaine and cannabis. The West, in turn, is accused of not doing enough to reduce demand for these drugs. Yet today, Pakistan has more heroin addicts per head of population than anywhere else in the world while Indonesia, Thailand and China are awash with ecstasy produced locally by European chemists and the smoking of methamphetamine is common right around the Pacific rim. Even so, the United Nations persists in political grandstanding over drugs which in 1998, saw a declared intent to eradicate coca and opium growing by 2008. The chance of such a policy succeeding was comprehensively debunked by the Catholic Instititute of International Relations in a paper which pointed out the futility of crop eradication and substitution schemes and other measures in desperately poor economies where the governments rarely control the whole country and which would collapse entirely without the revenues from the illicit trade.[3]

* * * * *

In the northwestern state of Sinaloa, the centre of Mexican drug trafficking, there has been a craze for narcoballads or *narcocorridos,* gangsta rap style songs with a polka beat written in praise of the heroic exploits of the drug smugglers like Baltazar Diaz, Lamberto Quintero and 'El Borrego' who consistently outwitted the Gringo and the Mexican police until dying in the inevitable hail of bullets from the guns of rival *narcotraficantes.* At least five different bands have recorded *corridos* about Amado Fuentes, the Lord of the Skies who died during a plastic surgery operation. Young people from the capital city Culiacan have adopted narcofashion – cowboy garb, gold chains, ostrich skin boots, silk shirts and suits with snakeskin lapels dubbed 'Chalinazo' style after Chalino Sanchez, the Tupac Shakur of *narcocorridos* who was mysteriously murdered after a concert in Culiacan in 1992.

Where the government totally lacks credibility and cannot provide schools, medicines and other basic essentials either because it is too poor or too corrupt, the drug producers step in. Like those who are dubbed terrorists by some and freedom fighters by others – one person's 'merchant of doom' can be another's local hero. As a young dental student told reporter Sam Quinones, 'Here these guys aren't enemies, they're friends. People know they (the narcos) are doing wrong… but people don't care where the money comes from if they've helped people'. One reason among many why drug wars as currently fought are doomed to failure, even if the flowers of evil are unlikely to show their faces to the sun again.

PART ONE

1 STEP RIGHT UP FOR GOD'S OWN MEDICINE

Nowadays, the public perception of heroin and cocaine is that they are dangerous, enslaving drugs which destroy young lives while making vast sums for the evil men who supply them; such men are often regarded as worse than murderers. The image of marijuana is not so destructive as it once was, but the belief is still strong that an inexorable path leads from marijuana use to heroin addiction.

It is hard to imagine that the situation has ever been any different, but up to the First World War, opium, morphine, heroin and cocaine were freely available to anyone who could afford them from respectable doctors, pharmacists and even street-corner grocery stores and business-men selling patent medicines. The famous herbalist Nicholas Culpeper remarked in his *Complete Herbal* that cannabis was so well-known to English housewives that he would not bother to list all its uses round the home.

For most of the nineteenth century, medical science was still wedded to the theories of the ancient Greeks, modified by the barbaric practices of so-called 'heroic therapy'. Driving out unpleasant maladies with even more unpleasant remedies was the guiding principle. Patients 'could expect to be leeched, cupped, blistered, amputated, sweated, trepanned, scourged and flayed to a fare-the-well'.[1] Small wonder that doctors in the eighteenth and early nineteenth century lost many well-to-do patients to fashionable herbalism, until the virtues of opiate drugs became apparent.

With so little knowledge of how the body worked, doctors could treat only the symptoms, not the causes of illness. Pain was the most distressing symptom and as the world's greatest painkillers, opium and its derivatives were a godsend to beleaguered doctors traditionally regarded as little better than butchers and charlatans. The noted English physician Thomas Sydenham spoke for all his colleagues when he said 'among the remedies which it has pleased almighty God to give to man to relieve his sufferings, none is so universal and so efficacious as opium'. Doctors prescribed it for ailments great and small and 'it would be almost easier to list those areas where it was never employed than to attempt to deal with every therapeutic possibility'.[2]

Today, a 'typical' heroin addict might be a young unemployed male (black or white) living in a deprived inner-city wasteland. The nineteenth-century addict was more likely to be a middle-aged, middle-class white female who had become dependent on her prescriptions of laudanum (opium with alcohol) or injectable morphine. The problems associated with long-term use of opium were well known but for the most part were regarded as the inconvenient side effects of an otherwise miraculous drug. In an era when self-control was a social necessity, some of those who became addicts felt a degree of personal shame and were regarded as self-indulgent or weak, but certainly not as criminals or social pariahs. Injectable morphine was really available only to those who could afford doctors, a rare and expensive service in the nineteenth century.

The patent medicine industry in Britain and America supplied the drug needs of the majority of the population. Thomas Sydenham's own laudanum concoction was the first patent medicine to make an impact in the late seventeenth century, and it remained a clear market leader for the next 150 years. Later it faced extensive competition from Godfrey's Cordial, Battley's Sedative Solution, Squire's Elixir, Mrs Winslow's Soothing Syrup, Daffy's Elixir and many others, all containing opium and on unrestricted sale.

Patent-medicine selling was big business. The manufacturers were the first to realize the potential benefits of advertising and, once the railways opened up distribution networks for the mass circulation of newspapers, the medicine men poured thousands of pounds into advertising. For many newspapers, the medicine business was their major source of advertising revenue.

The story was repeated in America, but on a much larger scale. The first American patent medicine was registered in 1796 – Samuel Lee's Bilious Pills, good for everything from worms to 'female complaints'. Three years later somebody else called Dr Samuel Lee began marketing his bilious pills and, through newspaper advertising, a commercial war ensued. Each attacked the other as a fraud and both made a handsome profit, setting the tone for the rest of the industry in succeeding decades: no lie too big, no claim too outrageous, no deception too dishonest. By 1900 some 50,000 preparations were on the market generating an income for the manufacturers of nearly $80 million. As with medicines in Britain, opium was a common ingredient.

In 1898 a German scientist working in the pharmaceutical laboratories of Friedrich Bayer produced a new derivative of morphine, diacetyl morphine. The new drug was tried with sensational effects on a number of intractable respiratory conditions. Bayer marketed this wonder drug as 'heroin', its name in German indicating a lot of power from a small amount. What pleased the research team was that those given heroin seemed free of the usual morphine side effects like nausea and constipation. They assumed that dependence would also be absent, but once adverse medical reports started coming in, heroin's career as a widely distributed legal drug was cut short. At about the same time a new drug, derived from a South American bush, burst on to the market as 'the real thing'.

Sigmund Freud was an early champion of cocaine. In his paper *On Coca*, he listed its uses as a stimulant, a cure for digestive complaints, asthma and even alcohol and morphine addiction. But the news wasn't all good: Freud warned that immoderate use could cause 'physical and intellectual decadence', together with 'weakness, emaciation and moral depravity'.

Cocaine found long-term medical favour as a local anaesthetic, but in the 1890s it was its stimulant qualities that encouraged the patent medicine industry to flood the market with tonics and 'pick-me-ups'. Some, like Dr Tucker's Specific or Agnew's Powder, were virtually pure cocaine. Bernay's Catarrh Cure came with its own drug paraphernalia kit – not a mirror, razor blade and spoon, but a small glass tube and short length of rubber tubing. One end of the tube went into the powder, the other up one nostril, relieving catarrh, sinus trouble, and doubtless a lot more besides.

Far more innocuous, containing very small amounts of cocaine, were the cola drinks (including Coca-Cola) and the coca wines. Vin Mariani's (named after its Corsican producer) was among the most popular and became a great favourite in royal circles. Mariani received enthusiastic testimonies from the Prince of Wales, the Tsar of Russia and the Kings of Norway and Sweden. Pope Leo XIII presented Mariani with a gold medal for being a 'benefactor of humanity'.

Like its British counterpart, the American newspaper industry flourished under the patronage of the patent-medicine advertisers. From twenty dailies in 1800, by 1860 America had four hundred and numerous rural and provincial papers, with some manufacturers spending up to $100,000 a year on advertising. But convinced though they were of the value of newspaper advertising, the medicine men were also showmen – they wanted to get out on the road and sell direct to the people. So was born the medicine show.

The 'show' might be no more than one man standing on a box on a street corner pitching his wares. At the other extreme was John Healy and Charles Bigelow's Kickapoo Indian Medical Company Show. This consisted of re-enactments of Indian battles, magicians, comedians, musicians – dozens of entertainers putting on a whole evening's extravaganza for crowds anything up to 8,000 strong.

But whatever the size of the show, the guiding principle was the same: the pitchman had to keep his audience interested but not critical, to convince them that it was only a matter of time before they would be ill and in dire need of his latest wonder cure:

> STEP RIGHT UP – HERE YOU ARE! No matter what it is, this little box will save your life. One dose alone irrevocably guaranteed to instantaneously eliminate, permanently prevent and otherwise completely cure toothache, sleeplessness, club feet, mumps, stuttering, varicose veins, youthful errors, tonsilitis, rheumatism, lockjaw, stomach ache, hernia, tuberculosis, nervous disability, impotence, halitosis and falling downstairs or your money back.[3]

To bolster the credibility of the medicine, the pitchmen would either pose as doctors or take a doctor on the road. These were often sad cases who had lost their own practices through drink or drugs. Some of the performers were in an equally bad state: with opium and cocaine so close at hand, overusing them to relieve the boredom of travelling on the road was always a risk. And for the 'has-beens' or 'never-weres' that made up any troupe, these medicines would have provided an escape from the reality of being doomed to tread the boards in one grim hick town after another.

For a young nation with little history of its own, the imagery of ancient and mysterious races held a powerful sway. The Kickapoo Indian Company traded on belief in the healing powers of the American Indian. Many pitchmen donned oriental garb to weave tall tales about the exotic East. Exploiting the trust that the clergy engendered, the Quaker pitchmen spouted thees and thous and wore wide-brimmed hats. But at the most basic level, with so much ignorance about the fundamentals of health care, the pitchmen relied on fear.

> Do you ever feel like it is almost impossible to get up in the morning? You eat well and sleep well, but you hate to get up? Well, folks, you might not know it, but that's the first sign of gallopin' consumption!
>
> You laughing happy audience, you mother, you father, you young man, woman and child – within every one of you are the seeds of death. Is it cancer? Is it consumption? Is it perhaps some horrible unknown malady?

The medicine shows were full of larger-than-life characters: Big Foot Bill Wallace, Phenomenal Klaus and Wonderful Walton. Ray Black's Tour of the World pitch went on for five hours without a break. He said, 'If they stay with me till the end, they're sure to buy. When I get through with them, their heels are round … their backs are aching and they're certain they have kidney trouble or lumbago.'[4]

A handful of medicine men became very wealthy; the Rockefeller family fortune has its origins in patent medicine. Nelson's great-grandfather William Avery Rockefeller was as sharp and sophisticated a supplier of drugs as any latterday New York cocaine dealer. Like his criminal counterpart today, he dressed stylishly, travelled under assumed names and never had less than a thousand dollars in his wallet. Big Bill Avery, 'the cancer specialist', made enough money to back his son J.D. Rockefeller for a stake in the Cleveland oil business – and the rest, as they say, is history.[5] One of the very few women pitchers, Madame Dubois, left an estate worth over a million dollars. Another, Violet McNeal, told of life on the road in her autobiography *Four White Horses and a Brass Band*. Violet travelled as 'Princess Lotus Blossom' with her husband Will, who was one of the first pitchmen to develop the 'oriental' sales show. During their most lucrative period from 1906-14, Violet and Will and other successful pitchers could be regarded as the first media stars. Their shows were seen by thousands all over the States; they wore the best clothes, ate at the best restaurants, and sat at the best tables. 'I had twenty-seven diamond rings. I had diamond bracelets and lockets and one of them Hope Diamonds [sic] – a six-carat stone set in a brooch. We called them Sunbursts.'[6] And everybody called her Diamond Vi.

Diamond Vi mixed with the fringes of urban and small-town society – prostitutes, gamblers, bookmakers, hustlers – all making a living from the greed and gullibility of straight society, together with other travellers in the twilight zone – actors, prizefighters, gangsters and musicians. She learned of the pitchman hierarchy: the low pitchman who played from a box in the street and the high pitchman who played from a stage and paid large licence fees for the privilege. The high pitchman would mix socially with circus owners (never the performers), saloon-bar and gambling-house owners, madams, politicians, racehorse owners and the better class of thief.

The shows did best in the Middle West and Southern States. The unsophisticated rural crowds were more gullible than city dwellers and more grateful for the entertainment. Aside from the occasional touring minstrel troupe or tent show, the medicine show was one of life's few diversions. Generally modest affairs, they would be staged on a simple wooden platform backed with canvas and flanked by the company's transport vehicles. The show would feature the lecturer/manager, a sketch team who also did solo turns, a song-and-dance man, a pianist and other musicians, and a black-face comedian doubling as MC and producer. The bill often changed nightly, so the performers had to be very versatile. A show lasting two hours would run something like this: the black-face act or a song routine with the whole cast starts the ball rolling and settles the audience down. A comedy routine follows featuring a standard caricature of the negro – 'Jake' or 'Sambo' with big pants in loud colours and outsize shoes, with a straight man acting as 'feed'. More music, or perhaps a speciality act like ventriloquism comes next. Then the first pitch of the evening, selling to begin with some cheap soap, the more expensive stuff coming later. Then music and comedy, followed by the second pitch. There might be a Prize Candy Sale: buy some candy and you get the chance to win a bigger prize, ranging from cheap novelties to bedspreads. The Sambo act closes the spectacle.

Music played an important part in the medicine show, which enabled those struggling to earn a living as musicians to find regular work and gave them a chance to travel. Travelling was a part of the mythology of being a musician: it invoked the wayward spirit, the freethinker, the outlaw untrammelled by social conventions. Once illegal, drugs developed their own mystique which was embraced by the outlaw myth of the itinerant musician.

Before the mass migration to the North early this century, becoming a wandering minstrel or musician was one of the few options for blacks in the South who did not want to work the land as sharecroppers. For those who couldn't break free, the 'travelling coon', as immortalised in songs from around the Southern states, became a figure imbued with almost superhuman powers, fast-talking, free-spending and a hit with the girls. After emancipation in 1865, freedom was equated with mobility and thousands of questing Negroes took to the roads, establishing a pattern which was to become part of the black self-image in America. The travelling musician, who had taken on the role of truth-teller from the Black Preacher, and the role of trickster or 'bad nigger' from the Devil, became the ultimate symbol of freedom. Escape from the monotony and hopelessness of black employment, combined with the potential for earning a living without having to rely on the white man – beating the white man at his own game, in other words – kept the musician's status high.

'At one time or another, most of the top Memphis bluesmen and street singers worked the medicine shows,'[7] states blues writer Bruce Cook. The medicines show was regarded by the blues singers as 'a kind of paid vacation from the rigours of town life', something they did for fun. However, life for the black musician on the road at the turn of the century could be dangerous. With the Black Codes, anti-black legislation in force throughout the South, the rednecks had a field day. Black musicians got the worst lodgings if they got any at all, were refused service at restaurants, could expect to be ripped off by managers and agents, were generally subjected to routine harassment and intimidation, and occasionally lost their lives. W.C. Handy was almost lynched after he had saved one of his troupe from being killed, escaping only by hiding in a railway car's secret compartment. Louis Wright, a fiercely proud black minstrel, was not so lucky. Snowballed by whites in Missouri while out walking with his girlfriend, Wright retaliated with a few well-chosen insults. An angry mob quickly formed, but Wright dispersed them with shots from his gun. The sheriff arrived, arrested the whole company but 'released' Wright to the crowd during the night. His mutilated body was shipped home to Chicago for burial.[8] Despite these difficulties, musicians travelling with the medicine shows helped to spread knowledge of the blues throughout the South.

One of the very earliest blues singers was Ophelia Simpson, known as 'Black Alfalfa'. She worked for Dr Parker's Medicine Show, helping to mix a concoction which was supposed to eradicate tapeworms. This was a favourite pitch: the medicine man would suspend a huge tapeworm full length in a glass jar; by the end of the lecture most of the audience were convinced they had tapeworms. Black Alfalfa would sing ragtime songs as a crowd pleaser, but she was better as a blues singer. Her husband Henry worked in a fertilizer factory on the Ohio River near Louisville, Kentucky, which earned him the nickname Dead Dog. Early in 1898, Ophelia Simpson stood trial for the manslaughter of Dead Dog Simpson. She was committed to what the blacks called the Stoney Lonesome (jail) for a while and then released on the grounds that her husband was a 'no-count' and probably deserved to die anyway.

Plenty of no-hopers played in the medicine shows, but some famous names began their careers there up until the forties, when the medicine show effectively died out. (By then of course, patent medicines contained only water, herb and alcohol mixtures.) Buster Keaton's parents ran a medicine show. Harry Houdini and country stars Roy Acuff, Hank Williams and Jimmy Rodgers all paid some dues there. Even the King of Rock'n'Roll, Little Richard, did his time supporting the 'grinder' (medicine man).

> When I started getting into all this trouble at home, I left and joined up with Dr Hudson's Medicine Show. I didn't tell anybody I was going, I just went. Doc Hudson was out of Macon and he used to sell snake oil. He would go into towns, have all the black people come round and tell them that the snake oil was good for everything. Well, they would believe him. But he was lying. Snake oil! I was helping to lie … He had a stage out in the open and a feller by the name of James would play piano. I would sing 'Cal'donia, Cal'donia, what makes your big head so hard?'[9]

But long before Little Richard hit the boards, the writing was on the wall for the patent medicine industry as a significant force in American commercial life. The medical profession was growing fast and becoming increasingly well organized and self-assertive as new discoveries in clinical medicine stimulated the development of specialization. Meanwhile the patent medicine business had reached the point where only large companies could launch new products because of the massive capital investments required. Battle was joined for control of the market in medical services.

S.H. Adams, a journalist, fired the first broadside on behalf of the medical profession, with a series of articles written for *Colliers Magazine* entitled 'The Great American Fraud'. The first article appeared in 1905 and began:

> Gullible Americans will spend this year some seventy-five millions of dollars … in the purchase of patent medicines. In consideration of this sum it will swallow huge quantities of alcohol, an appalling amount of opiates and narcotics, a wide assortment of varied drugs ranging from powerful and dangerous heart depressants to insidious liver stimulants; and, far in excess of all other ingredients, undiluted fraud. For fraud, exploited by the skilfulest of advertising bunco men, is the basis of the trade. Should the newspapers, the magazines, and the medical journals

refuse their pages to this class of advertisement, the patent-medicine business in five years would be as scandalously historic as the South Sea Bubble.

A medical crusader, Dr Hamilton Wright, who figured largely in the eventual prohibition of narcotic drugs in America, seized on this opportunity and had 500,000 copies of 'The Great American Fraud' distributed round the country.

Of itself, the Pure Food and Drug Act of 1906 did little to help the doctor's campaign. The Act's architect, Dr Harvey Wiley, was much more concerned with food adulteration; the measures relating to patent medicines were an afterthought. All the manufacturers were required to do was to list and quantify the ingredients of any medicine that contained opium and its derivatives morphine and heroin, or cocaine. However, the Act did raise public awareness of the amount of opium and cocaine in circulation at a time when general fears about the consequences of addiction were being taken up by the more sensation seeking newspapers. The real crunch came on 1 March 1915, the day the 1914 Harrison Narcotics Act came into force. From that day on, as far as the Treasury agents enforcing the Act were concerned, those who had anything to do with narcotic drugs – suppliers, doctors or patients – were criminals.

2 FROM SAMBO TO SATAN

Most writers on the passing of the Harrison Narcotics Act focus on two key elements running in parallel. First, the medical profession's continuing fight to control prescribing, and second, the need for domestic anti-narcotics legislation to give America's international campaign against narcotics trafficking some credibility. But as John Helmer has noted in his book on drugs and minority oppression, the available history of drug use in those years and of narcotics policy appears almost completely divorced from the affairs of the rest of America, and as a result, the forces which shaped that history are not easy to see.

It is well beyond the scope of this book to examine all these forces, but because the story of popular music is essentially the story of black music in America, the changing attitude of the white community towards blacks after the abolition of slavery is of importance both for the history of drug legislation and in the creation of a high-profile bugaboo – the drug-using black jazz musician.

As the nineteenth century drew to a close, America underwent something of a spiritual and moral crisis. A national mythology existed, founded on the belief that 'cultural renewal depended upon movement in space'.[1] The progress of a nation founded on evangelical Protestantism and wedded to the work ethic drew much of its impetus from mobility. Open space and the battles fought against the Indians to win it, had provided a challenge which was supposed to have kept the nation young and vital. But after the last Indian wars of the 1880s, Americans reached the end of the trail. A people born to run and infused with the pioneering spirit had nowhere to go.

Reaching the edge of the frontier also had serious implications for American business. Still recovering from the shock of economic slump in the 1870s, domestic markets were reaching saturation point. For American politicians in the 1890s the search for new frontiers became a priority. Senator Orville Platt said in 1893, 'A policy of isolation did well enough when we were an embryo nation, but today things are different. We are the most advanced and powerful people on earth and regard to our future welfare demands an abandonment of the doctrine of isolation to the ocean that our children must look, as they once looked to the boundless West.'[2]

America's Holy War against international narcotics trafficking was part of a 'publicity campaign' designed to show the rest of the world that America was a world leader and therefore entitled to a share of the foreign markets carved up at that time by established colonial powers like Britain, Germany and Holland.

The problem on the home front was more intractable. While taking an expansive view abroad, the WASP culture at home closed ranks. America had no unified culture and the Civil War had shown how frail the Union was. The male-dominated WASP ethos, with its innate sense of superiority over the Indians, blacks, immigrants and its own women, was nevertheless insecure. From the earliest days of white settlement, deep fears had existed about contamination from undesirables. These fears were heightened as the crumbling of Victorian social and moral values coincided with a stagnant frontier, throwing up visions of slow decline into Old World decadence. From these anxieties came the idea of 'the enemy within', a useful device for uniting the nation, excusing failures or preparing the people for unpopular legislation. Twentieth-century enemies have included Jewish and Italian gangsters, communists, student activists, sexually and politically independent women and jazz and rock musicians.

Government propaganda often attempted to forge links in the public mind between those labelled 'beyond the pale' and illegal drug users. Thus there were drug-pushing communists and acid-crazed student activists. In the nineteenth century the press, police and politicians combined to generate public fear of two groups: Chinese opium-smoking white slavers and violent black cocaine users.

Chinese labourers were brought over in their thousands to the West Coast of America in the 1840s and 1850s, to work in the gold mines and build the railways in conditions and for wages that no white man would accept. As the mines were exhausted and the railways finished, America was shocked by an economic depression in the 1870s which compelled whites to compete with Chinese labour. Until then, the Chinese had at best been tolerated by the white community. Now a wave of anti-Chinese feeling swept the country and the Chinese, who had built up large, thriving communities in many American cities, found themselves the victims of legal restrictions and systematic harassment. A consortium of California cigar manufacturers were persuaded by a trade union leader to attach a label to their products proclaiming that the cigars were untouched by Chinese workers.[3]

San Francisco had the largest Chinese community. When William Randolph Hearst took over the *San Francisco Examiner* in 1887, he embarked on an anti-Chinese crusade and single-handedly evolved the crude mythology of the 'Yellow Peril' through sensational journalism. The Chinese had brought with them their opium-smoking habit and the social institution of the opium den. As early as 1875 the City banned opium smoking as a direct attack on the community. Hearst chose opium as a natural hook on which to hang his crusade. Everything there was to fear about the Chinese became embodied in the opium den.

Polite society steered clear of the Chinese community, but the white underworld and the artistic demi-monde had no scruples about fostering community relations. Unlike the solitary activity of morphine injecting, opium smoking was a social habit and the attractions of the amenable opium den enticed Chinese and whites alike. The paraphernalia and ritual of opium smoking, the sense of belonging and exclusivity felt by smokers, the use of esoteric jargon – 'hop joint', 'long draw', 'yen', etc – set the pattern that all drug subcultures would follow in the next century. The same fascination that drew people to buy patent medicines with an 'oriental' history drew them to buy Hearst's newspaper, to read about 'Ten Slaves of the Poppy's Spell', 'Sunday Vice in Chinatown' and 'Body of Opium Fiend Burned'. Well before the first Sax Rohmer stories about Fu Manchu were published in 1913, the public had a fixed image of devious, inscrutable Chinamen leading young virgins into white slavery and prostitution through addiction to opium.

Chinese immigration was stopped in 1882 and in 1909 the importation and use of opium for smoking were banned. Unlike tobacco and coffee in Europe, the fear was not of downward percolation through the social strata, but upward. The architect of all America's early drugs legislation, Dr Hamilton Wright, wrote in 1910, 'Smoking opium has spread steadily to a large part of our outlaw population and even into the higher ranks of society.' This was certainly true, in fact by the 1890s, there were probably more white smokers than Chinese, and so therefore ownership of the dens also moved beyond the Chinese community. On Forty-sixth Street near Seventh Avenue in New York was an opium den that catered strictly for wealthy clients. It was run by two white crooks and bankrolled by a third. Many of the wealthy clientele brought their own equipment, pieces made of gold, ivory and silver – much like the chic cocaine paraphernalia of a century later. The house itself was cloaked in heavy curtains, with heavily embroidered cushions scatttered across the floor and a piano for the entertainment.[4]

It took a district court in Oregon to discern the true genesis of the ban on opium smoking. The court, ruling on the conviction of a Chinese for selling opium, acknowledged that the target of the prohibition was not opium, but those most associated with its use: 'Smoking opium is not our vice, and therefore it may be that this legislation proceeds more from a desire to vex and annoy the "Heathen Chinese" in this respect, than to protect the people from the evil habit.' The conviction stood however on the grounds that the court could not take the possible motives behind the law into account.

For Hamilton Wright the devil's fork had two prongs: one was opium and the other cocaine, 'the most threatening of the drug habits that has ever appeared in this country', spread by those whom he imagined were the most threatening social group 'the cocaine-crazed niggers'.

When they were first brought to America as slaves, blacks were regarded as little more than savages. The first American slave owners had viewed slavery as a necessary expedient. The slaves' labour was essential and they themselves would benefit from enforced assimilation into Christian society. But from the turn of the nineteenth century, attitudes began to change: slavery became a necessary evil which must eventually be abolished.

As the notion of 'natural slavery' became increasingly disturbing to many Americans, apologists for slavery sought to change the image of the Negro from brute savage to innocent child. This child was Sambo, lazy, shiftless, ignorant, good-natured, docile and, above all, contented. Sambo became a stock character in tent and medicine shows, but it was the minstrel show that did most to perpetuate this crude caricature. Sambo, the white man with a black face, was presented to Northern urban audiences as the acceptable face of slavery, a safe and comfortable image of the blacks and their lives on the plantations.

The minstrel show presented the Negro as inferior, subordinate and Cupid. Black-face comedians played out ludicrous caricatures: exaggerated facial make-up to accentuate eyes and mouth, ill-fitting patchwork clothes, rolling eyes, jerky bodily contortions and heavy 'nigger' dialect. The visual stereotyping was complemented by idealised views of the plantation. In the songs of Stephen Foster, for example, everyone was happy, safe and free from worries – either content to be where they were or looking forward to returning 'home' to Africa:

> It was no accident that the incredible popularity of minstrelsy coincided with public concern about slavery and the proper position of Negroes in America. Precisely because people could always just laugh off the performance ... minstrelsy served as a 'safe' vehicle through which its primarily Northern, urban audiences could work out their feelings about even the most sensitive and volatile issues ...Like every aspect of the show, minstrelsy's racial content grew out of the intimate interaction between the performers and their vocal patrons. When public opinion shifted, the content of minstrelsy shifted.[5]

This meant that during heightened public debate about slavery an element of anti-slavery sentiment crept into the shows, but as soon as the slavery question threatened to tear the Union apart, such sentiments expunged.

In 1852, Harriet Beecher Stowe's *Uncle Tom's Cabin* was published. The first American novel with blacks as central characters, *Uncle Tom's Cabin* showed blacks to be human beings, able to feel suffering, misery and humiliation. But the producers of minstrel shows managed to sanitize this when the novel was adapted for the stage. Their message was that:

> there was no need to fight a war over slavery, no need to accept Negroes as equals in the North and no need to feel guilty for contradictions between slavery and the American Creed. Fulfilment for blacks ... came only within the subordinate roles of the plantation; blacks needed supervision and they got it in a benevolent atmosphere of a loving extended family.[6]

Emancipation changed everything. Although most blacks stayed in the South, they gained mobility and a new social and spiritual life through the rapid growth of the American black church. Even as sharecroppers they were not under the direct economic control of whites. Blacks became political leaders and were a presence in many white-collar and professional occupations. In response the whites, particularly Southern politicians, created a new popular image of the Negro – he changed from innocent child to malevolent rapist.

Spurred on by a fear that black voters would ally themselves with low-income whites and threaten the Democratic powerbase, politicians like Thomas Dixon of North Carolina engineered a virulent anti-black crusade in the 1890s, not dissimilar to Hitler's campaign against the Jews. This evolved into formal legislation, the 'Jim Crow' laws which institutionalised segregation in the South and separated black from white in every conceivable area of public life. Fear, harassment and intimidation were part of the daily routine for the black community. It has been recorded that between 1890-1917 a black man or woman was lynched every second day.

The Prohibition movement was particularly strong in the South, on the principle that booze turned Sambo into Satan. But it was his involvement with cocaine which gave the instigators of racial hatred their most potent symbol of black savagery.

Given the popularity of the medicine show among poor Southern blacks they were enthusiastic consumers of tonics, remedies and cola drinks containing cocaine. Moreover plantation owners often kept a supply on hand and passed cheap cocaine to their workers: a happy worker was more industrious, and as cocaine suppressed the appetite he didn't get hungry so quickly either. A shrewd boss doling out a quarter of a gram per man could keep sixteen workers happy and more productive for a full seven days on a single ounce. With cocaine selling at $2.50 an ounce, he could hardly go wrong. The difficulty of buying alcohol may also have diverted some blacks to cocaine.

The 'cocaine-crazed black' mythology served the purposes of both drugs campaigners and racists (where the two were not the same). Blacks used cocaine, blacks were a menace, therefore cocaine was dangerous; alternatively cocaine was dangerous and when taken by blacks it made them revert to their savage state. Newspaper reports began linking cocaine with black violence. In 1903 a Colonel Watson wrote to the *New York Tribune* warning that 'many of the horrible crimes committed in the Southern states by coloured people can be traced directly to the cocaine habit'. Report followed report: Atlanta's Chief of Police claimed that seventy per cent of all crime was cocaine-related, while Dr Christopher Koch, an anti-drugs campaigner, asserted that 'Most of the attacks upon white women of the South are the direct result of a cocaine-crazed Negro brain.' Under the influence of cocaine, blacks allegedly became unstoppable and superhuman. Writing in the *New York Times* of 8 February 1914, Dr E.H. Williams maintained that a 'cocaine nigger' near Asheville, North Carolina, stopped five men dead in their tracks using one cartridge per man. A policeman from the same town swore that a direct shot in the heart at point-blank range of a 'Negro in a cocaine frenzy' did not even jolt him. Police all over the Southern states used this incident as an excuse to issue themselves heavier-calibre revolvers.

In the 1890s, the Indian Hemp Commission set up by the British found no evidence for any of the claims made that marijuana drove men mad. The commissioners followed up anecdotal reports to check their validity. Hamilton Wright made no such checks; it suited his purposes not to. He assimilated all the unsubstantiated gossip about cocaine and translated it into part of the official and 'authoritative' rationale for curbing non-medical drug use.

'The corruption of youth' has always been an attention-grabbing rallying cry for campaigns in support of traditional values. For America, this was part of the country's moral 'crisis'. In the era of America's youngest President, Theodore Roosevelt, the youth of the country were revered as standard-bearers of future economic and military strength. The middle-class-based Progressive Reform Movement was active in legislation to protect young people against prostitution, abortion and drinking. With supporters in influential government posts, it now put pressure on Congress to move against drugs.

Much was made of the use of heroin among adolescents (a term first coined in 1904 by psychologist G. Stanley Hall, to denote those in the fourteen-eighteen age group). Most studies of the period, while acknowledging that heroin use did occur among adolescents, showed that it was far more prevalent among older age groups. Similarly, an outcry was raised about alleged drug use, especially cocaine, among servicemen. But again, from studies carried out it was found that there was no significant drug use in the armed forces, and the fact that so few young recruits had drug problems was further evidence that young people in general were not heavily involved in drugs.

In effect, whatever the parts played by medical self-aggrandizement, international diplomacy and genuine concern about public health, social disapproval was central to the banning of recreational drug use in America. Laws were enacted as demonstrations against particular user groups, their lifestyles and the threat they allegedly posed to white society.

Sambo became Satan when he became 'out of control' – on cocaine so they said, but actually out of the economic thrall of the white man. In consequence drugs went underground, an appropriate place for satanic pleasures. Equally appropriate was their association with the new voice of the black community- blues ('the devil's music') and jazz. Blacks, jungle rhythms and drugs: an unholy trinity to make the stiff-necked WASP quail, the gutter journalist rub his hands with glee and the thrill-seeker hit the streets.

3   LIGHT UP AND BE SOMEBODY –
MEZZ AND MARIJUANA

I's gwina save all my nickels and dimes/To buy me a Mary Jane
'High Sheriff Blues'

For the cats and kittens of the Jazz Age, marijuana was kicks, climbs, jollies and high times jumpin' to the beat of a hot horn or a mean licorice stick.
Albert Goldman

My … memories will always be lots of beauty and warmth from gage. Well, that was my life and I don't feel ashamed at all. Mary Warner, honey, you sure was good …

Louis Armstrong

Once the war in Europe was over and the boys were home. America experienced a period of spiritual emptiness. The new religion was materialism, accumulation, the worship of everything new and big. And as in the 1960s, the affluence and conspicuous consumption of the 1920s brought a reaction among a section of the younger generation who could afford the luxury of being unorthodox. They sought escape in anti-establishment music, sexual pleasure, alternative lifestyles and 'other worldliness'.

For the flappers 'other worldliness' meant a craze for ouija boards, rather than Eastern mysticism. And instead of 'back-to-nature' communes, the adolescents of sixty years ago turned to the 'loose passion' and vitality of black culture. The idealism of an earlier age gave way to realism: all the straight world had to offer was

26

disillusionment and stagnation; the past had been blown up in the trenches and the future held nothing but the dubious promise of 'progress'. Black culture seemed to offer honesty, spontaneity and even a new spiritual meaning to two groups in particular: affluent people looking for excitement where the rules and pretensions of polite society did not apply; and Jewish immigrant groups sympathetic to the problems of minority status.

Contrary to the expectations of the temperance movement, Prohibition encouraged the well-to-do to 'take a walk on the wild side'. Café, cabarets and restaurants had been a feature of urban nightlife for decades, but the speakeasies and basement dives selling illicit booze to the strains of jazz added a new dimension to the thrill of 'steppin' out down market'. Milton Mezzrow, jazz clarinet player and focal point of this chapter, summed up this situation in his autobiography *Really the Blues*, published in 1946:

'It struck me as funny how the top and bottom crusts in society were always getting together during the Prohibition era. In this swanky club which was run by members of the notorious Purple Gang, Detroit's bluebloods used to congregate – the Grosse Point mob on the slumming kick, rubbing elbows with Louis the Wop's mob. That Purple Gang was a hard lot of guys ... and Detroit's snooty set used to feel it was really living to talk to them hoodlums.'[1]

Among the young whites (often Jewish or Italian) in revolt against traditional values, the most rebellious were jazz musicians. Jazz had emerged as the urban voice of black culture, essentially a protest music in which blacks played out their daily experiences. This found favour with white kids seeking a vehicle for their own thrash against society, a music guaranteed to shock the squares, as rock 'n' roll did in the mid-fifties. One musician in particular epitomised the religious zeal that alienated whites felt for black lifestyles. He was white, he was Jewish, and he became the archetypal hip musician of the Jazz Age, the first White Negro.

Milton 'Mezz' Mezzrow was born 'on a wintery night' in 1899 to a respectable middle-class Jewish family on Chicago's Northwest Side. As a kid, he spent much of his time on the streets, getting into trouble, fighting, petty thieving and hanging around poolrooms. Throughout his early life he had an unfortunate knack of being in the wrong place at the wrong time. At sixteen, he was caught riding in a stolen car and sent to Pontiac Reformatory. 'During those months I got me a good solid dose of the coloured man's gift for keeping the life and spirit in him while he tells his troubles in music.'[2]

Inside Pontiac, Mezzrow met his first black musicians: Yellow, a cornet player, and an alto saxophonist called King. Race riots inside the prison (and later Chicago's four-day city-wide race riot in 1919), gave him a taste of Jim Crow, although on the streets of Chicago he'd bloodied himself often enough against shouts of 'Kike'. By the time he was released, Mezzrow had his life plan sorted out: 'I knew that I was to spend all my time from then on sticking close to Negroes. They were my kind of people. And I was going to learn their music and play it for the rest of my days.'[3]

The Great Migration of blacks from the South to the North saw Chicago's black population increase by 150% in the years 1910 to 1920, the largest influx coming after 1916, with the promise of high post-war wages. Blacks settled on the South Side of Chicago in such numbers that it became a city within a city, independent of the mainstream of Chicago life.

Along with tens of thousands of blacks looking for routine day jobs came musicians from New Orleans. 'Cook's Tour' histories of jazz set out an-over-simplified itinerary for the spread of jazz through America. The linear journey from New Orleans to Kansas City, Chicago and New York, prompted by the closing down in 1917 of black Storyville, New Orleans' red light district, ignores in Kenneth Allsop's words all the 'jazz, semi-jazz, near jazz and tributary jazz' heard throughout the South and Middle West. Brass-band music, ragtime, tent-show music, vaudeville, church music and a host of related localized musical idioms fed into the genre. Nevertheless New Orleans represented the best the new music had to offer and gave to jazz its sleazy reputation.

The New Orleans spirit was one of permissiveness and non-interference, very much a musician's creed. From its earliest days a city of low life, thieving, gambling and above all prostitution, New Orleans 'tolerated with impartiality small-time hustlers and high crimes, self-serving royal governors and fifty-cent whores'.[4] In a town of corruption and easy money, the establishments that thrived were bordellos, gambling joints, saloons, cabarets and dance halls. The customers needed entertaining, so music was a growth industry, although there were few professional musicians. In fact music was a subsidiary of the gambling business: 'The hustlers gamblers and racetrack followers were often hard-working musicians in their off-season or when their luck boned down and they needed a little ready cash.'[5] They also used drugs in a big way and naturally, before 1914, everything was there for the asking. But by the time war came, drugs were illegal and the Navy, worried about the moral well-being of young sailors, had Storyville closed down.

In fact the exodus of jazz musicians from New Orleans began much earlier. Mezz Mezzrow's ears were first turned by the Original Creole Jazz Band, who had been drawing in the crowds at Chicago's Big Grand Theatre and the North American Restaurant since 1913. Their star players included Sidney Bechet, Freddie Keppard, drummer Tubby Hall and pianist Lil Hardin, who later married Louis Armstrong. Initially, the Chicago Musicians' Union had made it hard for Southern jazzmen like Jelly Roll Morton, Keppard, Bechet, Jimmy Moore and Nick La Rocca to find regular work, but resistance crumbled in the face of an avalanche of public demand. Chicago jazz really started cooking when Joe 'King' Oliver, a superstar cornettist from New Orleans, arrived in 1918. He formed his own band in 1920, sent for Louis Armstrong, and drew a crowd of open-mouthed white kids like Mezzrow, Eddie Condon, Bix Beiderbecke, Dave Tough, Pee Wee Russell, Jimmy McPartland and Frank Teschemacher, who together pioneered the Chicago style.

Mezzrow was hooked by Bechet's soprano sax sound, rushed out and bought one, together with some sheet music, and declared himself to be a musician, spending every spare minute learning or listening to jazz.[6] On his twenty-second birthday, 11 December 1923, he became a fully paid-up member of the Local Tenth of the Chicago Federation of Musicians.

> I got to be part of the fixtures at the Pekin and a lot of other South Side spots. Making friends with Jimmie Noone, Sidney Bechet, Joe Oliver and Clarence Williams, I began to feel like I owned the South Side … Anytime I breezed down the street, cats would flash me friendly grins and hands would wave at me from all sides … I was really living then.[7]

One of the earliest white bands to copy Joe Oliver's style was the New Orleans Rhythm Kings. The clarinet player was 'a little hyped-up Italian guy with pop eyes' named Leon Rappolo:

> One night during intermission at the Friars Inn, Rapp took me into his dressing room, where he felt around on the moulding and came up with a cigarette made out of brown wheatstraw paper … He sounded more like he was sighing than smoking … After a lungful he closed his lips tight and held it until he was about choked and had to cough … 'Ever smoke any muggles?' he asked me. Man. this is some golden leaf I brought up from New Orleans. It'll make you feel good. Take a puff.' The minute he said that, dope hit my mind and I got scared – working in my uncle's drugstore had made me know that messing with dope was a one-way ticket to the graveyard. I told him I didn't smoke and let it go at that, because I looked up to him so much as a musician.[8]

In the early twenties, marijuana, muggles, muta, gage, tea, reefer, grifa, Mary Warner, Mary Jane or rosa maria was known almost exclusively to musicians. Hemp had been grown in the States since the oldest days of white settlement, as a valuable cash crop for clothes and rope making – so valuable, that the state of Virginia fined farmers for owning it. The plant grew wild in many regions, including along the banks of the Mississippi, but apart from the odd literary figure who picked up on the hashish experiences of French artists like Baudelaire, Gautier and Rimbaud, nobody knew of marijuana's other properties until the Mexican Revolution of 1910.

Marijuana smoking was commonplace in Mexico. The revolution sent thousands of Mexicans streaming over the border with the weed stashed in their packs. Smoking among Americans was initially confined to black soldiers living in garrison border towns like El Paso. Almost inevitably, marijuana found its way along the coast to New Orleans, a bustling sea port where sailors coming from the West Indies and Africa were the other major importers of the drug into America.

The story of marijuana in America was a rerun of Chinese opium smoking and the alleged over-use of cocaine by blacks. Marijuana was branded as an 'alien' drug (nobody made the connection with hemp) taken by a naturally excitable, volatile minority group (Mexicans), who turned nasty under its influence. Wherever Mexicans lived in any number, there were local ordinances against marijuana smoking. By 1933 seventeen states had banned the drug, but it was not regarded as a sufficient national problem to warrant its inclusion in the legislation of 1914 nor had the press latched on to it yet.

Organised crime was not a product of the Prohibition years between 1919 and 1933, nor was it always synonymous with the Mafia. Irish and American gangs had been operating in New York, Chicago and San Francisco for most of the nineteenth century. Southern Italian immigrants came to America after the civil war, but only in the 1890s did Sicilian gangsters begin to make their presence known on the New York waterfront. Jewish gangsters were also well represented in the underworld and the likes of Arnold Rothstein and Meyer Lansky ranked in notoriety with the top Mafia personalities.

Nevertheless Prohibition did secure the ascendancy of the Mafia in the underground hierarchy and allowed the organisation of an enormously profitable service industry, providing the nation with limitless quantities of illegal booze. The mob raked in millions of dollars during Prohibition and used the proceeds to fund every conceivable type of 'personal service': prostitution, gambling, loan-sharking, protection rackets and the supply of illegal drugs on a scale never before known, aided and abetted by corrupt politicians and policemen. It was Arnold Rothstein who during these years developed a new angle to mob operations: the 'laundering' and investment of money earned from the proceeds of crime into legitimate business. The Mafia made a major incursion into the entertainment business and, ironically much to the benefit of jazz, gangsters dominated the clubs, cabarets, dives and bars in many American cities. Indeed, if black musicians had needed to rely on legitimate ballrooms, theatres and restaurants for work, the story of jazz would have been very different.

The gangsters provided endless opportunities for musicians to play. John Hammond of CBS reckoned that three quarters of all the jazz clubs and cabarets were mob-controlled. In New York there were 1,300 licensed clubs and speakeasies, while Chicago boasted 24,000 night spots in 1926. Trumpeter Rex Stewart said musicians never had it so good in the twenties: 'You could get fired at 11 p.m. and by midnight be sitting on another bandstand blowing.'[9]

As most of the gangsters were immigrants, they felt an affinity both with the struggling white musicians from their own cultural groups and with the black musicians from the South. They were largely intolerant of racism and more than one offensive patron found his tyres slashed when he got back to his car. There was also an age affiliation; in 1925 Legs Diamond, Lucky Luciano, Louis Lepke, Vito Genovese, Al Capone, Carlo Gambino and Meyer Lansky were all under thirty. To musicians they liked they were generous. Earl Hines recalled 'Scarface (Capone) got along well with musicians. He liked to come into a club with his henchmen and have the band play his requests. He was very free with his $100 tips.'[10] When the mob moved in, no expense was spared. Louis Armstrong had a long residency in Chicago's Sunset Cafe; long residencies enabled bands to develop a style and make progress. When the Fletcher Henderson Orchestra from New York were booked to appear in 1927, the Sunset Cafe was redesigned to accommodate them. The mob owned the Lincoln Gardens, home of King Oliver, and Charlie's, whose main attraction was the Bud Freeman/Dave Tough Quintet. Like many establishments during Prohibition, Charlie's looked like a bomb ruin from the outside, so as not to attract roving Federal agents looking for booze, but inside was a sumptuously furnished, highly exclusive restaurant. The biggest nightspot owner in New York was Owney 'The Killer' Madden and the jewel in his crown was the Cotton Club. Sonny Greer, the house drummer, was given $3,000 worth of drums. Rival club owners fared less well. The owners of the Plantation Club, set up in Harlem in competition with the Cotton Club, were found dead and the club smashed to bits, two days after it opened – retribution for enticing away Cab Calloway and his Orchestra.

Musicians were allowed loans without crippling interest rates, given investment advice, access to drugs and a free rein for their own sidelines. Jelly Roll Morton sold drugs and ran prostitutes, while Duke Ellington was offered a piece of major bootlegging action in New York.

So what were the rules of the game? Basically, you kept quiet, kept playing, kept straight, did what you were told and didn't ask questions. The environment was tough, nerves were stretched to breaking point, physical injury was not uncommon. Muggsy Spanier saw two men shot dead in front of him, but had to carry on playing. Comedian Joe Lewis survived having his throat cut when he transferred from one gang-controlled North Side club to another. Pianist Pinetop Smith was shot dead on the stand and Bix Beiderbecke, the first of many music superstars to live fast and die young, died from pneumonia brought on by excess of bootleg gin.

Even the famous had to watch their backs: when Louis Armstrong changed managers, he had day-and-night bodyguards for months. It has been suggested that the careers of Fletcher Henderson and Joe Oliver went into steep decline after they fell out of favour with the mob. Oliver finished up as a janitor in a Savannah poolroom. Mezz Mezzrow once took his life in his hands with Al Capone. Told by Capone to sack his singer at the Capone-owned Arrowhead, Mezz screamed back, 'Can't sing?…Why, you couldn't even tell good whisky if you smelled it and that's your racket, so how do you figure to tell me about music?' Luckily Capone just burst out laughing. 'Listen to the Professor! The kid's got plenty of guts.'[11]

Mezzrow established himself running his own band, first at Capone's Arrowhead, then the Roadhouse and then the Martinique Inn, Indiana Harbour, all in the Chicago area. The Martinique was run by Monkey Pollack, a Jewish club owner who spoke Yiddish with a Texan drawl and fancied himself as a gunslinger. It was here that Mezz, albeit reluctantly, first smoked some New Orleans sweet leaf:

> After I finished the weed, I went back to the bandstand. Everything seemed normal and I began to play as usual. I passed a stick of gage around for the other boys to smoke and we started a set. The first thing I noticed was that I began to hear my saxophone as though it was inside my head, but I couldn't hear much of the band in back of me, although I knew they were there. All the other instruments sounded like they were way off in the distance; I got the same sensation you'd get if you stuffed your ears with cotton and talked out loud. Then I began to feel the vibrations of the reed much more pronounced against my lips and my head buzzed like a loudspeaker I found I was slurring much better and putting just the right feeling into my phrases. I was really coming on. All the notes came easing out of my horn like they'd already been made up, greased and stuffed into the bell, so all I had to do was blow a little and send them on their way, one right after the other, never missing, never behind time, all without an ounce of effort. The phrases seemed to have more continuity to them and I was sticking to the theme without ever going tangent. I felt I could go on playing for years without running out of ideas and energy. There wasn't any struggle; it was all made to order and suddenly there wasn't a sour note or a discord in the world that could bother me.[12]

Given Mezz's initial reluctance to smoke marijuana, it would have been no surprise if his first experience had been a bad one: expectations of a drug experience play a large part in how the experience actually evolves. But even allowing for Mezzrow's tendency to exaggerate (a further two pages of purple prose follow), his first taste of marijuana was obviously intensely pleasurable and convinced him that he played better for it.

Mezzrow's experience wasn't unique; it was widely felt among the jazz community that marijuana helped the creation of jazz by removing inhibitions and providing stimulation and confidence. Hoagy Carmichael described the influence of marijuana and gin while listening to another aficionado of the Holy Smoke, Louis Armstrong: 'Then the muggles took effect and my body got light. Every note Louis hit was perfection. I ran to the piano and took the place of Louis' wife. They swung into "Royal Garden Blues". I had never heard the tune before, but somehow I couldn't miss. I was floating in a strange deep blue whirlpool of jazz.'[13]

Mezz was an instant convert and quickly established a reputation for having the best weed around. In 1925, now based in Detroit, he found the local stuff decidedly second-class. 'A couple of times I had to make a trip back to Chi [cago] to pick up a fresh supply from my connection. a little Mexican named Pasquale. Chicago was home for high-class dope because thousands of Mexicans arrived in the twenties looking for work and traded it to supplement their meagre incomes. In those days we used to get a Prince Albert tobacco can full of marijuana ... for two dollars. The grefa they pushed around Detroit was like the scrapings off old wooden bridges compared with the golden leaf being peddled in Chicago.'[14]

The marijuana musicians soon formed a clique, sharing the experiences of the drug, writing songs about it, looking down on musicians who drank and the music they made (excepting Bix Beiderbecke, whom they worshipped): 'Their tones became hard and evil, not natural, soft and soulful, and anything that messed up the music instead of sending it on its way, was out with us.'[15]

Not everyone agreed with Mezzrow's view of the role of the marijuana in producing good music. John Hammond maintained that dope 'played hell with time' and Artie Shaw's view was that during the twenties and thirties, a lot of good jazz went down in spite of marijuana rather than because of it. The validity of either viewpoint is questionable; certainly nobody has proved that anyone actually plays better when stoned – the relaxation of inhibitions might push musicians to go for things they might not otherwise try, but if they are too stoned they won't make it and everything will collapse. On the other hand many musicians resent being linked with drugs and like Artie Shaw might play down or deny any possible advantages that might accrue from them.

While the musicians in Detroit used marijuana, the gangsters and (according to Mezzrow) most of the rest of the city had a yen for something more oriental. Despite the general legality of marijuana, as opposed to the total prohibition of opiate drugs, jazzmen got drawn into the illegal camp primarily because they relied on the largesse of the gangsters for continued employment. When a psychotic throwback who is paying your wages laughs at your joint and suggests you try something stronger, how can you 'just say no?' Mezz said 'yes' and from that first time, he liked it.

Moving back to Chicago in 1926, Mezzrow met a bunch of talented white musicians who first played together as a high-school jazz outfit called the Austin Blue Friars, eventually becoming Chicago's star white musicians – Jimmy McPartland (cornet and alto sax), Bud Freeman (tenor sax), Charlie Watts' hero Dave Tough (drums) and Frank Teschemacher (alto sax and clarinet), whom Mezz saved from alcoholism by turning him on to marijuana.

Playing up a storm and getting high with the renamed Austin High School Gang, the years 1926 to 1929 were good for Mezzrow. Then Depression signalled the end of an era on which the curtain finally dropped when Prohibition collapsed in 1933. The love affair with New Orleans jazz and the heyday of Chicago jazz were over; many musicians, including the Austin High Gang, headed for New York, the new jazz town. Mezz however stayed in Chicago vainly trying to keep the purist jazz flame alight, scuffling around the town to make a living for himself, his wife Bonnie (whom he married in 1925) and his stepson. Eventually the pull of New York was too strong.

One night, on impulse and wired up on cocaine to stay awake he drove there with a friend. On arrival he phoned the hotel where he knew the gang were staying. 'The first voice on the line was Eddie Condon. "Hey, Roll, where are you?" The next voice was Frank Teschemacher, "Hey Milton, did you bring any mula?" Then I knew I was home again, back among my own people. Solid…'[16]

All accounts of Milton Mezzrow give the impression of a life centred around joyful jazz and marijuana highs. But although he was never specific about them, he had a number of psychological and emotional problems. New York let him down (he couldn't find regular work) and in 1929 he fled to Paris to stay with Dave Tough, who found French audiences more appreciative and enthusiastic. He was trying to buy time, recovering from what appears to have been a nervous breakdown. But things were no better when he got back: the only work he could get was in dismal strip joints, watching leering white businessmen ogle at bored women. Depression got to him again and he resolved to move as close as he could persuade his wife to Harlem, for him the Promised Land. 'My education was completed on The Stroll (a famous Harlem street) and I became a Negro.'[17]

Mezzrow did not actually introduce marijuana into Harlem but the local stuff was poor quality and he still had access to the best Mexican grass. This was to be Mezz's calling card, his way into a community where he desperately wanted to be accepted. As a musician he was limited and could not hope to compete with black musicians, but as a marijuana dealer, he earned respect. Very soon the word got around and everyone wanted Mezz to light them up. He became a local hero. an overnight sensation. Like Biro or Hoover, 'Mezzrow' became a ubiquitous name, in this case for a quality reefer, fat and well-packed. Two dictionaries of jive defined the word Mezz as 'genuine', 'sincere' and 'anything supreme'.

Jive was a secret black language, a code with its roots in the plantation life of the South, allowing criticism or ridicule of master or mistress without fear of retribution. The word 'jive' itself appears to have African origins. A variety of African tribes and cultures were herded together on the plantations, 'but the Wolof seem to have played a particularly important and perhaps culturally dominant role in the early slave culture of the Southern United States'.[18] The linguist David Dalby has made some interesting comparisons between Wolof language and American slang closely associated with music:

Wolof	Slang
Jev – to talk disparagingly	Jive
Hipi – a person who has opened his eyes	Hip
Degga – to understand	Dig

The linguistic connection between Hipi and Hip was later extended to hippy whose lifestyle is often characterised by the psychedelic search for the inner self, using drugs as a means to achieve self-awareness. The language of drug subculture also fed into black jazz culture; 'hip' has been associated with the opium smoker's habit of lying on his hip in the opium den.

Jive talking among Harlem blacks was impenetrable to those not in the know. Two blacks might have been discussing how to kill the President, and a posse of policeman standing by would have been none the wiser. Whereas Southern plantation code was born out of fear, Northern city jive talk came from a sense of hope and spirit. Dan

Burley, editor of Harlem's *Amsterdam News*, called it 'the poetry of the proletariat' and Mezzrow described it as 'jammed with a fine sense of ridiculous that had behind it some solid social criticism…a whole new attitude to life.' Except for the honoured few, blacks kept whites out with jive. And as if the language itself wasn't obscure enough, prices and times were often doubled to add confusion. Mezz provides an example of jive and thoughtfully a translation to go with it:

I'm standing under the Tree of Hope, pushing my gage. The vipers come up, one by one.

First Cat: Hey there Poppa Mezz, is you anywhere?

Me: Man I'm down with it, stickin' like a honky.

First Cat: Lay a trey on me, ole man.

Me: Got to do it, slot. [*Pointing to a man standing in front of Big John's ginmill*]: Gun the snatcher on your left raise – the head mixer laid a bundle his ways he's posin' back like crime sure pays.

First Cat: Father grab him, I ain't payin' him no rabbit, Jim, this jive you got is a gassed. I'm goin' up to my dommy and dig that new mess Pops laid down for Okeh. I hear he rifted back on Zackly. Pick you up at The Track when the kitchen mechanics romp…[19]

Translation:

I'm standing under the Tree of Hope, selling my marijuana. The customers come up, one by one.

First Cat: Hello Mezz, have you got any marijuana?

Me: Plenty, old man my pockets are full as a factory hand's on payday.

First Cat: Let me have three cigarettes [*fifty cents' worth*].

Me: Sure will, slotmouth (*a private inner-racial joke, suggesting a mouth as big and as avaricious as the coin slot in a vending machine*). Look at the detective on your left – the head bartender slipped him some hush money, and now he's swaggering around as if crime does pay.

First Cat: I hope he croaks. I'm not paying him even a tiny bit of attention. [*Literally, 'father grab him' means Lord snatch the man and haul him away; and when you 'don't pay a man no rabbit', you're not paying him any more attention than you would a rabbit's butt as it disappears over a fence.*] Friend, this marijuana of yours is. terrific. I'm going home to listen to that new record Louis Armstrong made for the Okeh company. I hear he did some wonderful playing and singing on the number 'Exactly Like You'. See you at the Savoy Ballroom on Thursday … [*That is, the maids' night off, when all the domestic workers will be dancing there.*][20]

Although always a marijuana enthusiast, Mezzrow never tried to push it on people. He dealt mainly to friends and acquaintances; it was a family affair rather than a hard-nosed business deal. Ironically, when he was eventually busted in 1940 after the drug had been banned nationwide, he was caught giving it away.

Mezz was almost an underground national celebrity; visitors to New York sought him out to turn them on and no tea pad or rent party was complete without its stash of best-quality Mezz. Yet something was missing in all this adulation: the music. He was better known as a reefer man than as a musician. Mezzrow saw his marijuana-dealing as virtually a community service. Now, in the early thirties, the white mobsters (who owned many clubs in Harlem) were trying to turn it into a racket albeit on a small scale compared with the post-war years. Being dragged down to the level of white gangster scum enhanced the sense of inferiority Mezzrow already felt towards blacks.

In this state of rock-bottom self-esteem, Mezz met a drummer named Frankie Ward who reintroduced him to opium. His only previous experience of the drug had been with the mobsters back in Detroit: now he was more than ready to have all his fears and anxieties blotted out. From 1931 until 1935, Mezz spent a large part of his time in a cleaned-out six-foot-square coal bin which served as an opium pad. It had been set up by a dealer called Mike, in the basement of a tenement – where he was caretaker.

Mezz was in trouble. Even the guys whom he smoked with regularly begged him to give it up and not waste his talent as a musician. Like everyone who gets into opiates Mezz believed he could break the habit whenever he wanted to. Some can, and are able to use drugs like opium, morphine and heroin on a 'recreational' basis without ever becoming dependent. Mezzrow was not one of these. He tried hard to give it up and get his music together again. He made an appointment with a big-time radio booking agent to see if it was possible to fulfil his dreams of organising a racially mixed band. The agent greeted Mezz warmly, but all he wanted to talk about was setting up a marijuana distribution operation. When Mezz did get a contract he was allowed just one black singer. He had a black arranger as well though and everything looked fine until another bandleader poached his musicians: then it was back to the bunker for consolation.

In 1934 he tried again to come off and failed. Louis Armstrong, a long-time friend, offered him the chance of becoming his musical director. He gave Mezz $1,000 to clear his debts and meet his living expenses, but Mezz could not bring himself to tell Armstrong of his addiction. This time Mezzrow knew it was make or break. It is often the way that when there are more reasons for coming off drugs than staying on, a user will go for broke, however unpleasant the experience. And judged by his own description, Mezzrow had a tough time withdrawing from opium over several weeks. But he did it.

> One night I was sitting there listening and then I got up and took my docket and locked myself in my room. I put the horn together and looked at it for a long, long time . Then I raised it to my lips and blew. A beautiful, full, round and the note came vibrating out, a note with guts in it, with life and pounding strength. And then I started to cry. I had cried plenty the last four years, but this time my tears were tears of pure joy. I was human. I was awake. I was alive again.[21]

Busted for marijuana dealing in 1940, Mezz did a three-year stretch on Riker's

Island. His dealing days were over. Once outside, he carried on as musician and record producer, and married a black girl. Eventually he moved to Paris, where so many musicians, black and white, have gone into exile and seen their careers reborn among appreciative and receptive audiences. He died there in 1972 at the age of seventy-three.

4 CHANTS OF THE VIPERS

With so many musicians using drugs recreationally, it was hardly surprising that they should have written songs about them. In the thirties, the first heyday of songs about drugs, over one hundred containing references to the drug scene were recorded for the American black or 'race' radio-listening audience. In general the songs conveyed their message using the same 'hip' drug/jazz slang that the musicians used between themselves.

One hundred songs may be an underestimate for two reasons. First, after marijuana was banned in 1937, lyrics became increasingly obscure, so it is often impossible at this distance to be certain of the writer's meaning. Secondly, many songs had the word 'high' in the title, but no other lyrical clues in the song. A proportion of these would have been drug-orientated songs, but some writers just cashed in on the fashion for hip slang, to give their songs 'street credibility'. Further confusions arise from commentaries on drug-related lyrics. Charles Winick, a psychologist who has made a study of drug use among jazz musicians, maintained no doubt well-meaningly that Texas Tea Party' by Benny Goodman (1933) is not about drugs at all, but the opening lines are:

> Now, mama, mama mama
> Where did you hide my tea
> Now come on mama mama mama
> Quit holding out on me ...

So who goes to the trouble of hiding a tin of tea?

Marijuana was the drug most often referred to under its many slang names; weed, tea, gage, reefer and muggles, the title of one of Louis Armstrong's most famous recordings. The early 'viper' songs paid homage to the new 'social hero', the man who brought the stuff that people relied on to make their rent parties go with a swing. This was no evil mobster or sinister pusher, but a man like Mezz Mezzrow, regarded with affection and respect. He provided a public service in a city like New York where marijuana had an enormous impact, for not only was it the jazz capital of the thirties, but there were no local ordinances against marijuana smoking.

Musicians sang of the psychological and physical sensations of using marijuana, the illusions when you were high or, as they said, 'walking tall':

> *Dreamed about a reefer five foot long*
> *The mighty mezz, but not too strong...*
> *I'm the King of Everything...*
> *If you're a viper.*
>
> (If You're A Viper' 1938)

> *You never met the Reefer Man?*
> *Oh no? You never met the Reefer Man?*
> *And yet you say you swam to China*
> *And you wanted to sell me South Carolina*
> *I believe you know the Reefer Man.*
>
> ('The Reefer Man', 1932)

Some of the songs describe effects of marijuana which are totally at odds with the marijuana experience of the sixties. Then the drug was identified with peace, tranquillity and cerebral contemplation. But in the hysterical and dangerous anti-marijuana climate of the 1940s, (the subject of the next chapter) the singers related experiences more akin to the contemporary mythology of 'reefer madness'.

> *Boy, she's really frantic, the wildest chick in town*
> *She blows her gages flies in a rage*
> *Sweet Marijuana Brown*
> *In her victory garden the seeds grow all around*
> *She plants, you dig, she's flipped her wig*
> *Sweet Marijuana Brown*
> *She don't know where she's going, she don't care where she's been*
> *But every time you take her out, she's bound to take you in.*
> *Boy, that gal means trouble, you ought to put her down*
> *Get hep, take care, look out, beware of Sweet Marijuana Brown.*
>
> ('Sweet Marijuana Brown', 1945)

In the psychology of drug-taking, what the user expects to happen partly determines what actually does happen. This seems particularly true of marijuana. The drug features throughout the history of popular music, experienced differently by divergent subcultural groups: jazz-age swingers, cool beboppers, cosmic hippies and Trench Town roots rockers from Jamaica. Sociologist John Auld has discussed in depth the theory that the effects of marijuana are to a large extent a 'learned' experience, i.e. the novice user has to learn from others what he or she is expected to feel. (This may account for the fact that the first-time user often experiences nothing and wonders what all the fuss is about.) For somebody trying to be part of a social group as 'exclusive' and critical of outsiders as musicians, doing what the others do, saying what they say and feeling what they feel are of paramount importance. To stand a chance of being accepted, one had not only to use marijuana, but to appear to be affected by it in the same way as the others. Moreover, in the thirties, the belief that marijuana drives you mad was so widespread that users may have translated it into their actual experience, or said that they did, in order to emphasize their unorthodox outlook on life and consolidate their self-labelled outlaw status.

If the reefer songs reflected subcultural expectations of marijuana, they also reflected the legal response to the drug once it was banned in 1937. Now 'The Man' could mean not only the dealer but the government agent:

> *Light up, I know how you feel,*
> *You find what I mean in any old field,*
> *Now get your gig going,*
> *I'll say that's the thing,*
> *Don't let that man getcha,*
> *Just puff on your cig and blow those smoke rings.*

('Light Up', 1938)

Of necessity, songs' lyrics became increasingly obscure where drugs were involved. When Julia Lee sang her 'Spinach Song' (1943), she did not have Popeye in mind:

> *Spinach has Vitamins A, B and D*
> *But spinach never appealed to me*
> *But one day while having dinner with a guy*
> *I decided to give it a try.*

In 1933 Cab Calloway had been allowed to mention reefers in a big-budget Paramount film called *International House*. By the forties in-joke references to marijuana had to be slipped into Tin Pan Alley songs like 'Tea for Two':

> *Do you long for Oolong*
> *Like I long for Oolong*
> *Are you gone on Ceylon*
> *Like I'm gone on Ceylon?*

Marijuana found favour with most of the musicians who used it, although songs like 'Sweet Marijuana Brown' (1945) and 'Knocking Myself Out' suggested a downside to the drug and in 'Working Man Blues' (1937), Red Nelson declared 'reefers are made for doggone fools'. About cocaine, there was more ambiguity: several songs said how good it made you feel, but added that there was an eventual price to pay. Even a generally favourable song like Victoria Spivey's 'Dope Head Blues' (1928), has an air of desperation about the first two lines. The advertising for the record announced 'a record that groans with tragedy' accompanied by a suitably woeful drawing of a woman obviously wrecked by drugs:

> *Just give me one more sniffle*
> *Another sniffle of that dope*
> *I'll catch a cow like a cowboy*
> *Throw a bull without a rope.*
> *Just give me one more sniffle*

> *Another sniffle of that dope*

Less ambivalent was an up-tempo jaunt recorded by Chick Webb in 1938 and sung by Ella Fitzgerald called 'Wacky Dust':

> *They call it wacky dust*
> *It's from a hot cornet*
> *It gives feet a feeling, so breezy*
> *And oh, it's so easy to get.*

Possibly because most songs were negative about cocaine, writers were less coy about giving the drug its proper name and less often submerged the message in a welter of slang, like 'Wacky Dust'. In 1930 the Memphis Jug Band got straight to the point with 'Cocaine Habit Blues':

> *Cocaine habit's mighty bad, it's the worst ol' habit that I ever had.*

Cole Porter 'got no kick from cocaine'. Leadbelly and Sonny Boy Williamson sang blues about it and Dick Justice, Luke Jordan and Lil McLintock all sang a song variously titled 'Cocaine Blues', 'Cocaine' and 'Furniture Man', which further emphasized its perils:

> *I call my Cora, hey hey*
> *She come on sniffing with her nose all sore*
> *The doctor swore he wouldn't sell no more*

> *Coke's for horses, not for women or men*
> *The doctor said it'd kill you, but he didn't say when*
> *I'm simply wild about my good cocaine*

In 1941 'Can't Kick The Habit' was released. This was a decidedly sombre and pessimistic song about the problems of heroin addiction. To some jazz-age hipsters, opium and morphine users were right at the bottom, characters to be pitied rather than respected like the Reefer Man. 'Cokey Joe' and 'Jerry the Junker' were stock characters of death and degradation. 'Cokey' or 'Smokey Joe' turns up in Cab Calloway's 'Minnie the Moocher' (1938), delivered in a slurred, ponderous and tragic tone of voice:

> *She messed around with a bloke name Smokey*
> *She loved him though he was cokey*
> *He took her down to Chinatown*
> *Showed her how to kick the gong around.*

Smokey was doubly damned – not only an addict himself, but the cause of his girlfriend's addiction too. Hazel Myers' 'Pipe Dream Blues' (1924) is often quoted as sympathetic to opium smoking, but the good times are had only in reverie. When the singer wakes up, all her old troubles and some new ones, picked up through opium, come flooding back:

Dreamed I had a hot pipe in my hand
Owned a million dollars down in poppy land
I burn up ten-thousand-dollar bills
Everytime I light my pills
Someone woke me up
Now I'm crying
With the mean old pipe dream blues.

As jazz entered the fifties direct references to drugs of any kind virtually disappeared. In an era of anti-communist hysteria and draconian drug laws, it was very unwise of any musician to have too high a profile with the enforcement agencies. Drug references in jazz songs were largely confined to the titles of instrumentals in the drug slang of the fifties, like Harold Land's 'Smack Up' made famous by Art Pepper. You could never be too discreet; walls had ears and every careless word led back to the G-Man to end them all, the musician's nemesis, Mr Harry J. Anslinger.

5 HEY, HEY, HARRY J –
HOW MANY GUYS DID YOU BUST TODAY?

Opium? No! Cocaine? No! The Great American Brain Killer is Dance Music!

Portland Oregonian, *12 June 1932*

Jazz... the opiate that inflames the mind and incites to riotous orgies of delirious syncopation.

Harry Von Tilzer, popular song composer

Good jazz can be a wholesome tonic; bad jazz is always a dangerous drug.

Etude magazine, *January 1924*

For more than fifteen years before the 1937 federal ban on the possession of marijuana, State authorities in the South and West had been lobbying Washington to 'do something' about the drug. In the main, these were areas where Mexican immigrants had initially settled, and the campaign against marijuana was partly a reflection of what the indigenous population thought of the newcomers.

After the Mexican Revolution erupted in 1910, some of the fighting spilled over the Rio Grande. An attack by Pancho Villa on a small military outpost in New Mexico intensified antipathy towards Mexicans, already heightened by the influx of refugees. General Pershing led troops against Villa to the tune of:

> *It's a long way to capture Villa*
> *It's a long way to go*
> *It's a long way across the border*

Where the dirty greasers grow.

Pancho Villa's men had a different battle hymn. 'La Cucaracha' told of a cockroach who couldn't walk any longer because he didn't have any marijuana to smoke. (This song was regularly featured by Edmundo Ros and his Orchestra, a respectable middle-of-the-road dance band frequently heard on British radio in the fifties. Like Musical Youth's No 1 hit 'Pass the Dutchie', this celebration of an illegal drug slipped past the bat-eared radio censors.)

So closely were the Mexicans associated with the drug that, of all the names for it, the authorities and the press adopted the Mexican one, 'marijuana'. The newspapers of the South Western states carried regular stories about Mexicans driven crazy by 'locoweed' and committing assorted atrocities in familiar retellings of the 'cocaine-crazed nigger' scares. Resentment lay behind most of these stories; during the twenties, thousands of Mexicans moved north to Chicago in search of work, but when Depression struck they found themselves like the Chinese before them, in competition with dispossessed white labour.

But antagonism towards Mexican immigrants was not the immediate context in which marijuana became an outlawed drug. Mexicans were blamed for introducing the drug into America, but musicians were cited as the plague carriers, those who spread the disease and infected clean-cut white kids. The failure of Prohibition gave added impetus to the moral crusade against marijuana.

The quotes at the head of this chapter illustrate that drugs and jazz were so closely associated in the public mind that images of one were used to condemn the other. The pre-First World War dance craze brought with it dire warnings in fashionable women's magazines about the dangers of being seduced by stylishly dressed but lower-class 'tango pirates'. The word 'pirate' conjured up an image of an elusive rogue who stole money and virtue from helpless women beguiled by his charms, who 'trapped and tapped the sexuality of women'.[1] 'Worse than that, he used drugs as part of his arsenal of entrapment.' '[Cocaine] … is the stigma that classes him with the criminal of a lower and less alluring grade.'[2] Telling them the drug was for fun, the tango pirate allegedly inveigled women into sex and into squandering their money. Eliminate him, the reformers demanded, or the traditions of Victorian culture might disintegrate altogether.

It was but a quick two-step from the tango pirate to a new form of social menace, the jazz musician. Jazz was blamed for endangering the morals of young people by encouraging the release of animal passions through sensual dancing, boy-girl contact, the sexual content of jazz lyrics and, of course, the link with drug-taking. In 1922 Hartley Mann's play *The National Anthem* opened on Broadway. The essence of the plot was the debauchery and decadence of youth flying in the face of wise parent counselling. Jazz was implicated as 'modern man's Saturnalia', rhythm without soul. Pseudo-scientific studies purported to demonstrate its evil.

A report from the Illinois Vigilance Association claimed that in 1921-2, jazz had caused the downfall of 1,000 girls in Chicago alone. The leader of the State Hospital in Napa, California declared:

> I can say from my own knowledge that about fifty per cent of our young boys and girls from the age sixteen to twenty-five that land in the insane asylum these days are jazz-crazy dope fiends and public dance hall

patrons. Jazz combinations – dope fiends and public dance halls are the same ... where you find one, you will find the other.[3]

Attempts were made to ban jazz from places of public entertainment: some newspapers adopted a deliberate conspiracy of silence, others tried to wish it away by maintaining that jazz was a dying fad. Underpinning most of the objections to jazz was an antipathy to black culture and to the so-called Harlem Renaissance, whereby black artists were feted (or patronised) by a cross-section of affluent white bohemian society. Laurette Taylor, who played the lead role in *The National Anthem*, summed up the traditionalist viewpoint on jazz: 'Jazz, the impulse for wildness that has undoubtedly come over many things besides music in this country, is traceable to the Negro influence.'[4]

Some people seriously believed that if jazz was allowed to flourish, either the purity of the race would be contaminated by massive miscegenation or the epidemic would infect the sober white population, reducing them to the level of the savage black. No condemnation of jazz was complete without some reference to white kids going out of control to the beat of jungle rhythms.

The drug connection was central to the creation of the jazz (and later rock) musicians as outlaw figures. From the earliest expressions of concern about marijuana, musicians were implicated. On 21 August 1920, Dr Oscar Dowling of the Louisiana Health Board advised the governor about the increasing availability of the drug. This had come to his attention through the arrest and imprisonment of a twenty-one-year-old musician convicted of forging a doctor's name on a prescription. On 1 July 1928, under the headline 'New Giggle Drug Puts Discord in City Orchestras', the *Chicago Tribune* reported that marijuana addiction was common among local musicians. The paper noted that marijuana 'is an old drug but was generally introduced into the country only a few years ago by the Mexicans. It is like cocaine. In the long run, it bends and cripples its victims. A sort of creeping paralysis results from long use.'[5]

Several states banned the use of marijuana long before 1937. Usually these were in areas of Mexican settlement but, for some still unclear reason, California took the lead in 1915 at a time when there were virtually no Mexican settlers. Louis Armstrong fell foul of this state law in 1931, as he told Max Jones and John Chilton:

> It was during our intermission at this big nightclub which was packed and jammed every night with all sorts of my fans including movie stars. Anyway, Vic (Berton, a top drummer) and I were blasting this joint – having lots of laughs and feeling good, enjoying each other's company. We were standing in front of some cars. Just then, two big healthy Dicks came from behind a car nonchalantly and said to us, 'We'll take the roach, boys.'[6]

Fortunately Armstrong was saved from a possible beating, by the admiration of these two particular cops for his music. They were quite honest, regretting that Armstrong had been unlucky to get caught doing what many others were at. One of the detectives told Armstrong that a rival bandleader had 'dropped a nickel' on him, that is phoned the police to tip them off. Even though the police were sympathetic, Louis Armstrong faced a six-month sentence for possessing a cigarette stub, all that remained when he was arrested.

He spent nine days in the downtown Los Angeles City Jail waiting for his trial. The courtroom was packed and newspaper headlines had Armstrong serving time even before the case had started. In the event, he got off with a suspended sentence and was back playing that night. Movie stars, familiar with morphine, heroin and cocaine on the Hollywood film lots, didn't really know what marijuana was. It was obvious from the comments of some who congratulated Armstrong afterwards that they thought it was Mexican for an underage girl!

It was around the time of Armstrong's bust that the government began to change its mind about marijuana. Up until then, appeals from state legislators and moral crusaders had been ignored. The appointment of a new Commissioner of Narcotic Drugs and the reorganisation of narcotics law enforcement heralded the start of a new era in Federal drug policy.

In 1914 a narcotics division was created in the Inland Revenue Bureau of the Treasury Department to collect revenue from opiate sales and enforce the Harrison Act. In 1920 it merged into the Prohibition Unit of that department, which in turn became the Prohibition Bureau in 1927. The Bureau of Narcotics was formed as a separate bureau in the Treasury Department in July 1930.

Prior to the creation of the new bureau, the then Head of the Narcotics Division, Levi Nutt, was removed from office after a scandal involving the major gangster of the day, Arnold Rothstein, and some corrupt Federal agents. Rothstein was murdered in 1928. Among his papers was evidence linking him to Levi Nutt's son and son-in-law, both lawyers. Documents presented to a Grand Jury proved that both had been employed by Rothstein to defend him against the Treasury in tax cases, and one had borrowed money from him. The jury also heard that the local Federal narcotics office in New York had been instructed by Nutt to boost arrest statistics by falsifying records, and that agents from the same office had colluded with major dealers. Nutt was out, eventually relegated to the Alcohol Tax Unit until his retirement.

> ...[Anslinger] himself in appearance was a grotesquely ugly man. Frightening. He looked like the Swedish Angel – that wrestler. He was about six feet tall, with the biggest head I've ever seen on a person in my life... completely bald... very large ears.
>
> He had a disposition about him that used to scare the shit out of people who met him wherever he went... Whenever he came to the office, word would spread like word of a plague. Everybody had to be on his toes. He would say very little to any of the people. He just looked at you and he was a scary-looking guy... He had that kind of mystical quality about him and strange manners. I cannot emphasize enough the reverence everyone who worked under him held for him.[7]

On 25 September 1930 Harry Jacob Anslinger, 'the Swedish Angel', took over the newly designated post of Commissioner of Narcotic Drugs. There were narcotics laws, anti-marijuana laws and an albeit localized anti-marijuana campaign before Anslinger came to power (and if that makes him sound like royalty it's meant to). But it was Anslinger who orchestrated the national campaign against marijuana and determined the drug's image in the minds of the public for the next thirty years. The image changed only when Anslinger changed his tactics. Through a single-minded devotion to the greater glory of his department and to the moral crusade against drugs,

Anslinger manipulated politicians at home and abroad throughout his thirty-year reign in the Narcotics Bureau and afterwards as US representative on the UN Narcotics Commission.

Hardly anything is known about Anslinger's personal life. Born in Altoona, Pennsylvania on 20 May 1892, of dour, upright Dutch parents, he was as enigmatic and secret a figure as his arch-rival, J. Edgar Hoover of the FBI. No comprehensive biography of him has been written, although he remains the single most influential figure in the history of drugs legislation.

In *The Murderers: The Shocking Story of the Narcotics Gangs*, the second of two books he wrote, Anslinger recalled the incident which decided his destiny:

> As a youngster of twelve, visiting in the house of a neighbouring farmer, I heard the screaming of a woman on the second floor. I had never heard such cries of pain before. The woman, I learned later, was addicted, like many other women of that period, to morphine, a drug whose dangers most medical authorities did not yet recognise. All I remember was that I heard a woman in pain, whose cries seem to fill my whole twelve-year-old being. Then her husband came running down the stairs, telling me I had to get into the cart and drive to town. I was to pick up a package at the drug store and bring it back for the woman.
>
> I recall driving those horses, lashing at them, convinced that the woman would die if I did not get back in time. When I returned with the package – it was morphine – the man hurried upstairs to give the woman the dosage. In a little while her screams stopped and a hush came over the house.
>
> I never forgot those screams. Nor did I forget that the morphine she had required was sold to a twelve-year-old boy, no questions asked.[8]

When war broke out, Anslinger was employed at the War Department Ordinance Division, moving on to become a career diplomat with postings in Holland, Germany, Venezuela and the Bahamas, where he successfully stopped contraband whisky coming to the States from the West Indies. This earned him a transfer to the Prohibition Bureau where he rose to the position of Assistant Commissioner. His career was meteoric; he earned himself a reputation for being hard-working and unflinchingly loyal, with a remarkable flair for investigative work of all kinds. The years in government service had also attuned his skills to the art of the possible. Although a moral idealist, he was also a pragmatic bureaucrat, able to modify his policy when the situation demanded. Just as well, because the course of marijuana prohibition in the thirties twisted and turned like a rattlesnake.

Anslinger came into office decidedly unenthusiastic about a Federal ban on marijuana. When the Bureau of Narcotics was formed he was allocated only about 300 agents. As a member of the Prohibition Bureau he had seen the law fall into disrespect not only because it was unpopular but because lack of resources made it unenforceable. A rerun of that fiasco would kill his Bureau and career stone dead. For most of the thirties, few ordinary people had even heard of marijuana, let alone regarded it as a dangerous drug which should be controlled. It grew wild all over the country, so for all the bluster of state health officials and some newspapers, marijuana was not a public issue.

Anslinger wanted all the states to adopt a uniform State Narcotics Law and then define marijuana as a narcotic. This would mean that marijuana law enforcement would become a local issue, thus taking pressure off the Bureau who were busy enforcing the Harrison Act. Moreover, to define marijuana as a narcotic would establish it as a dangerous drug by linking it with true narcotic drugs like opium, morphine and heroin. In order to pressurize the States, much as they had been pressurising him, Anslinger began to orchestrate a national anti-drug campaign focusing on the marijuana menace and emphasizing how the drug was supposed to drive men to criminal acts. He whipped up enthusiasm for this campaign by speaking around the country to religious groups, temperance organisations, indeed any organization that invited him.

Although by his own admission the data were suspect, Anslinger built up a case file of crimes which purported to prove beyond a shadow of doubt the evil of marijuana. These cases he gave to newspapers to publish verbatim; nearly all the information on marijuana circulating in magazines and journals in the mid-thirties was supplied by Anslinger's office. The file of gory crimes was brought out at every opportunity and eventually formed the 'scientific' basis for the outlawing of marijuana in 1937. Among Anslinger's favourites was:

> Corpus Christi. Governor of Texas told me of a case he knew about personally, and one which in some measure influenced him to destroy 600 acres of hemp. An oil worker, good character, smoked a cigarette, raped his six-year-old daughter. When his wife returned home in the evening, she found him lying across the bed in a stupor and the little child torn and bleeding. He couldn't remember. Was sentenced to death.[9]

The pick of the crop, however, was the Victor Licata case in Florida. On 17 October 1933, twenty-one-year-old Licata killed his parents, two brothers and a sister with an axe while allegedly under the influence of a 'marijuana dream', as he explained to his arresting officers. This became the standard marijuana horror story repeated by Anslinger and the press time and again. Licata claimed that six months of marijuana smoking had unhinged his mind. Although the police were not convinced that marijuana was wholly to blame, police chief Bush used the occasion to condemn it as a dangerous drug, a theme taken up by the *Tampa Times* which had first reported the story:

> STOP THIS MURDEROUS SMOKE
> …it may or may not be wholly true that the pernicious marijuana cigarette is responsible for the murderous mania of a Tampa young man in exterminating all the members of his family within his reach -but whether or not the poisonous mind-wrecking weed is mainly accountable for the tragedy its sale should not be and should never have been permitted here or elsewhere… It required five murders to impress the Tampa public and Tampa officials with the serious effects of the habit.

As it turned out, Licata was diagnosed as criminally insane, a condition almost certainly inherited. His parents were first cousins and five close family members, including one of his brothers, were also insane. Licata remained in the State Mental Hospital until 1950, when he hanged himself. Marijuana was never mentioned in his case notes.

Anslinger's hope that the States would take responsibility for the marijuana issue was not his only reason for launching a scare campaign. A staunch Republican, he had been a Hoover appointee, an appointment not unconnected, some said, with the fact that his wife was the niece of Andrew Mellon, the Treasury Secretary. In 1934, Franklin Roosevelt became President. The Democratic New Dealers took great exception to Anslinger's comments about 'niggers' and how addicts were a menace to society. There were moves in high places to have him sacked, but he hung on thanks to the support of influential Republican Congressmen and of the even more influential Hearst newspaper group, which he assiduously cultivated.

All this meant Anslinger needed to divert attention away from his own right-wing attitudes and to prove the Bureau's worth. He was also anxious to steal some of the limelight away from J. Edgar Hoover and the FBI. The rivalry between the two was intense. Hoover kept his all-American boys away from the sleazy, slightly disreputable world of narcotics enforcement, fearful of corruption which would tarnish the FBI's image. Narcotics work is essentially done under cover; agents have to melt into the criminal background if they are to stand any chance of nailing big-time traffickers. Corruption is almost inevitable where poorly paid officers are mixing with wealthy dealers and the line between police and criminal can become very blurred. So Hoover stuck to 'ordinary' criminals who committed conspicuous crimes like bank robberies and whom he could apprehend with enormous publicity. In the thirties, the FBI netted two big fish, John Dillinger and Pretty Boy Floyd, making all the front pages.

The Narcotics Bureau faced additional problems when the wash of Depression hit it and wiped $200,000 off the budget for 1935 – all the more reason for Anslinger to find every means of demonstrating how well the Bureau was doing. In fact, Anslinger's campaign was bearing fruit. After a slow start, by 1936 thirty-eight of the forty-eight states had adopted the Uniform State Narcotics Law and many had added marijuana to their list of narcotics. In addition, all forty-eight states had enacted some legislation governing the sale or possession of marijuana completing the process started by California in 1915. So why was there a Federal ban on marijuana in 1937? What was the point?

In the first place, pressure was mounting on the Treasury and thus on Anslinger for the government to ban the drug. In effect. Anslinger's campaign was too successful. The press were saying that if marijuana was that bad, then not only the States, but the Federal authority itself, had a moral duty to take action and protect citizens. There was little confidence in the idea that marijuana could be controlled locally. Anslinger had to rethink his opposition to Federal action, realizing too that to have control of all illegal drug enforcement was the best way to win the approval of Congress in the light of recent budget cuts. A Federal law against marijuana would do wonders for the Bureau's arrest figures.

The passing of the 1937 Marijuana Tax Act, which effectively outlawed non-medical possession, brought with it a new problem for Anslinger. Again it arose as a result of his own campaign. So convinced were people that marijuana use led to crime, that defence lawyers all over the country were pleading insanity and diminished responsibility on behalf of their clients who claimed to have taken the drug. An important weapon in the lawyers' arsenal was Anslinger's own widely circulated article, 'Marijuana: Assassin of Youth', published in the *American Magazine* in July 1937:

In Los Angeles, California, a youth was walking along a downtown street after inhaling a marijuana cigarette. For many addicts, merely a portion of a 'reefer' is enough to induce intoxication. Suddenly for no reason, he decided that someone had threatened to kill him and that his life was in danger. Wildly he looked about him. The only person in sight was an aged bootblack. Drug-crazed nerve centres conjured the innocent old shoe-shiner into a destroying monster. Mad with fright, the addict hurried to his room and got a gun. He killed the old man and then later babbled his grief over what had been wanton, uncontrolled murder. 'I thought someone was after me,' he said. 'That's the only reason I did it. I had never seen the old fellow before. Something just told me to kill him!' That's marijuana!

Once he saw what was happening, Anslinger put the lid on all marijuana horror stories emanating from his office. Furthermore, he set out to discredit other moral crusaders who continued in this vein. This was not only to stop insanity pleas: to have people ranting on about the evils of marijuana would imply that the Bureau was not doing its job – definitely bad for business.

In fact Anslinger was not having much success in pulling off a major drug bust. In a sense, his trouble was that he believed his own propaganda. The drug was not in widespread use throughout the country as he claimed, but concentrated both geographically and socio-economically around certain cities like New York, Chicago, Kansas City and New Orleans. Anslinger had also hoped that local police would pick up small-time dealers and users, while the Bureau would grab the headlines by busting the big boys. The trouble was, there weren't any big boys; most of the marijuana dealers were, like Mezz Mezzrow, selling to friends, although there was some mobster involvement in places like Harlem.

So Anslinger adapted his policy once again. Leaving marijuana enforcement to the States, the Bureau concentrated increasingly on opiates, particularly after the war. Nevertheless, Anslinger still hungered after publicity for combatting marijuana, and began to target well-known personalities, film stars, musicians, to extract the maximum exposure for the minimum effort. This became known as the 'star-bust syndrome'.

Anslinger had kept a special file on musicians since the early thirties. A section contained details of musicians arrested for possessing and/or dealing in marijuana. In order to establish musicians as 'public enemies' he made a careful note of every case that came to his attention, however trivial:

> 1933:
> Three Negroes arrived (in Montreal) three days previously from New York to fill an eight weeks' dancing contract at the Frolics Cabaret, and one of them at least had immediately started in trafficking. In addition to several small buys, one transaction involved the purchase of fifteen cigarettes at a cost of $19.00. Owing to the necessity for not disclosing the agent, it was not possible to charge them with selling but two of the Negroes, Banks and Burnham, together with the Canadian Gravel, were found guilty and sentenced to six months' imprisonment with a fine of $200.00, the third Negro being acquitted.
> Banks and Burnham admitted using marijuana cigarettes and claimed to

secure their supply from a tobacco shop in New York City, but refused to give any further details. They arrived in Montreal by motorbus direct from New York City, and I understand have for some months past been filling dancing contracts in the United States.[10]

The press came to Anslinger's assistance in creating a musicians' 'pogrom' with stories like this from the *St Louis Post Dispatch*, 8 April 1934, headlined 'A drug menace at the University of Kansas':

> Everything points to the introduction of the drug Marijuana into the University by travelling jazz bands that come to play for large university or smaller fraternity and sorority dances. [Narcotics Investigator] Johns says that he has learned that many members of jazz bands not only in this section, but generally throughout the country, often resort to marijuana or some other drug to obscure the monotony of their lives, the ceaseless thumping of jazz night after night. 'They take a few puffs of a marijuana cigarette if they are tired,' Johns says. 'it gives them a lift and they can go on playing even though they may be virtually paralysed from the waist down which is one of the effects marijuana may have.' [No doubt another biochemical insight traceable to the Bureau of Narcotics.]

Lodged in Anslinger's file is a rare cutting from the British music paper, the *Melody Maker*, dated 22 February 1936. It is rare because it marks one of the very few instances prior to the rave era of the 1990s when the British music press has made editorial comment about drug use within the industry itself. Britain banned opiate drugs and cocaine with the Dangerous Drugs Act of 1920, adding marijuana in 1928. Statistically, the drug 'problem' in Britain was in decline through the twenties and thirties, not on the increase as the *Melody Maker* maintained. But among the small coterie of the rich and famous, writers, show people and musicians, illegal drugs remained in circulation, hidden from public view. Precisely which drugs were involved is unclear, because 'dope' could involve any or all of the major drugs covered by the legislation. Cocaine was the most popular illicit drug in London, circulating in West End bars and clubs:

> Drug peddling and drug-taking is growing in this country. It can no longer be denied that jazz clubs have been among the haunts of drug pedlars.
> It is right that the searchlight of publicity be turned upon clubs of this nature. It is unfortunate that the searchlight should sweep also across the many clubs that are guiltless.
> This newspaper has consistently championed the avant garde of dance music and its practitioners. It will continue to do so.
> Equally is it determined to stamp upon everything that will hamper the healthy growth of that music whether it be the policy of the BBC, the apathy of the recording companies... or those who would make jazz clubs the market-place of dope...

In America, musicians had been busted for marijuana offences throughout the thirties, but Anslinger himself did not clash with the industry until February 1938, after the Federal ban had been introduced. Two men were arrested near Minneapolis for growing and distributing $5,000 worth of marijuana. The Federal District Supervisor for the area, Joseph Bell, told the *Minneapolis Tribune* that 'Present-day swing music, the Big Apple Dance and orchestra jam sessions are responsible for increasing the use of marijuana both by dance band musicians and the boys and girls who patronize them.' Sidney Berman, editor of the predominantly white *Orchestra World*, fired off a letter to Anslinger complaining of this slur on musicians. Anslinger placated Berman by attributing the comments to those arrested and not to Joseph Bell. But Bell in his report to Anslinger said his own experience confirmed the widespread use of marijuana among jazz musicians and he quoted one of the men he had arrested:

> This person stated that the use of marijuana is quite prevalent among musicians, particularly so-called 'jazz bands', because, under the influence of the drug they seem to acquire a certain talent which they do not ordinarily possess. In the words of the individual I mention, they 'get hot'.[11]

Whether or not musicians actually did 'get hot' was itself a hotly debated issue. For Anslinger, the question was settled by the results of an experiment in 1944 involving marijuana and Carl Seashore's Musical Aptitude Test. Twelve volunteers were used, all prisoners serving sentences for marijuana offences with a 'mean' usage of about nine years. Of these twelve, only two were musicians, although two had 'musical ambitions', whatever that meant. First they were tested for their responses to pitch, tone, timbre, timing, etc. Then they were administered the drug and tested again. Nine out of twelve achieved poorer scores second time round, although eight thought they had done better. According to Anslinger this was conclusive proof that playing better under the influence of marijuana is an illusion. That may well be true, but the test proved nothing of the sort. What about the three who scored better under the influence? How did the two musicians score? Anslinger says nothing about this in his notes. In any case, it was plainly absurd to draw any conclusions about drug use and improvisational jazz playing from an artificial laboratory experiment.

Briefed by Anslinger, lurid press coverage of swing bands' marijuana orgies prompted a bitter response from *Keynote*, the magazine of the Detroit Federation of Musicians, echoing the *Melody Maker's* outburst five years earlier. 'Marijuana – a scourge' was a front page editorial in the January-February issue 1941:

> Marijuana – weed – grass – tea – reefers – call it anything you like – is classed by law and by effect in the same category as narcotics. For some reason or other – and no matter how it hurts, let's face it – the comparatively few musicians who are addicted to its use have gained for the entire music profession a reputation among law enforcement officers, and to some extent among the general public, that is most unsavory, and every day bring disgrace and worse to the good reputation of the great majority who do not use it.

On 15 January 1943 the prestigious jazz magazine *Down Beat* joined the war of words against musicians taking a 'tea break', after some soldiers, musicians and other entertainers were caught in a hotel room with marijuana. The editors faced a classic dilemma: they had previously killed similar stories for fear of bringing jazz musicians into ill-repute, as the mainstream press had done. On the other hand, they felt the need to be seen joining in the condemnation of those musicians who used drugs. So with great reluctance they ran the following editorial:

> This is one of the sorriest messes that we've seen. Immediately after the story broke originally, the *Beat's* New York office was deluged with requests for information... At first our attitude was 'we don't know a thing'; but when the big news weeklies began checking, we started thinking. And when one of the leaders concerned called up in a panic lest his band be ruined by adverse publicity as being a bunch of 'teahounds', we knew some action was in order... We know that there are musicians who smoke tea... We know that there is a select clique that has been working in the top bands for years who do it, and we know that they are going to get it in the neck if they aren't careful. And if the business as a whole isn't careful, it is going to take a bad rap along with them. Once more the old bogies are going to be floating around. 'Musician' is going to be synonymous with 'weed hound'. The business neither deserves nor can stand a national campaign of this sort... The Narcotics Bureau has the names and facts concerning many of the musicians who use tea. They aren't as interested in jailing these men as they are in finding out the sources of supply and the selling agents. We can only suggest to anyone who uses the stuff: STOP IT NOW, BEFORE YOU GET YOURSELF AND YOUR FRIENDS IN A POTFUL OF TROUBLE! We can only suggest to the AFM [American Federation of Musicians] that it pass a ruling calling for instant expulsion of anyone caught using tea.

Down Beat's attitude represents what is still the attitude of the music business in general to what it knows goes on in dark corners. This can be summarized as, 'Don't ask me because I don't know and even if I did, I wouldn't tell you.' This is part studied non-interference, part glamorization through mystique and part fear of attracting the attention of organized crime which runs the trafficking networks.

By 1943, it was clear that Anslinger's 'star-bust' policy had been a dismal failure His only big-name capture had been drummer Gene Krupa. In July 1943 during one of Krupa's engagements at the Hollywood Palladium and the Los Angeles Orpheum Theatre, Anslinger received information which resulted in Krupa's arrest in San Francisco for possession of marijuana and for sending his seventeen-year-old valet to his hotel room to fetch some reefers. Krupa was found guilty of possession, sentenced to ninety days in jail and fined $500. He was later found guilty of involving the minor in the unlawful transportation of narcotics and sentenced to imprisonment for a period of one to six years, but the conviction was reversed on appeal. Anslinger noted that after Krupa's conviction it was reported in a newspaper column that 'Gene Krupa's well-wishers are setting up a $100,000 fund for a public-relations build-up, so that Krupa's career won't be ruined by his present difficulties.'

In 1959, actor Sal Mineo made a reasonable attempt at playing the drummer in *The Gene Krupa Story*. Krupa is shown turning down reefers left, right and centre until his new girlfriend hands him one saying, 'Be somebody, Gino. Put your miseries out to pasture!' He then gets 'hooked', and when the police find thirty-nine marijuana cigarettes on him, his girlfriend is implicated After serving ninety days, Krupa is driven out of town, forced to play in any cheap dive he can find. Eventually Tommy Dorsey gives him a break and he finds his way back to the straight and narrow.

Exactly ten years after the film's release, the real Gene Krupa featured in a *Variety* story headlined, 'Gene Krupa Beating Drum Against Marijuana: Warns Youth of Illusory "Highs"'. 'According to Krupa. "I don't think that any person is greater than his talents and if you don't have your full faculties, your technique is not right... When you play the drums, you try to draw the sound out. When you're on drugs. you pound."[12] He illustrated a drum sound with an even roll as played by a skilled clear-headed skinster, and an uneven sound by a drummer on the weed.'[12] If Harry Anslinger heard about this 'confessional', his thoughts went unrecorded.

Ironically, Tommy Dorsey, 'hero' of the Gene Krupa film, was himself almost netted in 1944. He got into a fight at his birthday party and his opponent started shouting off about marijuana being present. However, when it came to giving a statement to the police, the informant denied ever making the charge and the case against Dorsey had to be dropped.

It was Anslinger's right-hand man, Malachi Harney, who concluded that if the Bureau was to have any success apprehending name musicians, it needed inside information. Anslinger regarded jazz musicians as hardly any better than criminals, notorious 'stoolies' if the price was right or the grudge big enough. He was easily convinced by Harney's argument that a system of informants was the answer. In fact it wasn't. Anslinger had not reckoned on the tightness of the jazz community. Worse still, from his point of view, musicians were blatantly admitting their own marijuana 'addiction' before the Draft Board. In this way, classified as 4-F, unfit for active service, they escaped the war.

To add insult to injury 1946 saw the publication of Mezz Mezzrow's autobiography *Really the Blues*. In an unpublished essay 'Marijuana and Musicians', Anslinger gave vent to his feelings: 'In addition to deriding the dangerous aspects and being a glorification of marijuana smoking and other forms of drug indulgence, the book reeks of filth in general. It seems incredulous [sic] that such an advertisement of narcotic addiction could overnight become a sensational bestseller.'[13]

Even without an effective army of informers, the Bureau managed to draw up a list of prominent musicians who were kept under surveillance, including Thelonious Monk. Anslinger also kept a special list of the orchestras containing musicians who had been busted for possessing marijuana. The list read like a pantheon of jazz, including the orchestras of Louis Armstrong, Count Basie, Cab Calloway, Duke Ellington, Dizzy Gillespie and Lionel Hampton.

In the late forties Anslinger tried yet another tactic – enlisting the aid of the unions. He sent the draft of a letter intended for the President of the American Federation of Musicians to his superior, Under-Secretary Foley, for approval. He didn't get it, perhaps for reasons of internal politics. Undaunted by this snub from his boss, Anslinger carried his campaign to the Ways and Means Appropriation Committee in March 1949, where his budget for 1950 was under review. His aim was to establish in the minds of Congress the notion that musicians were responsible for the spread of marijuana among young people:

> MR FERNANDEZ:　　　Then I take it there is more widespread use of it [marijuana] in the past two years than there was before the war?

ANSLINGER: I think the traffic has increased in marijuana, and unfortunately particularly among the young people. We have been running into a lot of traffic among these jazz musicians, and I am not speaking about the good musicians, but the jazz type. In one place down here in North Carolina we arrested a whole orchestra, everybody in the orchestra. In Chicago we have arrested some rather prominent jazz musicians; and in New York. It is pretty widespread. The musicians ought to do something about it. I have asked them to do something to see if they can't clean their own house a bit. And we have seized sources of supply from these musicians at different times. We have not made the progress with the marijuana traffic that has been made otherwise. You will notice, however, that in violations reported, our cases year after year seem to be about the same.

By making a distinction between 'good music' and jazz, Anslinger brought down an avalanche of protest letters on the Treasury. With one quote he had managed to alienate the music industry which he had been trying so hard to cultivate. *Down Beat* made Anslinger's comment the focus of their next editorial after the hearings:

How confused can you get?…
The bad time given to musicians by the daily press in the general run of things is serious enough. But when a government official in a report to Congress divides them arbitrarily into two groups, 'good' and 'jazz', it is going a little too far.

Realizing now that any systematic attempt to enlist the co-operation of any sector of the business was hopeless, Anslinger went back to a more direct approach. He proposed that the Department of State revoke the passports of all musicians who had appeared in court on marijuana charges. Again, he picked on Thelonious Monk. While obviously no fan, Anslinger had noted the significance of Monk for other musicians and fans and this seemed to single him out for special scrutiny. The same applied to Charlie Parker and Billie Holiday. Thelonious Monk was subject to harassment over many years, but he never had his passport cancelled, because again, Under-Secretary Foley refused to back the proposal.

Musicians were at the top of Anslinger's hit list. He tried to get them informed on, kicked out of their union, grounded in the USA and pilloried in the press. He had his victories and probably did more than anybody to establish publicly the link between drugs and musicians. But it was no easy fight; the jazz community closed ranks and his own boss pulled the rug from under his feet on at least two recorded occasions. Yet perhaps the heaviest body blow that 'the Swedish Angel' had to take was dealt by Fats Waller. He was asked to record a song for the troops, a morale booster for 'our boys over there'. The song, an Armed Forces Radio V disc, was distributed by the thousand to all the overseas bases. It began:

Dreamed about a reefer five foot long
Mighty Mezz but not too strong …

6 GOLDEN HORNS, GOLDEN ARMS

They can get it out of your blood, but they can't get it out of your mind.

Charlie Parker

We all find ways to try and destroy ourselves. Drugs – it was the rage. It's still the rage. It's the rage when you're not happy, not confident, when you can't deal with life. It's a death wish. I'm speaking from what I know not something I've read.

Sheila Jordan

The only jazz has come out of oppression and drug addiction …

Archie Shepp

The economic situation in which many black musicians found themselves during the Depression years of the thirties encouraged the younger generation to isolate themselves from the mainstream of white culture. Work was scarce and white musicians were always favoured over black in radio session work. The purge of top-flight gangsters through arrest or assassination closed a number of clubs in New York and Chicago, putting musicians out on the streets. The 'race' record market had been buoyant, but at a time of crippling stringency, 'disposable' income was at a premium and the market declined. So on the air, on the road and in the studio, job opportunities for black musicians were much reduced. In addition, touring bands were playing to increasingly segregated audiences, exacerbating the polarisation between black and white musicians.

But the divisions went still deeper; younger black musicians resented and mocked those of an older generation, 'Uncle Toms' who continued to dance to the beat of the white man's rhythm. As pianist Hampton Hawes put it, 'Our rebellion was a form of survival. If we didn't do that, what else could we do? Get your hair gassed, put on your bow ties and a funny smile and play pretty for the rich whitefolks? We were pilgrims, the freaks of the forties and fifties; our rebellion was a lonely thing.'[1]

The rebellion was bebop, built on the tradition that the black man had to prove that he was better than the white man on the white man's own terms, because only by being better could he be accepted. But revolutions need environments to ferment and develop, and perhaps one significant factor in the emergence of bebop and its 'hipster' jazz musician, was that few of the trials and tribulations of the professional black musician applied to those working in Kansas City.[2]

Under the patronage of Mayor Tom Pendergast and his Mafia supporters. every kind of 'public service' was readily available. The booze flowed like water, women were on every street corner and the city was the key drugs-distribution point for the whole of the South Western United States. Prohibition and, to some extent, Depression were events the citizens of Kansas read about in the newspapers. Kansas was a wide-open city with a proliferation of night spots where jazz could flourish as it had done in New Orleans and Chicago. The Pendergast political machine collapsed in 1939, but not before managers, agents and promoters had beaten a path to the city where it was all happening.

New jazz warriors like Lester Young, Walter 'Hot Lips' Page, Ben Webster and Count Basie provided a much-needed injection of freshness and excitement into a music becoming cliched and clinical with the passage of time. Sax heavyweights like Coleman Hawkins and Chu Berry came to do battle in 'saxophone city'. And hanging over the balcony of the Reno Club intently watching and listening to everything about Lester Young, down to the way he held his sax, was an earnest fourteen-year-old who shouldn't even have been there, as he was under age – Charlie Parker.

Jazzmen of Lester Young's generation were more sophisticated than the early New Orleans/Chicago crowd, but they were not yet ready to fight back against the white establishment. Kansas City may have provided plenty of playing opportunities – for black musicians but in every other respect it was a no-nonsense Jim Crow town. So what these musicians tended to do was to bury themselves in an exclusive, bohemian style of living. The stance they adopted was unapproachable, arrogant, non-conformist and inward-looking. Later, the barriers deliberately erected by bebop musicians between themselves and the audience created a romantic, tantalising image: the street-wise, world-weary Byronic shadow, the Wandering Jew with a saxophone. Central to the creation of this tragic hero and the whole process of cultural isolation was an overpowering need to alter the distasteful reality of everyday consciousness. Lester Young was the first and his isolation tank was full of whisky; but Charlie Parker became regarded as state-of-the-art, because his shield to the outside world was heroin.

Unknown numbers of jazz musicians, black and white, got involved with heroin to a greater or lesser extent in the forties and fifties. It was said that if you wanted to recruit the best band you had to go to the Public Health Service Hospitals at Lexington and Fort Worth, where many narcotics offenders were sent, supposedly to clean up.

Heroin was cheap; even those in the lowliest paid jobs could afford a habit without resorting to crime. The drug came in pharmaceutical No.5 capsules, ranging from $1 to $3 each. Ten of these capsules contained one gram of heroin. This would constitute a fairly heavy daily habit, but some musicians claimed habits in excess of four or five grams a day. When the Pendergast gravy train ground to a halt in 1939, several musicians moved to New York. Night spots on 52nd Street such as Minton's, the Royal Roost and Smalls' Paradise played host to bebop and to every drug dealer in the city. During the war years, soldiers coming back to base from a night out on the street stoned and/or robbed of their money led the military to put pressure on the city authorities to tighten up law enforcement. In consequence many establishments were closed down and both the music and the drug action became concentrated around just a handful of clubs. After the war the availability of heroin increased dramatically when the Mafia re-opened the supply routes from Turkey and the Far East, via Marseilles to New York, to meet the rising demand from the city's growing black and Puerto Rican communities. Dealers would gather in the men's room at Birdland, openly displaying their wares on the window ledge. Pianist Billy Taylor recalls: 'Around 1948, everything was concentrated on the Royal Roost. I'd come back from Europe in 1947. I thought I was sophisticated, but I stood there with my mouth open. All you had to do was walk behind the bandstand and guys were doing whatever they wanted to.'[3]

The owner of both the Royal Roost and Birdland was Morris Levy, who had 'practically grown up in the company of mobsters' working in Broadway nightclubs from the age of fourteen. By his mid twenties he was running or co-running a number of cabaret clubs and restaurants plus the top jazz clubs in the city. From there he built up a music business empire which included Roulette Records whose biggest star was Frankie Lymon and a network of smaller labels, publishing companies, artist management companies and concert and radio promotion activities. Levy was feared both for himself and his mob connections. There would have been no drug dealing at Birdland or the Roost without Levy having been involved. In association with some of New York's major crime bosses, he was later to be charged with attempting to extort money from MCA Records and was sentenced to ten years imprisonment. However before he could start his sentence he died of liver cancer in May 1991.

For the musicians who became dependent on heroin, including some of the finest players jazz ever produced, the process of dependence involved far more than the physical sensations of being stoned. The pharmacological impact of heroin (or any mood-altering drug) on the person using it is only one part of a complex interaction between the chemical properties of the drug, the physiological and psychological complexion of the user, the user's expectations of the drug and the cultural and social environment in which it is used. Heroin served the symbolic, functional, psychological and social needs of the cool, aloof hipster jazz musician and the whole added up to what might be called the heroin experience. It was this total experience rather than the drug alone upon which musicians became dependent.

Heroin use by black musicians was only the most visible manifestation of what was going on in the black community as a whole in the early fifties. In *Soul on Ice*, Eldridge Cleaver stated that 'prior to 1954, we lived in an atmosphere of novocain. Negroes found it necessary, in order to maintain whatever sanity they could, to remain somewhat aloof and detached from the "problem".' Hampton Hawes was less circumspect: 'All niggers are involved with narcotics ... you had to act a different way around white people and it was all that fear and oppression which made niggers get high. Especially musicians, because if a musician wants to play what he feels, he has to escape all that shit. It's happened to damn near everybody I know.'[4]

The terrible public image of heroin and those who used it made it a perfect vehicle for a trip to the margins of society and confirmed the status of black musicians who, as members of the black community, were already there. Heroin was tailor-made for inducing a sense of emotional distance, a central tenet of the hipster ethic. It remains the most effective physical painkiller ever developed. The feelings are not euphoric or high in the active sense, but cool and detached; some users have likened it to being wrapped up in a huge ball of cotton wool.

If for black musicians heroin symbolized the flight from white society, for white musicians it symbolized the flight *towards* black society. To enter the closed world of the jazz community white musicians had to transcend the distinct disadvantage (in this one respect) of not being black. Jazz was the music of black society; when the white musicians of Bix Beiderbecke's era, feeling alienated from their own culture, had looked to ally themselves with the jazz/black life, that very act had marked them out as 'social deviants'. In fact for young whites to become jazz musicians was a significantly more deviant act than for blacks. Traditionally, music has been one of the few career options for those in the black community looking to break free from a system eager to condemn them to a life of menial, unskilled labour. Black people have no more 'natural' capacity for making music than Jewish people have for making money. Both aptitudes are consequences of minority status in racist and anti-Semitic communities. Aspiring white jazz musicians often found themselves in an uneasy no man's land, rejected by the society they had turned their backs on, but only very rarely accepted (like Mezz Mezzrow) by the group whose approval they anxiously sought. Many black people thought that whites were attracted to the romantic idea of being black as a political or subcultural statement, without actually relating to black people as fellow human beings. White musicians tried to 'outhip' the real hipsters, to become blacker than black or, in Norman Mailer's terminology, 'White Negroes'. Their self-conscious aim was 'to live with death as an immediate danger, to divorce oneself from society, to exist without roots, to set out on that unchartered journey into the rebellious imperatives of the self ... one exists to be in the present'.[5] Which is a pretty fair description of the heroin experience and part of the reason why many white musicians took up heroin – as the ultimate expression of being hip.

Jazz musicians were faced with a myriad of everyday problems, both personal and professional. Travelling on the road put enormous strains on personal relationships. There were managers, promoters, agents and record companies of dubious integrity to deal with; sometimes hostile or inattentive audiences; ego clashes in the band; the uncertainty of work; declines in popularity; the glare of public attention. For those musicians who found all this too much to handle, heroin provided a functional solution: instead of having to deal with several problems, one problem-maintaining the habit – took over. 'Junk could provide a dream world. The daily process of living was dull and you had to scrounge for an income, when you just wanted to play your horn. Junk seemed to help in a bad time.'[6] (Gerry Mulligan)

This was, of course, an illusion. Heroin might block out the other problems, but its use created more than just one problem. Regular users were often irregular musicians. 'If I had to go to Watts to cop and the cat said "the Man will be here in an hour" and I had to be on the gig in an hour and a half – and the Man didn't get there for two hours – then the arithmetic was simple. I'd be at least a half hour late on the gig. If the Man didn't show, I didn't play ... keeping my ass normal took precedence; everything else had to wait – music, food, home, sleep.'[7]

Those with a bad reputation for reliability had a tougher time finding work than most and could get caught in a downward spiral of using more heroin as finding work became increasingly difficult. Many bandleaders refused to hire 'ex-users' in the belief there was no such thing. Health problems were inevitable in the process of injecting heroin of unknown quality and strength in unsterile conditions, using dirty needles. Personal, domestic and financial problems would escalate and at the end of the line, if you were still alive, came prison. And naturally none of those original problems ever went away; some time or another they had to be faced.

Thus the idea of heroin as a means of collapsing several problems into one was always a chimera. But it did have a more basic functional use – it got the addict musician to work. No musician could play blind drunk, but plenty played well while stoned on heroin. But the belief that you had to have a habit that would fell an ox in order to play like Charlie Parker was the classic mistake many of his acolytes made. What they failed or chose to fail, to comprehend was that Bird played brilliantly on heroin because he was dependent on it, that was the only time he felt well enough to play normally – i.e. better than anyone else. He wasn't playing better because of heroin; he was just playing normally because he didn't feel sick.

This was borne out by American psychologist Charles Winick in 1954, in the only study ever carried out on the use of drugs by jazz musicians. He interviewed 409 New York musicians and analysed their comments about drugs and their own drug habits: '32% pointed out that if a musician is a regular user of heroin, his musical norm would have to be his behaviour while on drugs. Such a person can only function and play when he is taking heroin.' While 53% regarded the drug as dangerous, there was a view among some that heroin was a 'working drug'; and that's exactly what it was for musicians like Charlie Parker and Hampton Hawes.

Heroin got those already dependent on to the stand to play the gig, but it performed another service which eventually brought several non-addicted musicians to dependency. Musicians are especially prone to colds and flu, moving as they do from freezing tour buses into sweltering club environments and then back out into the night air, for weeks on end. This was a particular problem for singers; if their voices went, the whole gig was in jeopardy – the rest of the band depending on the singer appearing. If you want to stay working in the music business, you cannot ring in sick like other workers. No matter how bad you feel, you've got to be up there. Nobody on heroin gets flu, coughs or colds; the membranes are dried out and the cough reflex suppressed. Eventually, of course, many musicians found they had a heroin habit instead of flu.

Allowing for the pitfalls of lay psychology, even a superficial examination of the belief systems of musicians seems often to reveal a bedrock of decidedly adolescent attitudes. In those with the strongest adolescent traits these attitudes were served by the use of heroin and other drugs including alcohol. Part of the hipster ethic was founded on control, being strong when everyone else was weak, not becoming a fall-about junkie, seeing how far you could go in order to come all the way back. Those who came back were heroes; those who didn't were legends. Hampton Hawes said of Thelonious Monk: 'If Wardell (Gray) was like my older brother, Monk was my father – and he never interfered in my life or put me down for being strung. But the following year when the shit really got bad, he would be there to reach out a helping hand. If he was using himself, I didn't know it and he didn't show it and that's what being cool is about.'[8] Even the very act of hero-worship has a childlike quality about it, the urge to be like somebody else where a strong personal identity has yet to develop. It is doubtful whether the example of Charlie Parker had much impact on the young black community at large, many of whom had probably never heard of him. But he had an enormous influence not only on the way musicians played, but on the way they lived their lives. The first three notes of 'Parker's Mood' were a signal between users in Los Angeles, a call sign sung outside the dealer's house when they wanted to score in the dead of night.

Paradoxically, those who imagined they were most in control, the prime hellraisers on the jazz scene, often suffered from low self-esteem, a common characteristic of chronic drug users. By his own account Art Pepper, for example, was denied any familial affection. 'I was terrified and completely alone. And at that time, I realized that nobody wanted me. There was no love and I wished I could die.'[9] By his logic, if he was worthless, it didn't matter what he did. Normal restraints were off; he felt, and was regarded as, powerful and potentially dangerous. He ran with street gangs became a jazz musician, used heroin, committed robberies and had a criminal record.

Although staying in control was the ultimate in cool, the macho test incarnate, it does not appear that credibility was lost by admitting you were not in control. Drugs users have a large vocabulary of rationalizations to fall back on. Many musicians blamed the pushers for causing their problems. Ray Charles was more honest. Living in Seattle when the Royal Roost was playing host to all the dealers, Charles had a heroin habit when he was eighteen: 'It happened because I wanted it to happen … there wasn't no pusher hanging round the back alley … no white or black cat got me hooked or encouraged me to turn on.' He was young, wanted a piece of any action that was going and in response to warnings about the dangers replied: 'If it's so bad, why are you using it?'[10]

Of course, once a musician had lost control of his heroin use, the 'control ethic' of hipsterdom gave way to the symbol of the doomed hero. Musicians declared they had 'a monkey on their backs', carried like a badge of honour. Where the expression came from is unclear; Possibly a reference to the monkey carried around by organ grinders to collect money from passers-by. The monkey demanded money from customers and feeding from its owner – just like the heroin habit for a jazz musician. The status of being a junkie was not something easily surrendered.

Another factor common among children and those indulging in compulsive behaviour is the demand for instant gratification. In many ways the musician 'addict' is just the same as any other 'addict', but writ large, magnified by the pressures and anxieties of being, or not being enough, in the public eye. Some musicians went for the instant gratification of the needle when they realized they were not going to be superstars overnight. For the hipster living for the present who happened also to be a famous musician, a cohort of star-struck acolytes were ready and willing to supply any need the minute it was articulated. This has been taken to ridiculous lengths in the indulgence of rock megastars, but in relative terms the jazz stars of the fifties were similarly feted.

Richard Freeman, a psychiatrist who treated Charlie Parker, said that but for the music, Parker was just another potential mental patient dumped in a hospital, forgotten by everyone.

> But with Charlie Parker it is the music factor that makes all the difference. That's really the only reason we're interested in him, the only reason his followers are interested in him, the reason we're willing to stop our own lives and clean up his messes. People like Charlie require somebody like

that to follow them through life and clean up the shit.[11]

Trumpeter Kenny Dorham played with Bird from 1948-50:

> [Parker] was all music. He needed to have everything. When he played he couldn't play long enough and nothing stopped his playing. The more drugs he took, the more he went on playing. Bird was a high-starred person … he always had a crowd around him and he gave different jobs to each one. 'You go and get my horn. You get me some pot. You do this. You do that.' And they would jump.[12]

In the 'gimme it now' department, Bird was again fairly unusual. Unlike those of most heavy users of heroin, Parker's other appetites were not in the least diminished. Prior to a gig, he might consume two three-course dinners or two dozen hamburgers, washed down with torrents of whisky and followed by a gargantuan whack of heroin. After the gig, the women who had taken his fancy that night would follow him to bed. Parker grabbed at every piece of life and stuffed it in his mouth whole.

As well as being a symbol of the urban outlaw, the ultimate test of dues paying, the means to make the gig and the dream ticket out of misery, the social environment of heroin and rituals of its use also fed the demands of musicians for whom the normal support systems within the music community were insufficient. During the fifties that group seemed to be in the majority. One jazz musician has commented anonymously:

> To me, the reason musicians got into drugs so heavily was that, as artists and performers, they wanted to get closer to each other, to communicate as intimately as possible, and at that time shooting up seemed the best way to do this. It became such a habit with so many of them, that it was almost expected for any new man in the band to show his sense of brotherhood by sticking that needle into his arm, just like his buddies would.

The relationships between musicians are probably unique in the world of work. People who would not necessarily be friends, let alone close friends, find themselves incubated together for weeks or months on end in tour buses, hotel rooms, studios and dressing rooms. They can get to know each other better than family or friends. In such claustrophobic environments, relationships can become very intense, volatile and unpredictable, particularly if one or more of the band are heavily involved in drugs. Often the drug users form an inner clique or, as in the case of many jazz big bands in the fifties, represent the majority of musicians.

Bill Harris, trombone player with Woody Herman's Herd, would travel on the band bus for fifty weeks a year out of fifty-two, the only non-user in a band of heroin users. He sat alone on the back seat with his booze reading the paper, books and generally entertaining himself. The rest all sat up front except Herman who travelled alone. Nobody cold-shouldered anybody; it was just that the drinker and the heroin users inhabited different worlds. They had nothing to say to one another.

In the same way that drugs could take precedence over music, so musicians sometimes adopted very different attitudes to each other as professionals and users. As a musician, Hampton Hawes revered the very ground Charlie Parker stood on: 'We'd be willing to do anything to warm ourselves by that fire, get some of that grease pumping through our veins. He fucked up all our minds. It was where the ultimate truth was.'[13] But as a fellow user, he felt he couldn't trust Parker. This was a parallel world where the rules of musicians-in-arms did not necessarily apply:

> [He'd say] the cat's out in the alley, you can cop for twenty-five cents (meaning dollars). I'd say I didn't have twenty-five cents which may not have been true … If I said, 'I only need a dime's worth,' he might say. 'Well, I'm low myself, make it two dimes and we'll cow [pool resources]. Of course if I went for that it was unlikely I'd ever see that second dime. It was the survival of the fittest in those days and you had to know where people were coming from.[14]

Nevertheless in most instances addict-musicians felt more at ease with other addicts than with non-using musicians. Art Pepper found self-esteem as a musician, but also as a heroin user. Nothing to do with the physical sensations of the drug, but the social experience of using it. Within the drug-using fraternity he found a ready-made family who understood one another. In their company he was neither terrified nor alone. He took as much pride in being a 'righteous junkie' who did not inform on others to save his own neck, as he did in being a great musician – possibly more so, because like many great artists, he took his talent for granted. 'I've never studied, never practised … I knew it was there. All I had to do was reach for it, just do it.'

Pepper spent nearly ten years in prison; sadly, he seemed to be most at ease in institutions. Inside, he had no responsibilities, his daily routines were planned out for him. Narcotics offenders had a certain degree of status inside and he could enjoy the adulation of being a famous musician without all the hassles associated with it outside: 'When I started using drugs, I ran into a different kind of person. In jail I found people who had honour. They were real. They said what they thought … the dope fiends were warm to me and open with me, I felt.[15]

In the world of jazz, where the daily mundane concerns of 'the squares' were scorned, the addict-musician had nevertheless to establish an elaborate set of routines and rituals in order to ensure continuing supplies of his drug. Connections had to be made, pick-up points arranged, places for fixing organized if home was not possible, followed by the cycle of preparing the heroin for fixing, getting high, then becoming sick or strung out and starting all over again. Nina Simone once said, 'Jazz is not just music, it's a way of life, a way of thinking.'[16] And what did Williams Burroughs say about heroin? 'Junk is not a kick. It is a way of life.' Musicians often had to make the choice during their careers and they didn't always choose music.

The personal investment in the heroin experience can be very strong: the whole routine of heroin use can be a powerful social and behavioural reinforcer. Heroin users have been known to inject warm water when they couldn't afford drugs, just to go through the ritual of fixing up. Ex-users have experienced some of the physical symptoms of withdrawal just by walking past a place associated with their former life.

Art Pepper was 'hooked' on the social rituals associated with maintaining a habit. His description of this may sound sordid and tragic, but to him it represented safety, security, simplicity and order – cocooned in the 'cosy' world of the heroin user. On the road with the Stan Kenton band in the early fifties:

> Me and Andy Angelo roomed together for a long time … and we each had

our own outfits. I had a little carrying case, like an electric razor case. I had an extra eyedropper and my needles, four or five of them. I had my little wires to clean the spike out in case it got clogged. I had a little bottle of alcohol and a sterling silver spoon that was just beautiful and a knife to scoop the stuff on to the spoon ...I would set up my outfit next to the bed in the hotel ... I'd wake up in the morning and reach over, get my little knife, put a few knifefuls in the spoon, cook it up and fix. It was beautiful.[17]

The lifestyle of the heroin user and the attendant health risks could sideline a musician from time to time. But just as hazardous to the long-term development of any jazz career in the fifties was a narcotics conviction. Under American law at that time, being a heroin user was by definition a criminal offence. Unlike the system in Britain, it has never been considered legitimate medical practice in America to prescribe drugs to users with the purpose of stabilizing their lifestyle and removing the need to become involved in the black market. It was for this reason that many American jazz musicians would stop over in London en route to European engagements or on the way home to obtain legal supplies of heroin from London doctors like Lady Isobel Frankau whose prescription list read like a *Who's Who* of modern jazz.

Gerry Mulligan made the point that 'we all started to feel like criminals and had to hide our addiction. After a while, our whole way of life became involved in our habit and we were thrown into contact with people whom we'd usually go out of our way to avoid. Instead, we had to cultivate them as friends.'[18] Addict musicians were vulnerable to unscrupulous gangsters who ran the clubs and controlled the heroin trade. A musician in debt could become much sicker than he ever was on heroin.

Although the number of jazz musicians using heroin in the forties increased, there seemed to be a decline in the overall numbers of heroin addicts. In the early years of World War II, heroin use was less of a public issue as the fire of the marijuana debate raged on. Art Pepper's early playing days were around Central Avenue, Los Angeles – 'The dope thing hadn't evolved into what it is now, with all the police activity. I'd never heard of a narc, didn't know what that word meant. Nobody wanted to rat on anybody or plant their car with a joint or with some stuff'[19]

After the war, addict figures did not rise dramatically even though heroin supplies were resumed – or rather they did not rise dramatically enough for Anslinger. He was anxious to head off any notion that the Bureau might be dispensable.

The figures were actually massaged upwards, the spectre of enslaved adolescents raised once more and demands for stiffer penalties rang in the ears of the judiciary. Since the mid-thirties, Anslinger had held a monopoly over any public information on drug misuse. He could say anything and be believed. He now claimed that heroin was responsible for rising crime because it was used to induce 'dutch courage'. Alcohol or amphetamines can provide such a stimulus, but certainly not dope – the very word is indicative of its soporific effect. Gang-fighting dropped off as young people discovered a new 'high'. Some black commentators have opined that widespread heroin use has kept the lid on the ghettos and so the police have turned a blind eye.

The key plank in Anslinger's anti-heroin campaign was a harsher sentencing policy. In 1951, as a result of Anslinger's testimony to the Kefauver Senate Committee on Organized Crime, Congress passed the Boggs Act. This compelled Federal judges on first, second and third offences for possession to give minimum jail sentences of two, five and ten years respectively. From a second offence onwards there would be no parole, probation or suspension. Legal devices which were granted to traitors and murderers were denied to drug users.

The Daniel Subcommittee report of 1955 led to the even more draconian Narcotic Control Act of 1956. Under the Boggs Act, the maximum sentences for first, second and third offences had been five, ten and twenty years respectively. These were increased to ten, twenty and forty years respectively. These sentences applied only to possession, not selling and applied to all drugs, including marijuana. There was a separate penalty of five to twenty years for a first dealing conviction, and ten to forty years for any subsequent conviction. Anyone aged eighteen or over convicted of selling heroin to a minor could expect a minimum ten years with a possible life sentence or even death upon a jury recommendation. Narcotics and customs agents were given guns and could make arrests without warrants. Black jazz musicians were prime targets for harassment. The police hated seeing black and white mixing together, especially if a white girl was on the arm of a black musician. Successful musicians driving new cars could expect regular shakedowns and the sudden appearance of drugs in the car once the officers had done their 'search'.

Perhaps the most extraordinary law passed in 1956 stipulated that not only those who had been convicted of a drug violation but any current non-convicted users had to register with customs and obtain a certificate to *leave* the United States. The certificate had to be surrendered on return and the minimum sentence for failing to register was one year. The law makers actually believed drug users would turn themselves in.

During the fifties and early sixties a number of musicians were arrested on drugs charges (either marijuana or heroin) and some served time in prison. Together they included Gerry Mulligan, Stan Getz, Tadd Dameron, Anita O'Day, Billie Holiday, Art Pepper, Lester Young (a cocaine charge while in the army), Red Rodney, Hampton Hawes, Chet Baker, Thelonious Monk, Miles Davis, Art Blakey, Percy Heath, Phil Urso, Milt Jackson, Elvin Jones, Charlie Persip, Curtis Fuller and Philly Joe Jones.

Amazingly, Charlie Parker was never even arrested on a drugs charge, surviving numerous searches and pat-downs. Some of his sidemen were less fortunate. His star trumpet player in the quintet, Red Rodney, copped a maximum five-year sentence for heroin possession after building up a $75-a-day habit. Like Stan Getz and Art Pepper, he had resorted to petty crime in order to raise money when work was hard to come by. He was sentenced in January 1953 to a term in Leavenworth. Under the terms of the Boggs Act he was out on parole in 1955, but with no therapy available in prison he was back on heroin inside two weeks. Coming out of prison and resuming heroin use can be particularly dangerous, because users often go back to the dose they left off when arrested, forgetting or not knowing that the body can no longer tolerate the same amount. Overdosing is common among this group. Rodney survived, however, to commit more burglaries until he was apprehended for parole violations. The rest of his sentence was served out at the US Public Health Service Hospital at Lexington, Kentucky.

Anslinger's informer system did not net the large haul he had hoped for, but a number of well-known musicians were trapped in this way. In 1953 Art Pepper was set up by an unnamed musician and, in the true spirit of McCarthyite America, was pressurised into naming others in exchange for his freedom. His refusal earned him nine months in the Los Angeles County Jail, the first of six spells behind bars. He also spent time in Fort Worth Hospital, the other major public institution housing narcotics offenders. His refusal to inform put him inside when others went free, but not being 'a rat' was an important point of principle for him.

A bass player whom Hampton Hawes named as 'Wally Shade' was an example of a musician who informed on others. Shade was a heavy user who had been busted many times, but who never served time. Ironically, Hawes was entrapped by a Mexican agent named Vince who got in with Hawes by warning him that Shade was an informer. Vince won Hawes' confidence and had the luckless pianist buy heroin for him on two occasions The second time Hawes climbed into Vince's car only to have a .38 pistol jabbed at his head and a badge flashed in his face.

Because Hawes had been trapped into selling heroin, he was treated like an 'evil pusher' and sentenced in 1958 to a staggering ten years in prison at Fort Worth. In 1960, Hawes started the tortuous process of applying for a Presidential pardon from newly elected John F. Kennedy. Three years later, just ten weeks before he was assassinated, President Kennedy granted executive clemency to Hampton Hawes.

Although Charlie Parker avoided a drugs arrest, he had his New York Cabaret Card revoked from 1951-3, on the recommendation of the Federal Bureau of Narcotics, who always had him high on their suspect list.

During this time, he could not work in New York. Anyone who worked for more than three days where alcohol was being served had to obtain a cabaret card from the division of licenses in the police department. Each applicant was photographed and fingerprinted and charged $2 for the card which had to be renewed every two years. A musician with a narcotics violation record would automatically be denied a card and anyone busted while holding a card would have it revoked.

New York was the world's major showcase for jazz; a musician's out-of-town reputation meant little unless he could win New York. All the best clubs were there and the top money. To be denied the chance to play there was a serious blow to a musician's career from which some never recovered.

Thelonious Monk suffered badly from a vicious system wide open to bribery and corruption. In 1951, a friend accompanied by two other people called at his flat. As the apartment was tiny and his widowed mother bedridden, Monk suggested they go and sit in his car. They were approached by narcotics agents and somebody dropped a small packet of heroin on the floor which was found by the agents. There wasn't enough to charge Monk as a dealer, but he took a sixty-day 'rap' for his friend as a matter of honour. Worse than the sentence, he lost his cabaret card and it took him six years, until 1957, to get it back and only then with the influential help of Baroness de Koenigswater, the jazz aristocrat in whose flat Charlie Parker died in 1955.

Barely a year after his card was reinstated, the authorities got Monk again. He was driving home with the Baroness and tenor-sax player Charlie Rouse, from a week-long engagement at the Comedy Club in Baltimore. They stopped at a motel and Monk went in to ask for some water. He was a large man, six foot tall and over 200 pounds in weight. His dark presence must have frightened the owner, who called the police. The next minute he was being dragged from the car and beaten up. The police 'found' some marijuana in the car. Even though the possession charge was dropped, Monk still lost his card because he had been arrested on a drugs charge. Not until 1967 was the cabaret-card system declared unconstitutional and abolished by Mayor John Lindsay.

How did the jazz community at large react to what many privately thought was a cancer in the body of the music? There was an understandable reluctance to discuss the matter for fear of perpetuating the image of the junkie jazz musician. In the same year that Charlie Parker and Wardell Gray died, Frank Sinatra starred as Frankie Machine in the film adaptation of Nelson Algren's novel *The Man with the Golden Arm*. Dealing as it did with drug addiction, the film needed a Public Control Administration Certificate of Approval (PCA), before it could be shown. After the war, foreign films and television made an increasing impact on American audiences, but were not subject to the same restrictions as Hollywood. Taking a stand for greater freedom, director Otto Preminger released the new Sinatra movie without a certificate. As the film attracted a wide audience, rather than see the code fall into disrepute the PCA amended the regulations, allowing the depiction of drug addiction as long as there was no hint of encouragement, glamour, size of profits to be made out of drugs or any suggestion that the habit could be easily broken. The film caused a sensation, because it showed an addict jazz musician who was white. It probably fused in the public mind for all time (or at least until rock in the sixties) the link between jazz and drugs.

But in this respect the film was not a fair adaptation of the book. Probably because Sinatra was playing the lead, Frankie Machine's musical connections were given prominence, whereas the book hardly mentions them at all. Frankie is basically a hot-shot card dealer. He has a dream that one day he will have a legitimate job as a big band jazz drummer, but it's all a fantasy, constantly pushed out of reach by his heroin habit. (Interestingly, jazz is seen here as the distant 'straight life', rather than disreputably 'deviant'.) Frankie was a classic example of the aspiring musician who used heroin as a rationalization for failures but in purely dramatic terms the link between jazz and drugs was tenuous.

Similarly, in 1960, Jack Gelber's off-Broadway play *The Connection* was very well received by audience and critics alike. The play had a jazz soundtrack, but none of the users on whom the action focused were musicians. Nevertheless, the same inevitable connections were made.

When it came to illegal drugs, whatever they were, the music industry was caught in a dilemma. The standard response tended to be 'Why pick on jazz musicians when there are far more doctors who misuse drugs?' This may have been fair, but it was hardly going to deflect attention away from the problem or silence the critics of jazz. In any event, a jazz musician arrested for drug possession was news; newspaper proprietors wanted to sell papers, policemen wanted high-profile publicity for star busts.

The industry could not be seen to condone drug use. Cab Calloway was one of the old school; the hipster ethos which embraced heroin was alien to him and he gave vent to his feelings in an article entitled 'Is Dope Killing Our Musicians?' published in the black magazine *Ebony* in 1951:

> A spectre is haunting the American music industry, the spectre of narcotics, destroying the talents of many of our finest performers, breaking up some of our best bands...
>
> Am I overstating the dope menace in music? I think not. As a practising musician for over twenty years, I know the situation as intimately as most members of the profession. I have watched an entire generation of American jazzmen develop during my career and I have seen scores of these promising artists struck down by an evil that is as cruel and

relentless as a deep-sea octopus. Some of my dearest friends have been trapped by this insidious habit, which has fastened itself upon them like a plague ... Drugs have caused a disturbing number of good musicians to deteriorate into hopeless has-beens. Many a fine young musician who has switched to heroin to get 'turned on', has discovered to his agony that his entire creative life has been stopped cold by a terrible habit which he cannot control.

In 1953 a half-hearted attempt was made to expel from the Hollywood Local 47 of the American Federation of Musicians any member convicted of drug offences. Fortunately no such action was taken. By contrast, jazz writers were incensed at the savage sentences handed out to musicians convicted of possessing drugs for personal use only. The dilemma was highlighted in the following *Down Beat* editorial of January 1962 on the occasion of Ray Charles' arrest for possession.

THE RAY CHARLES CASE
When Ray Charles was arrested recently in Indianapolis, on a narcotics charge, the singer reportedly told police he had been addicted since the age of sixteen. The arresting officers said they discovered in his room a quantity of marijuana and heroin, plus the paraphernalia used by a drug addict.

There is evidence of another kind in the case, too. Human evidence. Charles is blind and has been since he was six.

So what do you do with a blind man held as a heroin addict? Toss him in jail as a social menace? If he is a law breaker, as the police charge, then the statutes are explicit; he must be punished. Punishment in itself is held by many to be rehabilitative, the premise being that if you are punished for an offence, you may not repeat. But somehow this premise has been proved hollow where the vast majority of addicts is concerned. Besides, Charles had been arrested previously for violation of the narcotics laws.

Now, let's assume for the sake of argument that Charles is not punished if convicted. On compassionate grounds, let's say. Wouldn't this leave us with the question: where do you draw the line? If Charles should be exempted from the usual penalty of the law because of his blindness, why should not other addicts, handicapped in other ways, say by mental or emotional disorders, also be set free? They're sick, too, aren't they?

On the other hand, if Charles is convicted and jailed as an addict, what is the law proving? That it is inflexible and unyielding? Or that it is brutal and blind to the call of compassion? Charles' alleged need for drugs will certainly not be eliminated by serving a jail sentence, just as the craving of thousands of convicted addicts is not allayed by prison terms. Is there, then, a difference between the addiction of Ray Charles, artist, and the addiction of John Doe, car-park attendant? Of course not. Charles' case merely dramatizes in the most human terms one of the crucial problems confronting society. His physical affliction is obvious and inspires sympathy and understanding. In John Doe, car-park attendant, the affliction may not be so readily perceivable or permit of quick understanding, but it exists nonetheless.

In jazz we are prone to feel sympathy and tell ourselves we understand when a musician is jailed for narcotics violations. The empathy between jazzman and a just-plain-lover of the art serves as an excuse here. But too often there exists a tendency among jazzfolk to exempt a musician addict from the strictures of society and from the penalties his addiction incurs. The case of Charlie Parker is probably the outstanding example of this attitude in operation. But this tendency to excuse has deeper and more serious implications when jazz heroes such as Parker and Charles are the objects.

We are tragically familiar with the many literal applications of the faulty syllogism: Bird is a genius of jazz; Bird cannot live without heroin; therefore, heroin is essential to jazz genius. Just as Parker was hailed and enthroned on Olympus in his lifetime, today Ray Charles' music is marketed on record and in person with unstinting employment of the noun, Genius. Whether Charles believes his publicity matters as little as whether Charlie Parker did. The difference between Parker and Charles in terms of general influence however, should be obvious. Charles is reaching more people with his music and with his personality than Parker ever could. And an astonishing number of Charles-worshippers are kids. It would be tragic indeed if the mass-worship of Ray Charles were to result in just a single literal application of a similar syllogism. Because if one youngster is motivated or influenced to try heroin as a result of the story of Charles' arrest, then what the law may demand of the singer just won't mean a thing.

Industry concern for those musicians who provide the basis of the wealth for the industry, but who also get into trouble with drugs and alcohol, has usually fallen far short of any practical assistance. No doubt the musicians who were paid off in heroin by one small jazz label of the early fifties were eternally grateful, but this hardly constituted a planned response to the problem the industry was facing. In a letter written to *Variety* in March 1954, clarinettist Buddy de Franco called upon all those with connections in the business to start giving serious consideration to the issue of drug use among musicians.

Three years later, despite being strenuously urged to drop the idea, jazz critic Nat Hentoff arranged for a symposium on addiction at the 1957 Newport Jazz Festival. And from that session evolved the Musicians Clinic in New York, funded on a grant from the festival.

The chief psychiatrist was Dr Marie Nyswander, one of the pioneers of methadone maintenance treatment who died in 1986. In 1960 together with psychologist Charles Winick, she presented a paper which examined the progress of musicians who went through the psycho-therapeutic regime. In a controlled (clinical) study involving the clinic patients and a group of addict musicians who did not come for psychotherapy, the clinic patients improved significantly over the others in relation to stopping drugs, adjusting to a non-addict lifestyle and getting work. Numbers coming to the clinic in the first year were small – only fifteen musicians came for treatment, whereas in a separate study Winick had estimated that there were probably over 750 regular users of heroin among the New York jazz community.

Outside this one clinic, the narcotic rehabilitation prison hospitals at Fort Worth and

Lexington provided what little psychotherapeutic help was available, but notable successes were achieved including Gerry Mulligan and Red Rodney, who told *Down Beat.*

> I fought it, I didn't want any part of analysis. I even volunteered for narcotics tests. I figured I would get good and high all the time I was in, and ride through the three years But just before I was to go into the tests, I changed my mind. Maybe I finally realized that I had thrown too much of my life away. But I know that from then on, I began to really live like a human being again.
>
> Analysis is the greatest thing I ever went through. I began to grow up. At first, I lied and told wild stories. Then I wondered, 'Who am I lying to?' The answer, of course, was that I was lying to myself again. When I got straightened out on that score, the analysis began to help me. I saw for the first time how low I had fallen. I was ashamed, more than I had ever been in all my life.[20]

The study done by Winick and Nyswander demonstrated that addict-musicians were constitutionally stronger than the 'typical addict', in that many had withdrawn themselves from heroin on more than one occasion prior to coming for treatment. After a four-year habit during which he sank as low in the gutter as you can get, Miles Davis (not one of the patients) just decided it was too much trouble, sweated it out for twelve days and never went back on heroin. John Coltrane, too, kicked the habit on his own through his strength of purpose, filling the ensuing vacuum not with alcohol as many others did, but with spirituality and music.

Others did not fare so well. Through interviews which appeared at various stages in his disjointed career, *Down Beat* tried heroically to suggest that Art Pepper's troubles were behind him. He had a spell in Synanon, a rehabilitation house which had recorded successes with other musicians but he could not break his compulsive behaviour. Eventually, in 1982, his body just packed up.

What conclusions can be drawn from the use of heroin by jazz musicians in the post-war era? According to Hampton Hawes, '...the casualty list in the fifties – dead, wounded and mentally deranged – started to look like the Korean War was being fought at the corner of Central and 45th.'[21] Directly or indirectly, long-term misuse of heroin starting in the forties or fifties claimed the lives of – among others – Billie Holiday, Fats Navarro, Sonny Berman (Woody Herman's brilliant trumpet player), pianist Carl Perkins, Wardell Gray, Tadd Dameron, Shadow Wilson, British drummer Phil Seaman and Tubby Hayes. The record books show that by some strange coincidence both Charlie Christian and Jimmy Blanton succumbed to TB in 1942. One jazz musician commented however: 'There are a number of boys who would be living today if not for the pushers – Charlie Christian and Jimmy Blanton Duke's bass player. They weren't very strong and they allowed bad cats to take advantage of their weakness.'[22]

The need to maintain regular and – for successful musicians – expensive heroin habits, drove some into crazy situations; Charlie Parker actually signed over half his Dial Record royalties to his main West Coast dealer, Emry Bird. Musicians saw their careers ruined by long jail sentences and coming back was not always easy. Street credibility was not much use if you were also regarded as an employment liability. As advances against salaries, gig money got spent before it was earned and many a trusting musician has lent his horn to 'a friend' only to receive a pawn ticket in the post a few weeks later.

Heroin use hurt bebop because many club owners associated the 'new drug' with the 'new music' and banned both. The arrests of Elvin Jones and Tony Williams on drugs charges in Japan in 1966 caused the cancellation of Art Blakey's summer tour of 1967 and with it the loss of nearly $30,000.

But some might argue that all the problems caused by drugs were the price which had to be paid for classic, timeless jazz. Perhaps the same adolescent characteristics that made Charlie Parker a compulsive drug user, drinker and eater gave him the free unself-conscious flights of imagination to produce the music he did. To quote Robert Reisner: 'Bird was a neurotic, but the great strides in art are not made by happy well-adjusted people. Art is a form of sublimation and is created by neurotics and compulsion-ridden people.'[23] Art Blakey observed:

> You do not play better with heroin, but you do hear better. Bird said he wanted to kick the habit so that he could tell people what he heard … While he is suffering, he cannot produce; but reflecting about his pain, he can create. Musicians who have been junkies and then rid themselves of the habit have sometimes really then come into their own musically.[24]

A good example of this was Miles Davis. Ian Carr, his biographer, noted that the effect of Davis' heroin experience on his subsequent life and work cannot be overestimated. During his years of inactivity Davis was often to be found on the bathroom floor of Howard McGhee's apartment with a needle in his arm. The chances are that musicians who come out the other side will be stronger, more resilient, more disciplined and able to exploit a major experience for the purposes of artistic creativity. Davis had the talent to capitalize on that; his genius as a musician never deserted him, it just lay dormant.

7 LADY DAYS

It's like they say, there's no damn business like show business. You had to smile to keep from throwing up.

Billie Holiday

The dominant psychiatric model of female addiction (formulated largely by men) has stereotyped women heroin users as natural victims – passive, insecure, vulnerable, dependent creatures. Their family backgrounds are characterised as disturbed and chaotic, often containing episodes of physical or sexual abuse. Such women may get pregnant several times, as a way of breaking free from an oppressive family environment and gaining the security of a relationship. If she is 'taken on' by a man who also happens to be an addict, he will force her into addiction. For women, this is cited as the most common route to drug dependency .

Once hooked on heroin, the woman is stigmatized as more 'deviant' than her male counterpart, because she is seen to be challenging the *status quo* by not fulfilling her role as a dutiful wife and mother. But even if she wanted to fulfil such a role the law has decreed that drug use and parenthood are incompatible; Billie Holiday was turned down as a foster parent because of her drug convictions. Recent court decisions in Britain and America have determined that the unborn child of a pregnant addict is by definition the victim of child abuse, thus condemning the woman as unfit to be a parent. By contrast, the woman dependent on tranquillizers is not regarded (quite rightly) as beyond the pale, presumably because her condition is rooted in the 'legitimate' prescribing practices of respectable doctors, not the outcome of irresponsible hedonism.

In truth Billie Holiday and the other subject of this chapter, Anita O'Day, both jazz singers with heroin problems did fit this model in part, at a time when the social pressures on women to conform were not counterbalanced by an energetic and well-publicized women's movement. Billie Holiday suffered a highly insecure upbringing away from her mother in the charge of an uncaring aunt. She was subjected to sexual harassment and rape to the point where she became terrified of sex. Aged only ten, she was sent to a Catholic Reformatory after being found guilty of 'enticing' the man who raped her. By fifteen, she was a prostitute. Anita O'Day, dubbed 'excess baggage' by her mother, had to learn to be self-sufficient from an early age, fending off many unwelcome sexual advances. She endured over a dozen abortions, although she was never certain whether or not she was being conned by back-street abortionists, telling her that she had been aborted when she might not have been pregnant in the first place. She spent her middle-teen years roaming the dance halls earning money in the notorious dance marathons or 'walkathons' depicted in the film *They Shoot Horses, Don't They?* Not prostitution, but exploitation of the body for money in almost every other sense.

In sociological terms, just by being jazz singers Holiday and O'Day were 'deviant' long before they got anywhere near heroin. But in both women the pull towards tradition and conformity was always lingering in the background, in their autobiographies there are poignant and romantic reflections of the virtues of home, stability, family and children. But however much they might have conformed to some circumscribed image of 'damaged' women, Holiday and O'Day were most definitely not passive souls. Even being a prostitute was a matter of pride for Holiday; she knew she could make more in one night than in a whole month doing laundry and, as she said herself, she was never going to be anybody's maid.

First as professional female singers in the unrelentingly chauvinistic world of jazz and then as heroin users, both women had to cultivate a tough, hard-nosed attitude to business to keep working, obtain drugs and stay ahead of the law. Jazz singers were under particular pressure because the whole band often relied upon their appearance. Nobody would much notice a stand-in drummer or bass player, but the singers were the main attraction and their non-appearance could mean no gig and no money for anyone. Beyond this, however, the circumstances of O'Day's and Holiday's drug dependency differed. Holiday was a star – the dealers came looking for her and there was also a ready supply from the men in her life. O'Day never commanded that kind of status and often had to buy on the streets with all the attendant risks. The other crucial difference, of course, was that Holiday was black and the humiliations and indignities heaped upon her because of her colour were a source of deep bitterness and anguish throughout her life.

Racism threw up many ironies for Holiday; playing in Count Basie's band in 1937, she was actually asked to black up because she looked too fair skinned under stage lights and house managers were afraid of a riot should the audience think that a white woman was singing in a black band. She joined Artie Shaw the following year, not the first black singer to sing in a white band, but the first in a white band to take the risk of touring in the South. To his credit Shaw took that risk, but not surprisingly Billie received appalling treatment on the road, everywhere there were scenes with sheriffs, hotel and theatre managers. The direst roadside cafes wouldn't serve her even in the kitchen and sometimes promoters or club managers wouldn't let her sing and her place was taken by a white female vocalist. Once she mouthed back 'Motherfucker' at a Southern cracker who yelled out 'let the nigger wench sing another song,' and had to be rapidly escorted from the scene before the lynching party could be formed. But the final straw came in the so-called liberal North at the Blue Room of New York's Lincoln Hotel on 43rd Street. The gig was due to be broadcast coast to coast – a golden opportunity for maximum exposure. Claiming as an excuse the high percentage of Southern guests staying at the hotel, the management told Shaw that Holiday could not use the main entrance, travel in the main lift, mingle with the guests or even stay on the bandstand when she wasn't singing. Artie Shaw might have spoken out: he himself had known enough anti-Semitism to understand what Billie was going through, but he decided that he could not sacrifice the prospects of the whole band on a point of principle. As a result Art and Holiday parted company. There was understandable bitterness on the singer's part although it appeared to mellow with the passing years.

These ignominies were even harder to bear coming in the wake of her father's death in 1937, indirectly another victim of the innate racism of America's white majority. A travelling musician, he caught pneumonia on tour in Dallas, but didn't seek treatment believing that he would never find a hospital that would admit blacks. He was finally persuaded to try, and did succeed in finding one, but by then it was too late. 'Strange Fruit' was the externalisation in song of all Billie Holiday's rage about the inhumanity of white towards black.

Despair paved the way for Holiday's entrée into the world of heroin. She had a residency at the Cafe Society Downtown in New York, but although she was an acclaimed star, she had little money to show for a two-year, seven-nights-a-week engagement and by 1942 she was emotionally at a very low ebb. At this point Jimmy Monroe came into her life. Younger brother of Clark Monroe, owner of the Uptown House where Holiday also sang, Jimmy was generally regarded as bad news and Billie was urged not to get involved with him. But she ignored the advice and eventually married him, a union which turned out to be a cruel farce.

Holiday's relationship with men bore a striking resemblance to her love affair with heroin. Both were self-destructive yet compelling and all-embracing – she would move from one 'dependency' to another and back again without missing a beat. It was about as much good telling her not to get involved with somebody as it was to tell her to stop using drugs or getting drunk. Men and drugs seemed to perform almost the same functions in her life, superficially offering safety, security and escape. Social psychologist Stanton Peele has written very convincingly in *Love and Addiction* how similar the two states can be, applying equally to men and women.

Monroe was heavily into opium and Holiday went along the same road, not because he forced her into it, but because if she was going to stay close to him she needed to be on the same wavelength. However, for a touring musician, opium smoking was highly impractical – it was too easily detectable by inquisitive policemen, it made her sick and the smoke affected her throat so that her pre-performance warm-ups were taking longer and longer. So she switched to heroin, altogether more discreet and convenient, and took to wearing long evening gloves to hide the track marks that were evidence enough to get her arrested.

However, it was when Billie Holiday decided to come off heroin that her troubles really started. In the immediate post-war years work in the New York jazz clubs was hard to come by and Holiday took the opportunity to go into a clinic for three weeks at a cost of $2,000. From the moment she came out she had a policeman for a shadow. Back in the 1920s, the clinic had been involved in a deal with the city police whereby the police would threaten wealthy addicts with arrest if they did not go to the clinic for treatment. The clinic then made the appropriate pay-offs. Although the deal had been exposed, it is possible that the connection still operated, or perhaps informers anxious for reward or to keep the heat away from themselves had told police of Holiday's attempts to come off (before then her drug use had not been public knowledge). Only a few weeks after she left the clinic she was arrested, having gone back to using drugs. Assistant Attorney Joseph Hildenberger stated in court that Billie Holiday was a victim of the worst sort of parasite who charged her $100 for a $5 fix, but this did not prevent her from being sent to Alderson Reformatory in West Virginia for a year and a day.

Yet the worst parasites seemed to be those who professed their love for Billie; emotionally and financially, she was robbed blind by all of them. Joe Guy was an addict and Holiday had to take better paying but artistically less satisfying theatre gigs to pay for his habit as well as her own. John Levy, also her manager, had her tied up every which way with deals and contacts and threatened to inform on her ('drop a dime' as the saying went) every time they had an argument. Naturally, after her first drug conviction she lost her New York cabaret card, a serious blow to her attempts at winning national prominence, something she never achieved and another source of despair in her life. Although she never compromised her art if it meant dancing to anybody else's beat but her own, she was desperate to become 'popular' and win *Down Beat* polls. By judicious use of under-the-counter payments, Levy got her cabaret card back, but Holiday was convinced that he also deliberately set her up. One day in January 1949, he gave her some heroin in a hotel room and told her to flush it down the toilet. Just at that moment the police broke in and arrested her for possession. To prove she was clean, Holiday booked herself into a sanatorium to be supervised day and night by doctors looking for signs of withdrawal. She stayed there for four days at a cost of $4,000, but made her point and was eventually found not guilty. Later she saw photos of Levy, taken in the Uptown club, being very friendly with George White, the man who had led the raid.

Anita O'Day was encouraged in her singing by Lord Buckley, the ultimate jazz hipster eccentric, and she also fell for a musician named Don Carter, a brilliant drummer who somehow never made it. He taught her a lot about music and at seventeen she married him. She moved in with her new husband and his overbearing mother in their house in Chicago and fought for a year to prise him from his mother's clutches, during which time the marriage was never consummated. Finally it broke up altogether, mother and son leaving home and O'Day moving to the notorious Chelsea Hotel on Wilson Avenue in New York, home to itinerant artists of all kinds and the site where Devon Wilson and Nancy Spungen, the girlfriends of Jimi Hendrix and Sid Vicious respectively, both met their deaths.

Anita O'Day joined the Gene Krupa band in 1941 and began to move into the big time with two hits, 'Let Me off Downtown' and 'Thanks for the Boogie Ride'. That same year she won her first *Down Beat* poll as New Star of the Year and came fourth in the female vocalist section. She maintained her high position in the polls over the next few years and in 1943 married her long time 'on-off' lover, Carl Hoff, a golf pro and jazz fanatic. From Krupa she went to Woody Herman, then had two stints with Stan Kenton. But things were not as well as they seemed; the touring and the pressure from fans took their toll and O'Day hit the bottle in a big way:

> I should have been happy, but I was tired and depressed, drawing on energy I didn't really have ... I didn't eat regularly. But I drank. I even drank a little on the job. But I never thought of myself as looking for

booze. On the other hand, I didn't look for food either. I'd never been taught you had to eat. But I should have known I was heading for trouble.[1]

For six weeks in 1945, she suffered a nervous breakdown, spending much of the time in a wardrobe refusing to come out. As someone who felt she was born to fail, she couldn't handle success: 'Maybe I've been too happy … because I'm not used to that.'

In 1946, Carl and Ray Foreman, an old friend of O'Day's, tried to set up a jazz club in North Hollywood. Either they were incredibly impractical or their lawyer was suspect, because they had no building permits and failed to find out that the site of their proposed club had been earmarked by the city corporation for a water conduit. On top of that there were still restrictions on building inessential structures so that materials could be used for the war effort. Not surprisingly, the club did not materialize. Matters took another turn for the worse when Carl was busted by narcotics agents in March 1947:

> It was a dumb, nightmarish period. If only I'd been lucky enough to have been under contract to a movie studio or a big agency, I'd have placed a call to the head of publicity and he'd have known who to pay off. Around that time the only big movie star who landed in the headlines for using grass was Bob Mitchum, but he certainly was not the only one using it. There were lots of others whose drug use mysteriously never made the police records.[2] [Mitchum served a two-month jail sentence in 1948.]

Carl and Anita were released on $1,000 bail pending an appeal. Initially the bust seemed good for business. Crowds flocked to see her at a club in Milwaukee because as the club manager put it, 'dopers aren't that common around here'. However the appeal failed and O'Day spent ninety days in jail, although she seemed to regard this as a vacation rather than a punishment – for the first time in her life she ate regular meals. But out of prison, aged twenty-nine, she was stuck with a career that didn't seem to be going anywhere. Carl had another go at starting up a club, this time in Chicago, but it too failed and he and O'Day split up.

O'Day tended now to mix with the bebop crowd. Moving within Charlie Parker's sphere of influence, she was bound to discover heroin. In 1952 she almost shot up for kicks in the company of Stan Getz and Chet Baker, both users at the time. However, Gerry Mulligan was also on the gig and although a heroin user himself, he threatened to beat up anyone who showed O'Day how to fix. But Mulligan's gallantry notwithstanding, and in her own words, 'the "Bad Anita" began to take over from the "Good Anita"'.

In October, O'Day and her new lover, a young trumpet player called Denny Roche, were arrested for a second time, suspected of using marijuana. Driving home, they were followed by a police car. The police alleged that they saw O'Day throw a roach (the stub of a marijuana cigarette) out of the car window. She was released on bail; the case took four months to come to trial at the end of which Anita O'Day was found not guilty, because the police could not produce the actual roach she had thrown away. While waiting for the trial, O'Day had her first taste of heroin in the dressing room of Harry 'The Hipster' Gibson, who had a hit record with 'Who Put the Benzedrine in Mrs Murphy's Ovaltine?' but was more famous in the music business as a purveyor of chemicals.

Escaping that marijuana charge and her earlier run-ins with the law made O'Day something of a target at a time when the heat was on musicians and informers were everywhere. It was in fact a musician who set O'Day up for the more serious charge of heroin possession. A pianist passed her a packet of heroin at the Club Samoa and asked her to hold it for him until the end of the last set. Anita hid it in the ladies toilet, but as she left the stage after the gig she was grabbed by police. Denny was also arrested. The police made reference to the heroin in the toilet and tried to get Anita to admit she put it there. She and Denny were taken away and held on suspicion, during which time they were invited to pay up $2,500 to stay out of court. Anita refused and the hearing was set for 4 May 1953, after one postponement for a singing engagement. Following much legal wrangling, the trial eventually got under way on 8 July and dragged on for a month, ending in a retrial with the jury hopelessly deadlocked. Finally on 25 August, Anita O'Day was found guilty and put on probation for five years, on condition that she spent five months in the County Jail on Terminal Island. Again, like Art Pepper, she found that jail was not such a bad place to be – no responsibilities and, as long as you kept your nose clean, no problems either. The only really bad time she had was when her mother died and the prison authorities refused to let her attend the funeral because it was out of State.

The most ridiculous part of the whole business was that apart from an occasional sniff, there was no way Anita O'Day could be described as a heroin user, yet by virtue of her prison sentence and because there was little distinction made in law or public perception between a heroin addict and marijuana smoker, she was branded as a junkie and faced all the problems of having that label without actually being one. To blot out the reality of her fading career, which was crippled by legal problems and lengthy absences from the stage, she drank heavily. But she had acquired the reputation of a doper, not a drinker, and she resolved, in her own words, 'to play the game, if she had the name'. so it was that heroin came into her life, and with it a new man who became a crucial part of the equation.

For a jazzman, drummer John Poole was an unusual individual. He didn't smoke or drink and because of strong religious convictions he didn't believe in sex outside marriage – but he regularly shot heroin. O'Day and Poole were never lovers, but O'Day pestered him into injecting her. Possibly due to guilt feelings, he never showed her how to do it, but insisted on doing it himself.

As user-musicians on the road trying to find work, O'Day and Poole took enormous risks in order to obtain drugs, trusting unknown connections and even having heroin sent through the post. O'Day stopped drinking, which probably saved her from an early death, but of course injecting heroin brought with it its own potential hazards.

Inevitably, they were busted. They bought 84% pure heroin from an informer who had been supplied with narcotics by government agents. They never got to use it, which was just as well because with the average purity on the streets at that time around 20-30%, a dose that strong would probably have killed them both. Agents raided their room straight after the buy, but Poole put on an act of being completely mad, distracting their attention so that he could push the packet from the table to the floor and out of sight. The police left empty-handed, a very fortunate let-off because it would have meant a second conviction for Poole, after which in the fifties they threw away the key. O'Day would have gone to prison for five years for breaking parole.

Poole and O'Day lost their New York cabaret cards, but they were told that despite their convictions they would both be granted permits if they could pass Nalline tests. Nalline was the trade name for nalolphine, a narcotic antagonist: in other words a drug which reversed the effects of narcotics like heroin. One physical feature of opiate use is a constriction of the pupils in the eye. In the Nalline test, the person was seated in a darkened room, injected with 3 mg at Nalline and left for thirty minutes. If after this time the pupils dilated more than 0.5 mm, it was taken as proof that the Nalline had found some opiate to antagonize and had proceeded to reverse its action of constricting the pupils. More dramatically, the user would start going into withdrawal, perspiring and yawning. When the subject is clean, Nalline can paradoxically act as an opiate agonist, mimicking rather than combating the effects of heroin. Lenny Bruce took this test when he was off heroin and ended the session high as a kite. O'Day and Poole weaned themselves off heroin using an opiate-based cough medicine called Cosynal, took the Nalline test and managed to pass it. In being given the chance to 'win back' their permits, it might have been significant that both musicians were white.

To say that 1958 was a year of mixed fortunes for Anita O'Day would be something of an understatement. In May she very nearly died and by the end of the summer she was an international star. The turning point was 'Jazz on a Summer's Day', Bert Stern's film of the 1958 Newport Jazz Festival. Stoned on heroin, O'Day was hailed as 'the festival's outstanding act' by *Metronome* and 'the hit' by *Esquire*. Stern included two songs from Anita's nine-tune set in the final cut of the film, 'Sweet Georgia Brown' and a fast version of 'Tea for Two', bringing more accolades from the *New York Times* and *Newsweek* when the film was released. (Ironically, both these songs have drug associations.)

But it could all have been so different; one late afternoon in May that year, Anita had been in a hotel room with John Poole and a guy identified only as a 'very famous jazz drummer' who had a heavy heroin habit. For the first time, she allowed somebody other than John to inject her. But probably because the drummer's tolerance was much higher than hers, he gave her too much and she went out like a light. The drummer immediately shot her full of cocaine and between them, her male companions revived her by walking her up and down the room and showering her with cold water.

Anita O'Day met Billie Holiday only twice. The second time Holiday acted as though O'Day wasn't there, but on the first occasion they had pooled their money to buy heroin:

> I wasn't only in awe of her singing. I was in awe of her habit. She didn't cook up with a spoon. Man, she used a small tunafish can and shot 10cc into her feet. (Later, I understand she ran out of veins all over her body. So she used those on either side of her vagina. One sure thing, no narc was going to bust her for fresh track marks.)[3]

'Later' was 1959. For O'Day, the jazz film paved the way for tours to Europe and Japan, where she was a special favourite. Holiday was in a less fortunate position. In February that year, jazz critic Leonard Feather went backstage to visit Billie Holiday. What he saw drained the colour from his face. 'What's the matter, Leonard? You seen a ghost?' Feather didn't need to reply: the look in his face said it all. On the afternoon of 31 May 1959, Billie Holiday collapsed in a coma. She was taken to Knickerbocker Hospital in New York and then to the Metropolitan Hospital in Harlem.

The initial diagnosis of a non-lethal heroin overdose was changed to a liver ailment complicated by cardiac failure. She had actually begun to recover when police struck again. They raided the hospital room and claimed they found a small envelope containing heroin. It was pointed out that, wired up to a bank of equipment, Holiday could not possibly have reached where the drug was allegedly discovered. The police ignored this argument. She couldn't be moved, so a guard was placed outside the door as if she was a mafia mobster. Some claimed the drug was planted, others that it was left by a misguided well wisher. Her companion Alice stated in a BBC-TV documentary that the singer had asked for cocaine to be brought in and a nurse had noticed traces of it on her lips.

Whatever the truth, it was a blow from which Billie Holiday did not recover. Without her knowledge or consent, the police removed her few possessions from the room and further degraded and humiliated her by photographing and fingerprinting her in her sick bed. Doctors added cirrhosis of the liver to the diagnosis and her condition worsened. She died at 3.10 am on Friday 17 July 1959.

Through the publication of her autobiography *Lady Sings the Blues* in 1956, Billie Holiday became in her own way as much a public campaigner for the humane treatment of drug addicts as Lenny Bruce was for a reform of the laws on obscenity. Her much-publicized views hardly found favour with the police and yet another bust followed the appearance of her book, in which she wrote:

> People on drugs are sick people. So now we end up with the government chasing sick people like they were criminals, telling doctors they can't help them, prosecuting them because they had some stuff without paying tax, and sending them to jail.
>
> Imagine if the government chased sick people with diabetes, put a tax on insulin and drove it into the black market, told doctors they couldn't treat them, and then caught them, prosecuted them for not paying their taxes, and then sent them to jail. If we did that, everyone would know we were crazy. Yet we do practically the same thing every day in the week to sick people hooked on drugs. The jails are full and the problem is getting worse very day.[4]

In his book *The Murderers*, Harry J. Anslinger devoted a chapter to the use of drugs in the entertainment business. He wrote of the perils of being in the public eye: 'Billie Holiday was an example. The harpies were forever after this talented Negro singer. They not only put her on drugs, but would not let her get off ... Despite her addiction, she reached and held a high place in the entertainment world. But only a few years after she reached her peak, she was dead.'[5] Anslinger failed to mention those in authority who killed her career in New York and probably cost her the national acclaim she so desperately craved as well as several thousand dollars in appearance money (to add to the royalties lost to shyster record companies). Nor does Harry J. mention the brave and fearless officers who hounded a sick woman to her grave.

For Anita O'Day, life got worse before it got better. She was an international star, but like Holiday she had little money compared with more commercial singers and as the sixties progressed, she found herself losing out, as many jazz artists did, to the burgeoning pop and rock scene. She described her personal life at that time as a mess; by now heroin was a dominant feature of a life made complicated by affairs with a series of unstable men, including one psychopath who threatened to cut her vocal cords when she spurned him.

By the early sixties her health had begun to break down – prolonged heroin use, and her lifestyle with its unhealthy diet, interfered with her digestive and intestinal processes and she suffered from severe arthritis in her knees and right arm. She went through a particularly lean spell in 1966; money was tight and she was unable to buy drugs. Her 'hype friend', John Poole, the man who (in her terms) had cared for her for so many years, had given up drugs, got married and moved to Hawaii. She had no option but to try to 'cold turkey', but having been on heroin for fourteen years, she was terrified of withdrawal and the chances of her succeeding with no physical, emotional or financial support were slim. On 4 March 1966, having almost detoxified herself, she took a shot of heroin her body could no longer tolerate and overdosed.

A friend found her with the needle still sticking in her arm and got her rushed to hospital. On arrival she was declared clinically dead, but the staff at UCLA Medical Center managed to revive her. On being discharged she flew to Hawaii where John Poole helped her on the long road back to fitness. She said in her autobiography: 'I finally faced the fact that life was hard. I recognized that I couldn't continue running away from my problems. I realized that I was too old and too tired to do more than make the most of what I had.'[6]

PART TWO
INTRODUCTION

The 1950s saw a new generation of disaffected, alienated youth in Britain and America kicking against what their parents regarded as the trophies of victory over the Axis Powers and Japan – peace, safety, security and prosperity. For many fifties youngsters this meant a bland meaningless world where passions were stifled and the pace of life ticked to the beat of the factory clock. Britain was still rather austere and gloomy; rationing did not end with the war, the sights of war damage were inescapable and young people in the early part of the decade did not enjoy the economic freedoms of their American counterparts.

In America, the same stifling cloak of conformity throttled political radicalism in a wave of anti-communist hysteria; 'pinko' was the ultimate insult. In this respect at least, teenagers of all social classes did not demur from mainstream opinion in the fifties. They weren't interested in revolution, because people got killed in real revolution. What they wanted was safe rebellion – weekend unconventionality, crossing on to the wild side on the way home to mom's apple pie or fish and chips out of last Sunday's *Pictorial*.

Adolescent was the jargon of sociologists and psychiatrists – teenage was an entirely different concept, born out of market research and the economics of consumerism. Before the Second World War, those we now call teenagers existed in a demographic wilderness, not quite children, but with adulthood tantalisingly out of reach. A nineteen-year-old whizz-kid from Chicago, named Eugene Gilbert, changed all that. In 1945, he established Gil Bert Teen Age Services, promising hot advertising copy for manufacturers keen to reach this new and affluent market. But it was not until 1956 that the teenager became established as a cultural and commercial force in America. It was the year rock 'n' roll came of age to give teenagers a voice and stance that nobody could ignore. Even so, the phenomenon was not entirely new: like the post-war generation of the 1920s white kids turned to black music as a vehicle for the release of suppressed emotions and as a statement against cultural and moral 'norms'.

But they did not turn to jazz; modern jazz was becoming too introspective, complex and elitist. Moreover, you couldn't really dance to it and as dancing had always been the key to any number of post pubertal possibilities, jazz (and so jazz musicians) tended to be pushed out of the limelight as a source of public outrage at the behaviour of young people.[1] In indeterminate proportions the magic formula of rock 'n' roll mixed black r&b and urban blues with white country and Southern gospel. And the nucleus at the centre of popular music's Big Bang was a truck driver from Tupelo, Mississippi: Elvis Presley.

Much has been written about Presley, but it is worth restating that he was an icon of the new age, the apotheosis of everything that teenagers fantasized about and their parents hated and feared. Forty years on, when so much has developed out of those early rock 'n' roll records, it is impossible to imagine the impact Presley, Jerry Lee Lewis and Bill Haley had on a generation brought up on Tommy Dorsey, Glenn Miller and Benny Goodman. Here were white country boys not crooning ballads to virginal girls on distant pedestals but singing lyrics to earthy black music whose messages about love left nothing to the imagination. Mainly because of the black influence, rock 'n' roll was condemned in exactly the same tones as jazz had been. Such bastions of free thought as the North Alabama White Citizens Council declared that rock 'n' roll was a racial plot against the white community. Others condemned the music as 'aboriginal' and 'a communicable disease'. There were even Senate hearings on the sexual explicitness of r&b lyrics. However the record companies, RCA above all, were laughing all the way to the bank. 'Heartbreak Hotel' topped the pop, country and r&b charts simultaneously and sixty per cent of RCA's production output was given over to supplying the demand for Presley's music.

Presley also represented the chance for a vicarious experience of 'rebel chic'. Initially at least he was marketed as a new threat to right-thinking Americans whose children would be drowned in the sexual morass of rock 'n' roll. In fact, the dangerous, outlaw rabble-raising image of Presley and Jerry Lee Lewis merely capitalised on their heritage as white Southern boys. There's a long-standing tradition in the American South in which getting drunk and/or stoned and chasing women and shooting off pistols and racing cars around for the sheer hell of it are normal, everyday male activities, generally accepted with a resigned or amused shrug by much of Southern society. Through Elvis, the promise of 'Roarin' with the Billies' (as it was called) was served up for kids all over the country; to them, it was young and vital and all the frustrations of being a white teenager in the fifties were heaped on the shoulders of white rock 'n' rollers. Kids rioted when they played; public condemnation became the badge of teenage credibility.

Presley, Brando and James Dean were a new breed of working-class anti-heroes more potent than the black jazz hipster because they were white and thus embraced and lionized by the media who ensured their bankability whether alive or dead. Their attitude was instantly recognizable: the sneer, the curled lip, the slowburn cynicism and the black leather jacket said it all.

Speed informed the philosophy of youth culture; wheels were the essence of the fifties experience in America – bombing up and down in the '49 Ford, the '55 Chevy, the T-Bird and the Studey. Brando rode a bike in *The Wild Ones*, Jimmy Dean drove his way to immortality behind the wheel of his Porsche. But speed meant more than 0-60 in seconds and overhead cams. Rock 'n' roll needed high-octane fuel to keep it going – new music and a new generation demanded new ways of getting stoned. To keep the authorities off his back, American DJ Alan Freed maintained in the fifties that rock 'n' roll was good clean fun. And likely as not, the sea of acned faces out front was consuming nothing stronger than Pepsi Cola; but backstage everyone was wired for sound.

Neither rock 'n' roll, nor the mod or garage bands of the sixties, nor northern soul or punk in the seventies can be legitimately considered outside the context of amphetamine. The same applies to West Coast rock and acid, and to marijuana and reggae. But this is not to suggest that acid-rock bands used only LSD or that punks stuck only to amphetamine; far from it. Certain drugs influenced the sound and creative context of particular genres more than others, but as the pharmaceutical industry became more competitive and street chemists more sophisticated, so more drugs were added to the music pharmacopeia. There were sedatives, hypnotics and tranquillizers in a hundred different colours and dosages, notably methaqualone (Quaaludes/Mandrax); a range of synthetic painkillers like Dilaudid; an alphabet soup of hallucinogens – LSD, DMT, PCP, MDMA, STP etc. – and a variety of one-offs like amyl nitrate.

Then, of course there is marijuana, the drug for all seasons. A mainstay of jazz musicians and beat artists in the fifties, it percolated right through the popular music scene, the drug of relaxation, introspection, political statement and communal spirit, and became most closely associated with reggae once Bob Marley had won international fame.

Heroin and cocaine remained for the subterranean jazzman. They figured heavily in the street drug scene of black ghetto areas and so also in the lifestyles of many popular black musicians from Frankie Lymon to Marvin Gaye. These two drugs, supposedly at the heavy end of the drug spectrum, also became seemingly mandatory for the burgeoning white rock elite, as musicians took over from film stars in the early seventies as the new aristocracy. The new stars needed either to be coked up to their eyes to face the microphones and cameras, or to be locked up in heroin hide-aways to enhance their Svengali reputations, ready for the comeback tour and album. They also became the focus of attention for social revenge as the white pop star toppled the black jazzman as public enemy number one.

8   WIRED FOR SOUND

In Kerouac's *On the Road*, Neil Casady appeared as Dean Moriarty, a composite of the rebel without a cause and the arch villain of Conan Doyle stories. Everything about Casady was 'mad', 'crazy' or 'wild'. He was probably the greatest driver literature has ever seen. Kerouac has Moriarty ripping through the country at ninety miles an hour in search of America. (What he found was Kerouac's *version* of the American Dream. Hunter Thompson, author of *Fear and Loathing in Las Vegas* did no better; at the end of his rainbow were Hell's Angels waiting to beat him up.) But speed meant more to Casady (and Thompson) than a gas pedal jammed on the floor:

> He rubbed his jaw furiously, he swung the car and passed three trucks, he roared into downtown Testament looking in every direction and seeing everything in an arc of 180 degrees around his eyeballs without moving his head. Bang, he found a parking space in no time and we were parked. He leaped out of the car. Furiously he hustled into the railway station; we followed sheepishly … He had become absolutely mad in his movements; he seemed to be doing everything at the same time. It was a shaking of the head, up and down, sideways; jerky, vigorous hands; quick walking; sitting, crossing the legs, uncrossing; getting up, rubbing the hands, rubbing his fly, hitching his pants, looking up and saying, 'Am', and sudden slitting of the eyes to see everywhere, and all the time he was grabbing me by the ribs and talking, talking.[1]

One could not wish for a more vivid or more accurate description of an amphetamine freak.

Originally synthesized in 1887 by the pharmaceutical manufacturers Smith, Kline and French, amphetamine was launched on the market in 1932 as a Benzedrine nasal inhaler to relieve the symptoms of colds, hayfever and asthma. Noting amphetamine's stimulant effect, in 1935 the manufacturers launched a campaign promoting the efficacy of the drug in combating a chronic sleeping disease called narcolepsy.

As with other drugs like morphine and cocaine, amphetamines garnered often inappropriate clinical acceptance in the treatment of nearly forty conditions, ranging from radiation sickness and persistent hiccups to, yes you've guessed it, opiate addiction. At the same time there were reports about Benzedrine misuse in the British press and in 1939 amphetamine was added to the UK Poisons List.

Almost as soon as Benzedrine hit the streets, young people looking for new ways to get high discovered the rejuvenating effect of removing the Benzedrine strip from its casing and drinking it in coffee. This was Charlie Parker's earliest introduction to drugs.

Despite some medical misgivings, soldiers in all the fighting forces during the war were liberally supplied with amphetamines to boost morale and fight battle fatigue; seventy-two million tablets were issued to British forces. Kamikaze pilots and German panzer troops went to war with their nervous systems kick-started by speed. Medical records revealed that throughout the war Hitler was being injected with methamphetamine up to eight times a day, which would more than account for his increasingly erratic and unpredictable behaviour, acute paranoia and evermore unrealistic battle plans.

American soldiers continued to use speed during the Korean War, but being in the Far East gave them the chance to try something new. Amphetamines keep you awake and alert, but also very edgy and nervous, in Korea they mixed speed with heroin to smooth off the jagged edges. Thus was born the 'speedball'. Cocaine later replaced amphetamine as the 'up' side of the equation among the cognoscenti; according to the coroner, such a concoction killed Meatloaf drummer Wells Kelly in London in 1984.

The function of amphetamines as appetite suppressants enabled the pharmaceutical companies to market speed as diet pills. Those in the public eye anxious to stay trim swallowed amphetamines like sweets, but whether you were using them to stay awake, stay sharp and confident or stay slim, there was always a down side. More than any other drugs, stimulants like amphetamine and cocaine epitomize the saying that there is no such thing as a free lunch.

Stimulants give you energy, confidence, make you talkative and stop you feeling hungry. You feel witty, clever, amusing and powerful. But tolerance builds very rapidly. The more you take, the more you need. With amphetamine, regular high doses can turn the confident energetic user into a neurotic paranoiac, constantly living on the edge of psychosis. Speed does not in fact give you any energy, it takes from the body's resources. Stop the drug and a heavy lethargy and depression or crash takes place needing lots of rest and recuperation. But most problematic is the risk that the user will turn to more dangerous sedatives like alcohol or barbiturates to counteract the effects of the amphetamine. In combination such sedatives can be lethal; for example they cost singer Dinah Washington her life in December 1963. She had been desperately trying to get her weight down for an upcoming concert date, using amphetamine diet pills. Elvis Presley took to speed for two reasons – to keep him awake on tour and later to 'help' his battle against weight. Again, it was in an effort to counteract the stimulants that he embarked on a chemical grand tour which took him to the farthest reaches of the Merck pill index, consuming every painkiller, sedative, hypnotic and tranquillizer that the men in white coats could concoct.

Back home after the war, the American GIs brought their government-issue drug habits with them. Those who could not face the straightjacket of life on the factory floor took to the freeways as truckers, transporting the products of America's post-war prosperity across the country in their beloved rigs. Amphetamine became the trucker's friend. He needed less sleep and less food, while more mileage meant more money. He felt good, too. The redneck Southern truckers, fuelled on amphetamine goodwill, hit the bars and dives of dusty rebel towns like Natchez, Mississippi, to hear country boys belt out their favourite songs and to catch some of the raucous Saturday-night special sounds of this new thing called rock 'n' roll. At the Wagon Wheel in Natchez, Jerry Lee Lewis, then a raw nineteen-year-old, played to truckers who showed their appreciation by tipping him in fifteen-milligram Benzedrine capsules.

Speed stood at the crossroads of early rock 'n' roll and country music consumed by performers, roadies and audience alike. Johnny Cash got hooked on amphetamines while hanging around the drivers who ferried the Grand Ole Opry stars across the country. At first his performances were pin sharp, his timing excellent and he was confident to bursting point. But before long his voice was shot, he had that lean, hungry, wasted look and his behaviour became violent and erratic. Barred from the Opry, it took a long time to find his way back as a hundred Dr Feelgoods handed out pills on request. Rarely did Cash have to seek illegal supplies in Mexico or through drug thefts. Although a former truck-driver himself, Presley apparently did not get his first taste of amphetamines until a sergeant gave him some to stay awake on guard duty during his army days. Amphetamines were still regular US army issue in the sixties. Between 1966 and 1969 US troops legitimately consumed more amphetamines than British and American troops combined during World War II.

The little magic pills also got rockers to gigs and gave them the confidence to tear places apart. Years before the Who's speed-driven auto-destruction and Hendrix's amphetamine pyrotechnics with a flaming Fender, Jerry Lee Lewis set fire to his piano during Alan Freed's Big Beat tour of 1958. As the fire raged, he bawled at the stage crew, 'I'd like to see any son of a bitch follow that!' Jerry Lee and Elvis became rock 'n' roll models, but they had their own burnout guru in Hank Williams, acknowledged as one of the finest songwriters and performers country music ever produced.

Williams died of a heart attack at the age of twenty-nine, on New Year's Eve 1953. His alcohol and speed intake had been increasing in direct proportion to his meteoric rise to fame, bursting on to the country scene only four years before his death. It was a fame that this semi-literate son of a lumber worker could not handle. As Carl Perkins said about his own drink problem:

> When you're a country boy just a month from the plow and suddenly you're a star with money in your pocket, cars, women, big cities, crowds, the change is too fast. You're the same person inside, but you're a star outside, so you don't know how to act. You're embarrassed about the way you talk, the way you eat, the way you look. You can't take the strain without a crutch.[2]

The timeless quality of his simple, sincere songs of great lyrical beauty meant that Williams did not need an early, tragic death on the backseat of a car to ensure legendary status. But in a sense his life, and the lives of all those to follow who creamed down the fast lane, was defined through its temporal nature. It is difficult to escape the notion entirely that he was ultimately fulfilled at the moment of death. Hank Williams never made it; Jerry Lee Lewis, Johnny Cash and the Everly Brothers all fought long battles against amphetamine. Cash found religion, but Jerry kept finding John Law round the corner.

When a big bust meant Marilyn Monroe and speed was something the traffic cops got you for, Lewis and his band, the Memphis Beats, were charged with possession of 700 amphetamine capsules after a raid on their motel in Grand Prairie, Texas. In fact, amphetamines were not brought under strict Federal control until 1970, but Jerry Lee and the boys fell foul of existing legislation dating back to 1951, controlling sales of non-prescription over-the-counter drugs. And that's how it went for the next twenty years. Persistent speed-taking made Lewis unpredictable, violent and paranoiac, shooting off guns in hotel rooms and beating up his wife when she flushed his stash down the toilet. On finishing a one-year probationary sentence for possession in 1980, he was busted again at his home in Hernando, Mississippi. Inland Revenue Service agents had to come to seize property in lieu of tax payments and discovered an amount of cocaine. At forty-four, Jerry Lee Lewis was still a marked man.

The history of amphetamines and popular music takes us from the American Deep South to the English South, or more specifically to the club scene in London's West End.

Notwithstanding the *Melody Maker's* hysterical outburst in 1936 about drug-using musicians, not only was drug-taking in England actually very circumscribed, but the illicit use of drugs in Britain as a whole was not a social issue. Those addicts notified to the Home Office were generally middle-class, middle-aged morphine users, often professionally employed, receiving maintenance prescriptions from their GP. Most (if not all) were therapeutic addicts; that is, they had become dependent on opioids through GP prescriptions for pain. Their numbers were small and falling; from around 700 in 1935 to fewer than 300 in the early fifties. The figures began to rise sharply only in the early to mid sixties, when the addict ranks were swelled by a younger group of largely working class males using heroin rather than morphine and 'recreationally' rather than as a result of a dependence derived from pain relief.

Nevertheless, there was evidence after the Second World War of a drug-using sub-culture which operated mainly outside the network of GPs, involving first marijuana and then heroin and focused around musicians living or working in London. Drugs like opium and marijuana had for years been smuggled into Britain by Chinese and African sailors for use within their own small communities in London and Liverpool. But from 1947 drug offences, particularly involving marijuana jumped markedly, suggesting that the drug was being distributed outside such discrete communities.

Detective Sergeant George Lyle of Scotland Yard described the following incident at a talk he gave in January 1953:

> In 1950 complaints began to be received that Indian Hemp was being sold in certain dance clubs in the West End.
>
> On 15 April 1950, at 12.30 p.m. a large force of police, about forty, raided Club 11, a private dance club in Carnaby Street, W1. There were on the premises between 200 and 250 persons, coloured and white, of both sexes, the majority being between 17 and 30. All these people were searched. Ten men were found to be in possession of Indian Hemp. Two also had a small quantity of cocaine and another man had a small quantity of morphine. In addition, 23 packets of Indian Hemp, a number of hemp cigarettes, a small packet of cocaine, a small quantity of prepared opium and an empty morphine ampoule were found on the floor of the club. All

the cocaine had been adulterated with boric acid. All were later convicted and fined. The Indian Hemp cigarettes were being sold at 5/- a time and the adulterated cocaine at 10/- a grain.[3]

The report does not name names, but included in the haul were Ronnie Scott, who already had a cocaine conviction; and the bassist Lenny Bush. The excuses presented in court ranged from, 'I had no idea how the cigarette came to be lying at my feet,' to a plea that the defendant had no idea that cannabis was an illegal drug. Someone claimed that the cocaine found on him was for his toothache. The judge was not impressed. Ronnie Scott's drug conviction was particularly unfortunate because, denied a US visa, he forfeited any chance of a Stateside career.

A second major case of dealing (major for its time, that is) occurred, in 1951, when the pharmacy of a hospital near London was raided and large quantities of morphine, heroin and cocaine were stolen. Shortly afterwards, the Metropolitan Police became aware that a man known as 'Mark' ,was dealing in drugs in the West End. He was arrested and identified as a former employee of the hospital where the break-in had happened. Interestingly enough, of the fourteen people known to have obtained drugs from 'Mark', only two had been previously notified. By the end of 1954, thirty-six people associated with 'Mark', had been notified, twenty-one of whom were musicians.

The first white teenager caught with marijuana in Britain was arrested in October 1952, 'having acquired the habit through frequenting "be-bop" clubs and cafes where addicts congregated'.[4] Marijuana was used most among the jazz and folk musicians and their educated middle-class-audience. The heroin users, too, were a literate bunch. Devouring De Quincey, Burroughs and others, they knew more than most doctors about the nature of addiction. The jazz musicians who followed in Charlie Parker's faltering footsteps included two of Britain's finest, Phil Seaman and Tubby Hayes, both now dead.

Until the late sixties, the drug scene was tight, in its geographical location, in its elitist, exclusive attitude and in its numerical strength. Users knew each other and the Home Office Drugs Inspectors knew all of them, the dealers and the doctors. Amphetamines helped change all that .

Although amphetamines and mods were almost mutually dependent, mods were not the first 'deviant' subculture to start using them. Social workers in the late fifties noted fairly extensive use of Drinamyl, blue triangular-shaped compounds of amphetamines and barbiturates known as purple hearts, among East End prostitutes. Drinamyl, Dexadrine and other amphetamines were so common in the West End in the early sixties that pills were crushed underfoot in the toilets of Leicester Square underground without anyone taking much notice. Speed was also popular among those members of Soho's itinerant teenage population who were gays, lesbians and/or heavily involved in petty crime or prostitution .

Nor was speed exactly unknown among British musicians. Amphetamines in various shapes and colours kept the pop and rock 'n' roll tours moving in the fifties and sixties and Phenmetrazine, marketed as Preludin, was consumed by the handful by bands, most notably by the Beatles, on their trips to Hamburg. Stuffed to the gills with 'Prellies' bought at the chemist, the Beatles played hour after hour seven days a week in the Indra, the Bambi, the Top Ten and Manfred Weissleder's Star Club. Prellies kept them awake, frantic enough to whip up the crowd and free from hunger, which was useful because they had no money to eat. According to Peter Brown, former business manager of the Beatles, 'John was so out of control one night, that when a customer over-enthusiastically approached the stage, John kicked him in the head twice, then grabbed a steak knife from a table and threw it at the man.'[5]

The Beatles discovered what the rock 'n' rollers already knew and the rock musicians of the future would soon find out, that amphetamines were 'working drugs'. Nobody can play blind drunk and those who tried playing on acid often found themselves deep in conversation with microphone stands and speaker cabinets. Speed (and later cocaine) works by giving musicians the courage to get out there and sufficient edge to keep going throughout the performance. But trying to talk to the audience can be a mistake, when Elvis was taking large amounts of speed to trim down for a tour, fans were subjected to long rambling monologues between songs.

This is amphetamine use in a purely functional role. For the mods, amphetamines were symbolically enshrined at the heart of their subculture, fitting into a discrete universe, a system of magical correspondences in which all objects – clothes, music, scooters and drugs – had a precise relationship with one another. Each item was taken from the straight world and redefined within a homogenous cosmos; amphetamines were the subcultural adhesive which joined lifestyles and values the functional springboard for the frantic activity of staying up, buying clothes, riding and fixing scooters, and dancing.

'Mod' was a catch-all phrase which encompassed a variety of styles contributing to a media-created image of 'Swinging London'. It should have been called 'Speeding London'; the amphetamine-induced arrogance, edginess, narcissism and freneticism of mod culture was reflected right through the art, music and fashion of the period. London's Pop Art scene was like a giant Roy Lichstenstein painting – POW!! ZAP!! But as with all amphetamine 'runs' there came the inevitable crash. Like the merry-go-round at the end of Hitchcock's *Strangers on a Train* the scene collapsed and London was probably a duller place for it.

But when it all started, the mods were the upfront ambassadors. By the time the style had been castrated by the High Street entrepreneurs for furious but safe consumption, the mods had 'turned neatness into an art form'.[6] They came from a post-war British working-class attitude to smartness, best described as 'flash'. The spivs (George Cole as 'Flash Harry' in St Trinian's films, Arthur Daley as a young man) were followed by teds who hijacked a failed attempt by Savile Row to revive Edwardian elegance for the aristocracy, adding string ties and slick hairdos to a taste for American rock 'n' roll and the Mississippi steamboat gambler. Mods, too, took some inspiration from the States in taste and their attempt to re-create the sartorial coolness of the black hipster. However, they looked to the Continent particularly Italy, for the clothes themselves.

Amphetamines promote a sense of controlled anger (which is why they have proved so popular among American footballers). The mod stance was undeniably uptight. They looked normal, but they weren't. They made wearing a suit and tie seem aggressive and threatening. Somehow too smart and too neat, they caused consternation among 'the straights', who saw their own conservative dress sense mocked. The worst thing that could happen to a mod was to have his parents understand him.

In 1961, 2½% of all NHS prescriptions were for amphetamines. Even so, Mods made speed their own: it was youthful recreational use amphetamines, not over-prescribing by GPs, that caused them to be controlled in drugs legislation passed in 1964 especially created for purpose. Getting blocked on pills at weekends was what separated 'them from us', and it so happened that one of 'them' turned out to be Lee Harris, who quite possibly was the catalyst for the passing of the '64 Act outlawing unauthorised possession of amphetamines. There is an irony here; Lee became a staunch supporter of law reform and still runs a 'head-shop' in London's Portobello Road which the police have tried unsuccessfully to close down under the Drug Trafficking Act which bans the sale of drug paraphernalia. But back in the early 1960s, Lee was by his own admission, "something of a moralist".

Lee came to England from South Africa on the run as a teenage political activist from the apartheid regime. He settled in London as a playwright and actor and was a regular visitor to all the seedy dives and clubs of Soho playing r&b. Although by the time Mod hit town, he was in his late twenties, he embraced the culture, and had friends who were running the clubs where drug dealing was going on – until he saw what was happening on the streets, "There were all these young kids wandering about the streets at five in the morning completely out of it on pep pills". He met with young people who were becoming seriously addicted to the drugs, becoming very paranoid and anxious. He mentioned this to the Labour MP for Paddington, Ben Parkin, who had recently exposed the notorious slum landlord Peter Rachman, but who knew nothing about amphetamine.

> "He told me that he would raise it in Parliament, but that if anybody wanted to know more about what was happening, he would give them my phone number. I got a call from Ann Sharpley who was a top investigative reporter on the *Evening Standard*. She said, 'Would you like to show me round the West End?' I took her on a tour of the dives and introduced her to this young speed addict I knew called Johnny Colfer. She saw all these young people and the dealers passing the pills. That Monday, at the beginning of 1964, there was a headline in the *Evening Standard*, 'I see Soho pep pill craze'. In the evening, Soho was deserted. There was a terrific hue and cry – this had to have been the first big drug story ever to hit the British press. Up to that point, the general view was that the only people who took pep pills were housewives in the Rhondda Valley."

The relentless pursuit of fashion eclipsed everything else; food, drink and women didn't matter because speed killed the appetite for all three, which may account for the fact that the mod cult was predominantly male. Many mods had office jobs, paying around £11 a week, most of which went on clothes and pills. Mod fashion was a microcosm of an industrial society which paid homage to the sacred cow of built-in obsolescence. A mod would spend three weeks' wages having vents put in or taken out of jackets, lapels widened or narrowed, knowing that three weeks later something else would be 'in', and mods would rather stay home than be seen out in last week's fashion. Probably no teenage style has paid such meticulous attention to the minutiae of its uniform – an obsession which had its counterpart in the way amphetamine users can get totally absorbed in mindless and trivial occupations like washing a plate.

For mods, speed also had purely functional applications. First was fighting. The early mods had no time for violence but the hysterical press reporting of the first major mod-rocker clash at Clacton on Easter Monday 1964 became a self-fulfilling prophecy. Mods had been going down to the coast, using it is a 'chill-out' zone after the clubs closed in the early hours of the morning. Lee Harris recalls, "What happened was suddenly all these kids aged 15 and 16 with short hair and Parkas were out on the streets of Soho at two and three in the morning. They were all chewing gum with big dilated pupils and I started finding out about Purple Hearts at 6d each and some of these kids were taking 80 or 90 over a weekend and having amphetamine psychosis. The clubs would end at five in the morning and these kids stoned out of their minds would be out on the streets with nowhere to go. So they would all go off to the seaside; you'd see these great gatherings at Liverpool Street Station – and that was the beginning of the Mods and Rockers thing."

Easter '64 was the first time most people had heard about mods or rockers and the press instantly created a new breed of 'folk devils' to rival the similarly speed-driven teds and razor gangs. The press reports were littered with words and phrases like 'battle', 'attack', 'siege', 'screaming mob' and 'orgy of destruction'. The press exaggerated and distorted every aspect of the confrontation, conveying the impression that the fracas was strictly polarized on mod and rocker lines. Initially the clashes were more between rival gangs from London and the Home Counties. Only later, in some of the more bloody disturbances when it had become fashionable to be either mod or rocker, did these battles take on the lines of a clash of subcultures. At that point, the mod underground, a cool, understated bunch of natty dressers, became media darlings. Nothing really subversive ever got the *Sunday Times Colour Supplement* treatment. In the hunt for the ideal mod to interview, the *Sunday Times* came up with 'Denzil', who said 'Pills make you edgy and argumentable'; it made them hyper-sensitive to the possibilities of action and generated the desire to go looking for trouble. Having got totally wired up on pills, mods had to find trouble to release the frustration of what felt like an arrested orgasm. And after the way the press handled the Easter/Whitsun '64 incidents, it was obvious that any right-thinking mods or rockers out for some free publicity to shock the nation would get together at appointed times and places 'predicted' by the press, in the sure knowledge that the cameras would be ready and waiting.

Denzil had more to say – an average week in the life of the ideal London mod:

Monday night	Dancing at the Mecca, the Hammersmith Palais, the Purley Orchard or the Streatham Locarno
Tuesday	Soho and the Scene Club
Wednesday	Marquee night
Thursday	Washing hair (which had to be dried using a dryer with a hood)
Friday	Back at the Scene
Saturday afternoon	Clothes- and record-buying
Saturday night	The All Nighter at the Flamingo

It is unlikely that any mod ever kept up a regime like that for long however much speed he took. It all cost money and although mods were the most affluent teenagers to date, the money had to run out some time. Nevertheless the diary does demonstrate the importance of music and the club scene to all mods, whether 'hard core' or 'weekenders'.

In Britain, the club scene has always provided the main platform for the development of the new genres of musical taste from traditional jazz to punk rock. The only significant competition has been from the college circuit in the affluent late sixties, where many of the underground or 'progressive' bands like Jethro Tull built up their early following. The clubs and pubs also suffered in the early seventies from a vacuum which was left after most British rock bands went to play large arenas in America. Pub bands like Dr Feelgood and Kilburn and the High Roads helped promote a small-venue revival which finally took off with the arrival of punks. With the Beatles, northern clubs like the Cavern in Liverpool and the Twisted Wheel in Manchester, had already carved out for themselves a significant place in rock history, but much of the media and business interest during the sixties focused on London and the Soho club scene. That's where the music was to be found. And the drugs. Dark, subterranean dives, packed with people frantically dancing to loud music were an ideal setting for drug-dealing.

One of the main centres for speed-dealing was the Scene Club, situated in Ham Yard at 41 Great Windmill Street. The club was run by Ronan O'Rahilly, one-time manager of Alexis Korner's Blues Incorporated and a pioneer of pirate radio with Radio Caroline. Although O'Rahilly ran the Scene, it was part of the Nash gang club operation in Soho and hence a dangerous place to be.[7]

The club had an interesting history. Several venues had existed on the site, including the Cy Laurie Club and the Piccadilly Jazz Club, where music entrepreneur Giorgio Gomelsky first saw the Rolling Stones. Back in the forties and early fifties, it was none other than the Club Eleven, where that first London club bust had taken place in 1950. As the Scene, it was the place to be seen, as far as Mods were concerned. The DJ was Guy Stevens who had the best American record collection in Britain. chock full of rare soul, blues and r&b discs. He co-ran Sue Records with Chris Blackwell and later produced for Mott the Hoople and the Clash.

O'Rahilly had the walls padded and cushions strewn everywhere, so that those who speeded to exhaustion could crash out. Two cousins who manned the door for a time had a habit of relieving patrons of their pill stash as they entered, pretending to flush them down the toilet and then recycling them. The dealing went on in the club, safe from prying eyes; Drinamyl pills were sold at 1/3d. (c. 6p) each, but were normally bought in fives, tens, twenties, fifties and hundreds.

In March 1967, *Oz* magazine spoke to two twenty-one-year-old dealers called Paul and Cliff. They had a joint income of up to £400 a week and both owned '66 Ford Zephyrs. A third of the money was passed to a godfather figure they called 'Big Sid', and they employed two West Indian 'minders' with whom they shared a twenty-guinea-a-week flat (£21) in Chelmsford:

> Starting their work at the Marquee club they sell to a market of thirteen-year-old mods; after a meal they move into the clubs around Greek Street; then to a stand just outside Tiffany's at about one in the morning. When necessary they work a pitch in the Lyon's Cafes around Trafalgar Square; if on Sunday morning they have any pills remaining, they move into Chelsea where apparently tired debs are always a ready market. In conversation with one reporter as to the origin of the amphetamine, they said that some of their pills were knocked off, but most came as a regular supply through London docks – they weren't sure where, but 'Big Sid looks after that end.' In one weekend they never sell less than 3,000 pills

and sometimes in excess of 6,000, undercutting other pushers by selling at 1/- each.

Another key club for the speed dealers in the early sixties was La Discotheque in Wardour Street. It was originally called El Condor, and from 1957-61 operated as an exclusive night spot frequented by British royalty. The club was owned by Raymond Nash and Peter Rachman who sold the club to Tommy Yeardye and one of Rachman's own proteges, Peter Davies. However, the new club went bankrupt and reopened as the far more downmarket discotheque; hordes of young people replaced the upper middle class and the smattering of aristocrats. Rachman and Nash resumed control as joint shareholders. They installed a powerful lighting and sound system. Drinks were 5/- but the place was more awash with cheap amphetamines. A dealer dubbed 'Peter the Pill' forged another link between Rachman and the London amphetamine scene, as he was both a (if not the) major dealer in speed and one of Rachman's loyal soldiers, later to become a road manager for the Animals and Eric Burdon's War and an associate of Jimi Hendrix's manager Mike Jeffrey.

The question of supply during this period is one that has never been fully investigated. Certainly most of the amphetamines in circulation around the clubs were manufactured drugs, not the product of illicit street laboratories. Nor, in view of the huge number of pills involved, could they simply have been spillage from over-prescribing by doctors. Individual youngsters may have obtained some from the medicine cupboard at home, but not dealers.

As these drugs invariably had the manufacturer's name SKF (Smith, Kline and French) stamped on them, those working with chronic amphetamine users in Soho came to the not unreasonable conclusion that vast quantities of drugs were finding their way directly to dealers via SKF employees pilfering from the factory and warehouses. At a meeting of the Society for the Study on Addiction in September 1966, one worker, Judith Piepe, got up and said so in public:

> Extensive security precautions in a factory cost a great deal of money. It is easy for anybody on the production line quietly to take a handful and augment their wages by selling them. The production cost of drugs like Drinamyl are very low and the cost in money to ensure better security arrangements is considered too high by the manufacturers. They do not consider the cost in suffering to young people.

Replying for SKF, a Mr Schrire said:

> In regard to the accusation that tablets are being stolen from the manufacturing companies, I regard this as nonsense. The tablets are manufactured under stringent supervision and it is highly improbably that any quantities could be stolen from the factories in these circumstances.[8]

At about this time, the press reported a Gloucestershire doctor as saying that amphetamines were being made by teenagers with O-level chemistry. He offered no evidence for this and the *Daily Mirror* rang various experts to check the story. One GP, Ian Pierce James, stated that he was sure anyone with O-level chemistry could make amphetamine pills, but wondered how they managed to make the little moulds and stamp SKF on them!

Who were the dealers? To judge from Paul and Cliff's story, the operation was very lucrative and involved some crude dealer hierarchy. At the top may have sat members of Britains' most notorious criminal gangs of the sixties. They owned many of the West End clubs and would be unlikely to allow any profitable side action to be carried out in those clubs without taking some of the profits for themselves. In 1968, the Government introduced a system of NHS clinics supplying drugs to addicts in the hope of preventing organised crime setting up a wide-spread black market in illicit drugs. As we know, at best this system merely postponed the event, but it may have been that the gangs had already staked a claim in the illicit market prior to '68.

The clubs where speed was used and dealt ranged from the world famous to the here today, gone tomorrow. Despite its clean-cut image, the Marquee was a pill palace, catering for a younger mod set who were on the way home to bed, before the All Nighter session at the more sophisticated Flamingo Club got under way. The Flamingo provided mods with a chance to rub shoulders with black American airforce men on forty-eight-hour passes and dance to the black-inspired r&b of Georgie Fame and Zoot Money. Mods frequented the Last Chance, Le Kilt, La Poubelle and the Roaring Twenties, a basement place in Carnaby Street, before the street became fashionable. Originally a failed attempt to persuade Jewish teenagers from the more expensive parts of North London to part with their money on Saturday nights, the club reopened as the Roaring Twenties, a black club where bluebeat first appeared together with pimps, prostitutes and the general melée of Soho wide-boys selling stolen watches and dodgy Jags, the 'Mod Cons' as Lee Harris called them. Tiles was another important venue, providing the meeting place for a lunchtime mod culture which Tom Wolfe called the Noonday Underground.

The Reverend Ken Leech was a well-known figure around Soho in the sixties. He cared for young people in trouble at the Centrepoint night shelter at St Anne's Church, and was a keen observer of life in Soho at the time, trusted and respected by all the disparate and volatile elements that made up the fascinating community.

> As you walked up Wardour Street and turned into D'Arblay Street, there was a very small area which you could walk round in ten minutes where there was a very heavy concentration of amphetamine clubs. Within yards of each other you had in 1961, Le Douce, a gay club, directly opposite you had a club which changed its name several times but was most famous as the Subway. Then you had the Coffee Pot, which never closed (and where according to Richard Neville's *Playpower*, I'm always to be found!) Underneath that was the Huntsman and then opposite, in a smelly cul-de-sac between Wardour Street and Berwick Street, was Wardour Mews with the Limbo Club, the Granada and the Take Five.[9]

And what of the music itself? There was really no such thing as mod music, rather music that mods liked. Mod was originally short for modernists and in musical terms that meant modern jazz. They also picked up on black r&b, soul and Jamaican bluebeat and in the tiny clubs mentioned above, danced frantically to chart stuff from the jukebox. But if any music came to represent the anger, frustration, brashness and arrogance of the mods, it was that of the Who.

Right at the start the Kinks were in competition with the Who to be the mods' living identification, the people's band, but in the end they couldn't compete with the Who's auto-destruction and Townshend's anthems for a teenage wasteland. Nor did they have a Pete Meaden or a Kit Lambert.

Between them, Meaden and Lambert fashioned the Who's mod image; by inclination none of them was a mod. Meaden, a Drinamyl disciple and a face among the faces down at the Scene, became the Who's publicist and began the image-building whereby mods came to identify with the band. His shortlived renaming of the Who to the High Numbers was meant to indicate the state Meaden and the Who were in most of the time. Kit Lambert, who seemed to be able to function only under the influence of uppers or downers, depending on what image he needed to project at the time, completed the process with trips to Carnaby Street and the hairdressers. Townshend later said, 'The mod image was forced on us. It was dishonest.'[10] To keep their credibility intact, the band would watch what dance steps the mod audiences were doing and re-create them on stage, so that another audience would think the Who had invented them. The management of Kit Lambert and Chris Stamp was ideal, as Keith Moon explained: 'These people were perfect for us, because there's me, bouncing about, full of pills. full of everything I could get my hands on ... and there's Pete, very serious, never laughing, always cool, a grasshead ... Kit and Chris were the epitome of what we were.'[11]

The audience responded to the Who on a number of levels. First there was the aggression. 'We were all pillheads,' said Daltrey. 'We were probably the most aggressive group that's ever happened in England.'[12] But the truth was they were not all pillheads to the same extent, Daltrey least of all. The root cause of much of the frisson which sparked off fist fights in the band and generated such excitement on stage was precisely Daltrey's anger at Townshend's and Moon's drug intake, which often sent them out of control. But after Townshend had hit his guitar on the ceiling of the Railway Hotel in Wealdstone, Harrow and had to finish the job by wrecking it to save face, being 'out of control' became the Who's trademark – swirling arms, swirling mikes and a demolition derby driven by the immense volume. The fans responded to the physical presence of the Who; shrill, cutting guitar over a raw, open-nerved tension-ridden pounding and crashing. The Who always had more amplification than anyone else and along with Ginger Baker, Keith Moon pioneered the use in rock of huge double bass drumkits with a forest of tom-toms and cymbals. Then there were Townshend's songs; 'I Can't Explain', in retrospect not the Moon-and-June love song Townshend thought he'd written, but a statement on the inability to communicate much about thoughts and feelings; 'My Generation', with the stutter of an amphetamine freak which Daltrey didn't want to sing at first 'Anyway, Anyhow, Anywhere' – 'Nothing gets in my way, not even locked doors'; 'Substitute', about all the insecurities beneath the desperate need to keep up appearances and stand behind the image.

The mods were regarded, and regarded themselves, as an army, a unified body which often acted as one. Yet at the same time each mod saw himself as an island; speed gave each individual a razor-edged identity and a pin-sharp sense of his place in the world. And this was the achievement of the Who, the reason why, despite the manufactured image, they symbolized to mods what being a mod was all about, 'the ultimate instance of individuality acquiring its deepest meaning from inter-action with others'. The Who 'balanced the tension between individual vision and collective achievement without ever bothering to conceal the stress it caused – and this became part and parcel of their image.'[13]

Although the Kinks had initially vied with the Who as the mods' band, it was the Small Faces who carried the flame for mod subculture in its death throes, inevitably sucked into the mainstream of sanitized pop. The Small Faces were genuine mods and, just as the Yardbirds took over from the Stones, the Small Faces assumed cult status on the club circuit from the Who. They didn't stay there for long. Their first single, What 'Cha Gonna Do About It?' reached Number 14 in the charts in August 1965 and in January 1966 they had a major success with 'Sha La La La Lee'. But from the point of view of this story, 1967 was their most important year. In June 1967, with words like 'hippy', 'joint', 'acid' and 'psychedelics' dropping from everyone's lips, the Small Faces brought out 'Here Comes the Nice', an anthem to the pill-popping heyday of the mod. With the police and the media witch-hunting the Rolling Stones as satanic junkies, the Small Faces calmly strolled on to 'Top of the Pops' with 'Here comes the nice/ He knows what I need/He's always there when I need some speed,' the rest of the song being one of the more blatant rhapsodies to the drug dealer as cult hero. Stevie Marriott said later, '"Here Comes the Nice" was a drug song, but no one sussed it, the whole point being if they don't suss it, it's cool ... we could do it on "Top of the Pops" and we did it to be rebellious in a way – to see what we could get away with.'[14]

During the same year there was an outbreak of intravenous amphetamine (Methedrine) use. The outbreak was not among pill users who had graduated onto the needle, but among the existing group of heroin and cocaine users who had been switched from cocaine to Methedrine by London's most famous (some would say infamous) doctor, John Petro. The Methedrine scene in London at that time had little direct connection with the music business, but it is worth pointing out that Petro was no Dr Feelgood. Misguided he may have been, but he did at least care for his patients. In New York, where intravenous Methedrine use was closely tied in with the music business, the situation was very different.

* * * * *

> I don't have a bedtime
> I don't need to come
> For I have become an amphetamine bum.
> If you don't like sleeping and don't want a screw
> Then you should take lots of amphetamine too.
>
> The Fugs – New Amphetamine Shriek

In the mid-sixties, the widespread use of amphetamine pills and injectable Methedrine among New York's artistic community created a highly disturbed environment, where being freaky and strange was 'in'. The focal point for this frantic subculture was Andy Warhol's Factory, located first on East 47th Street and then 33 Union Square, where artists, poets, writers, musicians, fashion models and others vaguely creative in indeterminate ways – groupies, hangers-on, serfs, sychophants and ciphers – foregathered in the desperate hope that Warhol the Wunderkind would give them their allocated fifteen minutes.

They were the mole people, vapid shadow folk seen only at night in de rigueur super-cool black, cultivating the elegantly wasted look (later patented by Keith Richard) brought about by a massive intake of speed which diverts blood from the surface blood vessels. Sleeping and eating went by the board. Heroin too, produced the same livid malnourished look with the skin drawn tightly across the face, cheekbones accentuated and eyes sunken.

In truth, however hip, fashionable and 'creative' they were, most Factory folk were damaged, unstable, volatile nonentities speeding like crazy to give them the confidence to project whatever image they wanted. Nobody slept in case they missed something. Everyone talked at each other for hours on end about grandiose schemes, fads and whims, forgotten almost as soon as they were uttered. 'Uptight' was the key word; speed made everyone paranoid about their position in the Factory hierarchy – why did Andy seem to like him/her more than me? In fact 'uptight' was very much the key to the whole music business in 1966 – a frenetic jockeying for position, a hunger for publicity. Nobody could see where they were going as they spent so much time watching over their shoulder.

The Factory was just that; people were picked up, processed, marketed to the devouring media (who behaved like the crowd in the story of the Emperor's New Clothes), then tossed aside like empty cans of soup. Some were hounded out or found that their only reality was drug-induced. Stopping speed, for instance, brought unbearable depressions and many hit the bottle or turned to heroin or barbiturates

Edie Sedgwick was a classic Warhol protege. Her sad biography tells of a beautiful, doomed, poor little rich girl, speeding through a Warholian maelstrom, 'star' of his movies, crazy for fame and adoration. Factory life went sour for her and she fled to the Dylan camp where she endured more drug madness and then got dumped. At twenty-eight she was dead from an overdose of barbiturates. Joel Schumacher, director of *Batman Forever* and *Flatliners* and other films commented, 'She was the total essence of the fragmentation, the explosion the uncertainty, the madness that we all lived through in the sixties. The more outrageous you were, the more of a hero you became.'[15]

If Warhol was God, then Dr Charles Roberts was the ministering angel. From his surgery on 48th Street, he dispensed shots of Methedrine to the rich, the famous and the not-so-famous. The drug was dispensed indiscriminately for obviously non-medical reasons to whoever had the money. His surgery was packed with actors, models, businessmen and musicians, all lining up for their shots from a doctor who, to quote Schumacher again, 'was stoned all the time'. He had his favourites who could stroll in, sneer at the hordes waiting on the edge of their nerves and see Doc Roberts straight away for speed, debited on a prearranged charge account. Edie Sedgwick was one such favoured client.

Injected Methedrine is a turbo-charged form of oral amphetamine; prolonged use can lead to paranoid schizophrenia-like psychosis, delusions and hallucinations. Chronic users may stay up for days on end, eating very little, using anything up to 5,000 milligrammes a day, when 250 milligrammes can be a lethal dose. After several months' use, it can take several more months to recover from the depressive stage of withdrawal – some never do. But nobody seemed to care much; perhaps it was only an extreme version of what living in New York was like anyway.

Doc Roberts shot up the whole cast of Warhol's film *Ciao Manhattan* to get it finished quicker and on the tapes of the movie, Edie Sedgwick is heard to comment on the simultaneous horrors and delights of speed for her:

That acrylic high, horrorous, yodelling, repetitious echoes of an infinity so brutally harrowing that words cannot capture the devastation nor the tone of such a vicious nightmare … [yet] it's hard to choose between the climactic ecstasies of speed and cocaine … oh they are so fabulous. That fantabulous sexual exhilaration.[16]

Probably the most able interpreters of the swirling vortex of bohemian life which sucked in Edie Sedgwick and others like her, were the Velvet Underground, blessed with the genuine talent of Lou Reed. With their acid-drenched lyrics, the muses of California offered escape and a promise of a better world, full of peace, love and harmony; Lou Reed offered a one-way train ride to hell. With the Velvet Underground there was no escape.

In 1966, a friend of the band, Tony Conrad, found a paperback lying in a gutter in the Bowery, a novel of sadomasochism called *The Velvet Underground*, and gave the band its name. That same year Andy Warhol wanted to present a multi-media event, a touring show featuring the band against a backdrop of dancing, slides, films and lights. Warhol's most famous actor, Paul Morrisey, recalled sitting around with dancer and poet Gerard Malanga and a Factory figure called Barbara Rubin:

> I picked up a record album with Barbara on the back massaging Bob Dylan's head (*Bringing it All Back Home*). There were some amphetamine-Bob-Dylan-gibberish liner notes. I looked without reading and saw these words appear; something 'exploding' something was 'plastic', something was 'inevitable'.[17]

So Andy Warhol's Uptight Show became 'Exploding Plastic Inevitable'. It went on the road during 1966-7. The band made a theatrical impact in their own right; a manic fiddler, a mysterious street-wise punk, a straight-looking guy, a drummer of indeterminate sex, plus for a while Nico, a stunning blonde German singer. They didn't need the light shows and films and deranged dancing. It was OK for the night to create some atmosphere, but all that remains for posterity are the music and demonic writing of Lou Reed. There is a freshness in the songs that is absent from much of the music of that period. The hippy dream is dead, but we are still living Reed's bleak, hopeless view of urban life. Drugs are sickness and love, life and death.

Each Velvet song used a small group of notes that kept battering against one another until feedback – the screech, the amphetamine shriek – was the only place to go. The rhythm never let go, it held you down while the lyrics swamped you with street images. The sound of the band was an aural presentation of the amphetamine experience. That was the band's context, the framework within which they operated Reed put an amphetamine stutter in 'Sister Ray' to emphasize the point. Against this, Reed sang of a white boy going to Harlem to score heroin ('Waiting for the Man') and of the all-consuming love affair between a heroin addict and his drug ('Heroin'). Despite its title, the song builds up on the crest of a Methedrine wave 'when I'm rushing on my run/And I feel like Jesus' son,' then winds down as the junkie looks for a release from a world where 'I just don't know.' With heroin, he is caught in the ultimate paradox '…Heroin/will be the death of me,' but 'it's my wife/and it's my life.' The maximum shock value of the song was played up on stage; Gerard Malanga would go through the whole fixing routine, heating the spoon, tying off and shooting up, finishing on the floor staring blankly up at Lou Reed.

For writing songs like 'Heroin', Reed got a reputation as the biggest junkie around. His comments on the subject have always been ambiguous, often leaving it at 'just because I write about it, doesn't mean to say I do it,' or words to that effect. On his 1975 album *Metal Machine Music*, the sleeve note read: 'My week beats your year', by the mid-eighties he was saying 'I'm not into dope. I don't smoke grass and I don't like things that everyone sniffs off a table. It is so common.'[18] However during a particularly low period in his life during the mid-seventies Reed did admit to shooting speed and drugs have been a central theme in his music. During this low period he dyed an iron cross in his hair and re-created 'Heroin' in his solo act, complete with tourniquet and syringe. The theme of *Berlin* (1973) was a doomed liaison between two speedfreaks and the title track of *Street Hassle* (1978) told of a young girl whose body was dumped in the street after she had overdosed.

The first Velvet's album was originally rejected by Ahmet Ertegun at Atlantic on account of the drug content. Verve released the album in the United States in March 1967. By the time the album was released in the UK in October that year, Lou Reed's darkest New York subterranean vignettes were surfacing in sunny California. Already degenerating into a seedy tourist attraction, the Haight Ashbury district of San Francisco was witnessing the beginnings of a 'speed/heroin/epidemic'. The flower children climbed aboard Jim Morrison's Methedrine crystal ship and slowly the community began to sink.

From this developed the 'Speed Kills' campaign, which grew up on the West Coast. The counter-culture has always tried to look after its own where drugs were concerned; in 1969, some enlightened rock stations put out warnings about adulterated drugs in circulation. The Haight Ashbury Free Clinic, set up to deal with the drug casualties of the area in 1967 (and still going), received $5,000 from the Monterey Pop Festival and rock promoter Bill Graham put on a number of benefit gigs for the clinic when the finances were shaky.

In a strictly clinical sense, speed kills only very rarely, but it was an effective slogan around which to rally support from the music business. A street information service called Do It Now was set up in Hollywood to give out accurate information to drug users. Radio allocated the service slots and musicians would speak on the dangers of drugs. Frank Zappa featured in one slot, saying, 'I would like to suggest that you don't use speed and here's why: it will mess up your liver, your kidneys, rot out your mind: in general, this drug will make you just like your father and mother.'

To raise further funds Do It Now knocked on the doors of several record companies, asking them to donate tracks for an album. The record was called *First Vibrations* and among the tracks featured were 'Amphetamine Annie' (Canned Heat), 'The Pusher' (Hoyt Axton), 'Flying on the Ground is Wrong' (Buffalo Springfield), 'Artificial Energy' (the Byrds) and 'Roses Gone' (Peanut Butter Conspiracy). RCA donated 'Somebody to Love', as Grace Slick wanted to tell kids what Jefferson Airplane thought about speed. 'One pill makes you larger, one pill makes you small, but if you shoot speed, you won't be here at all,' she said at the time.

Two points to note about the involvement of musicians in the Speed Kills campaign. First, it was a significant gesture on the part of musicians and demonstrated through the release of *First Vibrations* that, contrary to public opinion, most rock songs about drugs took a negative view or at worst a neutral one. This will be examined more closely in Chapter Eleven. Secondly, musicians felt comfortable about being involved in anti-drug campaigns only when the focus was a drug they had never used or had stopped using. The same year as *First Vibrations* was released, Canned Heat were singing about 'Amphetamine Annie' with their guitarist Al Wilson subject to bouts of deep depression and finally overdosing on barbiturates. Grace Slick could take a hard line on speed, knowing that her major weakness was alcohol. This story has been repeated in the recent wave of musicians' statements in Britain about the evils of drugs. Many have made flamboyant anti-heroin statements as representatives of a business literally snowed under by cocaine.

In the seventies, cocaine tended to replace amphetamine as the favoured stimulant among those musicians with sufficient funds to be conspicuous consumers. But for musicians who still considered themselves spokesmen of the not-so-laid-back tradition of American rock, whose music demanded a jagged edge, and certainly for fans who could not afford cocaine, speed (and heroin) remained important elements in the polypharmacy of rock.

Heavy Metal has been home to speed since the days of Blue Cheer, a favourite band of the San Francisco speed-freak scene. For a band like Blue Cheer (whose name actually derived from a reputedly extra-potent strain of LSD) there was no such thing as too loud – legend has it during one gig a dog wandered on to the stage and dropped dead. Led Zeppelin fused the blues-rock initiatives of bands like Blue Cheer and Iron Butterfly and presented the result for an international audience. The atmosphere of a mass Zeppelin gathering was altogether more threatening than the days of peace and love. The Stones at Altamont had set the agenda for heavy metal/heavy rock concerts to come – a brooding sense of violence bubbling under the surface whether or not anybody actually got damaged. To get in touch with the uncompromising, high-energy hurricane of sound, the audiences arrived in various states of chemical readjustment a sea of working-class long-haired lads in denim mixing speed with booze and showering each other (and unwelcome support bands) with beer cans and bottles.

The Haight Ashbury Free Medical Clinic usually ran a MASH style unit at major rock events and in 1973 they logged an account of two concerts they attended at Kezar Stadium, San Francisco, one involving the Grateful Dead and the other Led Zeppelin. The clinic assembled a team of thirty to deal with the 20,000 crowd that showed up to see the Dead. The atmosphere was generally warm and mellow, with picnicking, dancing and sunbathing creating a carnival mood. The 55,000 who came for Led Zeppelin presented an altogether different profile; 'commercialised, bottled and over-sold to a horde of out-of-town teeny boppers who had never experienced the expectations of a love generation, this crowd seemed curious but sullen.'[19] Harmony and conviviality were replaced by a mood of restless discomfort. Alcohol and speed were mixed with a new drug, methaqualone.

Marketed in Britain as Mandrax and in the States as Quaaludes, 'mandies' or 'ludes' were similar to barbiturates in their hypnosedative effect, but less likely entirely to douse the spirits. 'Luding out' became a standard rock 'n' roll phrase. Combined with booze and speed at the Zeppelin concert, ludes produced a tense feeling of repressed anger and irritation. Of that crowd of 55,000, clinic staff calculated that at least 40,000 had taken some drugs during the day. The preponderance of sedative drugs, however, kept the lid on actual violence while leaving vibes which the staff described as 'barbed wire'.

Heavy metal slipped from public view in the mid-seventies but enjoyed a renaissance in the eighties on both sides of the Atlantic. New-wave heavy metal in Britain was spearheaded by Motorhead; SKF never had a more effective team of travelling salesmen. Everything about the band was fast; the music, the name (American slang for a speed-freak) and the leading light, Ian 'Lemmy' Kilminster, bass guitarist, singer and self-confessed devotee of amphetamine sulphate. It was this last credential that hastened his his exit from Hawkwind. In 1975, Canadian customs caught him with a quantity of white powder. Fearing that this would jeopardize their future in America, Hawkwind sacked him. He came home and put together Motorhead. The album titles speak for themselves: *Iron Fist, Overkill* and *No Sleep Till Hammersmith*. Says Lemmy, 'My favourite drug is speed, 'cause it gets me up on stage in a good mood, but I really wouldn't recommend it to most people because most people who do it go completely over the top, given a couple of weeks on it. It's not good for most people, but my metabolism seems to have adjusted.' But speaking for the band about heroin, he says 'We hate heroin and always will ... heroin always fucks people up.'[20]. To a degree, Motorhead were the advance guard for the return of the Wasted Rock Star fronting HM and its offspring – Grunge, Thrash, Doom, Death and the rest. Lemmy's views were not to be shared by the likes of Guns 'n' Roses and Kurt Cobain who, however much they sneered at the Stones and Led Zeppelin, took all their travel hints from the Keith Richard's inner space guide to the Planet Zog.

In England, Motorhead were coming up just at the time when punk rock was establishing itself and there was a good deal of cross-fertilization between the twos, both feeding off the energy of the other. Motorhead often appeared on the same bill as bands like the Damned and the Adverts. But in eschewing heroin, Motorhead distanced themselves from a strong tradition of heroin worship in punk, the legacy of nihilism given to American and British punks by the Velvet Underground. The mantle of outrage passed to Iggy Pop, the MC5, the New York Dolls and Johnny Thunders and the Heartbreakers. Max's Kansas City was joined by CBGBs as host venue to the sound of trash aesthetic.

The New York Dolls best typified the amalgam of the Velvet's urban nightmare the relentless thud of hard rock, the cult of bisexuality and the reckless pursuit of doomed intoxication that so influenced punk rock in Britain. Or to put it another way, r&b with make-up and high heels. The band was formed in 1971 with bassist Arthur Kane, guitarist Johnny Thunders and drummer Bill Murcia, to which were added Sylvain Sylvain on guitar and vocalist David Johansen. It took only a short while for them to become the darlings of the New York club scene, following in the path of Velvet Underground with a stint at Max's Kansas City. In 1972 they received a major boost to their career when the Faces invited them to play Wembley. Tragically, however, on 6 November 1972, drummer Billy Murcia died of an overdose of pills and booze. In an interview with Robert Christgau, Arthur Kane, wearing red lipstick and a sweatshirt over white tights, bemoaned their image as a bunch of 'transsexual junkies'. What also probably slipped his booze-fuddled brain, was that during a song called 'Looking for a Kiss', David Johansen did the old Lou Reed routine with a hypodermic. Meanwhile, backstage, they were all doing it for real: watching from the wings was Joe Perry and the rest of Aerosmith,

> This was the first time we saw drugs kill a band. Their first drummer had OD'd in London. Johnny Thunders was a heroin addict who was always shooting up in the back of wherever we were. He'd trade his guitar for drugs when he ran out, and I kept thinking, Boy, that'll never happen to us ... They'd cancel gigs when they ran out of drugs, fly back to New York and

score. Seven days on the road was all they could do because they'd get sick. We'd hear that Johnny and the drummer had to go back to New York because they were 'tired'. Yeah, right.[21]

In his autobiography, *Poison Heart,* Dee Dee Ramone recounted that in the early days of the Dolls then drummer Jerry Nolan (who used to inject an amphetamine called Dioxin) and Johnny Thunders would call on him to go and buy drugs, 'I guess those guys were all dope fiends then... Richard Hell had mentioned to me that he was going to write a song better than Lou Reed's "Heroin", so I took his idea and wrote "Chinese Rocks" in Deborah Harry's apartment.'[22]

Listen to the Sex Pistols and you hear the New York Dolls' basic rock 'n' roll riffs, played hard and fast and overlaid with snarling, sardonic vocals. In fact, it wasn't that much of a coincidence. In an attempt to revitalize a sagging career, the New York Dolls appointed a young Englishman as their manager in 1975. He tried to re-establish their anarchic credibility by spreading a rumour that they were all communists The attempt failed and the manager, Malcolm McLaren, went back to London to try again.

Malcolm McLaren maintained that there was nothing new about punk: 'I don't see it as a fad, because it's such a simple attitude; it's the same attitude, I think, that Eddie Cochran had, that any real rock 'n' roller had.' Yet the context in which punk sprang up was different from those which spawned all previous post-war adolescent movements. The mods in their smart suits and ties were not even pseudo-anarchists; they declared their intention of making it in the world on their own terms. but it was the same world as everybody else's, a world that provided jobs. While Mum and Dad could aspire to fridges, TV and even a car, the media pandered to Junior's tastes in transitory fashions and music.

Britain in the late seventies and early eighties was a very different place. The cut-up punk uniform derived from the throwaway and disposable garbage of a crumbling industrial society with no future. Punks represented to the media the embodiment of Anthony Burgess's vision of an aimless, violent droog army.

Punk angst was directed not only at straight society, but at a previous rock generation which in its time had been considered anarchic and subversive. Nothing new there: mods had been equally dismissive of chart dross and men in funny hats playing trad jazz. But what was new for Britain was the explosion of independent record labels providing the only consistent outlet for home-grown three-chord products. As McLaren acknowledged, the music itself was basic rock 'n' roll and the band line-ups – guitars, bass, drums – were equally conventional. Punks had the Sex Pistols- mods had the Who – bands that led the army into the fray. Both subcultural sets had strong affinities with black music and culture – blue beat and soul in the sixties, reggae in the late seventies. The mods looked to the black hipster for sartorial inspiration; punks reinterpreted dreadlocks in spikey gelled mohicans, picking out in them the colours of Jah. However, punk was the antithesis of mod (and seventies disco) designer chic. There was nothing 'flash' about punk dress; it took its cues instead from the sexual ambiguities and fetishes of the Velvet's sadomasochistic vision and the visual drama of glam rock.

Since rock 'n' roll began, the ultimate aim has been to get a reaction, any reaction. Jerry Lee stood on his piano, Elvis wiggled his pelvis, the Who smashed up their gear, Reed and David Johansen shot up on stage, the Stones pissed against walls, the Pistols threw up in airports. Sid spat at the crowd, covered in blood, while Johnny Rotten sneered at the audience, 'ever been 'ad, you fucking idiots?' 'Summertime Blues', 'My

Generation' and 'Pretty Vacant' – all anthems for a caged adolescence banging about through the teen years like balls in a pinball machine. Eddie was too young to vote; Pete seemed concerned about people putting him down; Johnny couldn't give a damn.

And in all this frustration and anger, this frantic effort to validate being young, by being outrageous, was speed – a cheap proletarian passport to self-esteem and social mobility. Speed was the subcultural constant linking '56, '66 and '76.

By the seventies amphetamine meant (as it still does) illicitly produced amphetamine sulphate powder rather than pills diverted from doctors, chemists and factories. The effect, however, was the same and Johnny Rotten was the role model of the speed-shot punk: 'Spikey, dyed red hair, death-white visage, metal hanging from lobes, skinny leg strides ... he looks like an amphetamine corpse from a Sunday gutter-press wet dream.'[23] Staying up all night in music clubs was back in vogue; to be a Face at the Roxy or the Nashville you needed the appearance of advanced amphetamine psychosis, even if you never went near the stuff.

But there were plenty of kids who did go near the stuff and plenty more who then switched to more dangerous, but still cheap, barbiturates such as Tuinal to slow themselves down and to take the edge off the amphetamine 'crash'. And for punk rock stars with money to spend there was also heroin. Topper Headon of the Clash and Keith Levene of Public Image Ltd (to name but two) narrowly avoided succumbing to the ultimate rock 'n' roll cliche. Malcolm Owen of the Ruts and Sid Vicious did not.

The *Sunday Times* ran a feature called 'All Dressed up and Nowhere to Go', about being a punk on the dole. It interviewed 'Keith': 'I was taking acid twice a week and it was making me crazy. I knew what it was like to go crazy.'

LSD was back, not as an artefact of anybody's political ideals, but as part of the self-centred pursuit of getting wrecked. But had it been so different in the sixties?

9 I HAD TOO MUCH TO DREAM TODAY

The first Prankster rule is that nothing lasts.

Ken Kesey

The real power behind the acid revolution came from the record companies. . .
acid music was album music and an album cost four times the price of a single. If
ever a drug was aptly named it was LSD. The pounds, shillings and pence it
produced began to affect the industry from top to bottom.

Simon Napier-Bell

But for LSD, the name of Albert Hofmann would have probably remained unknown
outside his family, friends and fellow chemists working in the laboratories of Sandoz,
the Swiss-based pharmaceutical company.

Hofmann joined the company in 1929 straight from the University of Zurich, in
order to work on natural products within the chemical industry. In the early thirties,
two Americans had successfully isolated lysergic acid as the nucleus common to all
alkaloids of ergot, a fungus found on rye. Most of Hofmann's work up to 1938 was
spent investigating the medicinal potential of lysergic acid. He was trying to develop
lyserg-saure-diathylamid (LSD) as a circulatory stimulant, but after twenty-five
different types of LSD had been synthesized by Hofmann the work was suspended in
1938 as unsatisfactory and inconclusive.

Yet his scientific curiosity would not allow him to abandon the work altogether and
in 1943, he again synthesised his last formula, LSD-25. Though meticulous in his
laboratory habits, Hofmann allowed his fingertips to come into contact with the
chemical and the result became enshrined in annals of drug subcultural lore:

Last Friday. 16 April 1943, I was forced to interrupt my work in the laboratory in the middle of the afternoon and proceed home, being affected by a remarkable restlessness, combined with a slight dizziness. At home I lay down and sank into a not unpleasant intoxicated-like condition, characterised by an extremely stimulated imagination. In a dreamlike state, with eyes closed (I found the daylight to be unpleasantly glaring), I perceived an uninterrupted stream of fantastic pictures, extraordinary shapes with intense kaleidoscopic play of colours. After some two hours this condition faded away.[1]

Concluding that the LSD had been responsible for his bizarre experience. Hofmann took the only course open to a true empirical scientist and ingested some deliberately to see what would happen. He dissolved one thousandth of a gram in 10cc of water and took off on a full-blown acid trip lasting several hours, some of it good, some not so good. Three of his colleagues tried with only one third of Hofmann's dose. The results were the same. Hofmann had stumbled on the most potent mood-altering drug ever known.

A year before Hofmann's momentous discovery and several thousand miles away in Washington DC, a group of American scientists were brought together under the command of the Office of Strategic Services, forerunner of the CIA. Their top-secret brief was to find a speech-inducing drug, a 'truth-drug', for use in intelligence interrogation. As the work progressed, caffeine, alcohol, barbiturates and mescalin were tried and rejected. At one time marijuana looked like the answer, but as with so many mood-altering drugs, the results were too unpredictable. Some OSS operatives who took part in experiments couldn't stop talking under the influence of the drug, others became paranoid in the austere, clinical surroundings of the laboratory and wouldn't say a word. The scientists were faced with a classic testimony of the role of environment and personal expectation in determining the effects of a drug on the individual. For any truth drug to work, the anxiety levels of an enemy agent had to be consistently raised, making him want to talk. Marijuana was dismissed as being ineffective in this way and the research committee wrote a report to that effect. One of the signatories to that report was the head of the Bureau of Narcotics, Harry J. Anslinger, brought on to the committee for his 'expertise' in the drugs field. So at the very time that Anslinger was waging a public war against marijuana as a destroyer of minds, he was signing a report which implied that the most 'psychotic' aspect of marijuana was its capacity to induce uncontrollable laughter in subjects.

The first published reports about LSD began circulating within the international scientific community during 1947. Having read these reports, the scientists working for the CIA (as it was now called), fervently believed that LSD was the drug that they had been looking for: a drug to unlock the mind. A number of secret projects code-named CHATTER. then BLUEBIRD, and ARTICHOKE, had been instigated to find a truth drug. Now a mountain of research money was poured into MK-ULTRA to test LSD under operational conditions. The CIA tried out the drug on its own agents with their knowledge and consent, but then carried out unauthorised tests on outsiders without their knowledge. In November 1953, the CIA LSD research team, led by Dr Sidney Gottlieb, dosed the drinks of army personnel at a remote hunting lodge for CIA and army staff in West Maryland. One officer, Dr Frank Olsen, became completely paranoid and a few weeks later crashed to his death from the tenth floor of the Statler Hilton Hotel in New York. It took twenty years for the story to come out along with revelations that the CIA had set up a brothel and paid prostitutes to spike customers' drinks while the CIA watched the results through two-way mirrors. Even today, the full story of the CIA's own LSD experiments has not been told.

But probably the most despicable aspect of the LSD research in the fifties was the work done by scientists whose experiments depended on CIA funding. LSD was tried out on those in no position to resist, such as prisoners and mental-hospital patients. Dr Harris Isbell was given the facility to test hundreds of different drugs on prisoners at Lexington. With heroin and morphine usually the reward for taking part, it is no wonder that the prison had a 90% return rate.

It was through CIA-funded work that Dr Paul Hoch discovered LSD to be a 'psychomimetic' drug – in other words, its action resembled the response of psychosis. Until the drug effects wore off, a doctor might have difficulty distinguishing between an LSD user on a bad trip and a schizophrenic. The CIA were interested in this angle and also in any potential the drug might have as a device for brainwashing.

The army too, got into the act. One army officer devised a scenario whereby an enemy would be bombarded with hallucinogenic gas. While the populace were talking to the trees, in would march the GIs and take over. Nobody would die and what's more, buildings and the national economy would remain intact. Another strain of LSD research theorised on the possibilities of the drug not as a weapon of war or counter-espionage, but as a therapeutic device to help those whose psychiatric problems derived from repressed emotions.

Noting, like Hoch, the schizophrenia/LSD comparability, British psychiatrist Humphrey Osmond began working with LSD and mescalin among psychiatric patients in Canada around 1951-2. He also treated alcoholics on the theory that some of them only genuinely try to give up drinking once they have reached rock bottom. LSD was the means to make 'rock bottom' happen. Osmond's work caused great interest in scientific circles and also caught the attention of Aldous Huxley, who had examined the spectre of drug-induced social control in his 1931 novel *Brave New World*. At his home in Hollywood, Huxley experimented with mescalin under Osmond's supervision. The results threw open a whole new vista on LSD, not just a drug with the potential to drive you mad, but one which allowed the existence of alternative or enhanced realities. Writing up his experience in *The Doors of Perception*, Huxley theorised that for the purposes of everyday living, the brain acts as a filter, allowing only essential information to pass through. LSD pushed back this mind screen; it was the key to the doors of perception and once opened, a torrent of sensations, colours, sounds and images flooded in. This, to Huxley, was nothing short of the ecstasies of mystical revelation and he predicted a worldwide religious revival should such drugs become freely available.

The experiments with Huxley also changed the emphasis of Osmond's own work. From Alcoholics Anonymous he learned that one of their major tenets for successful abstinence is a genuine religious experience. If LSD could provide that, then it was more than just a means of provoking a life crisis. This meant also that 'psychomimetic' was too narrow a descriptive term. Osmond first coined the expression 'psychedelic' to move away from the psycho' connotation. He announced his new terminology to a meeting of the New York Academy of Sciences in 1957. By then, a small group of scientists and literary figures had been experimenting with LSD at social gatherings. In a country obsessed by the virtues of psychoanalysis, LSD became all the rage among Hollywood psychiatrists and analysts tending the tortured psyches of the rich and famous. After a course of LSD treatment. Cary Grant said in a widely publicised statement, 'All my life I've been searching for peace of mind. I'd explored yoga and hypnotism and made several attempts at mysticism. Nothing seemed to give me what I wanted until this treatment.'[2]

So what was the LSD experience all about? As we have seen, only minute amounts are necessary for the drug to take effect. This can take anything from thirty minutes to two hours. A feeling of agitation gives way to a sense that the world is slightly out of alignment, weird visions can develop from the most mundane objects. Sensory awareness can be heightened to such a degree that colours are 'heard' and sounds are 'seen' a phenomenon known as synaesthesia. The most banal thoughts can appear profound, random noises extraordinarily knowing.

But the key to the LSD experience during the early stages of the psychedelic journey is usually termed 'ego death'. When experienced either in the company of a guide who has travelled this path before, or in convivial surroundings, or by those whose creative and intellectual abilities already give them a considered view of the world, 'ego death' need not be frightening. Quite the reverse; it stimulates a sense of oneness with the world, as the user lets go of the trappings of his or her ego. Where the user tries to fight the effects of the drug or is dosed unknowingly, the shattering of the ego can produce not beatific visions of 'one world', but the destruction of inner confidence and a feeling that you are losing your mind.

Towards the end of the trip, the user will often become deeply reflective, trying to consolidate the sensory bombardments of the previous hours. It is sometimes during his latter stage that important personal decisions are made. Finally the user will drift off, often into a long sleep.

Some researchers in the fifties, like Dr Oscar Janiger, wanted to explore the relationship between LSD and the creative mind. Volunteers for Janiger's experiments included Andre Previn, James Coburn, Lord Buckley and Jack Nicholson. (Nicholson later wrote the screenplay of a Roger Corman cheapie *The Trip* [1966], which never received a general certificate in Britain.) Dr Sidney Cohen turned on Henry Luce, president of Time Life and an ardent right-winger. His wife, a very influential political figure in her own right, was of the opinion that LSD was fine for doctors and their upper-class friends, but 'we wouldn't want everyone doing too much of a good thing.'[3] James I had uttered similar sentiments about tobacco over 350 years earlier. But while American bluebloods and intellectuals were tripping the light fantastic at cosy dinner parties, a Harvard psychiatrist was waiting to snatch LSD from behind hallowed doors and give it to the people as a panacea for the world's ills.

In 1959, Dr Timothy Leary, aged thirty-nine, author of a standard work of psychology and inventor of the Leary Personality Test (used for recruiting staff by the CIA among others), was undergoing something of a midlife crisis. He was feeling bogged down by university life and two previous marriages lay in ruins, the first having ended tragically when his wife committed suicide. On holiday in Mexico in 1960, Leary, who hadn't even smoked marijuana before, tried some hallucinogenic psilocybin mushrooms. The overwhelmingly religious experience that followed was to change his life.

Back at Harvard, Leary set up a psilocybin research project with Richard Alpert, an assistant professor of Education and Psychology. Together they conducted formal investigations into the hallucinogenic experiences and arranged informal sessions outside the laboratory. Beat poet Allen Ginsberg attended one of these sessions; at the time Leary had yet to try LSD, while Ginsberg had not had a mushroom trip. What seems to have happened is that during the latter stages of the psilocybin trip, Ginsberg had an apocalyptic vision of a new age in which peace and love would pervade the world, ending all war. To achieve this end, Ginsberg decided, all the world leaders had to be turned on so that they would understand and share his vision.

Leary was reportedly not over-enthusiastic at first while Ginsberg became a one-man psilocybin crusader. Among his closest friends were jazz musicians and it was they rather than rock musicians who first tried hallucinogenic drugs, including Thelonious Monk, Dizzy Gillespie and John Coltrane, who after an LSD trip said he had 'perceived the inter-relationship of all life forms'.

Ginsberg became a conduit through which artists, writers, musicians and poets plugged into Leary's research. From here onwards the LSD story becomes populated with all manner of eccentric people, literary visionaries, millionaires with time on their hands and money to burn, gangsters, renegade chemists, businessmen, conmen, CIA infiltrators and those who flit about in a shadowland of political intrigue and influence.

One such individual of indeterminate occupation was Michael Hollingshead who came to see Leary from England, toting a mayonnaise jar of LSD – enough for 10,000 doses. Having already initiated jazz trumpeter Maynard Ferguson and his wife, Hollingshead and the new converts turned up at Leary's house. Seeing the look on Ferguson's face, Leary tried some acid and became another instant convert. LSD now became the focus of his psychedelic research.

LSD was not yet illegal in 1962, but Leary's extra-curricular activities aroused the attention of the CIA. Government experimentation was still going on in the early sixties and the CIA were concerned about what they described as 'uncontrolled experimentation', ironic when one considers their own irresponsible testing on unknowing subjects. Leary had already been warned by somebody with CIA connections that he was being watched since it had become known that he was working with LSD. But a religious fervour had gripped him; religious imagery informed all he felt about LSD. He was a priest of the God Acid; there was a message to preach, souls to be saved, bibles and tracts to be written.

Leary's research was clearly out of step with the psychomimetic model of LSD adopted by all the major government agencies involved in drug research, monitoring and legislation. In 1963, he founded the International Federation for Internal Freedom and, together with Alpert, took a long sabbatical in Mexico to continue his research. He tried to involve both Huxley and Hofmann in his venture but, put off by Leary's blatant publicity-seeking, they refused. It is possible that pressure was put on the Harvard authorities to 'do something about Leary'; amid rumours of campus orgies both Leary and Alpert were dismissed *in absentia.*

Mexico, however, proved untranquil for Leary and friends. The Mexican authorities were unhappy about 'longhairs' hanging around and the researchers were expelled. They were rescued by a twenty-year old stockbroker millionaire, William Mellon Hitchcock, who in 1964 set up what was now the Castalia Foundation at Millbrook, a sixty-four room mansion set in massive grounds in upstate New York. Inevitably Millbrook became 'the place to be seen' among New York's bohemian community and many visitors arrived to be turned on, including the walking wounded from Warhol's Factory scene.

Also in semi-permanent residence were the media. Not only did Leary hype LSD as a short cut to mystical enlightenment, but he guaranteed himself banner headlines by marrying the idea to sex, inventing a concept called 'erotic politics'. Michael Hollingshead showed up again and became a Leary agent in Britain. Following the Millbrook model, he established the World Psychedelic Centre in the King's Road, attracting London's fashionable mid-sixties set including Donovan, The Rolling Stones, Paul McCartney and Eric Clapton.

It was largely through the interest of such trendy luminaries in things hallucinogenic that the mod scene in London dissolved in a haze of LSD and the swirl of marijuana smoke. Hollingshead was something of a drug hog, consuming vast quantities of acid, dope and speed. Eventually he was busted and spent twenty-one months in Wormwood Scrubs where he turned on spy George Blake to LSD that had been smuggled into the prison.

Back in the States, Leary was becoming a twenty-four-carat embarrassment to the political and academic establishment as his media circus rolled on. With his ready catchphrases like 'Turn on, Tune in, Drop Out', Leary became the media-appointed spokesman for anyone under twenty-five, although young people themselves, especially outside America, were not so enamoured of this forty-something Harvard academic. Inevitably, Leary was busted on a marijuana charge in December 1965 and from then on Millbrook was subjected to regular police harassment until, virtually under siege, the community broke up in 1967.

Although Leary was a publicity-seeker, he was fundamentally serious about what he was doing. LSD experimentation at Millbrook was a solemn affair, highly ritualistic, accompanied by earnest discussions among participants and meditation on the nature of the LSD experience. Millbrook was a psychedelic seminary. But like the division among academics in the fifties, there was disagreement among the creative spirits about the value of LSD. For acid veterans like Leary and Alpert, LSD was the psychic transporter for the journey into inner space and had to be treated with due reverence. For others, it was a recreational drug, one which encouraged social community and friendship and was, when all was said and done, an interesting way to get wasted.

Ken Kesey was another college boy turned on by Uncle Sam; he volunteered for LSD experiments at Menlo Park Veterans Hospital. Shortly afterwards he got a job as night attendant in the psychiatric ward of the same hospital. There he discovered a treasury of space-age drugs just asking to be lifted. It wasn't long before a select group at Stanford University and Perry Lane, the Greenwich Village-style community that surrounded it, got their first taste of LSD. A psychedelic commune grew up around Kesey and there were frequent takers for his famous acid-laced venison. On the proceeds of his novel, *One Flew Over The Cuckoo's Nest*, published in 1960, Kesey decamped to La Honda, a country home fifty miles south of San Francisco. Like Millbrook on the East Coast, La Honda became of a point of pilgrimage for a motley assortment of artists, poets, musicians and itinerants.

In many respects, Kesey represented a watershed between the angry 'No' of the Beats who turned their backs on a world they regarded as beyond redemption and the transcendent 'Yes' of the Hippies who believed in a better world attainable through peace, love and chemicals. The Beats had given up on American culture, its redundant materialism – Ginsberg's Moloch – which partly accounts for their adoption of the fatalistic religions of the East. They were also possessed of the old American vision of travel as a means of spiritual discovery, best captured in *On The Road*. But if you live on the West Coast where do you go? The answer for some was India. The Beats lived for any experience which would shut out what they despised; marijuana, booze, speed, heroin and LSD were all indispensable. Marijuana and acid opened whole new vistas for travel – journeys into inner space.

From the individuals gathered at La Honda came the Merry Pranksters, who criss-crossed America through 1964 in a psychedelic thirties bus driven maniacally by Neal Casady. The Beatles and Dylan blared from speakers, everyone wore funny clothes and were permanently stoned on acid diluted in Kool Aid orange juice. Back in California, Kesey had instigated the Acid Test, forerunner of the 'Be-in', the 'Happening' and eventually the rock festival. Participants, encouraged to dress up as weirdly as possible, paid $1 for which they could consume as much Kool Aid as they could manage. This formed a stoned backdrop to a totally free-form event; all kinds of musical and film equipment was left lying around for anybody to do what they liked with. A folk/rock band called the Warlocks would usually turn up. Their lead guitarist had been hanging around Perry Lane for the past few years. At the Acid Test, the Warlocks would play only if they felt like it. If they didn't, nobody objected or hassled them. Had they tried that a few years later the reaction would not have been so laid-back, for by 1966 the Warlocks had metamorphosed into the Grateful Dead.

Out on the road the Merry Pranksters hit the East Coast in search of Kerouac and Leary. Kesey envisaged a great meeting of minds, but he was disappointed on both counts. Casady set up a meeting between Kesey and Kerouac, but they had little to say to one another. Kerouac was one of the classic isolationist beats. He had no time for West Coast weirdness, acid sociability and stoned revelations. Burroughs, too, another beat guru, had been scathing about the psychedelic revolution and in *Nova Express* (1964) had warned about the use of hallucinogenic drugs as state weapons of social control. No flower children these. Clearly while the beat poets and writers exerted a measure of influence over musicians, the cultural heroes of the sixties, they had little to say to the masses of ordinary teenagers growing up in that same period.

The Merry Pranksters fared no better at Millbrook. For them the meditation sessions and earnest discussions about the nature of the psychedelic experience were just plain boring; they dubbed Millbrook 'a crypt trip'.

To extend a comment by David Pichaske in his study of the sixties, the Beats, the acid crusaders and the student radicals desperately wanted everything to mean something. By contrast, the rock audiences were just out for a good time. The musicians went for that, plus the money, which sat easy with establishment businessmen more than happy to finance the indulgences of rock stars so long as they got their returns.

Another sign that the beat star was on the wane was the break-up during 1962-3 of the North Beach area of San Francisco as a bohemian community. Tourists, hustlers and gangsters combined to drive beats and hipsters to another part of town where a warren of run-down ramshackle Victorian houses provided cheap accommodation. This was the district known as Haight Ashbury, eventually a state of mind as much as a place, which from 1964, became the new meeting place for all those who felt at odds with America's cultural and political mainstream. And the cornerstone of the Haight's counter-cultural position was rock music.

It would hardly be an exaggeration to say that the music was not just a record of the sixties, it *was* the sixties – not much else remains above the surface. The buildings are gone, the concert halls shut down, some of the best musicians of the era are dead, the fashions are outdated and rather than being expressed openly, the values of the period are locked inside the millions of people who lived through that time. But put on a Doors or Love album and the sixties live again.

In combination, the music and drugs served to bring together many undercurrents from the fifties; feelings against war and nuclear weapons, the growth of anti-establishment satire, poetry and folk music. As part of the youthful love affair with America's ethnic origins, and the 'back to nature movement' which idolised the American Indians and the time of the early settlers, folk, blues and 'hillbilly' music were very much in vogue. All the major San Francisco bands labelled as purveyors of acid rock had their beginnings playing roots music together in any number of loose permutations.

The Grateful Dead are the premier example of the combination of acid and electricity which brought about a musical revolution on the West Coast. The evolution of the Dead into one of rock's longest-running shows is one of those wonderfully twisted skeins of musical chronology that Pete Frame of Rock Trees fame is so adept at unravelling. After dropping out of school at seventeen, going absent without leave several times from the army, guitarist Jerry Garcia settled in Palo Alto along the San Francisco peninsula, home of Stanford University and Kesey's Perry Lane enclave. There he met lyricist Robert Hunter; together they scuffled around coffee bars playing folk songs and sleeping in wrecked cars. Garcia became hooked on bluegrass and in partnership with Hunter toured around the nightspots of Palo Alto, Berkeley and North Beach in a series of folk bluegrass bands like the Thunder Mountain Tub Thumpers, the Hart Valley Drifters (good enough to win the amateur bluegrass section at the 1963 Monterey Folk Festival) the Wildwood Boys and the Black Mountain Boys. Other personnel in these bands included David Nelson (New Riders of the Purple Sage), David Freiberg (Quicksilver Messenger Service and Jefferson Airplane) and Pete Albin (Big Brother and the Holding Company). In 1962 Garcia met drummer Bill Kreutzmann and both ended up working at Dana Morgan's music shop, where budding guitarist Bob Weir often hung around to pick up playing tips. Garcia and several other musicians lived in a pre-La Honda style commune known as the Chateau, to which a blues fanatic harp player named Ron 'Pigpen' McKernan presented himself one day. In 1964, Garcia, Weir and Pigpen conceived the short-lived Mother McGee's Uptown Jug Champions, but then the Beatles redrafted the blueprints for young white musicians and acoustic folk got left behind. The revelation of the Beatles was the fun and profit of playing electric rock 'n' roll. Pigpen took the lead; out went the washboards, in came Kreutzmann to play drums and the Warlocks plugged in. It wasn't long, in the close-knit Bay-Area way of things, for the Warlocks to become involved in Kesey's Acid Tests. Garcia was later to comment, 'The Acid Tests were thousands of people, all hopelessly stoned, all finding themselves in a roomful of other thousands of people, none of whom any of them were afraid of.'

There was no clear chronology to the development of the San Francisco rock scene – all the major bands came together at roughly the same time – but one West Coast band mentioned by many musicians as being a catalyst in the progression towards acid rock were the Charlatans.

Who?

Based in Los Angeles, the Charlatans were one of the first bands to play electric blues and rock 'n' roll smashed out of their brains on acid and magic mushrooms. They had an unlikely residency in 1965 at a rough-house bar called the Red Dog

Saloon, Virginia City, Nevada and the Bay Area musicians largely took their cue from this band. Unfortunately, it is often the way that the pioneers of rock music end up languishing in the footnotes of history. So it was with the Charlatans; once 'psychedelia' got under way, they were never able to land themselves a major record deal and disappeared from view.

It was during 1965 that certain individuals saw that all these musicians furiously forming bands were going to need somewhere to play. A would-be rock entrepreneur, Chet Helms, formed a promotions outfit called Family Dog and on 16 October staged the first of a series of highly successful concerts at the Longshoreman's Hall near Fisherman's Wharf. Star guests on that first night were a new band, Jefferson Airplane, named after their guitarist's dog. The Warlocks had already starred in benefit gigs for the San Francisco Mime Troupe (who were being regularly busted for obscenity), organized by the Troupe's business manager and treasurer Bill Graham.

In January 1966, the Merry Pranksters organized what amounted to a three-day acid test called the Trips Festival. Bands on stage included the Warlocks, Jefferson Airplane and Chet Helms' houseband at the Longshoreman's Hall, Big Brother and the Holding Company. Earlier in 1965, Helms had brought a singer, Janis Joplin from Texas, to play the Bay Area folk scene, but he shipped her back sharpish when she became hooked on Methedrine. He brought her back in June to front Big Brother, whose manager he had since become. The Trips Festival grossed $12,500 with few overheads. Two weeks later, Bill Graham started up at the Fillmore Theatre in the heart of San Francisco's black community and from then on every weekend was a Trips Festival. Chet Helms replied with concerts at the Avalon Ballroom on the corner of Van Ness and Sutter. Rock 'n' roll was here to pay.

Inseparable from the growth of the San Francisco music scene and rock in general was the widespread use of marijuana and LSD among the offspring of America's white middle class. If LSD was the icing on the counter-cultural cake, marijuana was its basic ingredient. As well as being central to the jazz scene in the fifties, it was enthusiastically taken up by white musicians on the folk-blues circuit. For those whose folk music was heavily politicized, smoking dope became integral to the protest movement.

The Free Speech Movement started on Berkeley campus in the autumn of 1964 and quickly became a focal point for the rising tide of student activism. Every issue from civil rights to the Bomb was up for grabs. By using an illegal drug like marijuana (LSD wasn't banned in the USA until 1966), cub activists made their first tilt at authority. For many, doing drugs would be their only 'political' statement. Shocking one's parents and teachers was the boundary of most acts of status-quo sabotage. The Left in politics failed to exploit the radical promise of acid, which while communal in its social context, was still far too individualistic and inward-looking an activity for the hardline politicos. The self-obsessed ME generation left outrage to the committed few. When Pete Townshend whacked Abbie Hoffman on the head with his guitar as the chief hippie tried to make an impromptu speech from the stage of Woodstock, the love affair between radical politics and the acid generation was over.

The claims for rock music as a revolutionary force have always been suspect, as protest rock courtesy of major record companies clearly demonstrates. A study which examined the attitudes of young people over a four-year period, from 1966-70, actually showed up rock as a vehicle for social control rather than anarchy. The authors concluded, 'our study suggests that rock music may have seemed to channel social unrest into a more politically passive direction. By helping to translate revolutionary opinions into rhetorical cant, protest rock facilitated token opposition to the status quo among youth....'[4]

From the early sixties the economics of the drug scene began to change. On the East Coast, for example, marijuana was relatively scarce unless you went to Harlem or bought poor-grade Mafia dope. But as the habit spread through white suburbs and college campuses, a new network of 'hippy' dealers grew up, distributing high-grade Mexican marijuana like Acapulco Gold with the same righteous air as Mezz Mezzrow. Organized crime syndicates like the Mafia gave up on the street marijuana scene to concentrate on drugs like heroin and cocaine, which were less bulky, more profitable, involved fewer dealers and were much easier to control.

But the true Mezz Mezzrow of his time dealt not in marijuana but in LSD. Augustus Owsley Stanley III was once described by a US government agent as the man who did for LSD what Henry Ford did for the motor car. Leary called him God's secret agent and to the hippy on the street he was the King of LSD. Grandson of a Kentucky senator, Owsley was a wayward boy genius of science whose natural home was a chemistry lab. Drifting around the West Coast in 1963, he took up a course at Berkeley and between then and 1965 operated a Methedrine factory, until police swooped and confiscated all his equipment. Fleeing to Los Angeles, Owsley set up an LSD operation which he took back north once the situation had cooled down. From there he began supplying 'Owsley tabs', white at first, then blue and then a whole variety of colours, designed to stay ahead of cheap imitations. Some had designs on them like Batman, others had special names like Purple Haze and White Lightning. All his products were top grade, purer than Sandoz LSD. Owsley had strong connections with the rock scene. Purple Haze was made for Jimi Hendrix: a special double-strength tab with an owl stamped on it. According to Lemmy of Motorhead, who was a Hendrix roadie in 1967, Hendrix bought 100,000 doses from Owsley. Hendrix had an acid-taster to make sure he wasn't being sold bad stuff; but with Owsley acid on offer he didn't need him. Owsley's closest association, however, has been with the Grateful Dead.

Owsley supplied most of the acid for the Acid Tests; here he made contact with the Warlocks, as they still were in 1965. Owsley had a keen interest in electronics and teamed up with electronics wizard Tim Scully, who in turn wished to know more about LSD. Together they supplied acid to the rock community and a mountain of electronic equipment to the Warlocks. The Grateful Dead owed much to Tim Scully for the creation of a sound described by Ralph Gleason as 'rolling thunder'.

Owsley became something of a patron to the band, channelling drugs money and equipment to them, providing accommodation and even becoming involved in their record production.

Owsley made a fortune from LSD, but like Leary he was an acid missionary, a psychedelic alchemist who probably gave away as much LSD as he sold. He had a 'righteous' view about acid, believing it to be a drug for the people. When criminal gangs tried to corner the Californian market in ergot, Owsley temporarily killed the market in San Francisco by parachuting into the 'Be-In' Festival at Golden Gate Park in January 1967 to give away 100,000 tabs of LSD.

By the time of the Festival, Owsley himself was a criminal as the unlawful manufacture and sale of LSD had been banned under Federal laws introduced on 1 February 1966. In the aftermath of the Thalidomide tragedy, the Federal Drug

Administration (FDA) greatly restricted experimentation with new drugs. From 1963, the FDA had to approve all Investigational New Drugs (IND) research in writing for each individual project. LSD was classed as an IND. At first this had limited impact on LSD research but then horror stories about the drug began appearing in the British and American press. The recreational use of LSD was spreading fast; in 1962 Leary estimated that about 25,000 Americans had tried it. A study conducted at the end of 1965 put the figure at nearly four million, of whom 70% were at high school or college. Bad experiences with the drug were inevitable, and not surprisingly the tiny minority of extreme cases made banner headlines; those who flew out of windows or committed murder under the influence of LSD. A heavily-publicized scare about chromosome breakage and deformed babies proved unfounded. One story that was widely reported involved a group of students who, having taken acid, looked into the sun and went blind. The doctor who submitted this story later admitted it was a lie intended to highlight the dangers of the drug. His retraction went largely unreported.

In the midst of all this hysteria Sandoz withdrew their IND application for LSD and took the drug off the market in May 1966 while Sandoz' American office, based in New Jersey, turned over all their supplies to the National Institute of Mental Health (NIMH) The government was now fully committed to the 'psychomimetic' model of LSD, anything else smacked of the dangerous subversion of Leary and his followers. Only those researchers seeking grants to study the adverse effects of the drug had their applications considered.

The Federal law of February 1965 did not outlaw possession of LSD, only its manufacture. But by late 1966 many states, including New York and California, had made possession a felony. Some state laws were particularly draconian; in Massachusetts, for example, simple possession could land you in jail for up to four years. Persuade someone to take it and you could be detained for up to twenty-five years. Yet it wasn't until 1968 that the Federal laws were amended to ban possession of LSD. That same year saw a reorganisation of the drug enforcement agencies; the Bureau of Narcotics and Dangerous Drugs was created from Anslinger's old Bureau and the Bureau of Drug Abuse Control (formerly part of the Health Department). Enforcement of the laws against psychedelic drugs was also switched from the FDA to this new powerful drug enforcement agency. The day the laws came into effect in California, 6 October 1966 (Britain banned LSD the same month), a large protest-cum-rock event was staged in San Francisco. The bands played and the counter-culture politicians and poets made speeches. One immediate impact of the acid laws was dramatically to increase the appeal of LSD for the 'generation in rebellion'. The Acid Tests petered out around the time Sandoz took acid off the market; Kesey had already fled to Mexico in the wake of a marijuana bust. But LSD became a permanent fixture, backstage and front, of all the major rock festivals of the sixties in both Britain and America.

The first rock festival to capture the attention of the media was the Golden Gate 'Be-In' of January 1967. Thousands of people came together to listen to music, make love, and (courtesy of Owsley's acid drop), get stoned. There was no trouble and no police. Despite the laws, the reputation of LSD as a drug of peace and love soared. But the importance of the concert was blown out of all proportion, possibly because the nation couldn't conceive that so many young people could come together to listen to the Devil's music and consume dangerous drugs without mayhem and disaster. When this didn't happen absurd ambitions were heaped on 'hippies' (as Herb Caen of the *San Francisco Chronicle* had dubbed them), as vanguards of the 'new generation', 'saviours of the world' and so on.

The record companies, too, were hailing a new age of increased profits. Jac Holzman, head of Elektra, told an industry conference at the time: 'To comprehend the music of tomorrow, expand your musical vistas, sensitize yourself, because the vibrations of contemporary existence cannot be had secondhand.'[5] The dark blue suit gave way to the Afghan coat, hair cascaded over ears, dope wafted from nostrils and 'hey man' fell from every corporate lip. Apart from that nothing much had changed.

The writing was already etched upon the wall at the 'Be-In' of January 1967. Jefferson Airplane, the headlining band, had been signed to RCA since August 1965, the same month that the Byrds' 'Mr. Tambourine Man' was in the British and American charts. RCA wanted their own Byrds and paid out an unprecedented $20,000 advance to secure them. Airplane repaid the debt with acid-drenched chart hits like 'White Rabbit' and 'Somebody to Love'. Grace Slick's brother-in-law, Darby had written 'Somebody to Love' after an acid trip taken to console himself at being dumped by his girlfriend. During the recording of Airplane's 1967 album *After Bathing at Baxters*, which also refers to acid trips, RCA set the band up in a Beverly Hills mansion complete with Japanese houseboy and rifle range, at $5,000 a month. Nevertheless relations with RCA were always strained; the company was only too eager to reap the profits from drug-inspired songs, but there were battle royals over album covers which were too 'psychedelic' for the company's liking.

The Monterey Pop Festival in June 1967 proved to be the launching pad for a number of other West Coast bands. Some were signed directly as a result of their appearance there, others gained from the international exposure Monterey gave to rock. Backstage was awash with Owsley acid and a new product for the hippy aristocracy, STP, an amphetamine with psychedelic properties. Hendrix, who became a star after Monterey, wrote 'The Stars That Played with Laughing Sam's Dice' as a homage to both drugs. Out front, Janis Joplin impressed Columbia, who already had the Byrds and later signed Moby Grape. Capitol paid out $40,000 in advance to Quicksilver Messenger Service and the Steve Miller Band; Vanguard signed Country Joe and the Fish, while Elektra snapped up LA's top acid bands, Love and the Doors.

But what of the Warlocks? During 1966 the band decided that a name change was in order. Talking to Michael Lydon in 1968 Jerry Garcia said,

> One day we were over at Phil's house smoking DMT. He had a big dictionary. I opened it and there was 'Grateful Dead', those words juxtaposed. It was one of those moments, you know, like everything else on the page went blank, diffuse, just sort of oozed away and there was GRATEFUL DEAD in big black letters edged all around in gold, man, blasting out at me. Such a stunning combination. So I said how about Grateful Dead? And that was it.[6]

The name change signified the move away from a rigid folk-blues formula to meandering, free-form rock improvisations. The Dead were probably unique among the acid-rock bands. Many merely jumped on the bandwagon, adopting fashionable psychedelic names and creating a drug atmosphere through judicious knob-twiddling in the studio, but all within the standard three-and-a-half minute format. Even on Jefferson Airplane's most overt drug album, *Baxters*, no track is longer than five minutes. The Dead were more of a touring community than a rock band. They arrived stoned, played stoned and their fiercely loyal fans, 'Deadheads', were stoned along with them. Acid stretched the length of concerts to legendary proportions. They could play five hours and when the promoter pulled the plug on them, they'd set up somewhere else and play for another three. Song structures were at best fluid. About acid, Garcia said: 'It was like another release, yet another opening. The first one was a hip teacher when I was in third grade; and the next one was all marijuana, and the next one was music and the next one was LSD. It was like a series of continually opening doors.'[7]

Of those bands signed up prior to Monterey, the Dead held out longer than most against the fluttering chequebook, but finally signed to Warner Brothers in December 1966. Even so, they made acid work for them. Up until then, bands were paid royalties based on the number of songs on an album, if the Dead were going to try and re-create their stage act on record, they would lose out. So a deal was struck whereby royalties were paid per three-and-a-half minutes of music instead of per song.

The Dead played music that was quite specifically aimed at those who used psychedelic drugs and marijuana. Indeed, some of their sixties material is almost unlistenable unless one is in an altered state of a consciousness. Similarly targeted was a classic album of the period, the debut offering from Country Joe and the Fish, *Electric Music for the Mind and Body*, with songs like 'Flying High', 'Section 43' and 'Bass Strings':

> *Hey Partner, won't you pass that reefer around*
> *My world is spinning, yeah*
> *Just got to slow it down*
> *Oh yes I've sure got to slow it down*
> *Got so high this time that you know*
> *I'll never come down – never come down.*

The 13th Floor Elevators were an unusual band in that they were the leading lights of a psychedelic rock scene based not in San Francisco but Texas. The Texan acid-rock scene was largely overlooked at the time because of the predominance of San Francisco and, in truth, the music world lost little. But the Elevators' first album, *The Psychedelic Sounds of the 13th Floor Elevators*, released in 1966, is probably the most reverential anthem to acid ever released and certainly left the listener in no doubt as to the source of its inspiration. The sleevenotes read, '…Recently it has become possible for man to chemically alter his mental state and thus alter his point of view… he then can restructure his thinking and change his language so that his thoughts bear more relation to his life and problems, therefore approaching them more sanely. It is this quest for pure sanity that forms the basis of the songs on this album.' The album is full of psychedelic references, both blatant and oblique. One song called 'Fire Engine' has the line 'let me take you to the empty place on my fire engine', but 'the empty place' came out as 'DMT place', the dimethylatriptamine under which 'Grateful Dead' was born.[8] Whatever came out of the 13th Floor Elevators, it certainly wasn't pure sanity – quite the reverse.

Although the horror stories about acid were exaggerated and most people suffered no ill-effects, some people took so much acid that, as in the words of 'Bass Strings', they never really came down. These were the 'acid casualties'. Their numbers were uncounted, but a disturbingly large number of people from that period, inside and outside the business, seemed to know of at least one. Exactly what happened in these cases is unknown, although the most likely explanation is that the action of LSD precipitated a latent psychotic condition.

Roky Erikson, vocalist with the Elevators, finished up in a mental hospital, where whatever damage had been done by LSD was compounded by the 'Cuckoo's Nest' treatment he received. It took three years and a court case to get him out. Some years later, interviewed on radio, Erikson claimed to be interested only in horror and the Devil and denied ever having been in the Elevators. The band's jug player, Tom Hall, went the same way. Other notable acid victims included Love's Arthur Lee, Skip Spence from Moby Grape, Pink Floyd's Syd Barrett, Mitch Ryder and Peter Green of Fleetwood Mac, while Jimi Hendrix ate acid tabs by the handful.

In 1968 writer Ralph Metzer interviewed David Crosby, then with the Byrds, for a book called *The Ecstatic Adventure*, a log of chemical journeys taken by people from all walks of life . Asked about using drugs while creating music, Crosby said that he had been using LSD since 1964 and had learned to play guitar on speed: 'I don't know any good guitar players who haven't taken speed... I play most of the time high and I always write high (on psychedelics or marijuana).'

Crosby once spoke to Bob Dylan about acid and Dylan asked, 'Man, haven't you done that enough?'[9] The answer went unrecorded, but time was to reveal that for Crosby there would be no such thing as enough.

Dylan, on the other hand, was speaking from the point of view of somebody who, by the late sixties, had done it all before. As Michael Gray observed: 'The attempt to learn from drugs, the attempt to create drug experiences, the rejection of common sense, logic and the acceptance of mystery – Dylan accelerated the awakening to all this.'[10]

Dylan went through some profound drug experiences during 1964-5, taking up Baudelaire's formula for immortality: 'A poet makes himself a seer by a long prodigious and rational disordering of the senses.' He surrounded himself with 'the mindguard' equivalent of Presley's Memphis Mafia and tried just about everything he could to 'open his head' as biographer Tony Scaduto puts it. He talked about recapturing spontaneity and about writing songs that matched his thoughts at the age of ten, which was not going to happen while he was the doyen of protest folk. So he turned his back on politics as marijuana and acid turned him in on himself. Within a few short months the hard-nosed political reality of the 'Lonesome Death of Hattie Carroll' and the 'Ballad of Hollis Brown', gave way to expressions of drug experiences like 'Chimes of Freedom', 'Lay Down your Weary Tune', 'Subterranean Homesick Blues' and 'Mr Tambourine Man'. Michael Gray cites 'Lay Down Your Weary Tune', written in 1964, as Dylan's first acid song, 'the first concentrated attempt to give a hint of the unfiltered world.'[11] In 1964, Dylan refused a request from Ginsberg to lead a peace rally at Berkeley and earned the unbending enmity of singer Phil Ochs, who called him 'LSD on stage'. Dylan reported that Ochs was writing bullshit because politics were absurd and the world was unreal. Dylan took his personal drug-inspired search for freedom and escape through 'Mr Tambourine Man' and 'Highway 61 Revisited', to the ego-dissolution of 'Like a Rolling Stone' and *Blonde on Blonde*. Nevertheless, claims that all references to 'railways' and 'tracks' and capitalised H's on lyric sheets demonstrate that Dylan was a heroin addict or that 'Blowin' in the Wind' was secretly a song about the wonders of cocaine are probably

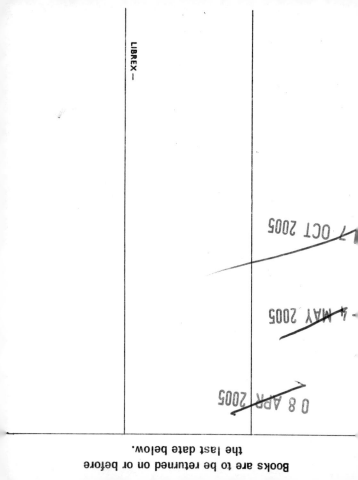

LIBREX—

Books are to be returned on or before
the last date below.

0 8 APR 2005

- 4 MAY 2005

1 7 OCT 2005

best led in the more extreme realms of Dylanology.

In the early sixties, sharing the experiences of marijuana and LSD between creative spirits had a missionary zeal about it. Rock writer Al Aronowitz turned both Ginsberg and Dylan on to marijuana; Dylan in turn introduced dope-smoking to the Beatles. They met him on their first tour of America. Dylan was 'anti-chemical' at the time, probably due to a surfeit of amphetamine, and suggested that the Beatles try something more natural. Dylan rolled the first joint and passed it to Lennon, who, too scared to try it, passed it on to Ringo. The episode ended with everyone rolling round the floor in hysterics.

It was during the filming of *Help* that LSD came into the Beatles' lives. A dentist friend threw a dinner party for them at which the conversation focused on a renegade academic called Timothy Leary, whom only John had heard of. The host passed round the LSD with none too beatific results. The Beatles left the party and drove from night club to night club in a very peculiar state of mind. Driving at 10 m.p.h. they somehow managed to get back to George Harrison's place, by which time neither his girlfriend Patti Boyd nor Lennon's wife Cynthia believed they would ever be sane again. While under the influence of acid, Lennon started drawing and perceived Harrison's house as a big submarine where they all lived.[12] This child-like acid imagery soon grew more pronounced as Lennon became obsessed with acid, taking hundreds of trips which undermined his already volatile personality. Probably acid and a destructive affair with heroin did more to push Lennon and finally the Beatles to the final collapse than any other outside influence.

Like Dylan's, the Beatles' drug adventures soon showed in their music. First *Rubber Soul* (1965) and then *Revolver* (1966) saw the release of Beatles songs in this new context. A concept of love that goes beyond a quick one behind the gasworks appeared in 'The Word', while 'Nowhere Man' examined the inner mental workings of the individual as revealed by psychedelic drugs. 'She Said, She Said' was inspired by a conversation Lennon had with actor Peter Fonda during his second acid trip, and Leary's psychedelic version of *The Tibetan Book of the Dead* provided the material for 'Tomorrow Never Knows'.

In June 1967 came the release of *Sergeant Pepper's Lonely Hearts Club Band*. Quite apart from being one of the most significant albums ever recorded, *Sergeant Pepper* galvanised the acid subculture and gave LSD an international platform. Whether or not 'Lucy in the Sky with Diamonds' really meant what it looked like is irrelevant; fans looked at the cover, read the lyrics, heard the studio effects and made up their own minds. The BBC also read the lyrics and banned 'A Day in the Life' because of its favourable reference to 'a trip'. In any case, Paul McCartney let the cat out of the bag when he admitted to *Queen* and *Life Magazine* in 1967 that not only had he used LSD, but 'it opened my eyes. It made me a better, more honest, more tolerant member of society.' In the ensuing furore, Brian Epstein tried to salvage the situation by saying that he had been using LSD as well: 'I did have some apprehension but I took that risk. I think LSD helped me to know myself better and I think it helped me to become less bad-tempered.' In truth, Epstein was not floating through life on a sea of acid, but committing himself to a roller-coaster existence on barbiturates and amphetamines.

The release of *Sergeant Pepper* seemed to accelerate the rate at which the moths of popular culture flapped round the flame of LSD, in a desperate attempt to cash in while it all lasted. If nothing else, LSD brought colour into the lives of many young people, most of whom never touched the stuff. Hippy fashions in ethnic textiles swirled through the streets to the jangle of bells and beads. There were psychedelic films, rock light shows, often unreadable underground newspapers in multi-coloured prints and, of course, the music. Pop co-opted and sanitized acid. The very word 'acid' sounded hard and dangerous, a corrosive element in society; flower-power, on the other hand, was safe and innocuous – one of the biggest hits of 1967 was Scott McKenzie's 'San Francisco', with the benign lyric, 'Be sure to wear some flowers in your hair.'[13]

The Beatles also helped to put London on the psychedelic map and there were many attempts to re-create Haight Ashbury in W10 and SW6. For the *Berkeley Barb* and the *Oracle* read *International Times* and *Oz;* the Roundhouse, UFO and Middle Earth for the Fillmore and the Avalon Ballroom; Ally Pally for the Be-In; Pink Floyd, Soft Machine and Cream for the Dead, Airplane and Quicksilver. Cream and Hendrix straddled both continents, representing acid rock on a scale unmatched by any other band, either for power or virtuosity.

In London it was amusing to see r&b artists like Zoot Money and Graham Bond playing the same r&b songs in Hawaiian shirts and calling them 'psychedelic' (or 'psychodalek' as Bond dubbed it). A sign of the times was the opening of the Temple, a seedy rock venue frequented by the capital's acid casualties, on the site of the famous Flamingo jazz club. But acid had a much more profound effect on the music business than the spawning of transitory rock clubs and one-hit wonders like Scott McKenzie. After *Sergeant Pepper*, straightforward 'one for the money/two for the show' rock 'n' roll was brushed aside. Over the next few years albums outsold singles for the first time; there were doubles, triples, boxed sets, concept albums, tracks lasting a whole side, gatefold album sleeves, the album cover as 'art', groups working with orchestras, rock operas and a slew of pretentious and obscure lyrics.

Acid also played a significant part in the development of FM radio in America, in the shape of Tom Donahue. Already a veteran DJ in Philadelphia, Donahue arrived in San Francisco in 1961, worked on KYA for a couple of years and then became involved in concert promotion and record production. As head of Autumn Records, he had eighteen national hits of which two got into the Top Ten. Then in 1966 he gave it all up. His partner in Autumn Records was dying of Hodgkin's disease and not surprisingly had lost interest. Donahue was taking a tremendous amount of acid. 'You know, you're taking acid three or four times a week and it's very hard to talk to thirty-seven distributors and ask them the first day where your money is, the second day what they're doing about your records and the third day where your money is.'[14]

Donahue dropped out for about eighteen months and hung around his apartment doing more acid, trying to conceive where next to go. From his psychedelic musing came the notion of using the FM waveband to play all the 'head' music that AM Top Forty radio wouldn't touch. KMPX started up in the idyllic summer of '67 and became a spectacular success. But although business was good, the acid spirit in San Francisco was already dying. Haight Ashbury was going the way of North Beach, drowning in a sea of tourists, weekend hippies, hustlers, police harassment and bad acid. Injecting Methedrine became popular, serving only to heighten the level of paranoia and suspicion. In London, acid euphoria cooled with the coming of winter. Between August-December, pirate radio stations like Radio London, 270 and Scotland closed down,[15] Brian Epstein died, and the Beatles' attempt to film their own Merry Pranksters trip, *The Magical Mystery Tour* ended a shambles.

Throughout 1968 violence was the new radical pose. Jefferson Airplane said goodbye to the white rabbit and hello to *Volunteers* and 'Up against the wall, motherfuckers'. After the debacle of *Their Satanic Majesties Request*, the Stones gratefully (and wisely) ditched flower power for 'Street Fightin' Man'. Woodstock showed it was all still possible, but in December 1969 came Altamont. The Rolling Stones had come to the end of their American tour and Mick Jagger was determined to hold a free concert in California, the home of free concerts, and to release a film of the tour and the concert before the Woodstock film was released. A date had been fixed, but only at the eleventh hour could a venue be found – the Sears Point Raceway at Altamont.

Everyone involved knew the crowd would be vast and so it was – at least 300,000 people turned up. To cater for a crowd that size needs time and the careful planning of safety, security, staging and on-site facilities. None of this happened. To compound what was potentially a very serious situation, the site was awash with very poor quality LSD. The medical team very quickly ran out of Thorazine, the drug used to calm people down on a bad trip. Fights broke out over food, water and in the long queues which formed for the few toilets. In this atmosphere, the appearance of Hell's Angels as security guards for the stage area only served to make matters worse.

At the Golden Gate Park concert in 1967, there was plenty of acid around, the Angels were on duty and there was very little trouble. On the strength of that experience, Grateful Dead manager Rock Scully recommended the Angels to the Altamont concert promoters. This time, however, it all went horribly wrong. By noon, well before the first band came on, the Angels had consumed volumes of alcohol and bad acid thought to have been cut with speed. They were already fighting with members of the audience down near the front of the stage where most of the trouble happened. Nor were the artists safe: Marty Balin of Jefferson Airplane was smashed in the face during their set for trying to stop the Angels beating somebody up.

It was after dark when the Stones finally came on stage. Five songs into the set with fights going on all around him, Jagger had just uttered the first line of 'Under My Thumb', when he spotted a man in the audience waving a gun. He yelled at guitarist Mick Taylor and the music stopped. Holding the gun was Meredith Hunter, an eighteen-year-old black man, who had come to the concert with his white girlfriend. This had angered the Angels; they taunted Hunter and a fight broke out. Hunter was stabbed, but still managed to pull a gun. He was stabbed again and fell to the ground where he was kicked repeatedly. For several minutes, the Angels allowed nobody near him to tend his wounds. Eventually, he was taken to the medical tent, but the promised emergency facilities were not there – there was no equipment and no helicopter to fly Hunter to hospital. He died.

Meredith Hunter was not the only fatality at Altamont; two people were killed in their sleeping bags by a hit-and-run driver and somebody drowned in a canal during a bad acid trip. The Angels were blamed for everything, but in truth the concert should never have taken place under such shambolic circumstances.

Coming on the edge of the new decade, it was inevitable that Altamont would be played up as a *fin de siécle* for the sixties. Even so, with most of the acid crusaders out of the picture by then, either on the run, in prison or in retirement, it is hard to escape the feeling that as the life ebbed away from Meredith Hunter, the spirit of the sixties went with him .

Acid subculture was bound to dissipate because the whole structure was underpinned by rock music, a business which thrives on instant mass communication and international markets for its survival. In the process, however, LSD did create a new environment for rock to develop; it had a significant impact on already creative and talented minds and it is highly probable that without it the best of sixties rock music would not have emerged. Inevitably, LSD took its toll; with it Hendrix wrote some of the most powerful rock of all time, but it also made him malleable in the face of business sharks.

LSD was and is a drug that demands respect. William Blake knew nothing of it, but he encapsulated its power when he wrote,

> *To see a World in a grain of sand*
> *And a heaven in a wild flower*
> *Hold Infinity in the palm of your hand*
> *And Eternity in an hour.*

10 STAR WARS

If I smoke, will I get caught? Only if you're stupid, unlucky or a pop star.

Richard Neville, Playpower

When I wasn't high, I was in court ... you try saying twenty-five times 'Guilty, your honour' in Marlborough Street and keeping a straight face ... it was a game, nothing to do with justice or law.

Keith Richard, New Musical Express

Getting arrested on drugs charges is as much an occupational hazard for rock musicians as it ever was for the top-flight jazz stars of yesteryear. The context may be different, but the logic of moral outrage remains the same. In jazz's golden days, the spokesmen of 'right-thinking' citizens, the clergy, police, politicians and the press, could conveniently combine their entrenched racism and their disapproval of a delinquent generation by blaming black jazz musicians. If it wasn't for the jungle rhythms of licentious dope-smoking jazzers, they reasoned, young people would obey their parents and not expose themselves to mortal danger and ruin.

But as jazz gave way to rock as a music of mass popularity the moralists were faced with a puzzle; not only was the new breed of musicians white, but the kids were using more drugs than ever. Moreover, a new element entered the analysis: being a long-haired rock star wearing outrageous clothes was bad enough, but the real red rags to the bullish moral establishment were the money and the adoration surrounding the new stars. Some of these yobbos were millionaires. God damn it, their pictures in every paper, on television, the media hanging onto their every word. These publicity-seeking oiks had to be taken down a peg or two. The trouble was that being a teenage idol was not a criminal offence. Taking illegal drugs, on the other hand, was another matter. Busting musicians serves a number of purposes. First, particularly since the beginning of the new era of heightened public concern over drug use back in the 1980s, musicians have been an easy target, handy folk devils for the new moral panic. *The London Evening Standard*, for example, ran part of its story about Boy George and his heroin problem underneath a typical piece of unfounded hysteria about the threat of a 'crack' epidemic hitting London (10 July 1986). In the wake of the Boy George revelations, both Baroness Trumpington from the DHSS and the then Conservative Party Chairman Norman Tebbit railed against 'junkie' pop stars setting a bad example. Mr Tebbit raised the question of whether known drug-using stars should be banned by the BBC, and voiced the opinion that 'twenty or thirty years ago people were perhaps more permissive' (*Oxford Mail*, 5 July 1986). Not necessarily so; or at least, certainly not Mrs D. Baylis of Noss Mayo near Plymouth. The wheel has turned full circle in Britain since 1967 and the *News of the World*'s first 'shock expose' of drugs in pop. Mrs Baylis then wrote to the paper saying 'Pop stars should be subjected to a system of tests – like horses and greyhounds – before they go on stage.' (*News of the World*, 26 February 1967).

Musicians are also good copy in the propaganda war against drug users, showing that fame and fortune are no protection against drug problems. Indirectly, the bust is a means of exercising unadmitted social revenge and in default of the Mr Bigs, who are rarely apprehended, nabbing Mr Pop Star ensures the police front-page headlines. Attention is thus diverted from the palpable failure in reducing the numbers of people with drug problems, so that the musician in the dock becomes part of the symbolic fight against drugs in lieu of any significant successes in law enforcement, treatment or prevention.

And of course, there's nothing like a good star bust to keep the newspaper proprietors happy. Whoever gets the scoop can be pompously self-righteous in the editorials, while printing a juicy story to sell thousands more copies. It must be said too that musicians are often their own worst enemies in this respect. This was especially so in the 'hang loose' sixties. As Julie Burchill observed, for Traffic to release 'Hole in My Shoe' with the lines 'I looked in the sky/while an elephant's eye/was looking at me/from a bubblegum tree' was tantamount to writing to the drug squad, 'I use illegal hallucinogenic drugs, please arrest me.' And much the same applied to many of those who churned out 'windmills of your mind' acid imagery.

Musicians tend on occasion to be ludicrously careless. While in England in 1968 recording their first album *Children of the Future*, the Steve Miller Band received a box of chocolates sent through the post and stuffed with marijuana. Attached to this box was a customs officer; the whole band were busted and sent home.

On account of two previous marijuana convictions in 1972 and 1973, Paul McCartney had been denied a Japanese visa on a number of occasions. However, under pressure from music promoters anxious to book Wings, Japanese immigration officials relented and on 16 January 1980, McCartney and the band flew into Tokyo airport. Japanese customs are legendary for their scrutiny of incoming musicians – the police are known to follow them around the streets. McCartney was bound to be a target, but there, lying neatly on top of his luggage, was about seven and a half ounces of marijuana. Nine days later, in a flurry of international publicity, he was deported with the loss of the whole tour, £200,000 to compensate the promoters and a further £100,000 in lawyers and sundry expenses.[1]

Because of their high-media profile, musicians are particularly vulnerable to the vengeful impulses of ex-employees, sacked band members, disgruntled former girlfriends and anyone else wishing to bask in the fall-out from chequebook journalism while sticking the boot in at the same time. The police read newspapers too, and arrests have often followed tabloid exclusives. More sinister, there have been examples where it would appear that a musician has been set up by his management to bring an internal row to a 'satisfactory' conclusion.

On 3 May 1969, Jimi Hendrix landed at Toronto airport en route from Detroit. Under normal circumstances baggage at airports is searched by customs and if anything untoward is discovered, the individual is escorted into a side office. But on this occasion the Mounties were waiting. They searched Hendrix's luggage as if they knew what they were looking for, duly found some hash and heroin and then began an interrogation in full public view for maximum effect. A heroin charge was serious; at a time when most musician arrests were for possession of marijuana or LSD, Hendrix was one of the first rock stars to be caught in possession of heroin. Yet he had had no need to take such a risk. In the first place, it was usual for other members of a rock entourage, roadies or road managers, to carry any drugs, as they were less likely to be searched. Second, fans were always thrusting drugs on Hendrix wherever he went.

There was a strong feeling among those close to Hendrix that he had been set up by his manager Mike Jeffrey, who at the time was afraid of losing his hugely successful star to his former co-partner, Chas Chandler. Hendrix had been increasingly unhappy about the way Jeffrey was handling his affairs, but if he became embroiled in a drugs case he would need Jeffrey's help. All talk of leaving would cease. If Hendrix got off he would be grateful. If not, there was still an awful lot of mileage to be made from a rock star out of circulation. Imagine, for instance, the fees for a comeback tour.

It took nine months for the case to come to trial. Hendrix, who was facing a minimum seven years behind bars, was adamant that he did not know the drugs were there and his defence argued a *mens rea* case ('the guilty mind'). in other words, if Hendrix did not know he was carrying drugs, how could he be found guilty of deliberately intending to possess them, or of having them under his personal control? After deliberating for eight hours, the jury returned a verdict of 'not guilty'.

There is an adage in the entertainments industry that asserts there is no such thing as bad publicity. As far as drug busts are concerned, one could indeed take a cynical view of, for example, the intense publicity in 1986/7 exposing Boy George's drug problems and subsequent recovery. Here was a world-famous pop star who had 'over-exposed' himself to the media, had had a flop record after a string of hits, and disappeared from the public eye. George claimed that concert promoters wouldn't let him tour in Britain because of his recent history (*Sunday People*, 19 April 1987). But his first 'post drug' single, 'Everything I Own', went to Number One. Boy George did not become addicted for publicity purposes, but tasty headlines like 'Junkie George Has Eight Weeks to Live' (*Sun*, 3 July 1986) didn't exactly harm his prospects. Or consider the revelations in 1984 that Duran Duran were cocaine-crazy: nicely timed, it seemed, to coincide with their attempt to break into the adult album market and gain acceptance as pukka musicians. Nevertheless, drug busts are usually bad news for musicians; great lengths are taken to avoid close encounters of the unwelcome kind.

Many a European concert itinerary has been planned according to particularly lax border checks. One band employed a private detective to scout around the airports of Europe to ascertain which airport staff would cause the least hassle to the passengers of a private jet landing at some remote spot on the airfield. Other musicians would try and bluff their way through. In his less coherent moments, British r&b star Graham

Bond, all eighteen stones of him, would shout at the top of his voice going through customs, 'You won't find any drugs up my arse. You can look, but you won't find any!' But often as not, especially where the most famous musicians are concerned, roadies, personal managers and the like will do the carrying, some willingly, others not so. One road manager says 'I have always refused to carry stuff through customs, although some idiots do it, because they get threatened with the sack if they don't.'[2]

Once convicted, international rock musicians can find themselves denied access to countries like America and Japan and lucrative tours will go by the board. Paul McCartney, John Lennon, Brian Jones, Johnny Rotten and Joe Cocker are just a few of the stars who have been inconvenienced in this way. Joe Cocker was lucky first time around; busted at the height of his fame in December 1968, his girlfriend 'took the rap' and charges against him were dropped. However, as his career slumped, his legal problems grew. In 1972 he was busted in Australia and deported; in 1973 he was arrested on marijuana charges in Sheffield; America threw him out on grounds of illegal entry in 1977 and in 1984 he had his collar felt yet again. More recent arrestees have included David Gahan of Depeche Mode, a member of the Stone Temple Pilots and the infamous Bez from the Happy Mondays and Black Grape. Liam Gallagher was arrested in possession of cocaine, but was simply cautioned – of which more later.

In court, defence lawyers use limitations on touring in appeals for leniency. In 1980, former Led Zeppelin guitarist Jimmy Page was arrested in London for possessing 198 mg of cocaine. By the time the case came to trial in October 1982 his new band the Firm, with singer Paul Rogers, was being launched with projected tours in America and Japan. The defence QC argued that Page stood to lose millions should he be convicted. Moved by this plea on behalf of Britain's invisible exports, the judge conditionally discharged Jimmy Page for twelve months.

The experience of John Lennon showed how a drug conviction can reverberate down the years. In October 1968, John and Yoko were arrested in Ringo Starr's basement apartment after cannabis resin had been discovered in a police raid. Following the famous Rolling Stones bust of February 1967 (of which more later), it was generally accepted around the pop fraternity that the drug squad had targeted those they regarded as big-mouth pop stars who needed sorting out. Most zealous of the boys in blue at the time was Detective Sergeant Norman 'Nobby' Pilcher, who became the scourge of London's drugs/ music scene. Several musicians were on his hit list, including Eric Clapton. In 1967 Pilcher led a raid on Clapton's studio flat in the warren of residencies in the King's Road, populated by artists and known as the Pheasantry. Calling out 'postman, special delivery' into the intercom, Pilcher & co. burst through the door and up the narrow passageway to cries of 'Where's Eric Clapton? Where's Eric Clapton?' Fortunately for Eric, he was out. In fact, despite all his well-publicized drug problems, Clapton has been busted only once. On 20 March 1968, he was arrested in North Hollywood for possessing marijuana in the company of three members of Buffalo Springfield, including Neil Young. Clapton got off, but not before spending a night in jail wearing prison denims and his pink boots, trying to convince his cellmates, Black Panther members, that he had a genuine interest in American blues.

Lennon had been warned that Pilcher was waiting for an opportunity to pounce, and said that he was especially careful not to have drugs in the flat, particularly as the previous occupant had been Jimi Hendrix (Lennon claimed he went to some lengths to make sure the place was clean). So it was hardly surprising that Lennon should allege that the resin which was 'found' had in fact been planted. Although never proved, such action would have been in keeping with some of the more suspect methods of the drugs squad at that time. John Lennon testified in court. 'He [Pilcher] said, "If you cop a plea, I won't get you for obstruction and I'll let your missus go." I thought. "It's a hundred dollars [i.e. the potential fine for pleading guilty], it's no skin off my nose."'[3] Pilcher had arrived mob-handed with forty officers. This led to questions in Parliament about why forty policemen were needed to arrest two unarmed suspects and how come the cameras got there first.

In August 1971, John and Yoko moved to New York, where Lennon began to develop more overt links with radical politics. In December he took part in a benefit convert for John Sinclair at Ann Arbor, Michigan. Sinclair was a radical writer, so-called Minister of Information for the White Panthers (formed in 1968) and manager of a politically-orientated rock 'n' roll band called the MC5. He was a wild enthusiast and serious believer in rock as a political force. He wrote a manifesto to accompany the release of the band's first album *Kick Out the Jams* (1969), in which he declared 'We don't have guns because we have more powerful weapons – direct access to millions of teenagers is one of our most potent and their belief in us is another.' Since the mid-sixties, Sinclair had been under the same kind of police scrutiny in his home town of Detroit as Lennon had been in London. He was told to his face repeatedly that it was only a matter of time before they would have him 'banged to rights', as London underworld slang puts it. In July 1969, he was sentenced to an outrageous ten years in prison for selling two marijuana joints to an undercover agent. He continued his political activities in jail, but the MC5 split from him because they decided he was too political, while all they really wanted to do was have a good time. Later they signed to Jon Landau who became Bruce Springsteen's manager and Wayne Kramer, the band's guitarist, was to serve a ten-year sentence for cocaine dealing. Sinclair served two and a half years of his sentence, being released only three days after his benefit concert. The FBI duly noted Lennon's involvement and added this to what became twenty-six pounds of documentation on the ex-Beatle.

1972 was election year in the States and there was genuine paranoia in the Administration that Lennon represented a threat to Nixon's reselection chances. Early in February, Republican Senator Strom Thurmond sent a secret memo to Attorney-General John Mitchell, saying that on the basis of Lennon's publicised plans for anti-Nixon rock rallies, 'if Lennon's visa is terminated, it would be a strategic counter-measure'. At the end of the month, Lennon's work visa expired and his application for permanent residence was turned down by the Immigration and Naturalisation Service (INS), on the grounds that Lennon's 1968 drug conviction made him ineligible to remain in the States. As mentioned above, drug convictions can make entry into America very difficult. However, the INS can issue discretionary waivers and many musicians have managed to get their HI (work permit) visas on that basis, including John Lennon. Of course, the INS can go the other way, and under political pressure they began the process of forcing Lennon out of the country. Deportation hearings took place in March, April and May 1972. Meanwhile Lennon appeared in anti-war demonstrations in New York and a benefit concert for a mentally handicapped foundation with Stevie Wonder, Roberta Flack and Sha Na Na. This was Lennon's only properly rehearsed concert between the Beatles' final US tour of 1965 and his death in 1980, and it was a great triumph.

Nixon was reselected in November 1972 and in the same month, back in England,

Norman Pilcher was charged with other officers of 'conspiring to pervert the course of justice'. Lennon's defence team, Leon Wildes and Nathan Lewin, entertained the rather fanciful idea that should Pilcher be found guilty Lennon's conviction would be overturned – even though the background to Pilcher's trial had nothing to do with the Lennon bust – and the INS case would collapse. Pilcher was in fact convicted, but the judicial process in America rolled on and in March 1973 John Lennon was given sixty days to leave the country, while Yoko Ono was granted permanent residency. Lennon appealed against the decision, claiming (correctly as it transpired), that the US government was using the bust to rid themselves of somebody it found politically undesirable. After a long battle which put an incredible strain on John and Yoko's relationship and sent him on another drug binge the US Court of Appeal overturned the deportation order on 7 October 1975, and in July 1976 John Lennon got the all-important green permanent resident's card.

Presiding Judge Kaufman had ruled against the INS on a very slender point of law, similar to that invoked in Jimi Hendrix's case. Knowledge and intent are important elements in American drug law. At Lennon's trial in 1968, the prosecution could not actually prove that Lennon had intended to possess a controlled drug, merely that both drug and defendant were found together. While that would have been sufficient grounds for a conviction in Britain at the time, it was not enough for Judge Kaufman. As the charge would not have stuck in America, the INS had no grounds for denying Lennon his resident's status.

Once a drug case involving a musician comes to court, a judicial *pas de deux* is often played out. The defence leads by saying the accused is fully aware of the dangers of drugs and in the intervening period (usually months), between arrest and trial, the contrite musician has given up. This can be crucial to staying out of jail, but is more often than not an economic rendering of the truth. It formed part of Hendrix's defence, yet he got totally smashed on his way home from court. Judges and juries like to see humility and deference from those who could buy them out many times over – perhaps a power trip for the common man. A frequent conclusion to musician-centred drug trials is the standard homily delivered from the bench on a pop star's responsibility to society.

An early pop bust was Donovan in July 1966, fined £250 for possessing marijuana and told 'I would like you to bear in mind that you have a great influence on young people and it behoves you to behave yourself.' Pop stars like to think they are influential, but where is the actual evidence that young people copy the behaviour of their idols? For youngsters to take specific drugs because a pop musician does, they should have to know about a part of the musician's private life which the musician is normally anxious to keep secret.

Aerosmith used to have lines of coke trailing across the tops of the amps during a gig, but for the most part, musicians do not snort cocaine on stage, nor do they smoke marijuana in the streets. The illicit nature of the act necessitates secrecy. In addition, musicians who have a drug problem become notoriously unreliable and can find it difficult to obtain work on a regular basis because nobody will take the risk of hiring them or forming bands with them; concert promoters and record companies may be similarly reluctant.

Occasionally the desire to cover up a drug problem can have tragic consequences. Deep Purple guitarist Tommy Bolin was discovered unconscious in a Miami hotel room and put back to bed in the hope that everything would be all right. It wasn't.

In the mid-seventies David Bowie was as popular as ever. His concerts sold out, the audiences dotted with Bowie clones. His records sold by the truckload, his pictures were pinned to countless bedroom walls. But who, outside the business, knew that the Thin White Duke persona on *Station to Station* (1976) was a reflection of Bowie's coke-fuelled existence in Los Angeles? This was revealed only much later in the flurry of Bowie biographies and by Bowie himself (*Daily Mirror*, 18 March 1983).

Despite the rumours flying round the business and Fleet Street for months, who would have known about Boy George but for the *Sun* and reporter Nick Ferrari? Once the story broke, everyone was looking for George including the police. Having tracked him down to drug treatment specialist Meg Patterson via Richard Branson, they allowed him time to complete his treatment before interviewing him. Peter Bruinvels, Conservative MP for Leicester East, was reported as saying it was 'scandalous' that Boy George should be given what he regarded as special treatment (*Daily Telegraph*, 11 July 1986). What he and other MPs should have been querying was the appalling legal precedent of charging somebody with once having been in possession of a controlled drug. But as he admitted himself in a Radio One interview, by confessing to 'past possession', Boy George saved himself a long drawn-out court case, which in his vulnerable physical and psychological state he was ill-equipped to endure. Presumably the police needed his co-operation in order to bring charges against those accused of supplying him, including his brother Kevin, who subsequently claimed that he was being made a scapegoat for others. In that same radio interview Boy George stated that all his friends were avoiding him, particularly those involved in drugs. Who could blame them? Once the police latch on to a celebrity drug circle, the net widens; early in October 1986, former Culture Club drummer Jon Moss was arrested on a cocaine charge.

The Boy George saga is the most glaring example of the fact that from then on, the media rediscovered the news value of pop stars – very reminiscent of the late sixties, and of the days of the most famous and intriguing pop drug bust of them all.

In the wake of Donovan's conviction in July 1966, the *Melody Maker* ran an editorial headlined 'Drugs: is it true what they say about pop stars?' In contrast to its outburst against drug-taking jazz musicians thirty years earlier, the *Melody Maker* this time came to the defence of the beleaguered pop star: 'It is being insinuated in some quarters that drug-taking is widespread among singers and musicians. As a result, the public are being misled into thinking of pop stars and members of beat groups as being addicts or "junkies". This is dangerous, irresponsible nonsense.' The paper admitted widespread use of marijuana, but denied prevalence of speed, heroin or cocaine. It followed up in November with its own investigation 'Pot in Pop' (26 November 1966) interviewing among others, Eric Burdon, Eric Clapton, Zoot Money, Brian Auger and Spencer Davis. Everyone agreed that it went on, but nobody should admit to using marijuana themselves. Chris Britton of the Troggs denied ever coming across *anyone* who smoked.

However, as far as the *News of the World* was concerned, *it* published the first 'exposé' of drug-addled pop stars. The series (devoid of any byline) started on 29 January 1967 with a piece concentrating on Donovan and the use of LSD. This was hardly news of itself, as Donovan had already been busted several months earlier. Ashley Kozak, Donovan's manager, admitted that the singer's number-one hit 'Sunshine Superman' was about LSD. 'Of course,' said the report, 'to the uninitiated, the words are difficult to follow.' Ironically, with Paul McCartney's revelations about his use of acid only weeks away, the *News of the World* stated, 'The leaders like the Beatles derived their success from sheer native genius. But many others in the pop world needed or sought artificial means to gain recognition.' Ginger Baker said he'd tried everything, Pink Floyd and the Move were implicated in the use of acid (Floyd wrote to the *News of the World* two weeks later vehemently denying this). Also mentioned was a house in suburban Roehampton, to the south west of London, rented by the Moody Blues and allegedly visited by musicians to sample acid and other drugs. Pete Townshend and Mick Jagger were among those named. The paper went on to claim that they had tracked Jagger down to Blaises in Kensington, where he freely admitted using hash. Unfortunately the *News of the World's* intrepid reporters were talking to Brian Jones, not Mick Jagger. Compared with this monumental blunder the fact that the *News of the World* lads confused hash with LSD in their report hardly warrants a mention.

On 5 February 1967, an incensed Mick Jagger appeared on the Eamonn Andrews show, denying everything and announcing he was going to sue the *News of the World*. Two weeks later, on 19 February, the papers carried a front-page story headlined 'Drug Squad Raids Pop Star's Party'. No names or locations were mentioned. Two points of interest arose from this 'exclusive': first, the *News of the World* reported that, 'acting on a tip-off that one foreign national present at the party might abscond abroad, police have been keeping watch at major sea and airports'; second, just prior to the raid, 'one pop star and his wife drove off and so unwittingly escaped the net'.

The key names were Mick Jagger and Keith Richard and the location was Redlands, Richard's house in West Sussex. Richard decided to throw a select party; later he said he wasn't personally involved in sending out invitations, but the guests were Mick, his girlfriend Marianne Faithfull, art dealer Robert Fraser, photographer Michael Cooper, Christopher Gibbs and George and Patti Harrison. Fraser's servant Ali was there, plus two outsiders: a typical pop hanger-on called Nicky Cramer and a Canadian, David Schneidermann. Schneidermann, the 'foreign national', had won instant entrée as the bearer of all manner of psychedelic drugs, including Orange Sunshine, state-of-the-art LSD, produced by Owsley's protege Tim Scully and another chemist, Nick Sand. The group arrived at Redlands around 6 p.m. on Sunday 12 February 1967, but the Harrisons left shortly afterwards. About ninety minutes later nineteen police officers, led by Chief Inspector George Dineley, turned up armed with a search warrant issued by a Chichester magistrate. Three policewomen were in the party to search the three women who, according to the tip-off, would be found there – Marianne, Patti and Anita Pallenberg. Schneidermann's attaché case, full of drugs, lay in the middle of the living-room floor, closed but clearly visible Nevertheless the only guest really worried by the police intrusion was Robert Fraser, who had heroin on him supplied by Richard's main dealer Tony Sanchez, plus some hash and speed tablets.

The house was searched and the guests frisked. The police took away for analysis the 'white powder' found on Fraser, marijuana found on Schneidermann and four amphetamine tablets discovered in Jagger's possession (apparently these had been given to Marianne by a French doctor). Keith Richard was warned that should any of the substances turn out to be marijuana, he would be charged with permitting its use on his premises.[5] The police then left.

As the one facing the most serious charge, Robert Fraser was anxious to find a way to 'fix' the police laboratory analysis. Sanchez claimed that £7,000 would sort it out; the money was passed over, but this did not prevent summonses being issued on 22

March, the hearing being set for 10 May at Chichester Magistrates Court.

The charges were as expected and all three pleaded not guilty. They elected to go for trial by jury and to reserve their defence for then. Meanwhile they were each released on £250 bail. As in the Boy George case, there was a snowball effect: the same day as the three defendants were released, Brian Jones was arrested on charges of possessing hash, cocaine and Methedrine. He too was released on £250 bail.

The Redlands bust trial lasted three days, from 27 to 29 June 1967. Defending counsel for Jagger and Richard was Michael Havers (later Sir Michael, the Attorney General). As his clients had pleaded 'not guilty', Havers had to try and convince the jury that Jagger had got his drugs on the authority of a doctor, even though no written prescription could be produced. In Richard's case, Havers had to show that no marijuana had been smoked on the premises, even though it had been in the possession of certain individuals who were his guests. Robert Fraser had his own counsel who advised him to change his plea to guilty.

The cases against Jagger and Fraser were heard first. Both were found guilty. The judge had directed the jury that the phone call which the defence claimed took place between Jagger and his doctor did not constitute a medical prescription. Sentences were deferred until the case against Keith Richard had been heard.

It was during this part of the proceedings that the full story of the bust came out. The main thrust of the prosecution's case was that Miss X (the worst kept secret in legal history), had been smoking marijuana at Redlands. The press were more interested in the allegation that 'Miss X' had been wearing only a rug when the police arrived, which she deliberately let slip in order to embarrass them. A rumour was also circulating, seemingly at odds with the rug story, that Mick Jagger had been interrupted in the act of devouring a Mars Bar inserted between Miss X's legs.*

But things really started to warm up when Keith Richard got into the witness box and alleged that the *News of the World* had planted Schneidermann in order to get Jagger convicted on drugs charges, forcing him to drop proceedings against the paper. Until then Malcolm Morris, prosecuting counsel, had managed to keep Schneidermann's name out of the case. Presumably he did not want the jury influenced by talk of a drugs dealer, detracting from the far lesser offence of which Richard stood accused. The matter of the 'plant' was not pursued, no proof being offered. In his summing-up, the judge instructed the jury to disregard the evidence of Miss X that she hadn't been smoking marijuana. The unanimous verdict was guilty. Richard was sentenced to a year in prison with £500 costs, Jagger three months and £200 costs, Fraser six months and £200 costs.

The sentences of Jagger and Richard prompted the famous *Times* editorial 'Who Breaks a Butterfly on a Wheel' (1 July 1967), claiming that the sentence of Jagger was a reflection of who he was rather than what he had done. Interestingly. Keith Richard was not mentioned in this attack on social revenge, presumably because it would have diluted the argument – Jagger was only 'involved' with some amphetamine tablets while Richard had been linked to cannabis smoking and was thus less defensible morally. So it was rather ironic that, on appeal Richard's conviction was quashed whereas Jagger's stood, although the sentence was reduced to a conditional discharge.

Was there any truth in Richard's contention that they had been set up by the *News of*

---

* In her autobiography, Marianne Faithfull denies the Mars Bar story – and given what she does own up to, one is inclined to believe that the rumour was simply that.

the World? Following the allegation in court, the paper printed an editorial headlined 'A Monstrous Charge' (2 July). It was emphatic that there was no connection with Schneidermann, but admitted that it did tip off the police after somebody had phoned the paper on Saturday 11 February and then again at 3 a.m. on the Sunday with details of the party. The police moved in around 7.30 that evening. Obviously there must have been collusion; either the police or the mystery voice reported back to the *News of the World* the salient events of the bust so that the paper had its exclusive story ahead of the rest of Fleet Street.

Apparently, some time after the event, Keith Richard concluded that an employee of his had tipped the *News of the World* off about the party. That works as far as it goes, but the paper had reported that 'a famous pop star' and his wife (Mr and Mrs Harrison) had left before the police arrived. There were no minions present at Redlands who could have passed that information back. Indeed it seems that the police had expected Patti Harrison to be one of the three women present, because three policewomen were in on the raid. It is that fact which casts doubt on another theory put forward by ex-Beatles business manager Peter Brown in *The Love You Make*: 'Some newspaper accounts intimated that a famous rock star and his wife were at the house all day, but that the Drug Squad had waited for them to leave before raiding the house. This was assumed to be in deference to Brian Epstein's reputation as well as David Jacobs's expertise as a lawyer.'[6] Apart from the fact that the timing is wrong, how could the police or anyone else know that the Harrisons were going to leave, and what would have happened if they hadn't? Would the police let a headlining raid slip away in order to save the image of the Beatles? Unlikely. As for the expertise of the Beatles' lawyer, the Stones were hardly going to rely on a High Street solicitor should they ever appear in court on any charge, let alone drugs, and the police would know this.

Whoever gave the *News of the World* the tip-off and the follow-up story, must not only have known about the party in advance, but have been there at the time. The hanger-on, Nicky Cramer had his innocence established after a member of the Stones entourage beat him to a pulp, but failed to elicit any confession from him. This brings us back to the mysterious Schneidermann.

Schneidermann was a Canadian who arrived from the West Coast a few weeks before the party, having met Richard in New York several months previously. Apparently he had a number of passports in different names (one being 'English' or 'Britton'), spoke several languages and knew a lot about guns. He may have used the *News of the World*, but he doesn't sound like the average grubby informer out for a quick windfall, particularly as he seems to have had ready access to illicit drugs worth thousands.

Two patently suspicious aspects of the raid were that Schneidermann's briefcase was left untouched by the police and the fact that they let him get away. There was some speculation that he was a CIA agent or something of that ilk. This is unlikely, but for lovers of conspiracy theory, it *is* just possible that Schneidermann was working for the Bureau of Narcotics and Dangerous Drugs in Washington. There is no proof of this theory, merely a hypothesis in the absence of any completely satisfactory explanation of how the bust came about. (A key figure, who could have shed much light on this, refused to give an interview).

From about 1967 onwards, links were established between those police units at Scotland Yard involved in drug arrests and their American counterparts based at the

European office of the Bureau of Narcotics and Dangerous Drugs in Paris. The British police had little experience of dealing with the widespread use of illicit drugs which had developed only very recently. In contrast, their American colleagues were well versed in drug enforcement techniques like entrapment, paying informers in drugs by under-declaring the amount seized and using a system of 'licensed' or 'favoured' dealers who were allowed to deal with impunity in exchange for information.

In 1973, as a direct result of using such methods, officers of the Drug Squad including the chief, Vic Kelaher, and Norman Pilcher, found themselves in court on corruption charges. Back in 1968, it is just possible that Schneidermann was used either to demonstrate the value of these tactics or merely as an act of goodwill between two groups of police engaged in specialist activities in a climate of developing mutual interest.

The Redlands bust was the first in a long-running saga of police v. Rolling Stones cases that (if you include the publicity over Bill Wyman's affair with Mandy Smith) seems never to have ended. Brian Jones was busted by Pilcher on two separate occasions during 1967 and 1968, which did nothing for his disturbed mind. Ronnie Wood was allegedly set up for a cocaine bust on the Netherlands Antilles, but was later released and deported, and Keith Richard, of course, has had any number of run-ins with John Law, the most serious being his 1977 arrest in Toronto – almost ten years to the day after the Redlands bust. Anita Pallenberg was arrested at Toronto airport a few days before the arrest of Richard in his hotel room. At first he faced a charge of being in possession with intent to supply, because of the large amount he was carrying to feed his then enormous habit. Eventually this charge was altered to lesser charges of possession, for which Richard was put on probation and ordered to play a benefit concert for the blind.

The Stones weren't the only victims of media/police collusion in 1967. In San Francisco, the police were out to get the Grateful Dead as much as the London Drug Squad wanted to nail the Stones. On 2 October 1967, acting on a tip-off and with the press primed in advance, eight narcotics officers burst into 710 Ashbury without a warrant and arrested Pigpen, Bob Weir, equipment chief Bob Matthews and managers Rock Scully and Danny Rifkin, on marijuana possession charges. They would have had Jerry Garcia, but somebody in the house had seen him coming up the street, leaned out of the window and waved him away. Next day the band held a press conference and issued the following statement:

> As you know by now, the San Francisco Police Department and State narcotics officers invaded this house on Tuesday for the unpeaceful purpose of arresting ten persons on charges of possession of marijuana. We have invited you back to our 'way-out pad', as the *Chronicle* calls it, to discuss the meaning of this action. The arrests were made under a law that classifies smoking marijuana with murder, rape and armed robbery as a 'felony'. Yet almost anyone who has ever studied marijuana seriously and objectively has agreed that, physically and psychologically, marijuana is the least harmful chemical used for pleasure and life-enhancement. It is particularly less harmful than alcohol. But the law continues to treat marijuana smokers as felons. The president of a company that makes a defective automobile which may lead to thousands of deaths and injuries can face a maximum penalty of a minor fine. A person convicted of

possession of marijuana can be sentenced to life imprisonment. The real danger to society, as well as to thousands of individuals, comes from a law that is so seriously out of touch with reality.

The law creates a mythical danger and calls it a felony. The people who enforce the law use it almost exclusively against the individuals who threaten their ideas of the way people should look and act. The result is a series of lies and myths that prop each other up. Yet all we wish is to be free Americans – endowed with certain inalienable rights – among which, somebody once said, are life, liberty and the pursuit of happiness. Is this so frightening? The Grateful Dead are people engaged in constructive, creative effort in the musical field, and this house is where we work, as well as our residence. Because the police fear and misinterpret us, our effort is now interrupted as we deal with the consequences of a harassing arrest.

The police missed Phil Lesh and Jerry Garcia in 1967, but they caught up with Lesh in January 1973 and Garcia in March 1973 and again in 1984. By then, Garcia was in difficulties with drugs and he was busted on heroin and cocaine charges. He was ordered to attend a drug rehabilitation programme and play some benefit concerts – which he had been doing for years anyway. Talking to *Musician* in 1985, Garcia said 'I got busted under that new thing where they no longer need "probable cause", just this so-called "good faith". That means they can work backwards from what they find.'[7]

Once the police have grabbed one member of a band, others quickly follow -the Stones in 1967-8, the Grateful Dead in 1973, Boy George and friends in 1986. In 1969-70, it was Jefferson Airplane's turn. Jack Casady, the bass player, was first arrested at the Royal Orleans Hotel in 1969 for possessing marijuana. Some months later, other members of the band were caught in a wave of anti-rock hysteria orchestrated by proto-moral majority groups like MOTOREDE – the Movement To Restore Decency. Par for the course was their claim that rock was a communist plot glorifying 'drugs, destructiveness, revolution and sexual promiscuity'.

In May 1970, Marty Balin was arrested backstage at the Minneapolis Auditorium, along with two members of the road crew, on marijuana charges. He was fined $1,000 and given a one-year suspended sentence in the Minnesota Workhouse. The police had no warrant, but the judge refused query of the seizure by Balin's defending counsel. Four weeks later, Paul Kantner was arrested in Honolulu and later convicted of possessing marijuana. Kantner addressed the court: 'I only want to say the verdict and this court is one of the main reasons people have no faith in the government any more.' He then began to argue that the only evidence against him was a marijuana cigarette which vice squad officers *claimed* they saw him smoking at a private party the previous October. At that point his attorney cut him off.

It is the rock star drug arrests that make the headlines; apprehended roadies and road managers are far less newsworthy. However, these people are often the main conduits for drugs to pass between suppliers and musicians. They can be involved in negotiating deals, collecting supplies and making payments (creaming some profit off the top), as well as carrying drugs through customs and border checks. Lawyers who specialize in the music business are forever defending cases involving roadies and offensive weapons or excessive violence. Few of these cases make the news. One exception was in November 1983, when Michael Houchin, a former Stones road manager, was arrested in Hollywood for dealing cocaine and weapons from his house.

Those who supply drugs to musicians in order to bathe in reflected glory, to curry favour or to stay on the payroll, can come unstuck. Liam Kelly, a former roadie with Thin Lizzy, was sent to prison for two years in October 1986 for supplying cocaine to the late Phil Lynott, who died the previous January. In his defence, Kelly said he had switched Lynott to cocaine to get him off heroin. However, the only reason he was in court at all was because he had been informed on by members of Lynott's family. *The London Evening Standard* quoted a 'close friend' as saying: 'We were disgusted with what happened to Phil and took action to stop it happening to someone else.'

A similar defence was used in probably the most publicized of all roadie drug trials, involving John 'Scooter' Herring and the Allman Brothers in 1976. Even without the trial, which eventually helped destroy the band, the Allmans must qualify as one of the most jinxed bands of all time. In 1970, their road manager Twiggs Lydon was up on murder charges. Manager Robert Payne was shot by police in March 1971 and in the same month the whole band was busted in Alabama on drugs charges. Seven months later in October, guitarist Duane Allman was killed in a bike accident in Macon, Georgia. (This was followed by a bizarre damages case in which two women claimed to be Allman's widow.) A year later, on the same stretch of road, Berry Oakley, the bass player, also died in a bike crash. Astonishingly, almost on the same spot where Duane Allman died, drummer Butch Trucks broke his leg in a car crash. In 1975, Gregg Allman's marriage to Cher collapsed in a matter of weeks and guitarist Dickie Betts was arrested on drugs charges.

The balloon went up for Scooter Herring in February 1976, when a pharmacist named Joe Fuchs pleaded guilty to a charge of conspiring to possess cocaine with intent to distribute it, for which he was sentenced to ten years in prison. He named Allman Brothers road manager Scooter Herring as his co-conspirator and struck a deal with the District Attorney that other charges pending against him would be dropped if he co-operated in the case against Herring.

So on 23 June 1976 Scooter Herring appeared before the US District Court in Macon, Georgia, charged on five counts of supplying drugs to Gregg Allman. He was a motor mechanic by trade, but got the nickname Scooter through his acrobatic skills as a child. It was in early 1973 at the garage where he was working that he first met Gregg Allman who had brought his bike in for repair. Said Herring: 'We get to know each other and became good buddies. Our friendship developed and when you get close to someone, you get to know a lot about them.'[8]

At the time, the Allmans were riding high with 'Ramblin' Man' at Number 2 in the singles chart and a Number 1 album, *Brothers and Sisters*. But Herring soon discovered that all the street rumours about Gregg Allman's drug habit were true: the guitarist was doing heroin in a big way. Although he had no formal links with the band during 1973, Herring hung around with Allman, savouring his tenuous hold on the romantic world of rock. He became involved with Allman's drug intake, somehow rationalizing that he would be doing Allman a big favour by getting him interested in drugs other than heroin – mainly cocaine, but also other opiate-type drugs. In retrospect, however, he admitted that he was really looking out for himself. 'There was no recognition or prestige in being a mechanic … I know that maybe I didn't have the right feeling in my heart for Gregg, but it was a good shot to make something of myself.'[9]

If Herring was going to provide Allman with drugs, then he needed a supplier. Joe

Fuchs, a local pharmacist, became the Man. Herring and Fuchs met at the same garage when Fuchs brought in his '68 Corvette. Herring sold him a number that here was once-in-a-lifetime opportunity to help out a famous rock star. Although initially reluctant, Fuchs too become intoxicated with the idea of being associated with the rock business. A deal was struck whereby Herring told Fuchs what drugs were needed, Fuchs supplied the drugs to Herring, who conducted the transaction, keeping a third of the money for himself and handing over the rest to Fuchs.

Top of the shopping list was pure pharmaceutical cocaine, supplied in bottles by Merck Sharp and Dohme at $22.50 an ounce and distinguishable from cut-street cocaine by its sparkling, fluffy appearance. The other drugs listed in the indictment were both powerful narcotic analgesic painkillers: Meperdine (marketed as Demerol) and a chemically similar drug, Anileridine (marketed as Leritine). Both were supplied to Gregg Allman in injectable form.

All pharmacies are required to keep records of controlled drugs ordered and dispensed. Therefore Fuchs had to devise ways of covering any shortages, should the Drugs Inspectorate arrive to conduct an audit of his stocks. In June 1973 Herring and Fuchs faked a burglary at the store, carried out by Herring while Fuchs was on a flying trip. Other shortages were to be accounted for by altering or forging doctors' prescriptions. A week later, Fuchs and Herring went to the house of another intermediary Paul Crawford and sold him one ounce of pure cocaine for $1,200. This was the first of thirty-five separate transactions between then and January 1975 involving the supply of drugs to Gregg Allman, for which he handed over about $10,000.

Once Allman came to know Fuchs, he started bypassing Herring and dealing directly with the pharmacist. Using a prearranged code, Allman would phone Fuchs at his store, Harrison's Pharmacy on Ingleside Avenue in Macon, either to ask him what was available or to order specific items. Allman would then drive to a particular street, Fuchs would follow in his truck and drop the drugs through the car window. No money changed hands – this was still managed by Scooter Herring. Later, at Herring's insistence, the deal reverted to the original arrangement, ostensibly because Allman was consuming too much when he made the collection himself.

It wasn't until the spring of 1974 that Herring was employed to accompany Gregg Allman on his first solo tour, at a time when relationships within the band were very strained, particularly between Allman and guitarist Dickie Betts. By September, Herring was a road manager with the Allmans' organisation and had a one-seventh share in the company which employed him, Great Southern. Other shareholders included the band's office manager Willie Perkins, Phil Walden, Gregg Allman's personal manager and boss of the Allmans' label Capricorn Records, and Bunky Odom, vice president of Phil Walden Associates, the band's management company.

All went well until January 1975, when the Drugs Inspectorate turned up at Harrison's Pharmacy and discovered a number of irregularities in the books. In his trial testimony, the officer who actually conducted the investigation, Ronald Byrd, said that they were acting on an anonymous tip-off that Fuchs was dealing in illegal drugs. So who blew the whistle? This was never established in courts, but at least one prosecution witness had a motive.

Janice Allman had married Gregg in February 1973. An admitted cocaine user herself, she testified against Herring under court immunity about collecting drugs from Fuchs for herself and her husband. It was clear from her testimony that she objected strongly to Herring bringing injectable drugs and needles to the house, and largely blamed Herring for the break-up of their marriage in December 1974 just prior to the exposing of Fuchs' drug activities. She knew that Fuchs and Herring worked together. Obviously if Fuchs went down he would try and take Herring with him, if by doing so he could lighten his sentence. It also transpired that she had discovered that Herring had tampered with her car to allow carbon monoxide fumes to filter through to the driver's seat. This matter was not pursued in court, but would have been reason enough for Janice Allman to have wished Herring behind bars.

There were other wild cards in the pack, like Bobby Wood. At the time of the trial, he was awaiting sentencing for distributing marijuana and like Fuchs, Janice and Gregg Allman, he testified against Herring under an immunity agreement which protected him from any further charges as a result of the trial. In his testimony, Fuchs said that he stopped supplying drugs to Herring in January 1975, when the Drugs Inspectorate came to call. However Wood said that Herring sold him two grams of cocaine from the Great Southern office in August 1975 and that the money had been paid over to Willie Perkins, the office manager. At the time of the transaction, Wood himself was a Great Southern employee, but testified that he was fired in December that year for dealing in cocaine. Despite the twisted logic of such a decision, Wood was unlikely to appeal to any industrial tribunal, so he took his revenge in court.

What it does show is that Herring had sources of drugs other than Fuchs and he may have been using them in addition to Fuchs prior to January 1975. One of these connections could have made the fateful phone call to take Fuchs out of the game. The names of other ex-employees of Great Southern were mentioned in court as drug dealers and the impression was clearly given that although the case focused on just two grams of cocaine plus some painkillers sold to Allman by Herring, there was an awful lot more going on. The Federal Grand Jury hearings which preceded the trial were not just concerned with the activities of a wayward pharmacist and a glory-seeking motor mechanic. This jury had 'been investigating possible local connections with an alleged multi-million-dollar drug ring'.[10] Witnesses had spoken of conspiracy to supply drugs to musicians throughout the Southern States of America. At the end of the Herring trial, Judge Wilbur Owens said to Herring; 'Now frankly, the Court is troubled by your case and all of its many ramifications. Without going into specifics, your case involves other cases. You know that, your lawyer knows it and the Court knows it.'

It took the jury of nine women and three men two hours to find Scooter Herring guilty on all five counts. Four weeks later, Judge Owens sentenced him to the maximum of seventy-five years, but said he would review the sentence in three months. During that period, the police and drug enforcement agencies were going to be seeking Herring's assistance in identifying other dealers. The reviewing of the sentence allowed for a deal to be struck.

The dealer is usually portrayed as the 'evil pusher', while the user is the 'victim'. In this case, however, local public opinion as expressed in the press sided with Herring as the scapegoat who had been forced into supplying drugs by Gregg Allman, the powerful and influential rock star. No doubt then, those who were well disposed towards Scooter Herring would have been pleased with the end of the story. Herring was freed on a bond while appealing against his sentence. Finally, in March 1978, the fifth Circuit Court of Appeal ordered a retrial because of a mistake during the original proceedings by Judge Owens. While the trial was in progress, a front-page story appeared in the *Macon Telegraph* stating that Gregg Allman was being protected by four US Marshals round the clock, because of threats to his life if he took the stand. According to the Court of Appeal, Judge Owens should have examined each juror in the presence of counsel, to determine whether the juror had read the article and whether it had prejudiced him/her against Herring.

After the trial, the Allman Brothers broke up; Allman's testimony against Herring had been the final straw. Dickie Betts formed a band called Great Southern, Allman went solo and the rest formed a fusion band called Sea Level, which Herring was road-managing at the time of the successful appeal.

However, Herring was not yet off the hook; he faced a re-trial. But possibly because he had something to sell, Herring waived his rights to a retrial and instead pleaded guilty to the much less serious charges of possessing cocaine and using a commercial facility, i.e. a telephone, to distribute the drug to Gregg Allman. On 14 August 1979 Herring stood before Judge Wilbur Owens who by then had definitely changed his tune about the relative culpability of Allman and Herring. Originally he had dismissed any notion that Herring was a scapegoat or in the thrall of Gregg Allman. Now he regarded Herring as a malleable underling and described Allman's influence over him as 'compelling, powerful and awful'. This *volte face* proved crucial for Herring in the final sentencing. Initially he was looking to die in prison, now he was down to thirty months in jail and five years on probation.

Reflecting on past events to a local reporter from his home town of Macon, Scooter Herring said with some conviction that he bore Gregg Allman no ill will. He was more concerned about looking after himself and his future: 'Sometimes I feel I'm reverting to the same old ways, but I'm fighting it ... I want to hold my head up and be who I've wanted to be for a very long time.'[11]

Despite all the media attention given to musician drug trials and the amount of public deprecation heaped on the offending star by politicians and others, judges have been singularly reluctant to send rock stars to prison for anything more than token periods. There may be a number of reasons for this attitude. Certainly most judges, having admonished a rock star for reneging on his duty to society's young, do not then want to make him a martyr in their eyes by putting him away. Others, for more laudable motives, make a specific point of not being influenced by public opinion baying for blood, nor do they succumb to the temptation of administering an unnecessary custodial sentence to make a moral point to someone in the public eye. Some, however, do seem to become star-struck when faced with anybody who has a public reputation – and defending counsel play on this.

Dennis Muirhead is a lawyer with a music management business and has a wealth of experience at representing people in the music business including Mick Taylor and Jack Bruce. He cites the case of drummer Brian Davison in 1974. Davison had been one of Britain's premier percussionists during his days with Keith Emerson and the Nice, but drug problems overtook him and by 1974 he was in serious difficulties. At that time he was in another rock trio, Refugee, with Patrick Moraz (later in Yes) and his bass-playing partner from Nice days, Lee Jackson. Davison was caught with a pound of cocaine – more than enough for a charge of possession with intent to supply and an almost certain jail sentence. Character witnesses included top rock journalist Chris Welch, the conductor Joseph Eger and the late Tony Stratton-Smith, boss of Refugee's record company Charisma. Albums were flashed around with the drummer's name and face on them and much to everyone's amazement, Davison kept his freedom.[12]

John Phillips of the Mamas and Papas also had a narrow escape. Phillips was a multi-drug user for several years and became a significant dealer in his own right to pay for it all, mainly cocaine, but also many thousands of barbiturates, tranquillisers, narcotic painkillers and methaqualone. Like switching on a light bulb Phillips turned anti-drug crusader as soon as the Drug Enforcement Agency caught up with him. Together with his daughter Mackenzie, who also had a serious habit, they turned up on every TV chat show, blaming everything on drugs. It paid dividends. Instead of eight years, he got thirty days, plus five years' probation and a promise to do 250 hours of anti-drug campaigning in the following year. Hugh Cornwell of the Stranglers was not so lucky – he wasn't nearly so famous, didn't do any breast-beating chat shows or have big guns to speak up for him to dazzle the bench.

Travelling back from a Stranglers gig in Cardiff in November 1979, Cornwell was stopped by a routine police traffic check on Hammersmith Broadway in West London at about 3 a.m. To the police, the girls travelling with Hugh and Paul Loasby looked under-age. .All the occupants were searched and from Hugh the police extracted a gram and a half of cocaine, 90 milligrams of heroin (about one syringe-full), half an ounce of hash and some marijuana. The cocaine was in two separate packets and taken with the other drugs made a total of five counts of possession. Paul Loasby was charged with possessing fifteen milligrammes of coke, a minute amount.

The case was heard at West London Magistrates' Court in January 1980. Both men pleaded guilty and the respective defending counsels went on at length about their previous clean record and impeccable behaviour. The fact that Hugh Cornwell has a degree in biochemistry was mentioned. Unfortunately all this backfired, as the magistrate remarked, 'All this good character stuff makes your behaviour more despicable. You should have known better if you are that intelligent.' Apparently this particular magistrate was usually quite fair, but when a drugs case came before him, something snapped. Loasby got two weeks for an amount of cocaine you could hardly get under your fingernail while Cornwell got two months in Pentonville, of which he served six weeks, fourteen days longer than John Phillips.

Cornwell wrote up his jail experiences in *Inside Information*, published by the Stranglers Information Service in 1980. His account of the stupidities and injustices inherent in the prison system is extremely sharp-witted. The magistrate made it clear that he was out to make an example of Cornwell – 'Young people today look to you for guidance' were his exact words. And Hugh Cornwell's conclusions? 'If they wanted to teach me a lesson by sending me down, they've failed. They ended up spending £140 a week keeping me in there, whereas they could have made me pay them money which would have crippled me a lot more. Actually, you could even say I benefited from it publicity-wise.'[13] In fact, in the next decade, rather than being bad for business, public revelations about drug use almost became part of the marketing.

11 ONE STEP OVER THE LINE

Name me one rock group that doesn't have in its repertoire hymns to LSD and marijuana.

Timothy Leary

I ask Congress to give thoughtful consideration to legislation entitled appropriately, the Banana and Other Odd Fruit Disclosure and Reporting Act of 1967. The target is those banana-smoking beatniks who seek a make-believe land ... as it is described in the peel puffers' secret psychedelic marching song 'Puff, the Magic Dragon'.

Congressman Thompson of New Jersey, Congressional Record *19.4.1967*

Between July 1969 and July 1971, rock suffered its first and arguably most significant losses to drugs. Barbiturates are potentially the most lethal of all mood-altering drugs in both overdose (particularly when mixed with alcohol) and withdrawal (during which users have died of convulsions). It was these drugs that were primarily implicated in the deaths of Brian Jones (3 July 1969), Al Wilson of Canned Heat (13 September 1970) and Jimi Hendrix (18 September 1970).

A few weeks after Hendrix died, Janis Joplin overdosed on heroin mixed with Tequila and Valium. Heroin and booze were also possibly implicated in the most mysterious of all rock deaths, Jim Morrison's on 3 July 1971. Only his wife Pamela and an unidentified doctor saw the body before it was buried in a Paris cemetery. Officially, Morrison died of a heart attack in his bath, retrieval of the body from a bath could also suggest an attempt to revive him from an overdose. Morrison's drinking and to a lesser extent his drug use were legendary. In the event Pamela Morrison took the secret to her grave. On 24 April 1975, she died of an overdose of heroin.

Together, this spate of major rock deaths, the musician-inspired 'speed kills' campaign, the anti-rock publicity of the post-Altamont period and the rising levels of adolescent drug use fed conveniently into a systematic attempt by the US government to generate public hysteria over heroin. In his twilight years, Anslinger was no doubt proud of his legacy. The impetus for the campaign came from Nelson Rockefeller, Governor of New York State.

At the 1964 Republican convention, Rockefeller was ditched in favour of Barry Goldwater. Thereafter, Rockefeller latched on to the drug issue as a means of toughening up his law-and-order image with Republican hardliners, while at the same time appealing to moderates by promising a reduction in street crime. His campaign got under way in 1966 and from then till 1973, in the time-honoured tradition of American drug law enforcement, 'the size of the addict population proved to be conveniently flexible.'[1] In New York, the figure swung between 25,000 and 200,000, depending on whether Rockefeller was trying to justify more judges or demonstrating that he had the 'heroin disease' under control. Rockefeller's 'finest hour' came in 1973, with the enactment of the most draconian drug laws ever passed in America. These laws 'made it mandatory that anyone convicted of selling or possessing more than a fraction of an ounce of heroin (or even amphetamine or LSD), would be imprisoned for life'.[2] Life was also mandatory for anyone ingesting a 'hard drug' up to twenty-four hours before committing any one of a whole list of (mainly petty) crimes. The laws proved unworkable and a later evaluation proved that they had virtually no impact in reducing either the level of drug use or crime in New York,[3] but as a political exercise to show that Rockefeller was 'tough on drugs' they served their purpose: under Nixon he became Vice President of the United States. While Rockefeller was preparing the groundwork for his reign of terror against users in New York, the Bureau of Narcotics was undergoing a reorganization. By amalgamating other drug agencies, including Anslinger's office, a Bureau of Narcotics and Dangerous Drugs (BNDD) was created in 1968. That drugs had become a law-and-order issue rather than one focused on revenue, was emphasized by the transferring of responsibility from the Treasury to the Justice Department. Also, much to the chagrin of the customs service, the BNDD was allowed to operate overseas: it was Bureau agents who broke up the 'French Connection' – the Far East-Marseilles-New York trafficking route for heroin.

Under its new director James Ingersoll, the Bureau grew dramatically in strength. Prior to 1968, there were never more than 330 agents on the payroll nor a budget greater than $3 million. By 1971, 1,500 agents were being paid out of a budget in excess of $43 million. Like Rockefeller, Ingersoll had a vested interest in the public regarding drugs as 'public enemy number one' and this inevitably meant massaging the heroin addiction figures upwards. An astonishing jump in the national statistics from 69,000 in 1969 to 560,000 in 1971 was achieved by the simple but fraudulent expedient of calculating a notional figure of those users who did *not* come forward for treatment and presenting this as an accurate count of the numbers of addicts. Congress swallowed it whole and agreed the appropriations.

The third and most crucial factor in the equation was President Richard Nixon. The anti-communist platform on which he had built his reputation in the fifties was on the wane, while much unwelcome attention was being focused on issues like civil rights and the Vietnam War. Once Nixon received the Republican nomination for President in 1968, he took his cue from Rockefeller and made the 'war against drugs' the key issue on which to fight the election. But what started out as a law-and-order electioneering strategy become something very different once Nixon took office in 1969. Gradually, under the guise of an unimpeachable battle against a social evil, the White House laid the foundations for acceptance by the people of a new all-powerful internal enforcement agency operating almost entirely outside the constitution. This evolved into the Office of Drug Abuse Law Enforcement (ODALE), established by Nixon in January 1972 without consideration or approval by Congress. The hope was that nobody would dare oppose Nixon for fear of being branded 'soft on drugs', an act of political suicide for any politician anywhere in the world. ODALE and BNDD were both subsumed in July 1973 in a new superagency, the Drug Enforcement Administration, which remains the major American agency for drugs law enforcement both at home and abroad. Probably only Watergate prevented the DEA becoming Nixon's personal shock troops. As soon as he was installed in the White House, Nixon immediately sought the help of the media in putting his message across, especially to young people. A special meeting was called of the country's leading disc jockeys; among those who attended were Murray the K and Cousin Brucie Morrow. The reception of some DJs was decidedly lukewarm, seriously doubting whether they could exert any influence over young people other than perhaps their listening habits. Others, however, like Bruce Morrow, became ardent enthusiasts. He began working with the National Institute of Mental Health, touring around schools to speak out against drugs. WWRL, a black soul station in New York, flooded Harlem with 'Help a Junkie – Bust a Pusher' badges; WKYC in Cleveland went on the air with a recorded suicide note from a nineteen-year-old addict, which WFMJ in Youngstown, Ohio, distributed around the schools. and there were similar radio campaigns from coast to coast. However, the Administration had been putting most of its anti-drug campaigning efforts into television advertising, slots in chat shows, etc. This upset the National Association of FM Broadcasters, who wrote complaining to the President that as broadcasters of rock music, FM radio stations could play a particular role in spreading the anti-drug message.

What happened next, began a process of claim and counter-claim which rumbled through the US justice system for three years. The Federal Communications Commission (FCC) is the government's broadcasting licensing body. On the 10 September 1970, FCC commissioner Robert Lee sent a note to Senator Frank Moss with a list of songs 'that would appear to be eulogizing the use of narcotics'. The list was apparently produced by an advertising agency and 'does not have any government sanction'. The list of songs was as follows:

'Happiness is a Warm Gun'	Beatles
'Everybody's Got Something to Hide Except Me and My Monkey'	Beatles
'With a Little Help from My Friends'	Beatles
'Cold Turkey'	Plastic Ono Band
'19th Nervous Breakdown'	Rolling Stones
'Let's Spend the Night Together'	Rolling Stones
'Don't Bogart That Joint'	Fraternity of Man
'White Rabbit'	Jefferson Airplane
'The Acid Queen'	Who
'Mr Tambourine Man'	Byrds
'Rainy Day Women'	Bob Dylan

'Cocaine Blues'	Johnny Cash
'The Trip'	Donovan
'Cloud Nine'	Temptations
'I Like Marijuana'	David Peel and the Lower East Side
'The Alphabet Song'	David Peel and the Lower East Side
'Walking in Space'	cast of *Hair*
'Heroin'	Velvet Underground

Each song title was accompanied by some indication of how successful the song had been, plus sample lyrics. It is a curious list, to say the least ranging from the obvious pro-drug material like David Peel's songs and 'The Trip' by Donovan, to the equally obvious anti-drug songs like 'Cocaine Blues' and 'Cold Turkey'. Note, too, the legalistic and pejorative use of the term 'narcotics' in Lee's note to Senator Moss referring in part to drugs which have no narcotic action.

Four days later, Vice President Spiro Agnew, speaking at a Republican dinner in Las Vegas, criticized rock music lyrics for glamorizing and promoting drug use, citing all the songs from the list which had 'no government sanction'. In what seemed like an answer to the FM Broadcasters' complaint, Agnew went on to suggest that television had a far greater role in drug reform than radio could ever have. Perhaps too, the powerful pharmaceutical industry lobby had been at work, as the speech coincided with the leaking of new National Association of Broadcasting guidelines aimed at curbing the exaggerated claims of non-prescription drug advertisements.

Surprisingly, the initial counterblast to Agnew's speech came not from the radio bosses, but from a dissenting voice within the FCC itself In a speech before foreign service officers of the US Information Service, Commissioner Nick Johnson cited several other songs like 'Amphetamine Annie' by Canned Heat and 'The Pusher' by Steppenwolf as examples of anti-drug messages in rock. He went on to attack television for promoting alcohol and prescription drug misuse and further noted that Agnew refrained from attacking those whose support was important at election time, like the beverage alcohol industry and other large corporations like Ford and TWA who were at the time using the imagery of illegal drugs in their advertising.[4] Finally, Johnson rounded on the tobacco industry: 'There are a lot of kids who are being exposed to drugs because of the deliberate efforts of greedy immoral television and tobacco company executives to hook 'em on nicotine – executives who are revered as the pillars of our society and whose activities are sanctioned by the Federal Government – than there are those who get pot "with a little help from their friends".'[5]

The presidential campaign moved up a gear when seventy radio station owners and managers were called to the White House on 14 October 1970 for a carefully stage-managed conference 'to urge increased drug education programming and to curb pro-drug music and jargon of disc jockeys'.[6] To add weight to the conference, Dean Burch chairman of the FCC, agreed to speak. Burch opened the proceedings by suggesting the FCC would look favourably on licensees who provided more airtime for anti-drug commercials. Nothing was said about the FCC's attitude towards those it felt were promoting drug use by playing certain records. For the rest of the day, the station managers were treated to the same show put on for the TV producers six months earlier – shock films, sniffer-dog demonstrations and a display of law enforcement techniques. As before, John Ehrlichman, presidential adviser on domestic affairs, announced dramatically at lunchtime that the dogs had actually discovered some marijuana during the demonstration. And again as before, Nixon addressed the meeting, not as part of the officially announced programme, but as if it was an eleventh-hour decision on the part of the President himself to grant the station bosses a special audience to emphasize the importance of his mission. Said Nixon (in apparent contradiction of his Vice President), 'No one is in a better position than you to warn our youth constantly against the dangers of drugs.'[7]

Nixon's Presidential adviser on Federal law enforcement and internal security, Egil Krogh, had told Nixon that there would be no press coverage of his remarks to the conference. However, *Billboard* magazine reported that Nixon had urged the broadcasters to screen the lyrics of all rock records to ensure that no songs favourable to drug use were given air time.[8] In the light of subsequent events, it was highly significant that Nixon should add that although the government (through the FCC) were the broadcasting licensers, it would never become involved in the programming content of a station.

The next step in the 'war' against drugs and rock came from within the music business itself. Early in November, Mike Curb, President of MGM Records, announced that eighteen allegedly drug-orientated bands were being dropped by the label. 'I'm not looking to go on a witchhunt,' said Curb, 'and we are not asking any acts to roll up their sleeves [but] MGM will not be used to further the use of drugs.' Curb was also seeking the support of broadcasters to ban songs with drug-related lyrics. Nixon praised Curb's actions, as did some record-company bosses. Others were more sceptical of Curb's motives: Gil Friesen, Vice President at A&M, and Columbia Records boss Clive Davis both accused Curb of exploiting recent rock-star deaths and taking a 'grandstand play', as Davis put it, to rid MGM of unprofitable acts. And there is a deal of substance to this allegation.

Back in the late sixties, MGM tried to cash in on the San Francisco sound by trying to hype Boston as the new rock capital of America. They spent around $4m launching the 'Bosstown Sound' with a bunch of no-hopers like Beacon St Union, Chameleon Church, Orpheus, Puff, Kangaroo and the marginally better Ultimate Spinach. The project was a disaster; MGM sacked the whole A&R department and brought in Mike Curb to try and salvage something from the mess. Curb was in favour of a new breed of record company for the seventies. Rock was getting a bad name after the 'anything goes' sixties and many of the true company hedonists of that period found themselves on the streets. Too many people were stoned and self-absorbed and spending company money as their own. Curb's move against drugs was thus partly symbolic of a new mood of austerity within the business which rebelled against excess and over-indulgence. MGM lost a reported $18 million in 1968-9: Curb's job was to put that right. Eric Burdon was one MGM artist who was not dropped, despite the release of drug-related songs like 'Girl from Sandoz' and 'San Francisco Nights'. Truth was, Burdon was still a good earner for MGM and his retention is perhaps the best indicator that Curb's motives were financial rather than moral. Eric, on the other hand, was supposed to be somewhat insulted that he was not considered druggy enough to be dropped. Burdon eventually did leave MGM which became a label for good, clean family acts like the Cowsills and the Osmonds. Yet despite paring down the roster of artists, the company barely broke even in 1970 and 1971. Curb was the last President of MGM before it was sold to Polygram. Quite possibly, he had one eye on his political career in supporting Nixon's drug campaign: when he finally left MGM in 1973 he became Reagan's right-hand man in California, as Lieutenant Governor of the State.

As well as criticizing Mike Curb, Clive Davis led a spirited defence of the music industry, flatly denying that rock music encouraged drug-taking: 'Music is a reflection of a culture – a footnote to the events within a society.'[9] He was supported in this view by Dr David Smith, medical director of the Haight-Ashbury clinic, who explained in a *Billboard* article how much rock bands had done to raise finds for his clinic, and then went on to say: 'I consider the current attack on youth culture and rock lyrics as not being an expression of concern over the tremendous problem of drug abuse [but] a political tactic, playing off the hysteria of the dominant culture in this area.'[10]

But the White House was not going to be diverted from its course by minor inconveniences such as the total lack of empirical evidence of a causal link between rock music and drug-taking. Nixon's special pleading to the radio station owners and the presence of the FCC Chairman at the same meeting, were the warning lights that sooner or later the question of stations playing 'drug songs' would become a licensing issue.

Sure enough, on 5 April 1971 the FCC issued a Public Notice which it claimed resulted from the receipt of a 'number of complaints' about the lyrics of some records being played on the radio. The FCC required stations to pre-screen all records before playing them on the air, work out what the lyrics meant and determine whether or not it would be in the 'public interest' to play the record. There was no further explanation of phrases like 'language tending to promote or glorify' drug use, nor was it at all clear how far stations should go in making 'reasonable efforts' to determine lyrics and their meaning. The sting in the tail, however, was unmistakable. Failure to adhere to these nebulous, ill-defined guidelines, would 'raise serious questions as to whether continued operation of the station is in the public interest'. So much for presidential reassurances about non-interference. One has only to remember the list of songs sent by the FCC Commissioner to Senator Moss, to realize that the FCC had a very clear idea as to which songs it regarded as unacceptable (i.e. *any* song that mentioned drugs). However, it saw fit not to relay this to those who depended on FCC licences for their livelihood.

There were many appeals for the FCC to reconsider its position and on 16 April the Commission issued what it called a Memorandum Opinion and Order. The FCC reiterated that it was not trying to censor radio playlists, merely that station owners should know whether or not any song tended to glorify drug use and if it did, make a decision against playing it. Again, requests that licensees should act 'reasonably' and in 'good faith' went unexplained.

Attached to the original Public Notice in March, came a highly publicized minority statement by Commissioner Nick Johnson, who had previously attacked Vice President Agnew. Johnson called the FCC Notice 'a brazen censorship move' which breached the First Amendment of the Constitution on Freedom of Speech and threatened the livelihood of radio station employees. He pointed to all the songs which glamorize drinking and again emphasized the heavy advertising of non-prescription drugs on television. In all this, Johnson saw a thinly veiled attempt by the Nixon Administration to attack the anti-establishment stance of American youth culture through its music and divert attention away from the real social evils of the day – racial prejudice, unemployment, poverty, urban decay, the Vietnam War and so on. He cogently argued that to expect licensees accurately to decipher which songs were pro- or anti-drug (or neutral), was ridiculous, particularly as the FCC refused to define its terms sufficiently. He made the obvious deduction that no licensee was going to risk getting it wrong, which meant that any drug song was likely to be banned from the airwaves; by any definition this was censorship. Undeterred, the FCC issued a second memorandum on 18 August 1971 refusing to clarify previous statements on the basis that a fuller explanation 'would not appear to be useful'.

How did the music industry itself react to the rubics from the FCC? As *Rolling Stone* succinctly put it, 'Rock stations, AM and FM are scared shitless.'[11] One of the first songs to suffer was Brewer and Shipley's 'One Toke over the Line'. Jeff Kaye, programme director of WKBW in Buffalo, told *Rolling Stone*, 'I frankly didn't know what "toke" was. So we did a street survey and 90% of the kids said it had to do with marijuana.' So just as the song was beginning to climb the charts, it was dropped by WKBW and several other Top 40 stations along with 'White Rabbit', 'DOA' (Bloodrock), 'Monkey Man' (Stones) and 'Eight Miles High' (Byrds). WDAS-FM in Philadelphia also reacted swiftly by dropping 'I am the Walrus', 'Let It Bleed', 'One Toke over the Line', 'Small Circle of Friends' and 'Needle and Spoon' (Savoy Brown). A major row broke out at WDAS-FM. One D,. Steve Leon, defied the order and played a number of drug songs on a particular show. His brother-in-law, Station Manager Robert Klein pulled the plug on him. Leon stormed into his office, dangled his privates in Klein's face, and got fired.

By not giving clear guidance the FCC were in fact playing a very clever game which attacked rock music in general, not just drug songs, because of the very subjective nature of song lyrics. As Commissioner Johnson predicted, no station boss was going to take chances with the station's licence. Therefore any song, whether containing intentional drug references or not, was liable to be axed. A song with the word 'high' or 'trip' in it, was an obvious target, station managers relied heavily on second-hand knowledge of drug slang to make decisions on records where they themselves were often completely ignorant. One owner banned *all* Bob Dylan songs because he couldn't understand any of the lyrics, and there were demands that lyric sheets be included in every album.

The FCC also relied on the fact that should any station take the FCC to court, even if the station won, it could be crippled by legal costs, absence of staff while giving evidence, and so on. However, a number of stations and individual DJs did decide to pursue the matter through the courts, represented free of charge by an ex-aide of Commissioner Johnson, Tracy Western. She declared to *Rolling Stone*: 'This is an insidious and underhand form of censorship, because the FCC has not had to guts to come out and say what they really mean. They are trying to scare private stations into doing censorship themselves and avoid the rap.'[12]

From the US District Court, the petitioners went to the Court of Appeal in March 1972. They accused the FCC of devising a policy that was deliberately vague and unconstitutional. Furthermore, based on affidavits received from many stations, they set out to prove that the policy was unworkable. Specifically they stated:

1. With most stations having libraries of up to 7,000 albums and receiving around 200 new albums a week, it was impossible to expect DJs to listen to every lyric on every record before playing it.
2. The lyrics of many modern songs were indecipherable.
3. Where the lyrics could be understood or were printed, there was still the job of determining meaning.
4. Having done that, the licensees still had to decide whether or not the

lyric actually promoted or glorified drug use.

The petitioners also asked the Court of Appeal to rule on the FCC's refusal to adjudge whether or not the uncensored musical programming of Yale Broadcasting Station, WYBC, would pass muster with the Commission. The station had actually asked the FCC to check its playlist, as a way of forcing it to issue specific instructions, rather than vaguely worded notices.

In January 1973, a three-judge panel upheld the FCC policy of requiring licensees to screen lyrics prior to broadcast and threw out any claims that the wording was vague and an infringement of free speech. The Court said the first Public Notice was confusing, but ruled that the follow up Memorandum clarified the issue. The Court was of the opinion that the FCC were merely requesting licensees to be aware of the drug situation and know what they were putting on air and could see no threat, implicit or explicit, not to renew licences. They further made the point that if a lyric was completely indecipherable, it was largely irrelevant as to its subject matter and would therefore fall outside the Commission's ambit. All that was required of a licensee was that he should know what he was allowing to be broadcast.

However, the story did not end there; while Tracy Western was planning an appeal to the Supreme Court, the Chief Appeal Court Judge, David L. Bazelon, in an unprecedented action, issued a warning, calling into question the legitimacy of the FCC policy on drug lyrics . The judge wanted the case reheard by the full nine-member Appeal Court, saying that the case raised many questions about censorship and possible political pressure on broadcasters. He disagreed with his fellow jurists that there was no implicit threat in the FCC pronouncements and felt particularly strongly that the court had dismissed the fears of broadcasters simply because nobody had yet lost their licence over the issue. Judge Bazelon went public with his views after failing to secure another hearing.

The broadcasters used Judge Bazelon's published opinions in their own submission to the Supreme Court in May 1973, that FCC policy contravened the First Amendment of the American Constitution. However, in a seven to two vote the following October, the Supreme Court refused to review FCC policy on drug lyrics. Of the two dissenting votes, Judge Douglas was particularly critical of the majority verdict:

> 'The Government cannot, consistent with the First Amendment, require a broadcaster to censor its music any more than it can require a newspaper to censor the stories of its reporters. Under our system the government is not to decide what messages. spoken or in music, are of the proper "social value" to reach the people.'[13]

FCC policy on rock and drug songs was based on the generally accepted premise that listening to such songs directly affects the decision of young people to use illegal drugs. What about songs like 'Lucy in the Sky with Diamonds' or 'Purple Haze'? Surely this is all the proof that is required to demonstrate the role of idolized pop stars in glorifying and encouraging teenage drug abuse. Certainly the argument seems very persuasive. Here you have the world's most popular rock musicians singing favourably, it seems, about the psychedelic experience at a time of increasing drug use among those most heavily committed to rock music.

But this causal link has yet to be established, something neither the White House nor the FCC attempted, presumably because the readiness of the public to assume such a link existed was all that was required for the Government's political purposes. In fact, a number of independent studies have been carried out and they all come to the same conclusion, that there is no empirical evidence to indicate that a pro-drug message will promote drug use among those who hear it.[14] If any link does exist it is probably symbiotic rather than causal, and even then it is probable confined to situations where the social environment is an important part of the drug experience, such as in the smoking of marijuana.

In 1977-8, a study was conducted to discover the facts about the 'Woodstock Generation's' drug use ten years previously. Forty-three per cent of the 1,000-person sample believed that much of the music of the sixties could only really be understood by those who had gone through the drug experience. The majority stated that their initial marijuana cigarette had been in the college dorm with a group of friends, with Dylan or Led Zeppelin playing in the background.[15]

Sociologist John Auld has tried to explain the interaction between music and drugs in this very common type of social setting. He has described how the suspension of normal communication in marijuana-smoking groups together with the redirection of attention to expected changes of mood, creates a 'space' for introspective concentration on the music that would otherwise be regarded as bad manners. In return, the music provided a focus and rationale for such introspection. The smoker is thus saved the embarrassment of sitting in strained silence with a group of other smokers waiting for something to happen.

As I stated earlier, marijuana smoking does appear to be a learned behaviour; among young smokers in any given group, the majority will be uncertain as to how they are supposed to react or how they appear to the supposedly 'drug-sharpened' perceptions of their friends. In this scenario, the relationship between drugs and music is symbiotic – interdependent elements giving the listener-user 'permission' to exist outside normal goal-orientated behaviour and thus the normal social pressures. And of course the music could be entirely instrumental or with minimum lyrical content or with lyrics which have nothing to do with drugs. Furthermore, in a truly symbiotic relationship, one could equally argue that drug-taking encourages people to listen to rock music!

Another fault in the anti-rock argument was the assumption that all rock songs about drugs project a favourable image, a point raised by Commissioner Johnson and others in defence of the industry.

A study conducted in 1972[16] examined the lyrics of several songs and classified them as pro, anti, descriptive or conjectural. This last meant that there were no explicit drug references, but interpretations had been imposed on the song (e.g. 'Lucy in the Sky with Diamonds'). (There were also categories for 'Alcohol' and 'Drugs' – not included here.) The results were as follows:

	Pro	Anti	Descriptive	Conjectural
Marijuana	43	7	29	21
Heroin	0	67	23	10
Cocaine	11	50	35	4
LSD	16	16	34	33
Amphetamines	1	4	3	1

What the lyrics of many of these songs showed was that they reflected the personal experiences of the singer whose opinions about drugs were not necessarily consistent. Country Joe McDonald, for example. could write songs like 'Bass Strings' which was obviously favourable to LSD, but also 'Here we Go Again' with the lines, 'Crystal got my woman/ dope's driving her insane/she used to be so pretty/Now she can't remember her name.'

Dion, who had a string of hits in the sixties including 'Runaround Sue' and 'The Wanderer' acquired a bad drug habit as his career began to decline. Coming out the other side he found religion and recorded 'Your Own Backyard', probably the most personal and straightforward song about drug problems ever released:

> *Since I've been straight*
> *I haven't been in my cups*
> *I'm not shooting downs*
> *I'm not using ups*
> *You know I'm still crazy as a loon*
> *Even though I don't run out and cop a spoon*
> *Thank the Lord I've had enough.*

Songs like this, Neil Young's 'Needle and the Damage Done' or James Brown's 'Heroin' are often meant to serve as anti-drug warnings as well as personal statements. The same applies to the almost universal anti-crack sentiments expressed in rap songs, discussed more fully in Chapter 13. All that can be said about them is that they prove the existence of anti-drug songs in popular music. There is no evidence whatsoever that they are any more effective in warning young people off drugs than pro-drug songs are in encouraging experimentation.[17] The truth is that no form of drug education. be it pop song, TV advertisement, poster campaign, shock film or pure information-giving, has ever been shown to be more or less effective in preventing drug misuse than any other. Take the shock film for example, much-loved by drug squad officers going into schools: those who will be genuinely shocked probably wouldn't try drugs anyway, while for some kids the dangers involved in drug-taking are precisely what makes it attractive. And for those who are tempted but put off by seeing a film, how much impact does it have three weeks later? How many people give up smoking for good after seeing an isolated documentary about lung cancer?

The issue of whether rock songs encourage drug-taking should be dead and buried. However, the emergence in the 1980s of 'moral-majority' style anti-drug parent groups in America has brought the whole debate back on to centre stage.[18] The National Federation of Parents for Drug Free Life aimed to force record companies to print all song lyrics on the record sleeves 'so parents will know the glamorization of the drug culture that some music represents'. The American Parents Music Resource Centre wants to 'clamp down on subversive pop'. In support of their crusade, they have used a paper called 'The Hurried Child' by David Elkind, a professor of child studies at Tufts University, Massachussetts. The following interpretations are seriously proposed by Professor Elkind:

> 'Hey Jude':
> Jude is the Judas who betrayed Christ under the guise of friendship. Heroin at first seems a friend until it betrays the user. In McCartney's

song, 'let her into your heart' means the drug.

'Bridge Over Troubled Waters':
(Elkind claimed that in a survey of teenagers, 15% thought the narrator was a drug pusher.) Silver girl is slang for the hypodermic and the line 'your time has come to shine' clearly suggests a drug trip. 'If you need a friend/I am sailing just behind', indicates that the pusher is always there when another fix is needed. These are only more extreme examples of what is still a generally accepted viewpoint.[19]

Most of the more recent furore over song lyrics have centred on the colourful, if rather limited expletives of rap and many discs now carry warning labels about lyrics – ensuring that any kid (who has to be over 18 in some US states and with some record retail outlets) wanting to ruminate over the linguistic possibilities of 'mothafucka' knows exactly which records to buy.

However, the 'drug song' controversy won't lie down. In 1992, avowed ecstasy champions The Shamen released 'Ebeneezer Goode' ostensibly about a guy who is the life and soul of the party, but with the less than subtle background refrain 'E's are Good, E's are Good'. It went to Number One in the Radio One charts nicely coinciding with the Radio One 'Drug Alert' campaign warning about the dangers of dance drugs. To her unprecedented credit, Auntie Beeb had obviously had a dose of the hug drug herself, because a spokesperson fully acknowledged the apparent paradox *and* the fact that the Corporation was fully aware of the 'double meaning' of the song, but decided not to ban it because this would 'fall too much into the category of preaching', (*Sunday Telegraph* 6th September 1992). Capital Radio, London's commercial rival to Radio One, wanted both its cake and the opportunity to eat it. The song was put on the station B list and played infrequently because as programme director Richard Park explained to the *Telegraph*, 'We appreciate with this drug that there is a great worry and that there have been deaths'. None of which stopped the station sponsoring a night at the Hippodrome club in the West End boasting as its headline artists for the evening – The Shamen.

Three years later, *The Daily Mirror* (20th September 1995) among others, took Jarvis Cocker to task for Pulp's 'Sorted for E's and Whizz', not so much because of the song – which if you read the lyrics also printed in the paper, was actually an anti-drug song – with lines like, 'I seem to have left an important part of my brain/ Somewhere in a field in Hampshire', but because of the small line drawings on the sleeve showing how to fold a wrap of amphetamine, dubbed 'a DIY guide for hiding illegal drugs'.

The fact that there was a three year gap between these two examples and none since, in an era of rampant drug experimentation by young people points up the blindingly obvious fact that most rave music, in whose hearing much current drug use takes place, is instrumental with no lyrical content whatsoever.

This of course, has not prevented the UK government being at odds with itself over the impact of song lyrics on the drug behaviour of young people. The UK drug czar Keith Hellawell (just before he got the job) believed that pop stars' 'obscene lionising' of drugs and the songs they wrote about them exerted 'a subliminal drip on young people's culture'. (*The Independent* 7 July 1997). Yet it was the government's own advisory committee on drugs, the ACMD which reports directly to the Home Office, which recognised the redundancy of the argument that tries to indict drug songs as exerting a baleful influence on young people. In its 1998 report, *Drugs and the Environment*, which attempted to look beyond drugs and individual pathology to the wider circumstances of drug use in society including the influence of popular culture, wisely concluded, '…the lyrics themselves are not, we suggest, something about which we need to be very concerned' and that 'rather than simply deplore this (youth) culture which every succeeding generation is tempted to do, we believe that it should be used as a resource for drug prevention.' (p74).

But still hope springs eternal that doe-eyed impressionable youngsters, Ovaltine to hand as they play Mega Mass Homicide 2 on the PC, might just listen to the lilting words of a song and refrain from evil deeds. Or so Home Office minister George Howarth must have thought when praising the Verve single, 'The Drugs Don't Work' saying it was an example of 'anti-drug messages working and being popular', (*Evening Standard* 2nd June 1998), only to be contradicted by Deputy anti-drugs coordinator Mike Trace, with bags of experience in the drugs field, who quite rightly said the government would look 'silly' if it thought that pop songs had any role to play in drugs strategy.[*]

In the final analysis, of course, it's all in the ears of the listener. Perhaps the best example of that comes from the pages of America's bible of the drug subculture *High Times*. The author of an article in the August 1982 issue was at a party where some premium-grade marijuana was being passed around and the subject of 'great songs of the dope culture' came up. The question was posed: 'What is the ultimate dope song, the single song that best captures the spirit and the soul of the smoker?' The list of songs to choose from could be long indeed, but the author finally picked on a song which has no drug references in it whatsoever. He cast his mind back to a marijuana 'safe house' in Greenwich Village, where people could smoke the finest Colombian Gold. The proprietor of this 'den' played one song over and over again until the grooves wore out and an assistant was sent to buy another copy. The song was an old Elmore James number made famous by Eric Clapton called 'Key to the Highway'. The author, pseudonamed 'K', was enamoured of this song not for any super subliminal messages about the drugs experience, but because 'that song has an undeniable appeal to a certain type of personality attracted to outlaw, adventurist intrigue … the true all-time inside smuggler song. What it's really about is moving. It's a classic road song. A driving song. A-driving-long-distances-for-forty-eight-hours-with-a-truck-full-of-trouble-if-you're-ever-stopped song. Majestic.'

---

[*] This one less than most, because the non-working drugs in this case were anti-cancer drugs. The song tells of their failure to help Ashcroft's father overcome the disease – nothing to do with drug abuse.

12   REDDER THAN RED

Whereas jazz and rock often reflect an amphetamine frenzy reggae tunes in to the slowness of ganja.

New Statesman, *8 July 1977*

...you can dance with ganja rock/grab your chance with ganja rock/jump and prance with ganja rock...

'Ganja Rock', Benjamin Zephaniah

The significance of ganja in Jamaica is not simply a matter of the massive financial worth of the crop. It is as much a question of who controls that money and what cultural significance the plant possesses on the island.

Tim Maylon, Big Deal: The Politics of the Illicit Drugs Business

It is always a dangerous game to credit any popular protest music with the capacity to propose serious political alternatives to the situation about which it is protesting, let alone actively to promote tangible change. More than most protest music, reggae has been over-romanticized in this way by gushing white journalists at the height of Bob Marley's fame (and in subsequent deifications), without making sufficient distinction between those artists who protested from the solid foundation of an organized philosophical or political structure (like Rastafari) and those who were merely 'bandwaggoning' as Rasta saxophonist Cedric Brooks put it. Writing in the *Kingston Daily Times* (27 March 1977), Trevor Fearon stated that distinctions had to be made between 'political protest' and 'social reportage' and pointed up the lack of principle among singers who cease to protest once their own place in the system has been improved by a successful career in music.

However, given these caveats, reggae did become the strident voice of Jamaica's impoverished majority, venting in 'dread songs' the cultural predicament of a country caught between poverty and a lack of national identity born of years of imperial control. Reggae attempts to resolve this predicament with anthems to the beliefs of Rastafari, the vision of the black redeemer and the Back to Africa Movement, and with public protest against political violence, poverty and hunger, the duplicity of politicians in the pocket of Jamaica's ruling families and the Americans, police harassment and the laws against marijuana or ganja.

The relationship between ganja and reggae is probably the most complex drugs-music nexus to be discussed in this book, going beyond the *prima facie* interaction between a musician and drugs to encompass many of the significant events of Jamaica's cultural, political and religious history. The first point to make is that ganja is neither reggae – nor even Rasta – specific; it was introduced into Jamaica around 1845 by indentured East Indian workers brought in to work on the sugar-cane plantations which had lain mostly idle since the abolition of slavery in 1830. The etymology is a little confused, but ganja is a Hindi word possibly derived from bhang or bhanga, the common word for marijuana in India. Other Hindi words which have become part of the lexicon of ganja include chillum (the pipe used for smoking ganja) and kali (a variety of ganja, nowadays rendered as colley or colly). The term ganja itself is now so closely associated with Jamaica that it has become enshrined in the language of Jamaica's drug legislation.

Together with their labour and language, the workers brought with them the cultural baggage of centuries of ganja use among India's rural communities. Ganja rapidly diffused into Jamaica's black working class where it has remained endemic ever since. Studies carried out in the seventies estimated that between 60% and 70% of the population used one form or another.

Like opium in nineteenth-century England, ganja became something of a universal panacea in working-class culture. Either smoked, drunk as tea, cooked in food or applied as a poultice, ganja is a multi-purpose drug – social relaxant, an aid to work, to sleep, to calming fractious infants and (according to one seventeen-year-old interviewed in a study) to success in sex and cricket.

To complete the 'ganja vision', it constitutes an important vehicle for the rites of passage of male adolescents and is, of course, the sacred herb of Rastafari. The hallucinatory effects of ganja are not usually sought by working people, who tend to eschew its hedonistic functions in favour of social and practical uses. Among Jamaica's middle classes, smoking ganja is very much frowned upon, associated as it is with the unruly mob of 'violent' Rastas. Discrete sipping of ganja tea behind closed doors is more acceptable, but among the young well-to-do smoking ganja has the vicarious thrill of the forbidden. Divorced from the long-standing cultural context of ganja in Jamaica, these sophisticates look more to the American experience of the drug which is almost entirely hedonistic; for them, getting 'out of it' is the key to the whole adventure.

History is replete with examples of how the authorities respond punitively to the use of a certain drug by working people where it is seen either to be a debilitating agent undermining the efficient working of the labour force or as a threat to law and order. In this the colonial power in Jamaica was no exception; as early as 1913 Jamaica had anti-ganja laws on its statute book, making it one of the first countries to do so and beginning an internal process whereby increased penalties for ganja possession, sale or cultivation followed hard on the heels of any explosion of social or political dissent. In the words of one academic: 'Outlawing a popular custom is also a very convenient control device. The ganja legislation in Jamaica is very clearly like the legislation against illegitimate children or against obeah, a particular form of lower-class religion. It can be used by the elite to control the lower classes with no loss in world opinion.'[1]

In 1937, the Jamaican government was bombarded by propaganda from Washington to promote America's Marijuana Tax Act. At the time Jamaica was in deep economic depression and there were many bloody encounters between workers and police, the most serious being the sugar-cane cutters' strike. On the premise that the troubles were inspired by a psychopathic minority driven crazy by ganja, in 1941 the government revised its 1924 Dangerous Drugs Law and introduced mandatory imprisonment for any first ganja conviction under the law. As the Rastafari movement grew in strength from this time on, the so-called 'mad few' and the Rastas became as one in the eyes of the authorities and so the war against ganja became synonymous with the war against Rastafari.

Out of the protests of 1937-8 came the Jamaican trade union movement, and from the two largest trade unions evolved the two political parties which have dominated the country ever since: the Jamaica Labour Party (JLP) founded by Alexander Bustamante, representing middle-class business interests, and Norman Manley's people's National Party (PNP), which gleaned most of its support from Jamaica's urban and rural poor. In 1960, following an abortive Rasta-inspired uprising led by the Reverend Claudius Henry and his son Ronald, a Detention Powers Bill was passed providing for the detention of suspects without trial. The laws against ganja were further tightened as a means of clamping down on the Rastas, who were increasingly viewed by the middle class as the vanguard of revolutionary conspiracy. The PNP were in power at the time and were, ironically, condemned by the JLP for failing to present any evidence to support their allegations of a link between ganja and crime. Ironic, because when the JLP took office in 1963, penalties were increased still further in the wake of unrest following independence in 1962. Arrests for possession shot up by 300% through the sixties as political violence increased. It wasn't until the PNP regained control in the early seventies that fines replaced imprisonment for a first offence.

In 1974, Norman Manley's son, Michael, by now leader of the PNP and Prime Minister of the day, brought in the Drug Enforcement Administration to try to end the ganja trade with America. Violence on the island had escalated to unacceptable levels as a consequence of the ganja-for-guns business that had been going on between the two countries. The purpose of Operation Buccaneer was a top-to-bottom assault on everyone from the farmers in the hills to the dealers in the towns and the smugglers in the air or out at sea. Dealer groups were to be infiltrated, air and sea patrols were to stop ganja reaching America and crops were to be destroyed where they grew. The exercise was a success. It took about three years for operations to start up again; but start up they did. A Congress study mission to Central America and the Caribbean reported in 1985:

> The Government of Jamaica has taken some positive steps in narcotics control. These include enactment of a new civil aviation law aimed at narcotics traffickers, agreement on a modest US assistance program, signature of an extradition treaty, some significant seizures, an aerial survey

of marijuana fields, and eradication of more than ten per cent of its estimated marijuana production. Nonetheless, these efforts have had minimal impact on illicit production in or trafficking from Jamaica.

Jamaica was caught in a bind. It had treaty obligations to combat the marijuana trade and was forfeiting valuable American aid so long as cultivation and selling went unchecked. However, like many Third World drug-producing countries, Jamaica's ganja brought in millions of dollars helping to maintain the country's fragile political and economic stability. In 1980, the government were seriously considering legalization to cope with Jamaica's foreign exchange difficulties. Tentative estimates put the annual export value of ganja at $200 million, roughly equivalent to the net deficit in foreign reserves at that time. As Prime Minister Edward Seaga made clear the same year: 'It (ganja) supplied black-market dollars which were then used by industrialists and other persons in the economy who wanted to import raw materials for which they could not get Bank of Jamaica dollars. On that basis they were able to avert a lot of closures and substantial lay-offs.'[2]

In fact Seaga was in a position to play the 'ganja card' should he so wish right up until 1989 when the PNP came back into power once again under Michael Manley. The Americans wanted Seaga's support because he was virulently anti-communist and supported the US invasion of Grenada. In Somoza's Nicaragua and in Burma, the CIA have supported drug-trafficking activities to keep anti-communist factions in power. Seaga could in effect have said to the Americans 'pay up or we legalize ganja,' for if Washington pushed too hard on eradication and Seaga fell, America would have lost an anti-communist bulwark in the Caribbean.[3]

Ganja cultivation is a poor person's enterprise which fits well into the island's pattern of mixed cropping. In a typical farming community, at least a quarter of all households cultivate ganja ranging from a small crop ('roots') for personal household use up to large-scale cultivation for commercial sale in Kingston. What this amounts to is about half a million small farmers earning most of their cash income from growing ganja. And some of them are doing very nicely.

Any general eradication of ganja trading or use seems impossible so deep is the drug embedded in Jamaica's economic and social foundations; even so, no opportunity has been lost to use the drug laws to harass in particular one sector of the island's population, the Rastafari.

Often regarded as the conscience of the country, the Rastafari movement came together in the 1930s at the confluence of several developments in Jamaica's religious and political history which can be sketched only briefly here. In 1655, the Spanish released a group of slaves who fled into the hills. Dubbed the 'Cimarrons' or 'Maroons' ('the fierce ones'), they waged a guerrilla war against the British which lasted from 1729-39 when the occupying army was forced to sue for peace. The black people of Jamaica never accepted their fate as slaves. The Maroons were the spiritual ancestors of the Rastafari and began a tradition of slave and plantation worker rebellions which flared up intermittently right until the last war, then metamorphosed into the popular protests of the post-war period.

In the Afro-Christian religious sects which proliferated in nineteenth-century Jamaica, there was a particularly strong rememberance of Africa. Drawing on this and his alleged Maroon ancestry, Marcus Garvey kindled a fire of Pan Africanism and black consciousness which found its most potent expression in Rastafari. Garvey was born in 1887 near St Anne's Bay in the north of the island, where the Garvey of his age, Bob Marley, was born nearly sixty years later. He went to London in 1912 and returned two years later with a deep interest in African history. He founded the Universal Negro Improvement Association (UNIA) whose purpose was to unite 'all the Negro peoples of the world into one great body to establish a country and government all their own'. To further his aims, Garvey spent the years 1916-27 in America. There he set up the Black Star Line, a shipping company which was an important symbol in the vision of a return to Africa, and the Negroes' Factories Corporation. An unyielding enthusiast for his ideals, he even went to the Ku Klux Klan for money to send black people home. This appalled prominent black leaders and white liberals in America and hostility towards him grew. Garvey was an inspirational leader, but he was no businessman and all his ventures collapsed. He was deported back to Jamaica in 1927 on being convicted of selling stock in the shipping company after it had gone bankrupt. Back home and later in London, Garvey's other enterprises to promote black self-awareness also failed and he died penniless in West Kensington in June 1940.

Garvey is best remembered for perceiving that black people could not fulfil their destiny while they remained displaced persons. They had to return to Africa, under the guidance of a black redeemer who would be crowned King in Africa. Although this prophecy was actually uttered by one of Garvey's associates, James Morris, at a UNIA convention in 1924, this was forgotten in November 1930 when Ras Tafari Makonnen was crowned Emperor Haile Selassie of Ethiopia. The coronation made front-page news in Jamaica; many regarded Garvey's prophecy as fulfilled, a feeling strengthened when Ethiopia repulsed the forces of Mussolini in 1935.

A further impetus to the development of Rastafari was the inspiration of two preachers, Charles Goodridge and Grace Jenkins Garrison. In 1925, they founded the Hamatic church in Jamaica and introduced a bible called the Holy Piby, compiled between 1913-17 and written in Amharic, the language of Ethiopia. Allegedly the Holy Piby was closest to the very first version of the Old Testament.

On the run from religious persecution, Goodridge and Garrison fled into the bush in the forties to be joined by other key leaders of embryonic Rasta groups, most notably Leonard Howell. Howell was imprisoned in 1933 for selling one-shilling postcards of Haile Selassie to Kingston's slum-dwellers and telling them they were now the proud owners of passports back to Africa. In 1935, the year Howell was released, the fledgling Rastafari movement received some bad publicity when it was linked to an allegedly secret society called the Niyabinghi Order, headed by Selassie and, according to the *Jamaica Times*, dedicated to the death of all black and white oppressors.

In consequence Howell formed the Ethiopian Salvation Society and took several hundred of his followers into the bush to an abandoned estate called Pinnacle. Because of the Niyabinghi scare and the general campaign of harassment through the ganja laws, the commune came under constant police surveillance. Howell spent another two years in jail for growing ganja and on his release he formed the Ethiopian Warriors, dreadlocked guards who patrolled the Pinnacle estate with dogs. The commune survived the hurricane of 1951 which flattened Trench Town and all but wiped out the ganja crop, but finally succumbed to intense police action in 1954.

Deriving fundamentalist interpretations from the Holy Piby, the Rasta preachers constructed a worldview in which Africa was Zion or the Promised Land and the world of oppression was Babylon. They formulated strict dietary laws ('Ital') and rules against cutting hair, both of which bore a striking resemblance to the tenets of orthodox Jewry. Alcohol and gambling were forbidden, but from references to the beneficial 'herb' in Genesis, Revelations and the Psalms, ganja was venerated as a sacrament. This was an important aspect of the Rasta creed because it bound the movement closely to people at the bottom of Jamaican society, where Rastafari found most of its converts.

When Pinnacle broke up, the Rastas returned to the wasteland of urban Kingston, notorious ghetto areas like Trench Town and Back O'Wall, 'a desolate war-zone of zinc, cement and spit'.[4] They came back with nothing but their faith, found nothing except desperation and endless pressure, and consequently had nothing to lose. The ruling classes were terrified of the influx and sent the police in to crack heads at regular intervals. The notion that the Rastas were indeed a bunch of violent criminals seemed confirmed for business interests when a small group went beserk, burnt down a garage, killed the owner and a guest staying at a nearby motel. The Coral Gardens Incident of 1963 went into the legend of Rasta 'violence', but in truth it was a very isolated incident. Most Rastas have no interest in violent action – and with such a devotion to consuming vast quantities of the very finest sinsemilla ganja in chalices, chillums or spliffs the size of ice-cream cones, how could it be otherwise?

In fact, the Rastas were the spiritual alternative to the real lawmakers of the ghetto, the rude boys, and it was the revolution in their music that eventually gave Rastafari its public voice through reggae. The rudies were Jamaica's equivalent of Britain's teddy boys, mods and skinheads with a slice of small-time Chicago hoodlum thrown in. Dedicated to violence and getting drunk, they hung around the shebeens and clubs in shades and 'stingy brim' hats, earning a living through ganja dealing, pimping, gambling, riding shotgun for political heavies and large-scale ganja traffickers, and general hustling.

Music was a very important feature of ghetto life, not the passive strains of calypso, 'which couldn't carry the weight of the folk-urban rebellion taking place in Jamaica',[5] but American soul and r&b, the sounds of one dispossessed black population speaking to another. The music blared out of the island's dance halls from the massive speakers of the Sound Systems, run by youth cult heroes like Sir Coxsone, V Rocket and Duke Reid who would stop at virtually nothing to ensure that *their* systems had the best sounds. Jamaica had no recording plant of its own and there were simply not enough good records from America to go round, so in the late fifties two studios opened to record new Jamaican music, Federal Recording Studios and Coxsone's Studio One.

The new music was ska, the derivation of the word, like 'reggae', being ascribed to as many sources as those who cared to express an opinion. Essentially ska was a loose r&b calypso which emphasized the off-beat. As the sixties progressed and particularly after Independence, a distinctly more African sound emerged, whose pulse echoed the beat of burra drums which welcomed freed slaves and released prisoners back to their homes in the urban sprawl. As ska and bluebeat gave way to rock steady, the beat slowed and the lyrics began to reflect matters other than sex and romance. The key to these developments was Rastafari, as increasing numbers of musicians began to embrace its theology and express the concerns and visions of Rastafari in song. Rock steady can be likened to the erratic spit of an engine kickstarted into action, the strains of protest beginning to come through before giving way to the rhythmic purr and persistent throb of finely tuned reggae, Rastafari's most significant contribution to the culture of Jamaica.

Jamaican musicians were no strangers to ganja. Until well into this century, the principal entertainment for country people had been the Quadrille bands, a kind of Jamaican bluegrass. Using two guitars, fife, banjo and sometimes a fiddle or rhumba box, these bands would play waltzes and polkas, the music of their plantation bosses, at local dances and fairs. One of Bob Marley's relatives was a 'katreel' player around St Anne, where a particularly potent form of sinsemilla was grown. These musicians, like many in rural areas all over the world, had a special status in the community and their appetite for ganja and rum was legendary. But it was the Rasta musicians who first articulated what they regarded as the wonders of herb and the injustices of the ganja laws which had plagued poor people for over half a century.

An early ganja hit was U Roy's 'Chalice in the Palace'. U Roy (Ewart Beckford) was one of the first DJs to rap over an instrumental dub version of somebody else's song; he took the Techniques' 'Queen Majesty' to tell how he shared a chalice with Queen Elizabeth at Buckingham Palace. The first hit for Sugar Minott was 'Oh Mr D.C.' in which he begs a policeman not to bust him because he needs to trade in ganja to feed his family. Both Black Uhuru and the albino DJ Yellowman have recorded songs about sinsemilla. Yellowman's version begins with a 'newscast' relating his court appearance on ganja charges followed by a shout of 'Cocaine will blow your brain, but sinsemilla is IR-IE!' The basic rhythm for the song was taken from the Mighty Diamonds' herb anthem 'Pass the Koutchie' (ganja pipe). This in turn inspired Musical Youth's UK hit 'Pass the Dutchie' (The name was presumably changed so that the BBC censors would miss any reference to drugs, although in the light of their past record it is hard to imagine either song attracting their attention). The Itals, led by Keith Porter and another reggae singer John Holt, have both recorded songs, 'Herb Pirate' and 'Police in Helicopter', which at the same time reflect the reasons for becoming involved in the ganja trade and the dangers of doing so.

In Bob Marley, reggae and Rastafari found an international voice; 'international reggae' was precisely the term used by poet Linton Kwezi Johnson to describe the Wailers' first Island Records album *Catch a Fire* in 1973. Once he began touring around the world as a superstar, Marley came under the usual pressures to try a variety of drugs like acid and cocaine. He always refused, but when it came to ganja Marley was the first ambassador. During his professional career he recorded several songs in praise of herb including 'Kaya', 'African Herbsman' and 'Redder Than Red'. From piecing together comments he made to various reporters about his ganja intake since he began serious smoking in 1966 until close to his death in 1980, it seems that he consumed over 300 kilos of the best ganja Jamaica had to offer. As a defiant gesture to those who claimed that ganja precipitated Marley's premature death, his widow Rita placed a stick of sinsemilla in his coffin and went on to score a hit single with 'One Draw', recorded with the same purpose in mind.

Public figures in Jamaica's tumultuous political arena are always likely to incur the wrath of somebody, and that somebody is always likely to try to settle the issue at the point of a gun. If Bob Marley was ever in any doubt that he was a potential target, they were dispelled in the most dramatic way when he narrowly missed assassination in December 1976. Possibly for reasons of personal safety, he confined most of his public comments on ganja to the parameters of Rasta theology although he was in any event drawn more to the mystical rather than the political aspects of ganja use. He told reporter Richard Cromelin: 'When you smoke herb, herb reveal yourself to you. All the wickedness you do, the herb reveal it to yourself, your conscience, show up yourself clear, because herb mek you meditate. Is only a natural t'ing and it grow like a tree.'[6] Occasionally, however, Marley did respond to questions about legalisation, especially when Michael Manley's PLP were in power in the seventies and there was an influential groundswell in favour of legalizing the trade:

> Herb is the healin' of the nation. Manley can say whatever, but police still get their order from somebody. I mean ... there are people who live in evil and think it is right. For instance, now, a Rastaman sidding and smoke some herb, with good meditation, and a policeman come see him, stick him up, search him, beat him and put him in prison. Now, who is this guy doing these t'ings for? Herb just grow, like yam and cabbage. Policemen do it for evil. Dem don wan' know God and live, dem wan' ha'fe dead yunno![7]

Peter Tosh took an altogether more militant stand. Possibly, once he had lost the protection of being part of 'Bob Marley and the Wailers' and went solo, he became more vulnerable. In 1975, he was beaten up by the police and the song written to record the events 'Mark of the Beast', was banned in Jamaica, as was his personal herb statement 'Legalize It' (this despite the fact that the government had the same action in mind). He was on the receiving end of more harassment following the release of 'Equal Rights' in 1978, culminating in a police beating which almost killed him. He described what happened in an interview for *High Times*:

> TOSH: Well, I was standing at an office arranging a European tour. I was waiting for my musicians. I had a joint in my hand. Two guys came up behind me. One guy came behind me and just took it out of my hand. He was there looking at me. I took it back from him. He didn't tell me who he was. I just see him standing there smiling. I just took it from him and said, 'What happened?' And he was trying to get it back from me. When I see him trying to get my stick from me, my mind told me he was a beast, so I just tore it up and (blows) threw it away. He didn't like *that*. So he started up his aggressiveness and tried to do what he want, to take me to jail. But I realized he was a beast. He found out he couldn't manage me physically, so he went for his friend. His friend came with his gun and tried and failed, too. That didn't work so he went to find some more friends. And that still didn't work. Well, one of them closed his fist on his gun and punch at my face. I moved away and the one who was standing behind me, he got the lick in his face, and it cut him. It began to bleed.
>
> Well, one policeman in his uniform came I knew he was a police. He said, 'What happened?' I told him what happened. Well, he told me to walk with him to the station, and I walked with them to explain the situation. When I walked to explain what happened, they ganged me, put me in a cell. About ten of them ganged my head. And that is when I realized that I was in like Daniel was put in the lion's den. But Peter was put in the dragon's den. And because I was protected from the elements of death, see, I recovered. When they beat and beat and beat and beat for over an hour and found out I would not dead, they was beggin' me to dead. When I realized that they were determined to kill, I just took one blow,

another blow, and all those blows. I just lie down. They were convinced that I was dead because I didn't even wink an eye. I didn't shake a limb; so they was convinced that when I was lying there I was dead. Well, after they was convinced I was dead and left me, I got up like a lion. And they was marvelled. And they said, 'Take him to the dumb cell.'

Well, the dumb cell is a cell that when they put you in, there is not even a breeze come in. It is all concrete and a door. The only hole is a keyhole. And that is where they was taking me. When the guy went to the dumb cell and push his keys – he has about twelve keys together – none of them could fit the place, yet there was the right key there. But it was not spiritually designed for me to go into that cell because they wanted me to bleed to death because I was bleeding furiously. So the doctors came to the place when they heard of what took place. They said no, doctor cannot see me. Lawyers came. They said no, lawyers cannot see me. But when they realize that the news was getting spread all over Jamaica they got two lorries of soldiers to take me to the hospital. I went to the hospital. My hand was broken. This hand was broken here. And my head was properly hashed in.

Well, I went to the hospital and the doctor stitched it up, put my hand in plaster of Paris. They took me back to jail. Then I find that I could not go into the cell. They didn't want me among the prisoners. (The jailer) was asking me if I wanted to go among the prisoners. I said Yes. They are not criminals. You are the criminals – so I went among them and they used their hot coca tea and bathed my hand and bathed my head. One of the prisoners look inside and say he was seeing *inside* of my head and saw my nerve going up like this [wiggles his finger back and forth][8]

In an interview with the Legalize Cannabis Campaign, Tosh came to this conclusion: 'So the system continue, my brethren, and until I and I can tear it down physically, mentally and spiritually and make it look as if it wasn't there, boy, it will still be there, but as long man live in fear...the shitstem (system) will still be there. You see.'[9]*

Although the reggae-Rasta-ganja connection fed into youth cultures all over the world, England proved particularly receptive to the message. In the early eighties it was often easier to get hold of reggae records, even Jamaican pre-releases, in London than in Kingston. And of course, several top reggae solo artists and bands achieved international exposure through British record companies like Island and Virgin. Among black communities throughout the country, 'Reggae took hold and helped to inject a much-needed sense of ideological and cultural solidarity into the lifestyle and thinking of disaffected and anti-social young people, not only because it was an easy kind of dance music, but also because its messages and self-conscious critical and

---

* Around 8 p.m. on Friday 11 September 1987, three men on motorbikes rode up to Tosh's house. One of the men was a regular visitor to the house and so the trio were admitted without question. Once inside, the men shot six people, including Peter Tosh who died two days later. Of the remaining five, one died instantly and the other four survived. Although some jewellery and cash were stolen, there have been strong rumours that the murders were drug-related. In what turned out to be his last interview given to *Musician*, he said: 'If gunmen come tomorrow to get I, I'm not afraid. Jah will protect I... Bullets can't come through I because I'm a wall.'

political commentaries on society were relevant to ... particular needs and desires.'[10] Not least of these desires was the establishment of ganja smoking, not so much to go high or deep, but as the defiant political gesture which has proved central to many of the country's racial explosions in recent years.

Less dramatically, and more closely tied to fashion and style, reggae won back the hearts of a section of Britain's white youth to black music. In the sixties, mods and skinheads demonstrated a close affinity with ska and bluebeat. However, the 'Africanization' of the music as it metamorphosed into reggae alienated these groups and they switched their allegiance to mainstream rock, particularly heavy metal and glamrock. But it was the very ethnicity of reggae that attracted punks in the late seventies. Although it never informed the sound of punk, [reggae] carried the necessary conviction, the political bite, so obviously missing in most contemporary white music.'[11]* And with the music came the marijuana, back in fashion among a new generation of style-conscious youth normally contemptuous of any artefact of the sixties.

Notwithstanding the new heroes who emerged from punk, New Wave and New Romanticism, reggae retained much of its popularity in England through the eighties, both in its purer form (Bob Marley, Sly and Robbie, Misty in Roots, Sugar Minott, Burning Spear, etc), and as a rhythmic pulse informing the sound of white pop, from the Police and Madness to Culture Club. Undoubtedly, however, reggae has lost its political edge and, although the essence of ganja still permeates the sound and the religion, public affirmation of this from reggae musicians has subsided during the anti-drugs backlash.

The example of Jamaica has always been the best answer to those who claim that smoking marijuana leads to use of 'harder' drugs; despite such large-scale use of marijuana on the island, Jamaica has never had, for example, a heroin problem. And even though by 1993 Operation Buccaneer was on its seventh instalment, Jamaica remains the major source for marijuana in the region. However, in his eagerness to please his American sponsors, Seaga's anti-ganja crusade opened the doors for criminal diversification and the arrival of cocaine to the island. Now, in line with many Caribbean islands, Jamaica has become a stop-over point for cocaine passing from South America to Florida. Indeed, the island became something of a cocaine smugglers' paradise, because the ganja trade has supplied it with so many hidden airstrips. Inevitably, more of the drug has stayed in the country to supply the needs of both narco-tourists and the crack houses of Kingston. Always a violent country, gunplay in support of politics has been largely supplanted by the drug-related murders and shootings.

And with Seaga then Manley and his successor P.J. Patterson patently failing to get the Jamaican economy under control, the environment has been ripe for organised drug gangsters to become the most powerful group on the island, able in some cases, to bring some relief to the poverty-stricken ghetto areas, which like other regions where economic and social deprivation rubs shoulders with drug trafficking, is always guaranteed to get the locals on the side of the 'bad guys'.

Cocaine of course found its expression in the Jamaican music scene: Wayne Smith and Dillinger released the records; Gregory Isaacs' record was more criminal in

---

* This is debatable. The Clash certainly used reggae-influenced sounds as did many new wave acts.

nature. How the music industry in general responded to the snap of cocaine is the subject of the next chapter – so clap hands 'cos here comes Charlie.

PART THREE
INTRODUCTION

From about 1982 to 1986, the British government made several public statements which proclaimed that drug abuse was the nation's number one social problem, 'the most serious threat to peacetime Britain' as one politician put it. During that period, there was a steep rise in the number of heroin users and in the amount of drugs seized by police and customs.

Drugs were given the highest priority by those government departments dealing with health, education and law enforcement. More money was made available for treatment and counselling services, special drugs workers were appointed to schools, new anti-trafficking legislation was passed and the police intelligence network was strengthened. And in an attempt to get the anti-heroin message across, the government ran an unprecedented TV and press advertising campaign.

Beyond screening government warnings, the television companies became heavily involved in the drugs issue with numerous documentaries, anti-drug themes built into dramas and specific campaigns of their own, such as the BBC's 'Drugwatch' initiative.

In America, there was a parallel development, indeed the one from which British drug policy took its cue – the 'Just Say No' campaign instigated by Nancy Reagan. The US president met with television companies attempting to directly influence output while the music and film industries came under heavy public scrutiny accused of purveying pro-drug attitudes. Both were forced to respond with public declarations detailing what efforts they had made to de-glamorize drug use. So important had this issue become in America that Senate hearings were held in 1985 at which various media representatives were invited to provide depositions and statements demonstrating how they were 'doing their bit' to warn of the dangers of drugs.

Probably because of rock's long-standing pro-drug image, those musicians who went public in Britain with anti-drug sentiments received a high media profile and started a trend for pop celebrities becoming visibly involved in charitable works.

A prime mover for the public anti-drug face of rock in the eighties was Pete

Townshend. In 1984, he gave several interviews documenting his own problems with drink and drugs, and the help he had received from addiction therapist Meg Patterson. He was courted by government circles as a spokesman for young people (which shows just how out of touch they were) and was invited to speak at the Conservative Party Conference in October that year. However, it wasn't just speeches and good intentions; Townshend's Double O charity (for a short while anyway) put some real money into the drugs field.

The Double O was originally set up in 1976 by The Who (or the 'OO, hence Double O) to channel group funds into charitable works. When the band split up, the charity lay dormant, but was revived by Townshend in the aftermath of his own dependency problems. Nearly all of the charity's money went to drug agencies who, between 1985-87 received around £150,000. Inevitably, once Townshend has publicly exorcised the ghosts of his addiction, his enthusiasm for financially supporting the drugs field waned to the point where funds just dried up.

However, Townshend wasn't alone in supporting anti-drug efforts. Dire Straits became involved in sponsoring an Australian-inspired project called Life Education Centres which use visual aids to demonstrate the effects of drugs to young children. There were also several 'one-off' events in the mid-eighties such as the GLC anti-heroin campaign gigs in London and the charity concert given by Lenny Henry and starring Elvis Costello which raised £15,000 for Broadreach House, a rehabilitation centre in Plymouth. Feargal Sharkey was photographed wearing a 'Heroin Is A Life Sentence' T-Shirt, a slogan also taken up by Madness, Tom Robinson and Big Country. Even Ozzy Osbourne, who cornered the market in self-destructive habits, was reported to have recorded an anti-drug message for the Yorkshire Police. As *Rolling Stone* said, 'You know it's the eighties when even Sly Stone is getting off drugs'. And as if to drill home the point, the magazine that was the bible of sixties counterculture announced the right to test employees for drugs and alcohol.

What about within the business itself? Apart from the likes of Frank Zappa and Bruce Springsteen who always took a hardline on drugs in their bands, musicians generally were not likely to be too comfortable embarking on anti-drug crusades because the connections ran too deep for too long to be that easily broken. But while we would have to wait until the nineties for cocaine confession time from on high, the new urban black music of the late eighties had its own cocaine lament to sing.

Like the mantra of song lyrics and drug use, the belief that pop stars exert an influence over the behaviour of young people is another one of the drug chestnuts that is still hanging on in there.

To be fair, it is a common sense view. The most popular artists ship records by the truckload, their concerts sell out within hours of tickets going on sale and millions are generated through merchandising. The media-friendly utterances of musicians therefore inevitably get splashed across the front pages – especially where drugs are concerned. Noel Gallagher released the hounds of moral outrage when he declared that drug use was so commonplace, it was like 'getting up and having a cup of tea' (*The Sun* 30th January 1997).

His comments were in response to the revelation by Brian Harvey of East 17 that he had taken a faceful of ecstasy tablets in an evening and been fine. What was interesting about this revelation was that it came against a background of friction between Harvey and the rest of the band to the point where he was almost daring them to sack him. What better way to besmirch the 'clean-cut' image of the whole band and bring matters to a head than by a drug confession to the tabloid press, remarkable only for the fact that in the late 1990s, this still has the power to shock.

Despite the opprobrium heaped on Gallagher's head by the usual posse of apoplectic MPs, when the *Daily Mirror* polled its readers about Gallagher's view that there should be a national debate about drugs, 87% of those who voted came out in support (*Daily Mirror* 31st January 1997).

And some pop stars *are* 'bad'. Arguably, the likes of Noel or Liam Gallagher, Johnny Rotten, Keith Richard or Janis Joplin are blank slates on which young people inscribe a multitude of tantalising vicarious experiences. It's almost part of the pop star job description to be bad on our behalf, so that we can carry on as normal when the show is over. That's partly why so many of those with the worst reputations don't survive; they transfer those audience expectations into their own private lives and play out their own mythology. But however vicarious, surely young people look up to these glamorous ne'er-do-wells and actually ape the worst indulgences of stardom?

In fact, there isn't a shred of evidence that this actually happens in the young population at large. Across the world and down the years, literally millions of young people have been asked by thousands of researchers why they take drugs – none of them cite the drug habits of pop stars as a deciding factor, or indeed as any sort of factor at all. The reason young people take drugs is obviously bound with their personal and social environment; what's going on with family, friends, their community and the like. It is stretching the imagination to think that a remote pop star living a world of limousines, first class travel and bodyguards has anything to say to a kid living in a inner-city housing estate or in some of our less obviously impoverished rural areas. Given the widespread use of drugs by young people these days, it is almost tempting to suggest that when a rock star goes public on drugs, he (invariably it is a 'he') is actually trying to establish street cred by declaring, 'Hey, kids, I take drugs too. Please buy the record".

What we're into here is 'blame culture', a line of thinking which has underpinned so much social, political and moral thinking about drugs since the 1920s. Nobody has the foggiest idea how to stop young people trying drugs, so the next best thing to do is find somebody to blame for it – Chinese, Blacks, Mexicans, Communists, student radicals, drug gurus and pop stars.

Equally fallacious is the idea that you can harness 'the role model' effect in support of anti-drug campaigns. Noel Gallagher announced in October 1998 that (like tea, presumably) drugs were boring, so he'd decided to give them up. Is this likely to impress an adolescent half his age into spurning an activity which is almost a rite of passage for some many young people?

In the meantime, it came as no surprise to read revelations about the post-punk drug habits of Boy George, Modern Romance, Duran Duran, Julian Lennon, Topper Headon of the Clash, Keith Levene of PIL, and Nik Kershaw together with the drug-related deaths of two members of The Pretenders, Malcolm Owen of the Ruts and Sid Vicious. And as heralds of a new age of the wasted rock star, just as one lot were hanging up their syringes and going to AA meetings, The Mission, Guns 'N Roses, Nirvana, The Happy Mondays, Oasis, Hole, Primal Scream, Nick Cave, Evan Dando and a host of others seemed singularly bent on putting the sex and drugs back into rock 'n' roll. In hindsight such a development was predictable, but the drugs/music dynamic was about to take on a character and dimension that nobody could have foreseen.

13   CLAP HANDS HERE COMES CHARLIE

"Everybody is taking drugs. There's a blizzard of cocaine in London at the moment and I hate it. It's stupid. Everyone's so blasé, thinking they're so ironic and witty and wandering around with this stupid, fucking cokey confidence".
Damon Albarn, Q Mag, March 1996

"Crack cocaine is the genocide of black folk"

Paris aka Oscar Jackson

Day in and day out, the body provides a certain amount of energy chemicals which circulate around the body and help us stay alert and active for all the things we need to do during our waking hours.

Sometimes we need an energy boost for making love, for running away from danger or fighting. At such moments, the brain releases extra chemicals, in particular, adrenalin, like the cavalry coming over the hill. Once the moment has passed, the chemicals are reabsorbed back into the nerve tissues waiting to be called up again.

Now if you introduce a powerful stimulant into the body, such as cocaine, all those cavalry chemicals come charging into the bloodstream looking for some action, but nothing is happening. Not only that, the presence of cocaine in the bloodstream makes it very hard for these chemicals to be reabsorbed. So like any army with nothing to do and left hanging around, they go on the rampage and the user is rushing around like a lunatic, feeling superhuman, talking, partying or working like crazy but soon becoming restless, aggressive, very irritable and perhaps ultimately psychotic and paranoid.

But given that the music business thrives on aggression, hard partying and bullshit, it is hardly surprising that cocaine became the *sine qua non* drug of the industry, not only for musicians, but company executives, producers and managers alike. Cocaine imbues the user with a sense of supreme self-confidence, an illusion of clear-mindedness, a manipulative power over people, a control of yourself and a loathing for any kind of business etiquette. There is nothing emotionally sloppy about it; cocaine offers a spurious sense of invulnerability that meshes perfectly with a hard headed industry where the waving of a gun might make a point quicker than any lawyer's letter.

Cocaine first became fashionable as an illegal drug among the Hollywood film aristocracy; 'joy powder' was readily available on the film sets and stars had bowls full of the stuff lying around at parties. Aleister Crowley, whose book *Diary of a Drug Fiend* (1922) explored the effects of cocaine, wrote that Hollywood was populated by 'the cinema crowd of cocaine-crazed sexual lunatics'. The drug was also popular among the bright young things of London between the wars. By the end of the thirties, the fashion for cocaine had largely run its course to be replaced until the late sixties by amphetamines. Phil Spector buying cocaine in *Easy Rider* (1969) signalled that those in the music business, entertainment's new royalty, were setting the pace for cocaine's rediscovered popularity.

Although since then, cocaine has become very common on the US drug scene, it has retained its jet set image; as Robin Williams (among others) said; 'cocaine is God's way of telling you, you've got too much money'. In her book about club culture in the UK, Sarah Thornton demonstrates that the rave scene could equally fall foul of the banalities of the rock life. She described the Milleneum Club as a venue which imagines itself as entirely VIP chiefly because it's 'heavily into cocaine' while the owner of Cloud Nine 'snorts coke off a friend's Visa card'[1]. The exclusivity of cocaine is confirmed by country artist Steve Earle who battled for years with drug and alcohol problems, 'it created a caste system made up of people who could afford the drugs and people who couldn't'.

Marvin Gaye was totally besotted by the drug; he sniffed it, snorted it, ate it and rubbed it in his gums; 'No-one will ever tell me it's not a great feeling. A clean fresh high, specially early in the morning, will set you free – at least for a minute. There are times when blow (cocaine) got to me and sometimes I know it built up bad vibes inside my brain. I saw coke, though, as an elitist item, a gourmet drug and maybe that's one of its attractions'. [2]

Cocaine and sexual excess walk hand in hand. Movie star Tallulah Bankhead, an infamous bisexual, reportedly said, 'My father warned me about men and booze, but he never mentioned a word about women and cocaine'. Freddie Mercury's main dealer related to friends how he would turn up with supplies, to find young men being brought on dishes to serve up to Freddie in his bath; 'more sperm than water' was the dealer's cryptic observation. Elton John told *Q Mag* in 1995 that he used cocaine basically for sex, 'my sexual fantasies were all played out while I was on cocaine'.

Phil Spector had a photo of himself sniffing cocaine printed onto his Christmas cards with the legend, 'A Little Snow at Christmas Time Never Hurt Anybody'. He was probably right. But possibly more than most drugs (even heroin) there is often a significant payback time for those who overindulge themselves on coke. Why? Because cocaine acts on the brain's pleasure centres – those bits of the brain which give you those feelings that come from quenching your thirst, or from satisfying hunger for food or sexual desires. Cocaine pushes all those good time buttons at once without food or drink passing your lips or flesh brushing your skin; at the height of his cocaine habit, Elton John claimed he was doing a line every four minutes. One musician told the author that during the course of a two day coke binge, 'I couldn't stop, any more than I could stop breathing'.

Small wonder then, that some musicians have found themselves lost in a blizzard of the stuff. After all the ups, the sex, the status and the adrenalin of excess, come the downs.

Cocaine gave the American drug abuse industry a new lease of life. A number of doctors and academics built careers on the platform of, 'everybody thought cocaine was harmless, now we know it's not'. This, they argued, was because the symptoms which follow the cessation of cocaine use were not previously regarded as the true withdrawal symptoms on the heroin model. This removed the bogey of physical addiction which for many people, is the bench mark of a 'bad drug'. Also, of course, most cocaine users don't inject like the stereotypical heroin addict which tended to reinforce the notion that heavy cocaine users were not 'addicts'.

All of which was somewhat self-serving and disingenuous; Sigmund Freud changed his mind about cocaine back in the last century and blues and country musicians from Leadbelly and Champion Jack Dupree to Hoyt Axton have been singing about the perils of cocaine use for decades.

There are physical problems associated with regular cocaine use, the most fabled being the perforation of the membranes (known as the septum) separating the nostrils. Although rare, descriptions can be quite graphic; Little Richard recalled that 'My nose got big enough to back a diesel truck in... Everytime I blew my nose, there was flesh and blood on my handkerchief where it had eaten out my membranes'. Cocaine can also have a serious impact on the heart and heavy users can suffer fits and seizures as described by Elton John, 'I felt like Linda Blair in The Exorcist, like the top of my head was going right round. Terrifying... and still ten minutes later, I'd put coke up my nose. That's how bad it was'.

Like amphetamines, deaths from the stimulant effects of cocaine are relatively rare. However unlike amphetamines, cocaine has anaesthetic properties and in high doses these can depress the nervous system to the point where the heart starts skipping beats – known as the Casey Jones reaction after the chugging locomotive of the Grateful Dead song. Death can follow through cardiac arrest or respiratory collapse, and the risk is greater when cocaine is mixed with heroin to make speedballs. Most cocaine deaths recorded in America result from this concoction and also claimed the life of Meatloaf drummer Wells Kelly when the band were in London. Cocaine was also implicated in the deaths of The Pretenders James Honeyman-Scott and Peter Farndon.

However, for the majority of chronic cocaine users, the most intractable difficulties are psychological and as a result, regular cocaine use causes many problems for the music industry. One manager says he can always tell if the person he is confronting face to face or even on the phone is doing cocaine; 'They get impossible to deal with, they're all over the place and you can't talk to them'. According to Paul Kantner, the whole of the Jefferson Airplane album *Bark* was written under the influence of cocaine.[3] *Rolling Stone* asked Joni Mitchell what steps in the music-making process were most likely to prove the undoing of an album. She answered, 'Cocaine! There are entire albums that would be very different if that drug didn't exist.'[4] Steve Tyler of Aerosmith said, 'we would make sure that we had enough cocaine and do a lock-in for three or four days in Studio A at the Record Plant'[5], and in the band's autobiography, he recalled the making of the *Rocks* album, 'We'd do thirty takes – forty! – because we were *gacked*. Jack Douglas (the producer) would then take half of this take and half of that take and the bridge from Take 23 and put it together and nobody knew what was what when we finally heard the record. Today I listen to those albums, some of our best, and all I can hear are the drugs'.[6] Another former manager of an early nineties dance band who enjoyed chart success told the author that the band did so much coke, they were too paranoid even to leave their house and go down to the studio in the first place.

Because few people actually inject the drug, there is an unwillingness to believe that use can get out of control. As Stevie Ray Vaughan commented, 'I had conned myself into believing that I was controlling it... [but] I mean, doin' a quarter-ounce a day, snortin' it. I'd put a half-gram or gram into a drink, down that. Then take another drink'[7]

Once hooked, a chronic user can go downhill very fast. One musician who spoke to the author said, 'I had a twenty year heroin habit that I was managing quite well. Once I started on cocaine, it all fell apart inside six months'. Within the music business, it's not only musicians who lose control of their cocaine habit; former Aerosmith manager Tim Collins called himself a 'coke slut'; Oasis record label boss Alan McGee thought he was going to die in mid-air en route to the States as his coke-driven heart began to shed its cogs. A top agent sums up the cocaine scene from the suit side of the desk, 'coke is the music business drug; it's done in offices during the day. I know because I've seen it. It's quite sad really; they've been up all night at a gig and tonight they'll go to another gig. If you go to any of the Award ceremonies, you'll see all these A&R guys sitting there yapping away on their mobile phones, doing lines on the table'.

Clarence Paul, a Motown producer, says there were a lot of drugs around the company in Detroit in the early sixties and that he and Marvin Gaye did their share of cocaine during that time. Gaye's biographer David Ritz said that in all times he saw Marvin Gaye record, he was never straight; he was high for every major decison he had to take. On his 1983 tour, one of Gaye's musicians remarked, 'there was more coke on that tour than on any tour in the history of entertainment'[8]. The singer obviously suffered from a whole basket of emotional problems and regarded cocaine as his trusted companion and possibly his final way out, 'Blow is what really lets me fly. There were moments when I really thought I was gone. I'm talking about times, really down times, when I snorted up so much toot, I was convinced I'd be dead within minutes. I rather liked the idea of there being nothing left of me but my music'[9].

Before his tragic death, murdered by his own father in self defence, Gaye's behaviour became increasingly erratic. Oddly, Ritz doesn't seem to attribute this to Gaye's increasing consumption of cocaine, although a lay diagnosis of acute cocaine psychosis seems likely. Gaye hired a top lawyer to investigate alleged conspiracies to shoot and poison him. He would command his chauffeur to circle hotels several times before he would go in and in the last ten months of his life, he became totally obsessed with guns. Some of his friends tried to be light-hearted with him and dismiss his fears, but others had a vested interest in Gaye's paranoia and went along with all his demands in order to keep the gravy train rolling.

There is no reason to suppose that cocaine would cause any less problems for a black musician than for a white, but during the 1960s and 1970s, there was far less cocaine use in the black community as a whole because of its expense. All that changed in the mid 1980s with the introduction of a smokable form of cocaine known as crack.

* * * * *

There are different stories about how crack came onto the US drug scene. The technique is said to have originated in South America as a test of the purity of a drug purchase by separating out the pure salt from any contaminants using a strong solvent. The process of freeing the salt from its base was known as freebasing, and the end result, freebase. Crack was just the 'fast food' version, ready made for easy street sale. Another source says that crack was invented by accident. Dealers were trying to create cocaine base, a stage in cocaine production before final refinement, smoked in South America for years. Instead they created a much purer form of the drug. Yet another version says that base or freebase first appeared in the late sixties when users rolled the base into marijuana joints. The more elaborate form of freebasing using substances like ammonia to filter the drug apparently arose out of the belief that by removing the impurities from cocaine powder, the user would be smoking a more refined viz. 'healthier' product. But however it came about, freebased cocaine was a rare commodity until the early 1980s.

At this point, according to writer Terry Williams in *The Cocaine Kids*, a four year study of teenage crack dealers in New York, there was so much cocaine stockpiled, that importers feared the price would drop unless demand was rekindled. Therefore, small quantities of cocaine base were added to kilo shipments as a gift for dealers to use with buyers to entice them to use the new product. Acceptance of this type of cocaine took time to gain ground; it was initially expensive and so restricted to an elite group of big spenders – like Richard Pryor, gripped as much by the ritual of preparation as by the terrific whack to the brain delivered by smokable cocaine, smoking being the next most immediate route to a high after injecting.

Although it later transpired that he was actually attempting suicide, for many years the story went around that Richard Pryor badly injured himself during a freebasing session. It was said that he had been trying to filter the freebase in a pipe using a burning cotton ball soaked in rum. The cotton caught fire and Pryor suffered third degree burns from the waist up.

Less explosive, but equally destructive were the circumstances in which Dave Crosby found himself as a result of compulsive freebasing. Crosby had been involved with drugs since the earliest days of his career in the sixties and at times he got mighty annoyed at those who criticized his drug use, rationalising that he was stoned all the time his name was selling millions of records and nobody was moaning then.

However, once he got heavily into cocaine, he knew he was in serious trouble. In March 1982, he wrecked his car on the way to sing at an anti-nuclear rally and police found cocaine and a gun. From then on, he was a marked man. Three weeks later, he was caught freebasing in the dressing room of a Texas club, where police found yet another gun. When the case came to trial in 1983, he was sentenced to five years. Normally for the small amount of cocaine that Crosby had on him at that time, probation would have been considered sufficient, but the judge regarded him as a public figure whose actions would always be held up for closer scrutiny.

While free, pending an appeal, Dave Crosby was arrested yet again on drugs and weapons charges. His luck turned when the judge allowed him to go to a drug rehabilitation unit in lieu of sentence. He stayed there seven weeks before absconding and eventually served four months in jail in 1985, 'I know more about freebase than anybody! You think you plan to become an addict? It sneaks up on you. Oh, I'll just get a little high. I've kicked cigarettes, heroin, booze, everything, but this is the most horrible drug in the universe. It stays with you. I was in jail four months. Want to know how long I stayed clean when I got out? Two days. It never lets you alone. All I want to do is to be clean, man. But I'm scared I'm gonna crave it forever.'[10]

Shaun Ryder former leader of the Happy Mondays and nobody's vision of a jet set habituée, expressed virtually the same sentiments about his crack use in the late eighties, 'I was buying a sixteenth of a rock in the morning at eight o'clock and I'd smoked that by dinner time. I'd buy another sixteenth and then at night time I'd buy an eighth of a rock. I was just buying sixteenths and eighths and just smoking the fucker. Once you start smoking it's terrible. It's the worst, dirtiest drug in the world. We kept the smack thing quite well under control for years.'[11] But it was in between Crosby's earliest dalliance with freebase and Shaun Ryder's crack attack in Barbados during the recording of the disastrous *Yes Please* album that the real damage caused by crack was played out.

Initially, the dealers were reluctant to offer the new product because they could make more money with the powder form of the drug; if you take out the impurities in cocaine, you've got less weight to sell. They also objected to spending time on processing the powder into rocks; also you can cut powder several times to increase profits – you can't cut rocks.

However, in 1983, overproduction in the growing countries of South America forced a price cut. Dealers cashed in because they could buy at the new lower price, but still charge customers the same. Eventually prices did fall as the word got out, but even so receipts were down as sales lagged behind production.

And then a new product hit the streets – prepackaged cocaine at $5 a hit – a fraction of the minimum sale price for the powder. The Los Angeles *Sentinel* reported the first crack house in 1983; within a year few customers anywhere were asking for powder.

Inevitably this new cheap and potentially highly addictive drug found its biggest market in the worst of black urban ghettos areas of the USA; in New York, Chicago, Los Angeles, and Washington. These areas have traditionally been the target for large scale drug traffickers ever since Lucky Luciano cut a deal with the US to allow his heroin trafficking business to continue bringing the drug from the Far East to New York. This was in exchange for local Sicilian help to the Allies planning the invasion of Europe during the Second World War. Cheap heroin flooded into black areas in the fifties, sixties and early seventies to the point where it seemed like a conspiracy to keep the lid on the increasingly politicised ghettos by allowing unchecked drug dealing.

The Civil Rights movement attempted (among other things) to instill a sense of pride within the black community; to combat that sense of hopelessness and despair in which endemic drug use flourished. 'Black is beautiful' and 'I'm black and I'm proud' became the clarion calls for the hoped-for new age of equality. While white musicians considered the broader horizons supposedly offered by LSD and cannabis, black soul singers of the time tried to send out the message about the damage that very different drugs were doing to the community, James Brown's 'Heroin' being one example, 'Freddie's Dead' by Curtis Mayfield another.

But for a large percentage of the black community across America, the Civil Rights movement produced little in the way of tangible improvements to their living conditions, employment prospects or political empowerment. The main beneficiaries were the black middle classes; if anything, the lot of many working class blacks worsened. Come the years of Reaganomics and the worst off in society took the brunt of cuts in public and social welfare spending; politics was dominated by conservative politicians hostile to the interests of the black community. The statistics tell the story; more black men in prison than college; half of all black children living in the sort of economic hardship few western Europeans can imagine and ten million black people living below the poverty line[12].

'The aspiring working class of the black community found itself looking at white America across a growing cultural chasm and looking down at the poorest of the black poor with no social net below them. It was the children of this class that invented rap – the sound of black urban youth creating a musical and socio-cultural alternative to white radio, the integrationist policies of the 60s and the white backlash that followed.'[13]

It seems that every ten years or so after a form of black music has been tamed and co-opted into the American mainstream, the next generation of innovators come forward with a new style to recapture the identity of black music and the communities in which it is born. In succession soul, funk and disco were absorbed; by the early eighties it was time for something different.

In one sense, there was nothing new about rap. As David Toop observed in his book *Rap Attack 2*, 'Rap's forebears stretch back through disco, street funk, radio DJs, Bo Diddley, the bebop singers, Cab Calloway, Pigmeat Markham, The Last Poets, Gil Scott Heron, Muhammed Ali, acapella and doo wop groups, ring games, skip-rope rhymes, army songs, signifying… all the way back to the *griots* of Nigeria and Gambia'… *griots* being those who challenged social transgressors to listen to the will of the people.

Rap music as a 'labelled' distinctive musical form originated around 1976 among black street DJs in the South Bronx area of New York who discovered they could keep a dance crowd hopping by playing catchy instrumental breaks from popular records. They used two turntables and a sound mixer; the DJ could switch from one record to another to create a continuous dance groove while an MC would 'rap' over the rhythm, a tradition commonly found in Jamaican music. Who invented the form that came to be known as rap? Many pioneering DJs such as Derrick May, Clive Campbell (aka 'Herc') can take credit, but the name uttered most frequently has been Bronx River Projects resident Afrika Bambaataa who created a unique mix of that Jamaican 'toasting' tradition with electronic music actually inspired by the German band Kraftwerk at a time when (as Bambaataa noted) there was no black electronic music. In Simon Reynolds' history of Acid House, *Energy Flash,* Detroit DJ Juan Atkins made the interesting point that European electronic music appealed to aspiring black kids whose parents had jobs (even white collar jobs) at General Motors or Chrysler. Adopting such a Euro-centric music was part of their attempt to 'distance themselves from the kids that were coming up in the projects, in the ghetto'.

From this background emerged rap – embedded in a new young urban black lifestyle known as hip-hop. Initially at least, rap took black music away from corporate rock and created a whole new environment of home made music involving sampling, mixing and remixing. Using the rapid developments in computer technology, it was the aural equivalent of a William Burroughs novel – a cut up music taking from the whole of pop history, but nevertheless firmly grounded in its (often relentless) depiction of the grim realities of black American life in the 1980s.

The first commercial success came in 1979 with 'Rapper's Delight' by the Sugar

Hill Gang released by Sugar Hill Records, founded by former singer Sylvia Robinson. Also signed to the label was another Bronx rapper, Grandmaster Flash who put together the Furious Five which included the rapping talents of Melle Mel, responsible for the template of much of rap's outpourings of anger at the state of the black community, namely 'The Message' with its ominous warning to white society 'Don't push me 'cause I'm close to the edge'. The song was released in 1982, followed in 1983 by 'White Lines (Don't Do It)'. Although an anti-cocaine song, this was a time just before the crack explosion and so targets the warning not against using rocks, but the white lines of cocaine hydrochloride powder.

From here on in, as crack spread through the urban sprawls of America, rappers dogged its tail, telling of the damage done. New York produced Run DMC, LL Cool J, Eric B and Rakim, the Notorious B.I.G., Christopher Wallace aka Biggie Smalls, the more politicised Public Enemy and its leader, now solo artist, Chuck D and the recent hot shots, Wu-Tang Clan.

Across on the West Coast, an altogether more hard-edged and controversial rap style emerged, often celebrating the 'gangsta' life of LA's crime and drug-riven areas like Compton. Enter NWA, Cypress Hill, Ice T, Tone Loc, Dr Dre, Coolio – and further up the coast, Tupac Shakur, Tim 'Snoop Doggy' Dogg and the more spiritually oriented MC Hammer. But the east and west coasts did not have a complete monopoly of the music; Bone, Thug 'N Harmony hail from Cleveland, 2-Live Crew from Florida. And it was in Philadelphia that the hardcore 'gangsta' outlook first emerged in the shape of Schooly D's 'Saturday Night'.

Many rock stars have stated that it was music which saved them from a life of crime; within rap, the two have often co-existed side by side. This is hardly surprising given that many rap artists came from the worst areas of social and economic deprivation.

Ironically it was the harsh laws enacted by Governor Rockefeller of New York in the 1970s that helped create the army of teenage drug dealers. Rockefeller made a prison sentence mandatory for anyone over 18 caught in possession of drugs. So under-18s became the runners and street dealers.

In his study of teenage crack dealing in New York, Terry Williams meets with a young dealer called 'Master Rap' who is 'slick, articulate and cool...' 'Rap is my name, females my game'. Master Rap has his heart set on a career in music and wrote many rap songs which he hoped one day to record. He said, 'coke is just a way for me to make some money and so do some of the things I would otherwise not have the chance to do in the real world'[14]. By the end of Willams' study, Master Rap still hadn't made it, but many others did.

Former North Philly gang member Schooly D released his first solo album in 1986 rapping on a situation which was turning schoolkids into business entrepreneurs heavily involved in the dash for cash so much the hallmark of life in the 1980s. Tupac Shakur, Biggie Smalls, Coolio and Snoop Doggy Dogg all had their own histories of drug dealing and the street life followed them into their musical career; Tim Dogg beat a murder charge in 1995 while Smalls and Shakur were both subsequently murdered.

Much drug money was laundered through legitimate business, including music. It has long been rumoured that Ruthless Records set up by NWA member, the late Eric 'Eazy-E' Wright (who died of AIDS in 1995) was financed by drug money. Hip-hop critic S.H. Fernando describes Wright as sitting, 'Capone-like behind a huge desk in his Woodlands Hills office in LA'. Wright admitted to Fernando that the NWA crack dealer song 'Dope Man' 'was about me because that's what I was at the time', but wouldn't admit that Ruthless was established on the back of drug money, 'I don't know how Ruthless was formed. I think I probably did a little jackin' [stealing] for that money. I don't know. Or I have a money tree in the back yard. We'll never know anyway. Nobody can go back and find out how this money was made.'[15] Which seems a strange lapse of memory from the founder of the company, but not so strange when you realise that in some American states, you can lose your car if you are found sitting in it smoking a joint. These are the draconian forfeiture laws: that car would be impounded for being used to 'transport narcotic drugs'. These laws are helping to inject massive funds into otherwise under-funded state police operations, so you can imagine how much the LAPD would want to get hold of one of rap's most successful companies if they could prove its financial base was drug money.

A similar example comes from rapper 'Too Short' Todd Shaw who used to sell marijuana, but who became involved with a big time cocaine dealer who set him up with a state-of-the-art studio, rented him a cadillac and gave him money to put out some undergound releases.

Interestingly, however, for all the involvement in drug dealing and violence, few rap artists have gone on the record concerning any personal problems with drugs. Coolio's admission is probably a rare example, 'we started out on rock cocaine not really knowing what it was. By the time we realised, we were all hooked'. It took him over two years of hard struggle to clean up. But in the main, the code of the street gangs was to stay in control. For example, Young Boys Inc of Detroit who in 1982 grossed over \$400m in sales of heroin and cocaine, imposed a strict 'no drugs' policy on its members. There were no second chances.

Most rappers both before and during their music careers regarded crack users as losers because they were out of control and weak – De La Soul rap in 'Say No Go' 'push couldn't shove me to understand the path to a basehead'; one track on Public Enemy's 'It Takes A Nation of Millions to Hold Us Back' is called 'Night of the Living Baseheads', where the term 'basehead' replaces 'junkie' as the new insult for those hooked on drugs. More mainstream artists like Prince also had their say on a drug situation representing a sign of the times,

> *At home are the 17 year old boys*
> *And their idea of fun*
> *Is being in a gang called The Disciples*
> *High on crack and totin' a machine gun*

Women drug users are regarded with even greater disgust, especially those offering sex for drugs. Given that rap songs tend to divide women into 'hoes' (whores) or 'bitches', this reaction to women drug users is hardly any shock while at the same time it does recognise that cocaine is more of an 'equal opportunity' drug than say heroin, where chronic male users heavily outnumber women.

Donald D's 'FBI' ('Freebase Institute') talks of a drug that has women 'slobbin' the knob' in dark alleys. In the final verse;

> *Little Johnny and Tommy saw their mommy*
> *Hittin' the pipe with her best friend Connie*
> *She look like she suffers from malnutrition*

The kids are hungry, no food in the kitchen
Their gear's been worn for a month and a half
That was the last time they had a bath
Cause the crack has the man command
The welfare check to the dope man".

Live Crew's 'In The Dust' expresses a similar vision of maternal neglect; 'Babies cryin', I'm wonderin' where's the momma/She OD'd and got rushed to trauma' – without ever once asking, 'where's poppa?'

The misogyny that runs deep throughout rap has rightly come in for stinging attack both from white and black writers, although disgust at women drug users for seeming to turn their back on their 'rightful place' in the kitchen cooking with one hand and mucking out the kids with the other, is no less virulent for white women drug users than it is for black. And generally, the attacks in America on rap for its apparent glorification of violence are a bit rich coming from a society where the National Rifle Association has such political power and Hollywood's coffers overflow from the proceeds of Rambo, and all its shoot-em-up film and computer game offspring, not forgetting the whole Tarantino oeuvre. Britain, too, has seen plenty of press reporting based on the equation (to quote Ian Penman) 'black man + white powders x guns = end of civilisation'.

Heavy crack users are invariably condemned. However, when it comes to drug dealing, there is ambivalence within rap. The big drug dealers in the black community have always commanded much respect and admiration, especially from younger people, some of whom went on to become rap artists. Firstly because of the conspicuous material wealth that drug dealing brought. Secondly because of the respect that could be earned when you were holding the business end of a gun. Lastly because so many of the drug buyers were white, it seemed as if the black community was at last able to get some kind of revenge for all the damage visited upon the communities by the big time white drug importers. In 'Life of a Drug Dealer (1991) The Genius (aka Gary Grice) sang about the dealer who 'smokes' anything or anybody who gets in his way

I'll shoot up funerals, firebomb wakes
Vehicular homicides, whatever it takes...
You've seen my resume, that's just the half
I'm a bad motherfucker, just like Shaft

In Donald D's song quoted above, the dealer justifies his activities on the basis that 'a man has to do what a man has to do'. NWA's 'Dopeman' is written from the dealer's perspective, 'Well I'm the dopeman, yeah boy, wear corduroy/ Money up to here, but I'm unemployed/You keep smokin' that rock and my pockets get bigger/ Yo, got that 5-0 double up, nigger!

In the main, though, rappers regard dealers as those who have betrayed the black community. As Big Daddy Kane says in 'Another Victory',

I have to wonder, damn, how can lifestyle be fun to man
To see a brother get paid undercover
Sellin' drugs to one another

'Cause all the glamour you get is miscellaneous
And all the product you sell is real dangerous

Ice T's remedy in 'I'm Your Pusher', is to turn the dealer onto music instead,

The dope I'm sellin, ya don't smoke, ya feel
You wanna get high? Let the music play...

My dope hits the street with no doubt
Evil E add the cut, then removes it
Iz checks for purity, and then approves it
And then you get it, try it and like it
And if it ain't potent, we remix and spike it

During the 1990s, the worst of America's crack problem seemed to be abating. Why this should be is unclear. Certainly there were no improvements in the lot of those living in New York's Bedford-Stuyvesant area or LA's Compton or Oakland or Washington or any of the other crack-blasted areas of America. Nor did the Americans suddenly come up with some magic answer to the drug problem which had previously eluded them for the past ninety years. In fact, it does seem that irrespective of government actions, drug 'epidemics' of this sort have their own natural lifespan. Crack hasn't gone away, but use appears to have stabilised at a certain level within the drug scene.

The same applies to the innovatory honeymoon period of musical styles. Rap started out as an underground music, but was soon either assimilated by white corporate rock (who found a substantial young white audience for the music) or readily took on similar trappings through those black-owned rap labels. Bands formed and split, leading lights took off on their own solo careers; major artists faced criminal charges, some were gunned down in a hail of bullets.

Britain cottoned onto crack much later than America, but although it does create major problems in those areas where it has gained a foothold on the drug scene, overall Britain's crack crisis has not been anywhere near as acute as predicted for us nearly ten years ago. Nor has rap music in its purer forms proved as popular in the UK as other forms of black music such as reggae and soul. Instead, rap was integrated into yet another new form of music regimented by the beat of a very different drummer.

14   STONED IS THE WAY OF THE WALK

"We must make of joy once more a crime against the state"

Barney Hoskyns, NME *1991.*

"… there has always been a relationship between club culture and drugs. In the Seventies when I was immersed in the Northern Soul club underground, you would see clubbers who were patently addicted to the whole experience… Rave culture's hardcore is similarly addicted… Only there are a hell of a lot more of them and they take a hell of a lot more drugs".

Stuart Cosgrove interviewed by Sean O'Hagan, The Times *22nd February 1992.*

"… talking about ten years of dance music is simply not enough. Talk about five years of punk or indie. That makes sense. But not dance music. Dance music, like Ecstasy, have changed our very perception of time. In a decade, it has accelerated and mutated with exactly the speed and intensity you'd expect of music in the digital age".

Musik *magazine 1998.*

Yet it all started so slowly. In 1975, the police raided an amphetamine laboratory in the Midlands and came across a drug they couldn't identify. Tests showed it to be MDMA, an analogue of amphetamine that wasn't covered by the Misuse of Drugs Act. Therefore in 1977, the Act was changed so that any amphetamine derivative would be outlawed: before anybody in the country had ever heard of the drug, let alone tried it, ecstasy was banned. Eight years passed and then in October 1985, a journalist Peter Nasmyth wrote an article about ecstasy in the style magazine, *The Face.* He called it the 'yuppie way of knowledge'.

More prosaically, ecstasy is a synthetic amphetamine-like drug known chemically as 3,4, methylenedioxymethylamphetamine or MDMA for short. It belongs to a group of drugs called 'phenethlyamines'. MDMA was first synthesised early this century by the German pharmaceutical company Merck, who were looking to use amphetamine-like drugs to suppress appetite in overweight patients. MDMA was never marketed and, although it was one of a host of drugs tried out by the CIA as a truth drug, MDMA was largely forgotten about until the 1960s, when it was 'rediscovered' by Dr Alexander Shulgin, an American research chemist working for Dow Chemicals. Shulgin always tried out his experiments on himself and discovered that MDMA had a special quality in that it made the user feel very positive or 'empathetic' towards other people.

During the 1970s, some therapists who were counselling couples having problems with their marriage, gave the drug to them before the sessions and claimed that it helped each partner see the other's point of view and become less hostile. Inevitably, and like LSD before it, ecstasy (as it became known) leaked out on the streets of America, taken mainly by young middle class professionals in search of some kind of calming transcendental experience, although E is not hallucinogenic like LSD. However in 1985, just as the drug was becoming known about in England through Nasmyth's article, ecstasy was banned in the States, after some fears about brain damage in rats. From around 1982, the drug had been coming into Britain in small doses – some came direct from New York's club scene, some via the orange-robed disciples of Bhagwan Rajneesh. It was the gourmet delight for the yuppie seekers after truth, as well as Soho's elite group of fashion designers, musicians and journalists. But within a year or so of Nasmyth spilling the beans on E (for which he took some stick from the London glitterati, some of whom belonged to the Hug Club) another very different section of society discovered ecstasy. They were the largely working-class group, who became part of the regenerated British dance scene and created a bottom-up youth culture known as rave.

To date, there have been two major complementary histories of the rave or dance scene. Matthew Collin's *Altered State* (1997) book tells the military history of dance – its battles, its victories and defeats, set in the context of free parties, gangsters, police, outraged press and politicians. Simon Reynolds, in *Energy Flash* (1998) takes a different tack. The outline of events is there, but set much more within the framework of the music itself . He examines minutely, and with great perspicacity, the relationship between the sprawling behemoth of dance, and the drugs that made the music mad.

Reynolds writes that the music he describes in his book is shaped 'by and for drug experiences' believing that the essence of rave was not trippy hippy hoppy and ambient and 'intelligent' this that or the other, but what he calls 'hardcore pressure', 'the audience's demand for a soundtrack to go mental and getting fucked up'.

As such, it would have been equally valid to have discussed hardcore in the chapter on amphetamine because you could hardly have been more wired for sound than with this music. Just think about following a line from Sabbath and Led Zeppelin, through Guns 'n' Roses, Nirvana, death and thrash metal to hardcore ravers with a trail of booze, speed and then dodgy E's with all the downers to take off the edge. As Reynolds notes, 'By late 1991, you could see the walking wounded on the dancefloor'. Many of these were the so-called 'nuttercore' losing it at 140 bpm after necking up to 20 E's over a weekend including snorting the drug. Reynolds' ultimate dire observation of what happens if you position yourself 'permanently in rave's virtual reality pleasuredome...' is that 'the longer you stay there, the more likely it is that Ecstasy will degenerate into a dead(ening) end'.[1]

But having made the statement that it's all about 'tracks' and 'sounds' as the soundscape for excess without necessarily any intrinsic 'meaning', he still cannot bring himself to validate the rave experience just in terms of drugs, and this push-me pull-you is a recurrent theme. Reynolds makes it clear that while the ecstasy experience (both good and bad) underpinned all the music, the construction of rave's highways and byways, especially the speed of the music, changed as the purity of ecstasy diminished and ravers went from the ecstasy trip to the amphetamine stomp.

Yet he says, 'this begs the question of whether the meaning of rave music is reducible to drugs, or even a single drug, Ecstasy. Does this music only make sense when the listener is under the influence? I don't believe that for a second... [but] At the same time, rave culture as whole is barely conceivable without drugs, or at least without drug metaphors'.[2]

And there are plenty examples of those; Candy Flip named after an E/LSD cocktail; The Shamen supporting the views of latter day drug guru Terence McKenna and using some of his pro-DMT pronouncements on Top Twenty hit 'Re: Evolution'; Flowered Up having their video banned by the BBC for being too pro-drug; EMF, the 'Ecstasy Motherfuckers" 'Night of the Living E-Heads' as hardcore anthem; Xenophobia's 'Rush In The House' ringing out with 'Ecstasy, it's really got me now' to the tune of the Kinks 'You Really Got Me'; Goa Trance – heavily influenced by the LSD experience; the chilling out sounds of Intelligent Techno, Ambient and Trance – and so it goes, on and on and on...

Later in the introduction to *Energy Flash*, Reynolds is still clutching the worry beads because although he is a champion of the culture, 'there's a thread of doubt running through this book' as to 'whether recreational drug use is any kind of adequate basis for a culture, let alone a counterculture. Is rave simply about the dissipation of utopian energies into the void or does the idealism it catalyses spill over and transform ordinary life?'

To which the answer is 'yes' and 'no'. There have been a few but highly publicised E-related deaths and an unknown number of people who have suffered through overuse of the drug. On the other hand, the author attended a debate on ecstasy at Parallel Youniverse in Bagley's Warehouse behind King's Cross Station. One guy said that he had been very introverted and shy, unable to make friends. All that changed after he took ecstasy. Now he said, he had stopped using the drug, but retained the social skills gained under its influence. In a very real sense, ecstasy changed this person's life for the better.

Through the book, Reynolds cannot leave (what for him) seems a vital issue, 'Just as it seemed possible to make the case that electronic music could be more than a soundtrack to drugging and dancing along came 'ardkore: not so much music as a science of inducing and enhancing the E-rush. Could you even listen to this music "on the natural", enjoy it in an un-altered state? Well I did and do, all the time. But whether I'd *feel it*, viscerally understand it, if my nervous system hadn't been reprogrammed by MDMA, is another matter.'[3]

Why does the music have to mean something? This search for 'meaning' could apply to any largely instrumental music simply because there are no lyrics to interpret. And even when there are, does this make the music any more valid? Looking at all the cod symbolism of most of British progressive rock in the early-mid seventies – does this have more 'meaning' than Goldie or the Shamen or whoever.

There is also the issue of whether or not rave was/is in any sense political or countercultural. The Free Party community Exodus would probably view their activities in pursuit of political aims, even if it were simply to get up the nose of the authorities. The very fact of large numbers of young people gathered together to hear/ dance to music and take drugs is seen almost as a political act in itself simply because it is activity that society at large does not want to see happen. Of course, going mental on drugs and music would undoubtedly be seen by the majority of clubbers as completely the opposite of political action. They would see what they do as escaping from society, having nothing to do with a political agenda that (as they see it) is completely irrelevant to them. So, in the political jargon of the day, there is a third way analysis of rave – it was not avowedly political, but by default, it became political, both in the wider context of the social control of young people through legislation – and more specifically in the degree to which drugs is now an intergral part of the political agenda. But more of that later; in the meantime, where did it all come from?

* * * * *

The rave generation was fashioned from at least two distinct and broad-based strands – one whose cultural heritage was interior, the world of the club; the other being exterior, the free parties, descendants of the 'Be-Ins' and 'Happenings' of sixties west coast America.

Although ecstasy was first used recreationally in America, it never formed a core part of the club/dance scene to the extent that it did in Britain, and so that crucial link between stimulant drug and all night dancing was (apart from possibly on the New York gay scene) more tenuous. In Britain, that link was already firmly established, going back over seventy years. It is this tradition which helps explain why rave took off in Britain before anywhere else.

During the inter-war years, and with Britain's first drug laws in place, the illicit drug scene in Britain was limited to a few dance and drinking clubs in London's West End. The most popular illicit 'fun' drug of the time among the prostitutes, gamblers, theatre people and the more louche elements of the British aristocracy, was cocaine. *The Evening News* (14 March 1922) published an account of clubland and how women in particular were driven to prolonged wild dancing by the cocaine rush; 'One (of the "girl-addicts") was a frail-looking creature of about twenty in a flimsy frock that left three-quarters of her back bare. During the interval of her vivacious dancing in an underground room, she gave herself over to almost hysterical attacks of inane purposeless laughter...'[4]. The cocaine overdose death of dancer Freda Kempton in 1922 made the national press and prompted the *Daily Express* to run a campaign against drugs and 'dance dens' illustrated by a cartoon of a skeleton doorman standing outside 'The Dope Dance Club' beckoning in would-be revellers under the caption 'The Shadow of Death'. Apart from basement dives (and in images which resonate down the years) the *Express* also described dances held in 'unlit buildings in foreboding neighbourhoods' where the participants were 'perpetually seized with hysterical laughter and ogling foolishly'.

After that, apart from a few sensational tabloid stories about 'Indian hemp' in the early fifties and a drugs raid on a West End jazz club, the non-medical use of drugs was simply not an issue until the early 1960s prompted by the use of another stimulant drug by young people for all-night dancing, amphetamine.

Once the Mod era gave way to psychedelia in 1966, there was little in the way of a distinctive club culture in London to take its place. Rock music quickly outgrew clubs and became first campus and then arena-based. What remained were the mainstream discotheques, venues for the rock aristocracy such as the Speakeasy and Blaises and the regular clubs such as The Marquee, the 100 Club, Klooks Kleek and others which provided the launch pad for up and coming blues/rock bands.

For the next development in stimulant-based dance culture, we must look to northern England, to venues in Wigan, Blackpool and elsewhere and the phenomenon of the early 1970s known as Northern Soul. The devotees of Northern Soul were carrying on a long-established tradition whereby British music fans have embraced American black music often far more enthusiastically than the home base. During the fifties, for example, American blues artists were feted in Britain by white audiences at a time when young black American music fans regarded the blues as the best-forgotten sounds of slavery. The fifties blues buffs were primarily older middle-class whereas the fans of sixties soul music and West Indian-derived bluebeat and ska were often from working class backgrounds including, paradoxically, the skinheads who were otherwise implacably racist.

The driving force of similarly working-class based Northern Soul were so-called 'rare grooves', obscure American soul records, while the focus for this nocturnal dance culture were not only the pharmaceutical amphetamines of the sixties; 'bennies', blues' and 'bombers', but also illicitly manufactured amphetamine sulphate powder adding to the sense of exclusivity among aficionados.

Punk was the other speed-driven sub-culture of the seventies: club culture came much more to the fore and set the scene for the arrival of a 'new age' in the mid 1980s. Aside from Northern Soul and punk, there was a strong club network among the gay community and a post-punk club scene centred around 'New Romantics' and briefly neopsychedelia, an abortive attempt to recreate the sixties without the use of drugs. There were also the beginnings of illegal warehouse parties which owed something to the blues or rent parties and shebeens of the Afro-Caribbean community where alcohol would be served. However, by the late eighties, the club scene in the UK had run out of steam and was in need of fresh inspiration.

The source for the revitalisation of the UK club scene derived from a combination of two distinct but related developments – both from outside the UK. The first was House or Garage music from the USA. Named after the Warehouse in Chicago and the Paradise Garage in New York, this music came out of the same electronic melting pot that gave birth to rap inspired by key DJs such as Larry Leven, Frankie Knuckles and Ron Hardy.

Already well accustomed to absorbing the underground sounds of America, the north west of England readily accepted House music as it filtered across the Atlantic to venues like the Hacienda in Manchester. Opened in 1982 and owned by Tony Wilson, boss of the legendary indie label Factory, the Hacienda was to become the crucible for the whole rave phenomenon.

The other and far more unlikely source came from the Mediterranean island of Ibiza. A long-standing 'hippy hideaway', Ibiza developed its own dance club culture based on the House/Garage sounds of black urban America recast as the 'Balearic sound', not a sound style as such, more an approach to DJ-ing, a revolt against style and dress codes, against the rigidity and elitism which then gripped London clubland. The core of this largely instrumental music was a relentless and regular percussive beat by which all subsequent developments of dance music have been defined – from the almost beatless, melodic wash of 'ambient' music, through to Big Beat, Drum 'n' Bass, Techno, and out into the maniacal stratosphere of 'Gabba' and all the myriad offshoots and niches in-between.

British jocks, Nicky Holloway, Johnnie Walker, Danny Rampling and Paul Oakenfold, coming back from their 'Club Ibiza' experience, decided to try and stimulate the flagging London club scene by recreating the island sounds of summer. So in 1987, a whole new generation of clubs sprang up including the pioneering London venues of happy days Shoom, Future and Spectrum – and the more dodgy days of Clink St. Ecstasy was the centre stage drug for the Ibiza crowd, and already part of the London club scene, the drug was quickly assimilated to head the pantheon of dance drugs across the country and from there rapidly took its place as the cultural signifier of a generation.

From indoors to outdoors and the second major plank on which rave culture was founded – the tradition of open air music events inaugurated on the west coast of America in the early sixties as a prelude to psychedelia. The notion of young people gathering together in large numbers to dance and listen to music, take drugs and make love gained momentum through the sixties among mainly white middle class students in revolt against the monolithic straitjacket of American society in general and the Vietnam War in particular. From 'Be-In' and 'Happenings' in Golden Gate Park in San Francisco in the early sixties to Woodstock in 1969, spiritual and political aspirations were rapidly overtaken by commercial venality. But nevertheless, the tradition of transcendent hedonism combined with a hefty dose of spiritual, pagan and even paranormal desires and a polymorphous sense of communion was established and exported to Britain – not so much in the explicitly commercial environment of, for example, the Isle of Wight Festival of 1970, but beginning perhaps with the first free Stonehenge Festival of 1974.

Although much has been made of drug use in sixties Britain, the actual extent of use has probably been overplayed. From about 1966 onwards (when the 'sixties' as a socio-cultural phenomenon actually started) use of cannabis and LSD 'exploded', but from a virtually non-existent base, and was largely confined (sociodemographically) to elements of the student population and (geographically) to London and the Home Counties, where, by and large, the new high profile artistic elite lived (musicians, writers, painters, photographers etc) alongside the media who eagerly reported their drug use.

Among students there is some evidence to suggest that as artefacts of a past decade, drugs fell out of fashion in the early seventies, but over the UK as a whole, drug use began to permeate nationwide. However, the messianic/tribal aspects of the communal drug experience which surrounded the use of hallucinogenic drugs did decline except in pockets of the 'underground' which kept the spirit of the sixties alive at Stonehenge and Glastonbury right through to the 'new wave' open air rave parties. By the mid seventies, as Chris Stone describes it, 'Anger had replaced the placid self-indulgence of the hippie era, but the institution of Stonehenge fitted in well with the DIY punk ethos. It was anarchy incarnate, a riot of self-expression and celebratory culture. A new breed of punk was born from contact with the festival scene; the so-called rainbow punks, hippies in all but name. They bought trucks and took to the road. They became the core of what we now call New Age Travellers. The fusion of hippie idealism with punk politics is at the root of the counter-cultural scene' and the social cement of the underground was 'we all take drugs'.[5]

By the summer of 1991, the rave scene met the festival goers and travellers 'and a new philosophy was born'. This was based on the ethos of Spiral Tribe, one of a number of sound systems touring Europe as part of the free party circuit. They had a corporate identity, logos, uniform etc, but 'it was as if they'd learnt all the lessons of corporate capitalism, but to a different end. They aped capitalism in order to subvert it'.[6] Here perhaps is one of the paradoxes of the rave scene in nineties Britain. Arguably use of ecstasy and other drugs by young people was natural reaction against the hard-nosed materialism and insecurities of the 1980s – but also a strange endorsement of its hedonistic and entrepreneurial values. An explanation for these apparently contradictory viewpoints is required, but in the absence of hard evidence remains tentative.

The 1980s were a period of great insecurity for all sectors of British society – for the first time middle class professionals were experiencing the same kind of employment uncertainties as those experienced by the working classes. There was a sense of alienation, lack of community, looking after 'number one' – a sea of individuals each fighting for their own survival and fearful of what the future might hold. Young people entering their mid-teens at the turn of the decade were deeply cynical about the political process and found little solace in their own communities – nor did the Church have much to offer in the way of spiritual comfort. Thus we find a generation, not only looking for alternatives to reality, for altered states of consciousness, (like its predecessor in the sixties) but also in search of 'community', for almost tribal identification and a sense of belonging.

There are in fact, a number of parallels between ecstasy use and the early hidden rave venues and rites-of-passage drugs rituals of tribal societies. For example, young Huichol Native Americans make pilgrimages across the Mexican desert to secret locations where the hallucinogenic peyote cactus is found, locations known only to the initiates. The drug is taken in these secret places and the young Indians spend the night dancing and chanting to a repetitive drumbeat.[7]

Many young people found group comfort on the rave scene through the use of ecstasy with its capacity to promote empathy and fellowship among users. For those supporters of the drug, it would seem to be very much the right drug in the right place at the right time. To this search beyond the everyday and ordinary, of course, we might add the intense interest in aliens from outer space (*The X-Files*, *Independence Day* and other films) and 'virtual reality' on the Internet.

Reynolds seems to go along with the idea as propounded by sociologist Antonio Melechi, that rave culture represented a culture of disappearance, an internal tourism enjoyed by young people in a break from the tradition of youth culture as resistance-through-ritual such as punk and mod which were much more 'in your face' gobs at straight society. It is probably true that rave wasn't born as an escape valve from the tedium of capitalist-driven labours – because for many on the scene, there was no labour – which adds some weight to the vision of rave as some kind of holy communion.

But if the stance and attitude wasn't 'in your face' resistance, then what about the sheer numbers involved and the violence that ensued when the police attempted to intervene in dance events in the late 1980s, early 1990s – and ultimately – what about making joy a crime against the state?

There is also a version of the politics of ecstasy which as Reynolds points out, was far more in tune with the spirit of Timothy Leary, as the Parallel Youniverse environment indicated. The debate took place in the chill out area – with liquid light shows, films on the walls, a massage area and a general ambiance that took this author straight back to the Arts Labs of the late 1960s where everybody sat around stoned out of their box playing bongos. Even the smells were the same.

And then, there was what happened when you took too many E's and the amphetamine side of the drug kicked in. This places E culture firmly in the tradition of mod, punk, Northern Soul and the like – music to go mental on, a 'culture of consolation', a survival strategy to get a large section of Great British Youth through the Thatcher years and as Irvine Welsh puts it, 'the long, dark night of late capitalism'.

Then again, as Stone indicates, there has also been a seeming endorsement of eighties values; much of what goes on every weekend in venues and clubs up and down the UK is all about having a good time – and for many, a good time cannot be had unless drugs are involved. To an extent this mirrors the eighties era of the conspicuous consumption enjoyed by the lucky few. The abiding stereotypical image of eighties Britain was the 25 year old financial broker with mobile phone, Porsche sports car and unlimited supplies of cocaine. One might argue that many more are now joining the party – going to the 'in' clubs, helping to define the infinite varieties of dance music (an exercise in niche marketing which 'mainstream' business would be proud of), wearing the fashionable designer labels and taking the fashionable drugs. This has increasingly meant alcohol, as the breweries have fought back with drinks aimed at young people in a bid to retrieve customers from the other drug dealers. Alcohol is now routinely available at most dance venues. And as for the early entrepreneurs of rave who made large amounts of money from staging events, far from being dubbed 'bread heads' (the ultimate hippy insult) this motley crew of hooray henrys, gangsters and chancers became cult heroes. Only in the last few years has the corporate (for which read bland) face of rave come in for criticism in the letters pages of the dance magazines like *MixMag* and *Musik*.

At the beginning of this decade, there was a substantial new youth culture in Britain which dominated both the internal and external landscapes of the drugs/music nexus, drawing it closer to the mainstream of British youth culture than at any time this century. Dance music and ecstasy stood astride this new culture beyond the stimulant effects and empathogenesis even to the point of a palpable synergy between the rhythm of the music and the effect of ecstasy on the brain whereby the drug stimulates certain receptors which encourages the user to engage in repetitive acts without necessarily being aware of them. A combination of the repetitive 4/4 house music beat and ecstasy consumption produced dancers who entirely synchronised their bodies to the music.

Ecstasy and the dance culture it supported has opened the gateway to experimentation with a whole range of substances; established drugs on the UK scene such as LSD and amphetamine and new drugs (as yet uncontrolled by the Misuse of Drugs Act) such as ketamine, amyl nitrite (poppers) and gammahydroxybuterate (GHB). Ecstasy has informed just about every aspect of what has latterly been dubbed 'ecstasy culture'. This takes many forms, but for example includes the use of relaxing 'ambient' music, a gentle backdrop of 'easy-listening' sound, almost aural wallpaper in chill-out areas where people might be recovering from a long night of ecstasy-driven dancing. To take account of the fact that it can be dangerous to become overheated through taking ecstasy (with its effect of raising body temperature) in combination with extended bouts of non-stop dancing, club fashions in clothes changed to much looser, more 'baggy' styles. Before the drug element of rave became so public, High Street chains like Miss Selfridge and Top Shop were keen to exploit the 'smiley' logo on ranges of fashion clothing. This enthusiasm among retailers waned briefly, but the relentless pulse of rave culture and the sales revenue it promised proved irresistible, and now, for example, television and cinema screens throb to the beat of 'hyperreal' advertisements for soft drinks – another indication of how well-publicised health and safety aspects of drug use in clubs have permeated the commercial consciousness.

The 'new' drug users still believed that by using heroin (smoking or injecting) and/or cocaine (in its new formulation crack) that a line had been crossed and use of these drugs remains a minority activity among the 'rave generation'. But even here, ecstasy-inspired nineties rave music provided the soundtrack of *Trainspotting*, a film about the Edinburgh heroin scene of the mid-eighties. The upbeat soundtrack supplied ammunition for those critical of the alleged glamorization of heroin use in the film which also encompassed criticism of fashion photographers (most famously by Bill Clinton) for cultivating the much emulated 'wasted junkie' look favoured by young models like Kate Moss.

But the rave scene hasn't just been about beats per minute. Right from the start, there was a cross-fertilisation between the culture and sensibilities of dance and rock. There were DJs – but there were also bands. In the beginning was the war between the indie and the rave scenes, between studied misery and 'what the hell' hedonism. In the end, they all joined hands; fans moved between them with hardly a blink.

In the post-punk malaise of the 1980s, there was not a tremendous amount of music to stir the soul. Live Aid tried to make out that rock could still fulfil its promise of political influence and there was plenty of limp pop and rock fodder for those who bought one CD a year – usually Dire Straits. Most of what was vaguely interesting was happening in Manchester on the so-called indie scene where Morrissey and The Smiths indulged the arty long-coat student set with deftly wrought if rather fey tales of just how miserable life really was. If the 1960s belonged to London and Liverpool with London setting the pace in the 1970s (at least the second half) , then the 1980s (at least the second half) belonged to Manchester. Apart from the Smiths, local lads made good embraced the Fall, Joy Division, New Order followed by the Stone Roses and the band that eventually took the city into the nineties, Oasis. But there was one band that encapsulated both the benign and malign pulse of a city pitched briefly into the media spotlight – the Happy Mondays.

Lead singer and songwriter Shaun Ryder was brought up in the desperate reaches of Greater Manchester. Always rough and dangerous with high levels of unemployment and a rampant illicit economy, this area and many like it in northern England were laid waste by Thatcherism. Young kids got into glue sniffing and then (in much the same way as crack had done in the States) heroin stepped into the breach; it provided a routine where otherwise all there was to do was stare at the bedroom ceiling waiting to collect the benefit money; it provided a source of income and a way out of despair. Said Ryder, 'drugs were something to get you through. I've been on a drug trip since I was 12'. Living in areas like Salford and Eccles, 'the only buzz you could get was a 70p tube of gas'. So Ryder and his friends went on a criminal spree that included driving cars away, arson, poisoning pigeons and drug dealing. He has always been upfront about his criminal past. Many musicians prior to Ryder have said that music saved them from prison, although more recently (in line with many rap artists) confessing to misdemeanours has become part of the marketing armoury – witness the much vaunted burglary exploits of the Brothers Gallagher. Ryder even owned up to the fact that music was not necessarily the main driving force behind the Mondays, 'The Mondays weren't about making records, it was about living the rock 'n' roll life and getting out of our boring little existence' (*Q Mag* July 1996).

The band that played its first gigs in the summer of 1985 was a working class (perhaps even underclass) outfit bent on having a good time. In his biography of Shaun Ryder, Mick Middles described the band as 'the shambolic rumble of sordid camaraderie, teen angst, fumbling, artless musicianship, gibbering Salfordian street-speak, impenetrable in-jokes, punctuated by relentless vulgarities, profound hedonism, strange and deep-rooted musical knowledge and mod-ish sports gear casual fashion… this was all that would become the Happy Mondays.'[8]

Three members of the band shared a flat from where they would sell cannabis and heroin. Even though later Shaun Ryder was saying that heroin was an awful drug, 'the worst drug in the word and shouldn't be touched.' (*Arena* 1996) – the same as he said about crack – he also boasted that they sold, 'the best, the meanest skag around'.[9] Essentially the Happy Mondays were established on drug money; they traded drugs for instruments from musicians who had had their chance and blown it.

In their inaugural year, they signed with Factory Records; if it's true that having had Joy Division and New Order, Tony Wilson was looking for the new Sex Pistols, he certainly found them with Shaun and the lads. In 1986, the Mondays discovered ecstasy in Amsterdam and brought it back to Manchester going so far as to claim they introduced the drug to the city's drug scene, although in truth, they probably swallowed most of it themselves. By the time that the classic *Bummed* album was released in 1988, even Shaun Ryder knew they had to cut back. Although they had recorded the album 'absolutely caned on E', by the time it was released, 'I had already knocked down on my consumption of E. When we did that album, I could still eat three E's a day, but we were a lot calmer than before.'[10]. 'Wrote for Luck' on *Bummed* was Shaun Ryder's anti-drug song, 'drugs were something that gets you through'. Here was Shaun Ryder writing an anti-drug song, just as the rest of the country was beginning to catch on to a new chapter in the drugs/music dynamic. Because after 1988 came 1989 – and the conversion of Manchester into the media hype known as Madchester.

This was the stellar year for Manchester; both football teams were doing well, and another Manchester band was bursting through to recognition – The Stone Roses. As described by John Robb in his biography of the band, from their beginnings in 1986, the Stone Roses changed from 'amphetamine-driven rock to dope-smoke haze of more psychedelic pop'. Once 1989 came round, the Stone Roses joined the baggy culture of rampant musical eclecticism and mayhem. The Stone Roses played their now famous Blackpool gig in the summer and both they and the Happy Mondays appeared on Top of the Pops in November. For Chris Hutton, the musician who had the Oasis rhythm section in his band Rain, 'Manchester felt like the centre of the universe instead of a provincial outpost of drudgery'.[11]

Manchester became drug heaven, 'strung out, cabbaged whacked and plain weird was the mental currency of a city gone completely off its axis'.[12] Naturally, it couldn't last. Eventually rave culture would be rapidly hemmed in by a disingenuously outraged media on the one hand and the forces of law and order on the other. The drug scene, too, got out of hand. The gangsters moved in, but probably the collapse of the Happy Mondays in a miasma of heroin and crack most typified a smiley grin turned grim. Although *Pills, Thrills and Bellyaches* was dubbed by Shaun Ryder, the Monday's cocaine album, they were still holding it together then – just. But in an attempt to get Ryder right away from heroin influences in Manchester, the *Yes Please* album was recorded in Barbados. No heroin, true – but lots of crack and the story went that Ryder held the masters of the album to ransom until Factory Records sent out more money from drugs. Shortly afterwards, the bubble burst for Factory as well, a demise for which Shaun Ryder took an amount of blame, although unwise property purchases were more at the root of the trouble.

* * * * *

The media backlash against the dance generation took off with predictable swiftness, although perhaps not swift enough for some of the leading lights of the new scene who appeared anxious to receive the necessary press opprobrium in order to validate their underground status. The music press and the rave spokespeople played a strange two-step with the mainstream media. On the one hand, between February and August 1988, through the summer which became rave's 'Summer of Love' equivalent to the *Sergeant Pepper*/LSD season of 1967, *Record Mirror*, *New Musical Express* and *Melody Maker* (all owned incidentally by mainstream publishing corporations) were predicting that rave would be linked to drug use by the tabloid press. *Time Out* (17-24th August) even went so far as to helpfully write the headlines ('London gripped by Ecstasy' and 'Drug Crazed New Hippies in Street Riot'). For a time, the tabloids failed to rise to the bait. On October 1st *The Sun* ran a feature which set out a glossary of Acid House terminology and invited readers to purchase a Smiley logo T-shirt. However, only a week later the paper's resident doctor Vernon Coleman was warning about the dangers of ecstasy, followed by a plethora of the predicted headlines of which 'Dicing with a cocktail of death' (*Daily Star* 2nd November 1988) and 'Mr Big behind the latest frenzied pop party cult' (*Daily Mirror* 2nd November 1988) are but two examples. This latter was a reference to Tony Colston-Hayter, one of the earliest entrepreneurs of rave who organised large unlicensed warehouse parties. Immediately, party organisers and major drug dealers were cast as one and the same people (and it has to be admitted this was often the case). Although in practice, the police dealt with rave events as a public order issue, because they knew they couldn't possibly arrest every drug user, it was clear from the outset that the running battle between rave culture and their opponents among the mainstream press, police, local authorities and politicians would focus on the use of drugs.

Having achieved the notoriety they had arguably sought, supporters of rave culture began backpedalling to play down the drug connection. The immediate assumption about 'Acid House' was that it concerned LSD. In fact, this turned out to be correct, as LSD figured quite prominently in the early period just ahead or alongside ecstasy as a drug of choice. But at the time, the term was linked to the Chicago music scene which Paul Staines of the Freedom to Party Campaign later claimed he made up to put journalists off the scent. Staines was a good example of the strange bedfellows rave threw together, as his day job was assistant to David Hart, a rabid free market right winger who advised Thatcher. Staines linked the word 'Acid' to the technique of sampling in that 'Acid' was black American slang for stealing.[13] Radio One DJ Simon Bates for one was taken in, 'Acid is all about the bass-line in music and nothing to do with drugs' (*Daily Mirror* 12th November 1988).

Historically, however, while the Detroit house scene was relatively drug-free, in Chicago it was different. Cannabis was often dipped in angel dust to create 'happy sticks'; poppers, cocaine and LSD were all popular. The first Chicago music using the famous Roland 303 sound was Phuture's 'Acid Tracks' released in 1987 – the track became popular with the crowd at the Music Box as played by DJ Ron Hardy, a club where it was rumoured that the owners had spiked the water supply with LSD. The track's creators were at pains to point out the 'Acid Tracks' had nothing to do with drugs, instead the song was supposed to affect the listener like a drug, '… it takes you over. People go into a trance, they just lose it!' Phuture further pointed out that the flip side was an anti-cocaine song 'Your Only Friend'.[14]

Back in Britain, once the iniquities of rave were plastered all over the media, political pressure for a law and order response was sure to follow. Increasing or introducing penalties for drug use has been a key weapon of the state in dealing with youth movements viewed as a threat to society. In 1964, in response to mod culture, hastily conceived legislation resulted in the banning of amphetamine without a prescription. In the same year, it became an offence to allow premises to be used for the smoking of cannabis and in 1966, LSD was outlawed almost before it became established on the drug scene. In fact, it is particularly interesting to note that in a decade of unprecedented liberalising legislation in Britain which saw controls relaxed on gambling, censorship, abortion, homosexuality, the beginning of anti-discrimination laws in favour of women and ethnic minorities and even the abolition of hanging – the laws against drug use were tightened. This says much about the mythological and symbolic nature of drug use in society.

The early years of rave organisation and control can best be described as anarchic. Unlicensed events were taking place in any available location; fields, aircraft hangers, derelict buildings and motorway underpasses. Initially, the police and local authorities relied on legislation such as the 1967 Private Places of Entertaining (Licensing) Act which requires private (as well as public) events to be licensed by the local authorities and the Licensing Act of 1988 which gave the police greater discretionary powers in the granting of licenses. There was also recourse to various public order legislation, health and safety laws as well as the Misuse of Drugs Act.

The police and party organisers played cat and mouse with each other as a whole network of subterfuge was established. Convoys of young people would meet in cars at, for example, motorway service stations awaiting instructions as to the location of that evening's event. Where attempts were made to hold large open air festivals, police would cordon off roads and shepherd would-be attendees into neighbouring areas away from the site. The police set up a Pay Party intelligence unit based at Gravesend police station to monitor the activities of party organisers and over a two-year period from 1988-1990, there were some serious public order disturbances in locations around the country as police clashed with those either trying to reach sites or where police arrived to break an event already under way. Although much was made by the media of the risks posed to public order by these large outdoor events, most if not all of the violence occurred directly as a result of police intervention.

However, it was not strong-arm tactics that ended the illegal raves (if anything police action made activists even more determined) but new and much tougher licensing legislation. Under the Entertainments (Increased Penalties) Act of 1990 first tabled by Graham Bright MP, organisers of unlicensed parties could face fines up to £20,000 and six months in prison. This put most organisers out of business and some went abroad to the more liberal climate of European countries such as Germany. However, the free party movement was by no means dead in the UK and outdoor events continued around the country in Liverpool, Cheshire, Warrington, the Lake District, Wales, Gloucestershire and Southport often accompanied by violent clashes between police and ravers culminating in the rave 'Woodstock' held at Castlemorton in May 1992 attended by anything up to 40,000 people.

The organisers, the Spiral Tribe sound system were charged with public order offences and there were a number of other arrests over the ten day period of the event. In a trial costing an estimated £4 million all those whose cases came to court were acquitted, but the adverse publicity attending the event laid the groundwork for the Criminal Justice Act 1994 (CJA) which put the final nail in the coffin of the unlicensed event.

As with most legislation assembled in the white heat of media glare, the sections of the CJA which specifically refer to raves have been described as 'piecemeal'. For the purposes of the Act, a rave is defined as 'a gathering on land in the open air of 100 persons or more... at which amplified music is played during the night... and is such as, by reason of its loudness and duration and the time at which it is played, is likely to cause serious distress to the inhabitants of the locality'. This does not apply to events where public or private licenses have been granted. Under the Act, the police can intervene to stop an event from happening, even if only three people have gathered, if the superintendent has reason to believe that eventually more than 100 people *will* gather illegally. Police can also seize equipment and have the power to redirect people who may be on their way to a site. As it stands, the Act is open to interpretation. For example, there is no definition of 'night'; what about an outdoor event that started in daylight which would be quite common in the summer months? Would it be legal up to the point where it got dark? Nor is it clear whether a fully enclosed venue such as an aircraft hangar with doors would be exempt because the Act only mentions venues which are in the open air or 'partly open to the air'. How do you define 'serious distress'? The wording of the Act is vague enough to suggest that the complaint of one individual in an otherwise isolated rural location would be enough.

There is less controversy over the attempts of local authorities to regulate the activities of indoor venue owners where real risks to the customers exist in clubs where, in pursuit of profit, health and safety regulations have been ignored or violence allowed to continue unchecked. Certainly the lack of alcohol in rave clubs meant an absence of the usual type of customer-on-customer violence that is a regular feature of mainstream discos and pubs. However, any club or pub in an inner city area is a likely target for criminal gangs eager to provide protection. supply drugs or simply take over the business as 'sleeping partners'. Thus, for example, in Liverpool, a number of clubs hosting house music were closed down because of drug-related violence on the premises.

The city of Manchester, too has always been a hard and violent place. As the main focus for working class life, football has been also the main focus for violence in the city. In the 1970s, it was largely a disorganised rabble. In the 1980s, it slimmed to the more organised firms of dedicated psychopaths wreaking havoc in their own back yard. It was mainly the organised groups that were operating when the hangers-on and less dedicated let dope and ecstasy come into their lives during the Madchester days. You could stand on the terraces and inhale the passing cannabis fumes. The E grin was everywhere. But this was just an balmy interlude. In the mid-1990s, elements of soccer violence returned, but more significantly the drug gangs moved in on the rave scene turning Madchester into Gunchester. Drug shootings were often confined to turf wars over crack, but soon spread to the dance scene as ecstasy use continued to spiral.

Police and local authorities have objected to the license renewal for clubs where drug dealing is alleged – in January 1997, Club UK in south London lost its entertainment licence and closed down. Owners often counter criticism with assertions that they do all they can to stop drugs coming into clubs and employ security guards to search all customers, although they are not empowered to conduct intimate searches and the determined user or dealer can secrete drugs to avoid detection. Clearly the situation will vary from club to club. The larger urban venues have been tightening up on their 'no drugs' policies, and many venues now actively cooperate with the police. But there will always be circumstances where venue owners will be colluding in (willingly or not) or actually organising drug dealing on their premises. In addition, research indicates that it is something of a myth to indict rave venues as being 'drug supermarkets' because most drug users take their drugs before they arrive.

In May 1998, the Public Entertainments Licences (Drug Misuse) Act came into effect, allowing local councils to shut down clubs immediately if there is evidence of drug use and drug dealing. There are some councils who are used to dealing with club owners in urban settings and are aware of the virtual impossibility of guaranteeing a drug-free venue. Other councils, perhaps those outside the major conurbations who have less contact with dance venues, may take the opportunity of more stringent legislation simply to attack rave culture by closing down clubs.

Local authorities have been keen to act against those venues where health and safety regulations have been routinely flouted in respect of fire hazard, maximum numbers on the premises and so on. But the health and safety issue that has received most attention has been that related to minimising the dangers of drug use. As we have seen, dancing for long hours in packed venues sustained on stimulant drugs is nothing new on the British club scene. For all the untold amount of amphetamine consumed during the sixties, there is not one case report of an amphetamine-related club death recorded in the literature.

However, if ecstasy has a uniquely benign pharmacological action which has secured its popularity, then it also has a more malign property which has helped claim the lives of around eighty young people since 1989. To a much greater extent than amphetamine, ecstasy interferes with the thermo-regulatory mechanism of the body to raise body temperature, even when the user is at rest. Thus the combination of drug plus the circumstances of its use in hot ambient temperatures has caused the equivalent of heat-stroke type deaths as the major cause of fatality in those cases. However, thanks to the efforts of drug agencies such as the Merseyside Regional Drug Information Service (MRDIS now called HIT) and the Manchester agency Lifeline, club goers were warned about the dangers of overheating, and advised to wear baggy clothes and drink non-alcoholic fluids if they were going to take ecstasy and then dance for long hours in hot, humid and tightly packed venues. Club owners responded cynically by turning off the cold water supply in the toilets and then charging anything up to £2 a bottle for water.

The government and other authorities have been forced to take a more pragmatic view of drug use among young people in the light of the explosion of drug use through the nineties. This is best illustrated by what happened when the MRDIS published its *Chill-Out* leaflet in 1992, one of the earliest pieces of health and safety information about drugs and raves. There were front page exhortations from the tabloids for parents to go round to the agency and chuck the author of the leaflet in the River Mersey and funding was put in severe jeopardy. Within months, the same advice was appearing in the established medical press and was rapidly taken up by the government in its drug advice campaigns.

At a local level, too, the city authorities in Manchester, London and Scotland have all issued guidelines for making dance venues safer. In any event, both for humanitarian and commercial reasons, many club owners are taking on board the health and safety issues around drugs, following the guidelines and allowing drug agency workers in to offer advice and act as drug paramedics for those in difficulty.

After a decade of development rave culture, in all its manifestations, is now a legitimate and lucrative arm of the leisure industry with highly commercialised venue organisations such as Ministry of Sound and Cream, glossy magazines, record labels, merchandising and with the DJ (rather than the musician) as star. Inevitably, the rave scene has balkanised into many different genres and subgenres. The drug scene will almost certainly go down the same route. Certain drugs such as cannabis and LSD will undoubtedly remain central. But the demands of fashion, the search for some new experience and more prosaically, the controls on precursor chemicals which are used in drug manufacture, will mean that the underground chemists will be encouraged to become more ingenious in 'designing' new drugs. As drug use becomes increasingly a fashion accessory, it may be even more at the whim of fashion than in previous times – which means that mass consumption of 'dance drugs' as a normal activity of 'growing up' might go 'out of fashion' or that at least the experimenters and occasional users will become bored (or decide the legal risks are not worth the trouble) leaving the regular users to carry on. There are some signs in the UK that ecstasy use is not increasing at such a rate and that use may be levelling out.

On the other hand, ecstasy has created a 'platform of acceptability' among substantial numbers of young people who are now willing to experiment with all manner of psychedelic drugs which will no doubt dance hand in hand with whatever the music industry has to offer, be it top-down corporate product or innovations from the back bedrooms.

The culture has been exported the world over. Holland has a well-established rave scene, where drug users have an element of protection from the uncertainties of the illegal drug market through a drug testing programme available outside clubs. Rave culture has made inroads through much of Europe, and to Scandinavia despite the 'zero tolerance' to drugs in the Nordic countries. Even the Chinese are raving on E; the police there have recently made their first seizures of ecstasy or 'head rocking drug' as it's called. In those Chinese cities where adherence to western culture is at its most developed, the police have been told to stop any young person wearing shades on suspicion of being a drug user. In an ironic turn-round, Asia and the Far East, source of most of the world's heroin, is now being flooded with European ecstasy cooked up in jungle laboratories by Eastern European chemists. It's the top drug in Indonesia where the chief slang name is Bon Jovi.

In fact, in its latest world report on drugs, the United Nations expressed its concerns about the growth of synthetic drug use the world over, whether it's ecstasy, amphetamine, its smokable form 'ice' and other designer drugs. However, one drug has never gone away – as the beat changes, it just keeps reinventing itself.

15 THE BLUNT TRUTH

"*Older* was pretty much recorded on cannabis. I wasn't drinking – because I was
too stoned".

George Michael Q *Mag January 1998*

If it wasn't for cannabis, the world might never have heard of Christine Keeler or her
affair with Tory Cabinet Minister John Profumo and the Macmillan government might
just have survived.

The year is 1963 and a West Indian Johnny Edgecombe is on trial for the attempted
murder in November 1962, of a young cabaret dancer/model and general 'good time
girl' Christine Keeler at the Devonshire Mews flat of her mentor and protector, Dr
Stephen Ward. Ward was an osteopath and artist, but his claim to fame was as friend,
confident and 'fixer' to London society; politicans, celebrities and even royalty. What
he fixed was often as not, sexual encounters for those who could not afford to be
exposed to public scrutiny. He had a desperate need to be liked and respected and was
anxious to impress his high flying acquaintances at every turn.

One fateful day, he invited society artist Vasco Lazzolo to accompany him and
Christine down into Notting Hill, into the heart of London's West Indian community
for a little walk on the wild side. Keeler recalled in her autobiography that Ward told
Lazzolo, 'You've no idea what it's like there. There's always something going on…
You're always reading about the race riots, come and see for yourself'.[1]

They went down there, moved from one café to another, but nothing happened; even
Stephen Ward couldn't engineer a bit of inter-racial violence to impress his guest.
However, he had to salvage something from the evening to keep his reputation intact,
so he suggested to Christine that she try to buy some cannabis; 'it was just becoming
fashionable to smoke, but still quite daring'[2]

She approached a West Indian standing on the street, Lucky Aloysius Gordon, who
turned out to be not so lucky for Christine Keeler. She bought ten shillings (50p)

worth of grass from him and he was immediately attracted to her. She agreed to meet him again on condition he introduced Ward to a cannabis dealer in case any of Ward's society chums wanted a taste and also procured a black girl for Ward to sleep with. The deal was struck and Gordon brought a girl and a dealer to Ward's flat, but after that things started to go very wrong. Lucky Gordon became obsessed with Christine and on more than one occasion, according to Keeler, raped her and beat her up. Eventually she enlisted the aid of another West Indian, Johnny Edgecombe who supplied her with a 'hot' gun, previously used in a Queens Park robbery.[3] Although she doesn't mention this in her own book, another account of the Keeler affair says she went to live with Edgecombe in Ealing and he too become fixated on her. When she left him, he tracked her down and tried to shoot her. At the subsequent trial, he was sent to prison for possessing a firearm with intent to cause harm. But it was at this trial, due to behind the scenes political machinations, that Christine Keeler's brief affair with War Minister John Profumo and the link with a Russian diplomat, Eugene Ivanov, was made public. This was at the height of the Cold War, in the wake of the perilous stand-off between America and Russia over Cuba and the government still reeling from the Vassall spy case. Profumo resigned, Ward was the patsy, now totally isolated, and in the dock charged with living on immoral earnings. With his life in ruins, he killed himself before the verdict was delivered. The Profumo affair, the Great Train Robbery and the rise of the Beatles, all in various ways signalled that the Harold Macmillan's Conservative government was well past its sell-by date and on 17th October 1963, the Prime Minister resigned.

Christine Keeler's comment that cannabis smoking was only just becoming fashionable among the white smart set is indicative of how low a profile the drug had among the general population in the early sixties. It also shows up the complete fabrications of previous tabloid exposés of cannabis use among young people.

Up until the mid sixties, cannabis use was pretty much restricted to the West Indian blues and rent party scene and the West End jazz clubs. Only a small band of white musicians, students and sundry bohemians indulged in pot, reefer or charge, and it was only in 1964 that prosecutions for possession by whites outstripped those for blacks. Yet as far back as July 1939, the *Daily Mirror* was making the ludicrous claim that London had 'thousands' of 'addicts' taking this 'dangerous drug' under the banner headline, 'Just a cigarette, you think, but it was made from a sinister weed and an innocent girl falls victim to this TERROR!' with a photo, 'specially posed for the Daily Mirror'. The whole article centred on the use of the drug by young white women seduced into trying the drug by men 'usually coloured' in a 'reefer club'. There were also the Anslinger-inspired assertions that cannabis drove users to 'violence, even murder'. These themes were picked up in the early post-War period by articles in the *Daily Telegraph*, *Evening Standard* and *Sunday Graphic* of 1951 and in 'Indian Hemp: a social menace', published in 1952 from the pen of barrister Donald Johnson quoting wholesale from the tabloid articles as his key source of information on the growing 'problem'.

At one point, towards the end of the book, Johnson speculates on whether there might be a neurological link between cannabis and 'hot jazz'. He quotes Chapman Pincher writing in the *Daily Express*, 28th November 1951. Basing his comments on research conducted by the Burden Neurological Institute in Bristol, Pincher wrote 'Reefers and rhythm seem to be directly connected with the minute electric waves continually generated by the brain surface. When the rhythm of the music synchronizes with the rhythm of the brainwaves, the jazz fans experience an almost compulsive urge to move their bodies in sympathy'. Sound familiar? Ex-Superintendent Robert Fabian of Scotland Yard in his mid-fifties reminiscence, *London After Dark,* had clearly been reading the same reports,

> There is, I believe, some scientific foundation for the claim that marijuana addiction can help a musician, for this drug has some effect upon that part of the brain which responds to rhythmical vibrations, and it is as a result of this that the cult of 'reefer' smoking has been so closely bound up with jive musicians and coloured men.[4]

As in the USA, the idea that cannabis was of itself a dangerous, maddening drug, began to lose some ground in the British press, athough the overriding fears about miscegenation remained. Just days before the new PM, Harold Macmillan delivered his famous 'You've never had it so good' speech, *The Times* (15th July 1957) opined that hemp smoking wasn't that injurious to health. This view that the drug posed little in the way of a public health problem in Britain, was actually reflected in the government's attitude to the international treaties about cannabis. Reluctantly, in accordance with treaty obligations, Britain had outlawed cannabis possession in 1928, and was equally reluctant to sign up to the Anslinger-driven UN Single Covention on Narcotic Drugs in 1961 which put cannabis in the most dangerous drug category.[5]

However, there was more enthusiasm for a new law brought in during 1965 making it an offence to allow premises to be used for the smoking of cannabis. Up to then, this only applied to opium and was a direct attack on the opium dens. The premises offence for cannabis could be seen as another burst of racist-inspired drug legislation, aimed at the black community. According to one of the Home Office drug inspectors of the day interviewed by this author, this new law was born out of the fact that if the police raided a club or a party everybody dropped their dope on the floor and so nobody could be charged with possession. Under the new law, the police could now arrest the club owner or whoever owned the house where the party was taking place.

Once the waft of weed began to drift out of the black communities, there were the beginnings of dissenting voices about the drug's legal status. During 1963, there were calls for law reform from *The Lancet* (roundly condemned by *The News of the World)* and by Wayland Young in *The Guardian*. In 1965, the beat poet Allen Ginsberg founded LEMAR the first attempt to establish a campaign for the legalisation of marijuana. An offshoot met in London at the flat of another American beat, Paolo Lionni and included poet Dan Richter and Alex Trocchi, whose book on life as a heroin addict, *Cain's Book*, had been banned by Sheffield magistrates on the grounds that it would 'deprave and corrupt' those who read it. Support for the campaign came from the Reverend Ken Leech, quoted earlier in this book. Then assistant curate at the Church of the Most Holy Trinity in Hoxton, he gave a lecture at the London School of Hygiene and Tropical Medicine where he dismissed the commonly held belief that cannabis use led to heroin abuse except insofar as those who wanted to smoke cannabis had to come into contact with the underworld where they would find people prepared to sell them other more dangerous drugs; '... There is a strong, if not overwhelming case to be made for the legalisation of marijuana with similar restrictions to those appertaining to alcohol. Such a legislation would help cut the link which often leads to heroin and incalculable human misery.'[6]

As cannabis came more into the public conscience, mainly through arrests of pop stars, a more organised attempt at law reform was established. This was the SOMA, the Society of Mental Awareness founded in 1967 by an Oxford graduate, Steve Abrams. SOMA wasn't a campaigning group for legalisation as such, it was more interested in law reform to enable research to be carried out on a range of mind altering drugs, starting with THC, the psychoactive component of cannabis. In order to promote public debate on the issue, SOMA took out a full page advertisement in *The Times* of 24th July 1967 under the banner 'The law against marijuana is immoral in principle and unworkable in practice' and signed by sixty five of the liberally-minded members of the great and the good including two Labour MPs Tom Driberg and Brian Walden. The advert was paid for by The Beatles.

The immediate background to the advert was the nine month sentence meted out on 1st June 1967 to John 'Hoppy' Hopkins, for cannabis possession. Hopkins was editor of *IT* and organiser of the greatest of the underground events of the times, the '24 Hour Technicolour Dream' at Alexandra Palace on April 29th. The day after Hopkins was sent down, a group of his friends, including Steve Abrams, met at the Indica bookshop run by Miles. Steve Abrams takes up the story:

> I raised the idea of advertising in *The Times*. Miles said he thought he knew where the money might be found. His partner, Peter Asher, was half of the pop duo Peter and Gordon... Peter Asher's sister, Jane was Paul McCartney's girlfriend. McCartney had several times contributed small sums to keep *IT* going. By the end of the day, he had offered to guarantee the cost of the advertisement, which was £1800.[7]

Steve says he wasn't as surprised with the turn of events as he might have been. McCartney had only just revealed to the world that he had dabbled with LSD, and it would be a good way to deflect attention from the idea of mere pop star indulgence by linking The Beatles with leading figures in the world of the arts, science and politics in a legitimate protest from within the system.

> McCartney was well aware of the power of public statements coming from The Beatles. He realised that if they spoke out on too many issues, their influence would be diluted. But pot was going to be an exception. McCartney said that The Beatles and their manager Brian Epstein would all put their names to the advertisement and he agreed that the project would be left entirely in my hands. He hoped that his participation in the funding could be kept quiet.[8]

Needless to say, the press got wind of the story; Steve was phoned the very next day by *The Evening Standard*. Everything was progressing until the ad got to the proof page stage when the advertising manager of *The Times* got cold feet, delayed publication for a week while all the names were checked and then asked for payment in advance. Steve contacted The Beatles' office and Peter Brown of their publishing company NEMS, sent round a personal cheque for the full amount.

Steve thinks that it was the sensational events of the Rolling Stones trial that eventually persuaded *The Times* to publish the advertisment. The night that Keith Richard and Mick Jagger were released on bail, there was a spontaneous demonstration outside the offices of *The News of the World* which lasted another two nights, followed by *The Times'* own editorial of 1st July condemning the scapegoating of the Stones.

The last event preceding publication of the advert was the 'Legalise Pot Rally' at Speakers Corner, Hyde Park on Sunday 16th July. Like the Beatles and George Melly who signed the advert, musicians came in support of the Rally with Alexis Korner speaking from the platform.

Apart from raising the issues around cannabis prohibition, the prime objective of the advert was to influence a government committee recently established in April 1967 to 'examine the question of the misuse of cannabis and... LSD in the United Kingdom, and the problems arising'.

To summarise a fascinating episode in UK drug history, what became known as the Wootton Committee could not find any evidence that cannabis caused violent or anti-social behaviour, or that there were any obvious health problems from long-term moderate use. Accordingly, they recommended that a distinction be made in law between 'hard' and 'soft' drugs, that penalties for possession should be reduced and that the premises law should be scrapped. When the report was published, it was roundly condemned by the then Home Secretary, James Callaghan on the grounds that the committee had been nobbled by the 'pro-pot lobby'. From there, it has been assumed that the Committee's report was ignored. However, as Steve Abrams points out, much of what they recommended quietly found its way into the new 1971 Misuse of Drugs Act (MDA). And so, for example, while internationally, the UK had committed itself to the notion of cannabis as a highly dangerous drug, the MDA positioned cannabis in Class B with lesser penalties for possession. Unfortunately, the premises rule remained which was to have dire conseqences for public order ten years on.

As a consequence of the MDA, the reform movement had the wind taken out of its sails for some years. A short-lived organisation called CARO sent cannabis seeds to MPs which had no impact and so the baton was passed to the street agency Release who used the campaign for fund-raising purposes to keep their advice service going. The Legalise Cannabis Campaign began in 1978 and together with Release engaged the services and support of many musicians who performed at a number of fund-raising events and/or who made donations including individual members of The Beatles after they broke up, Status Quo, Bad Company, Procol Harum, Graham Bond, Arthur Brown, Billy Bragg, Eric Clapton, Brian Eno, Pink Floyd, Hawkwind, Jimi Hendrix, Mick Jagger, Soft Machine, Alexis Korner, Prince, The Prodigy and Roni Size.

* * * * *

However, during the 1970s, while cannabis law reform was pretty much a dormant issue in the UK, in the USA, it was a major item on the political agenda and under the Presidency of Jimmy Carter, the States were a whisker away from major law reform. Carter put legislation through Congress to have cannabis decriminalised for possession – and got the support of the DEA, the State Department and National Institute of Mental Health. (Some eleven states had already gone down this route). Such a move was politically possible because heroin use was going down (probably because of the break-up of the French Connection with no other parties yet fully in control of the trade) while cannabis use was going up thus breaking the link between them.

Then heroin started coming in through Mexico and Carter's principal drug advisor, Dr Peter Bourne, authorised the use of paraquat weedkiller on poppies. Trouble was, the Mexican authorities started using it on dope. Unlike in the UK, the America reform movement was highly organised under the leadership of an ex-Washington lobbyist Keith Stroup and his campaign group NORML, which attracted many ordinary people to the cause by making the cannabis issue a simple matter of consumer rights.

But to the ultimate detriment of the campaign, Stroup fell out with Bourne over the paraquat issue and set him up to snort coke with him and Hunter Thompson at a NORML function. There was also a scandal over a prescription that Bourne wrote for Valium for a White House employee. Bourne resigned and the Grand Coalition of Carter, DEA and NIMH collapsed. Once Carter was kicked out of office, in came Ronald Reagan with Just Say No Nancy right behind.

Again quietly in the UK, penalties for cannabis had been reduced under the Criminal Justice Act 1977 and in 1979, to a resounding media silence, the government-supported Institute for the Study of Drug Dependence published *Cannabis: Options for Control* based on the deliberations of a research group which considered the options for controlling cannabis under a legalised system. It was the quiet before the storm.

With the formation of drug squads and the revised dangerous drugs legislation of 1967 allowing police to stop and search specifically for drugs, prosecutions for cannabis possession skyrocketed, from 2393 in 1967 to nearly 14,000 in 1973. At the point at which otherwise law-abiding citizens were being persecuted for smoking cannabis, the subject became politicised. And not surprisingly, those most affected by the police action against cannabis was the black community.

As cannabis use spread throughout the 1970s, there were increasing incidents of police harassment against black youths on suspicion of being in possession of or dealing in cannabis. There were permanent tensions between the police and the local community in areas such as Brixton and Notting Hill. The Mangrove Restaurant in Notting Hill regularly played host to the local constabulary on fishing expeditions for drugs. It was the popularity of reggae that escalated the situation to boiling point. From the mid 1970s onwards, reggae achieved a growing international status, its artists feted as rock stars and many young people, both black and white, adopted the highly distinctive colours, sounds and look of Rastafari. One of the very few times Bob Marley was ever busted for cannabis possession, was sitting in a car in the All Saints Road in Notting Hill. A multi-coloured rag was waved at the bull of crass and racist policing.

The spark ignited on 2 April 1980, not in London, but the St Paul's area of Bristol after 40 police raided the Black and White café, an important local meeting place for West Indian youth, and left with 300 grams of cannabis which had been dropped onto the floor by café customers. A group of youths surrounded the police car taking the drugs away, clashed with plain clothes drug squad officers and the resulting riot caused up to three quarters of a million pounds worth of damage.

On 11 April the following year, a more serious riot flared up in Brixton after a stop and search drugs operation which yielded no drugs, but resulted in widespread looting and many injuries. There were strong rumours (that the subsequent Scarman riot enquiry neither confirmed or denied) that the real genesis of the riots was the fact that the police were favouring some dealers over others in exchange for information. This was picked up by *Now* magazine (April 1981) who interviewed members of the local community about the drug-related tensions between police and residents. There were claims of drug dealers paying protection to middlemen who passed the payments on to corrupt policemen and further allegations that cannabis seized by the police a week before the riots had reappeared on the market.

Another year further on to 20th April 1982, when more disturbances broke out, this time on the 'front line' of Notting Hill, yet again following a 'stop and search' incident on the streets. While two suspects were being questioned, a crowd gathered and helped them to escape. The inevitable escalation took place with petrol-soaked barricades going up in the streets. There were accusations of excessive force against the police and once more the Mangrove was trashed.

Since those troubled times, there has been almost *de facto* decriminalisation of cannabis with very few people nowadays actually imprisoned for cannabis possession, most being cautioned or fined. But as the young white middle class dope smokers of the late sixties and seventies ease their way into positions of power in politics and the media, so the calls for more radical reform of the laws against smoking cannabis have grown louder and more diverse.

In America, the debate has been regaining momentum for some years; there are now several law reform groups dedicated to the medical use of marijuana, to the release of loved ones handed down draconian sentences for possession and dealing and to reform in general. The Internet has played a major part in revitalising the reform lobby, linking groups throughout the States and across the world. The States of California and Arizona voted legislation allowing the use of cannabis for medical purposes while the billionaire financier George Soros has provided financial support to the pro-reform Lindesmith Center in New York.

In England, the 'broadsheet' newspapers, leading medical press and journals like *The Economist* and some judges and policemen have all called for the reform of the drug laws. The *Independent on Sunday* ran a campaign for law reform backed by Richard Branson and Anita Roddick, founder of the Body Shop. Both The British Medical Association and the House of Lords have called for proper research into the medical potential of cannabis while the Police Foundation are investigating the workings of the 1971 Misuse of Drugs Act.

All this activity has followed in the wake of a new interest in cannabis that has grown up in the UK on the back of the rave culture; cannabis has for some time been the number one 'chill out' drug to take the edge off ecstasy and a hard day's night. In fact, cannabis might actually be seen as something of a precursor to ecstasy. In the run-up to E, cannabis began to find favour with working class kids where before it was labelled disparagingly as the 'old hippies drug' – for which read, the middle classes.

The resurgence of interest in cannabis also has an eco-political dimension; Jack Herer's best-selling book 'The Emperor Wears No Clothes' claimed (although the evidence was circumstantial) that the outlawing of hemp in 1937 was a petro-chemical conspiracy to deny America the chance of a more eco-friendly source of fuel, clothes, paper etc, namely hemp. Licenses to grow hemp with very low THC content are now available in many parts of Europe and although the hemp growers distance themselves from the pro-reform lobby, nevertheless many of their products are advertised in the pro-reform magazines such as *High Times*.

So what about musicians and cannabis in the nineties? Many individual musicians still regularly turn to the drug to help free up their creative juices, especially for writing, although views are mixed. Sinead O'Connor readily admitted that, 'I smoke dope quite a bit and that really does help when I'm writing because it opens your mind up'. Joni Mitchell is more ambivalent, 'Pot tends to make you tactile, sensual. It warms your heart for about fifteen minutes. Then it starts to fog over. You've got fifteen minutes of really condensive creative thought and then it can flatten you. If you smoke that on a regular basis, you'd just be flattened and it's anti-creative. But if you do it knowing, "I'm stuck here", take some pot and you'll swing into the opposite of where you are and ideas will open up'. (*Musician* May 1992).

A number of white bands have been active in support of the revitalised reform movement including the Black Crowes, Blues Traveller, Jason Kay of Jamiroquai, and Pearl Jam. But undoubtedly it has been the new black music which has been at the forefront of the cannabis culture in the nineties.

What happened to reggae after Bob Marley died from cancer and Peter Tosh was shot was cocaine and with it came a hard-edged uptempo style of reggae known as dancehall or ragga. This developed in urban Jamaica and was very different in feel from the rural roots sensibilities of reggae. The music was the shortened, staccato percussive beats of the cocaine rush as Jamaica increasingly became a major transit route for cocaine bound for the States from South America and Jamaican gangsters began staking their claim in the cocaine/crack trade both in New York and London. Yet ironically, the big breakthrough for the music, the song that broke the style in America – was all about the delights of cannabis smoking, 'Under Me Sleng Tang' by Wayne Smith released in 1985. Rap followed soon afterwards. Although very much down on cocaine and crack, most rap artists have a very different take on cannabis. The distinctive green multi-pointed cannabis leaf turned up everywhere on hats, T-shirts, posters, album covers. Hip hop took over from hippie as the keepers of the marijuana flame.

Tone Loc (Anthony Smith) did a 1989 track 'Cheeba Cheeba' – one of the many slang names in rap for dope and 'Mean Green', 'I burn spliffs when I'm working. It's not the only way to be creative and it's not going to help anybody who wasn't creative to start with, but it does the trick sometimes. A lot more people know that than will admit it'. (*High Times* May 1992)

New Jersey hardcore rapper Redman recorded 'How To Roll A Blunt' on 1992 album *Whut? Thee Album*. A blunt is a large cannabis joint made of grass (cannabis buds) rolled in cigar tobacco leaf. Of all the many slang names for dope – blunt rose to the top. The hippest T-shirt of 1993 was an update of the old broken promise to freed slaves – 40 mules and a acre – 40 ounces and a blunt.

Dr Dre (Andre Young) named his album *The Chronic* yet another slang term, this time for extra strong weed – it went multi-platinum and took the chant of the vipers to its widest audience yet. Cypress Hill had similar album success rapping the delights of the chronic and songs like 'Something for the Blunted', 'Hits from the Bong' and 'Light Another' and ' I Wanna Get High'. Their first two albums sold five million copies and the band were tagged as the dope crusaders of the nineties, following in the steps of David Peel, Cheech and Chong and Bob Marley.

Inevitably, there have been clashes with the mainstream media. MTV blurred the hash logo on Snoop Doggy Dogg's baseball cap and changed the lyrics before playing 'Gin and Juice', the second Top Ten hit from Tim Dogg's platinum selling album

Doggy Style. Wu Tang Clan's 'Method Man' suffered the same fate – all dope references deleted. MTV also banned Fishbone's Angelo Morris fron wearing a hemp suit covered in pot leaves. Why? Fear of contravening Federal Communications Commission guidelines. What goes around, comes around.

This analysis of the revitalised cannabis craze in black music came from Grant Farred, a cultural critic from Princeton University. He claimed it marked a new direction in black consciousness, 'It harks back to an earlier moment before the collapse of the inner city, to the reggae of the late sixties and the earliest ganja smoking DJs like Herk. I think it's an attempt to produce a counter narrative to the one of black decline, it's like saying we want relief from the mad trade and gangster capitalism that comes with hard imported drugs. There's a lot more sense of process involved in cannabis – you can grow your own in your own back garden, it's natural, it's American... it harks back to an almost pre-industrial way of life, a sense of self-sufficiency' (*The Guardian* 23rd September 1993).

Yet the idea of staying in control still features heavily in black culture, even regarding cannabis. Although Ice Cube's screenwriting debut, 'Friday' owed much to the herb-smoking humour of Cheech and Chong, he said he doesn't write to heighten levels of creativity – 'I know some people who are dependent on weed. If they don't have it, they can't function in the studio, on stage, whatever. To me, it's a weak individual who goes into that and starts to be like, "I need this to do this". So I decided to write sober.' (*High Times* June 1995)

And if there is a darker side to ecstasy, no less with cannabis and the 'paranoia' vibe engendered by the industrial strength cannabis that appeared in the 1990s, so called 'skunk' designer dope grown in an artificial environment and genetically engineered to blow your head off.

Within rave, this was most manifest in 'trip hop', defined by one artist as 'the mixture between computers and dope'. Mainstream examples of this sensibility can be heard on, for example, Massive Attack's debut album *Blue Lines* 1991 with (what Simon Reynolds calls) 'spliff tempos' ranging from halfway between reggae and hip hop, around 90 bpm, down to a zomboid 67. This was nodding out music not dance music, little different in that way to Pink Floyd, cited by the band as one of its influences – when sixties and seventies students would gather in rooms to sit in circles, skin up and listen. Trip hop in the nineties is 'explicity designed to enhance the effects of marijuana' in the way, for example, the down, sluggish tempos correlate to the way in which time appears to slow down under the influence of the drug – or the way that perceptions of very small detail can be enhanced – hence where the music is reduced to simply bass and drums, the mind focuses on the minimalism as it slips out of temporal consciousness.

Tricky has bucked the trend with a general 'down' on the whole of the drug culture; he called his sub-label 'Durban Poison' after an especially potent breed of weed. The album, *Maxinquaye* includes 'Ponderose', a freefall into the bad end of booze and dope that Tricky says he fell into after working on *Blue Lines* when he had money but no more work – which leads to more general observations, 'Don't Dabble In Drugs. It Is A Social Evil and Crime'.

Similarly, there have been conflicting views within the British black press about cannabis – even within the same newspaper. In April 1997, Britain best-selling black newspaper *The Voice* ran a very sympathetic report of a new reggae pro-cannabis compilation album called *Legalise De Herb* with several quotes from reggae stars in support of the weed.

Yet eighteen months previously, *Voice* columnist Tony Sewell declared 'Ganja's making our young zombies'. Sewell objected to the fact that ganja smoking was giving the whole black community the reputation of drug users – if you were a young black male, you automatically smoked, knew where to buy it and so on. He also objected to the fact that too much smoking was destroying the motivation of young black males to fulfil all their oft stated hopes and dreams – and that those that are dealing are simply the puppets of the big white importers. He took a similar line to that expressed by Ice Cube, that anything which robbed you of control was bad for a community which had so little control over its life in the first place. He ended his piece, 'The next time you see a brother floating down a high street in Moss Side, Hackney or Brixton, wave him down and look into his eyes and after he tells you he's going to be the next Prime Minister, look carefully as you did in *Thunderbirds* and you'll see those puppet strings'.

Simon Reynolds goes down the path of equating the paranoia-inducing effects of the strongest weed with the unlikely philosophical alliance between America's extreme right, encompassing anti-government survivalists, conspiracy theorists and white supremacists – and those separatist-inspired gansta/rap artists predicting race conflict-driven Armageddon.

Reynolds contrasts the escapism of trip-hop UK and the 'realism' of hip-hop USA in relation to cannabis and asks 'how can this be?'. Leaving the difficulties of trying to surperimpose any aspect of American culture on the UK, we are back in the realms of cannabis as a drug for all seasons, tempered in this case by the fact that the Americans don't mix tobacco and dope – so they get more of the whack, and so possibly more of the paranoia. What you don't get is the notion that the weed is anything other than 'righteous'.

16   COPPING ...

Dealers rip off bands left, right and centre. They're probably doing even better now, because it's cut much more than it was – especially in the UK.

Tour manager

Alongside the changing nexus of drug/music fashions and the trials and tribulations of individual musicians, sits the interaction between the music business and the traffic in illegal drugs. Taking a wide view, pop and illegal drug use grew up together, parallel developments from the earliest days of New Orleans through Prohibition, the rise of organized crime and its increasing involvement in all leisure industries. Popular music is now the property of multinational corporations with many subsidiaries, thousands of employees and profits running into millions. It is impossible to place illicit drug trafficking on any commercial league table because dealers tend not to submit audited accounts. However, through the intervention of organized crime (which also has a stake in the music industry), drug trafficking has a worldwide complexion involving the economic and political stability of whole countries, widespread corruption from the highest levels downwards and financial transactions on a breathtaking scale.

The pathways of drug dealing within the industry are of necessity labyrinthine. At one end of the scale, musicians will deal informally among themselves, going out on the streets to score their own supplies or consorting with small-time dealers in limited amounts of money and drugs. Even those at the top of the tree will take incredible risks out on the streets, when you might imagine all they had to do was click their fingers; Steve Tyler of Aerosmith, at a time when they were one of the major arena rock bands, walked around the worst parts of New York, went up to a complete stranger to try and score and got mugged at gunpoint for his trouble.

Some musicians become known as people with especially good contacts which have developed alongside their need to finance a spiralling drug habit – Papa John Phillips was one such example. Jazz too has thrown up some notorious 'Jesuit junkies' well-known within the community. Musicians can also become conduits between dealers anxious for free-spending star business and those in privileged positions who need to keep more than an arm's length from their source of supplies.

Small drug-using cliques exist in all areas of the business including the record companies. A former employee of EMI remembers, 'We had this thing going in our department, just a few of us, and I was the person who knew how to get stuff. Outsiders didn't really know about it, but one day this guy comes up to me right in the middle of the office party and says he wants some dope. I mean, how stupid can you get, right in the middle of the office!'

Frederick Dannen's book *Hit Men* documents among other things, the excesses of Neil Bogart, label boss of Casablanca Records, whose star roster included Donna Summer, Village People and Kiss. Bogart died of cancer in 1982, but not before he had ridden the label on the back of the disco boom, straight over a cliff and nearly ruined the parent company PolyGram Records. The HQ on Sunset Boulevard, 'rocked with disco and rolled with controlled substances'. One employee commented, 'if you were into drugs, man, you were in Camelot'. The label motto was 'Whatever it takes' to sell records. Selling was everything – even if you spent more on selling than you made from sales. The office rang with ear-splitting music, dazzled with exotic decor and beamed with happy staffers who felt they had landed in never-never land. But if you weren't into drugs, like promotion man Danny Davis it wasn't so wonderful: 'Motown was the best work experience of my career... I must score Casablanca as the worst. With the abuses that were being perpetuated up there and the things that were being done... You can't do that twenty four hours a day. At three o'clock in the afternoon, an adorable little girl would come up and take your order for the following days' drug supply.' He goes on to talk of watching secretaries chopping up coke with their credit cards on the desks and going into meetings which didn't start until most of those present were fully coked up – 'and then nothing got done... And now the substance is gone, and they would go into their desk and pull out the ludes.'[1]

Clubs have always been notorious buying grounds for drugs; some club owners are big time dealers in their own right and use those lower down the scale to pitch the goods and attract the punters as described by this former UK band manager;

> There was this drug dealer in New York called Toast, a great fat guy who wore a flasher's mac. He would open one side of the jacket and he had all these compartments and pockets, 'I got E's, I got charlie, I got ketamine, I got heroin, marijuana.' And all these compartments were labelled, just shit loads of drugs. And the band said, 'Great...' Two of the roadies had tried some ketamine, 'Hey, it's really cool. Takes you on a different journey, really weird. Check it out, check it out'. So they take this and the gear's waiting to be loaded off. But all of them are sitting on the floor, nauseous, couldn't move a muscle. So I had to shift the gear myself.

Musicians in particular can always rely on 'well wishers' who want to bask in reflected glory, to supply them with tasty titbits, a situation which can rapidly get of control. Jimi Hendrix spent far too much of his time in an acid haze because he could not say no to the legion of camp followers eager to claim that they turned him on. So desperate was Free manager John Glover to keep parasites away from guitarist Paul Kossoff that he actually had policemen posted outside the dressing-room door. There was nobody like that to look after Nico; James Young, her keyboard player in the early 1980s wrote, 'There was a certain kind of person who thought it would be cool to share a drug with Nico. Or introduce her to a new one. It would make a good celebrity story. And Nico was something of a celebrity in narcotic circles. Queen of the Junkies. She was famous within a limited milieu, i.e. heroin users and those who thought self destruction a romantic vocation'.[2]

But sometimes it is the managers themselves who exploit a musician's dependency on drugs to keep them in line. Guitarist Steve Miller saw this happen to Barry Goldberg, keyboard player with Electric Flag: 'Barry really got into trouble. His manager tried to control him through drugs and he became a junkie for a while and he was down and out. His manager would go "That's great Barry, as long as you do what I tell you to do, here's a little smack, whatever you want".'[3] Miller also had this comment to make about Janis Joplin's manager Albert Grossman 'I was astounded by what I saw. When I saw Albert Grossman letting Janis Joplin play concerts because she was off heroin and only drinking a fifth of booze a day, I thought he should have been arrested.' Roadies, road- and tour-managers often figure as important intermediaries between dealers and customers. In fact their drug connections may be the main reason they get hired in the first place, like Scooter Herring. One tour manager who has been on the road for thirty years with several top bands recalled to the author, 'I remember being in Germany at a gig, sitting in the backstage office. On the table in front of me was a huge pile of coke about six inches high. I had to divide this for the crew and the band. I wrote down who was getting what and it came out of the band's wages. The crew got theirs free, but the band had to pay. On some tours I seemed to be doing nothing but sorting out drugs – on others, well they just turned up. Payment in kind to road crews is not uncommon, particularly with cocaine. Drugs represent more than just a perk of the job, they are a very bankable commodity. Cocaine can be resold as it is, or 'cut' to increase revenue. The entire crew of an American artist who toured recently in Britain was paid off in this way.

As this manager notes, drugs are there for the asking, 'The tour manager has to sort out the drugs as soon as they've stepped off the plane, and apart from Russia, it's so easy to get anywhere. We went to Spain with the band and they really liked their coke. We went to this bar and there were big lumps of hash and piles of coke available just in this one little bar. You just ask the promoter and he phones up the guy and he'll be there. And that's the same the world over. The dealer wants to get in with the promoter because he'll get his stash and all the freebies. And in the States, it's just scary, really scary, there's so much of it and it's so cheap and so many people have access to it'.

Record companies also play their part in the supply of drugs to their musicians. 'Hospitality' is normally taken care of by the Artists Relation Department (not to be confused with Artist and Repertoire or A&R). A band's special requirements are made known to AR and the rest is up to them. Promotion and publicity can also get involved. For example, when hijacking became a favoured means of attention-grabbing by political groups in the seventies, security was stepped up on internal flights in the States and a major record company was highly embarrased to have most of its promotions team busted for cocaine. An ex-AR man says he was most unhappy at having to score drugs for people:

> It was no good buying sub-standard stuff for the Americans, because they'd know straight away. you have to be very aware of connections.

Ludicrous things happen and they are taken as normal. When I was working for the company, this big name flew in to promote his latest solo album. We had to go to this massive suite at his hotel to see if he was okay, and if he needed anything. We get there and he's whacked out of his head. His small child, about four years old, looks me straight in the eye and says, 'Mummy and Daddy said I mustn't call them joints. I must just call them cigarettes.'

Drugs (along with women and cash) have always been part of the social grease of the industry. Journalists become accustomed to being offered drugs in the hope of eliciting favourable reviews. One British journalist who worked extensively for the music press in the seventies, was among this feted group:

It was all this 'let's be part of the hip drug circle' business. Early in the seventies, joints were being rolled the whole time; coke came in around 1974-5. This tended to appear more informally than in an office interview situation. You'd have a press do, a launch. Somebody from the record company would whip out some coke or you'd go back to the office at night or to the artist's home. It was no big deal.

The motivation of these executives was very transparent:

Mainly they are trying to look, do and feel right in an industry that's all about being chic and up to date. The drugs would change, so did the booze. It would be Southern Comfort, then gin and tonic, as the business got grimmer financially through the seventies. Same with the drugs. In '76 everyone had to be smoking thai* and nobody would be so gaffe as to bring out smack, although it was sniffed quite a lot then.

In turn, some of the journalists began to live the life they reported on:

It was a time of being elegantly wasted – all to do with snorting heroin, being fucked up, losing your teeth and being brainless. On the papers I worked for, cliques would evolve, a secret language developed and it would get quite complicated working out what level of consciousness different people were on. This code actually came out in the features – someone would write about 'traces of snow on the window' and so on. Then people started dying, friends of mine, the mood changed and those who were once elegantly wasted looked pathetic.

Nor are the company men themselves immune from the dangers inherent in regular drug use and believing you can be someone you are not. One band manager remembers:

This guy who worked for Atlantic in the mid-seventies is now a very bad junkie. He's been to every clinic, but nobody can do anything. He started

* Thai sticks – a form of marijuana

out as a young, dynamic, keen record guy. Then he started hanging round this one particular band on their tours – he wanted to be one of them and now he hasn't had a job for God knows how long. He's a real down and out, still on heroin.

Disc jockeys, too, particularly in America, have long been a target for company favours. In the early days of rock 'n' roll, money, prostitutes and gifts were on offer in exchange for playing certain records. The scandal which broke in the early sixties over what became known as 'payola' has since been interpreted by rock historians as an orchestrated attempt to shove rock 'n' roll off the air. It certainly destroyed the career of pioneering rock DJ Alan Freed, who was indicted twice, in 1960 and 1964, and died shortly afterwards, a broken humiliated man – while other non-rock DJs cashed in with impunity. With the increasing popularity of cocaine in the entertainment world, 'payola' gave way to 'drugola'.

Washington journalist Jack Anderson was the first to break the initial 'drugola' scandal in March 1972. Record company employees came forward with tales of drugs 'saloons' held by promotion staff, where cocaine, marijuana and assorted pills were handed out to DJs, station managers and performers. Unknown artists took it upon themselves to supply to DJs hoping to secure airplay for records that otherwise would have sunk without trace. The promotions man of a well-known record company bought plays with $20 lots of marijuana and then apparently complained that he was having trouble 'losing it' in his expense account.

Stanley Gortikov, President of the Recording Industry Association of America (RIAA), issued a trenchant statement calling for companies to sort themselves out for the overall good of the industry. Any pay-for-play policy was 'unconscionable, immoral and commercially self-destructive'. He went on to urge companies to conduct investigations and surveillances to root out those dealing in payola/drugola among their own employees and those working for companies as independent promoters and distributors.

When questioned by Anderson and others over exactly how records were promoted, the record companies proved singularly reticent about supplying information. However, it would appear that as a result of all this adverse publicity, salaried promotional teams shrank in size, while more independent promoters were engaged to get airplay for records. In such a cut-throat business, no company was going to risk another stealing a march by making any genuine attempt to stop payola. Instead, they adopted an arm's-length policy which in effect said, 'Here's the record, get it on the air, but we don't want to know how you do it. ' In consequence, the independent promoters became a powerful and feared force in the American music business during the seventies. Paid anything up to $15,000 a week for their services, these 'indies' used every means at their disposal to get records played on Top Forty radio – cash, women, holidays, threats of violence, but most usually cocaine.

Drug expenses money can be 'laundered' in a number of ways. If a slush fund is operated there are usually no receipts anyway; services like prostitution or goods like cocaine are bought and handed over. Supplies of drugs to musicians in recording studios can be lost on expense sheets under euphemisms like 'extra keyboards' or 'additional vocals' on the road, it's the accountant's job to do some creative accounting. One road manager said, 'I would purchase what was needed, put it through the accounts, tell the accountant what it was and ask him to hide it. Anything up to 10% of the whole tour expenses could go on drugs and with some of the bands I've been with, that could run into thousands. Drug requirements can appear, again euphemistically, as riders to tour contracts with promoters. Where the promoter gets his supply is his business, but one rider allegedly stated quite simply 'no snow, no show'. Some people make no attempt at euphemisms whatsoever. I have seen a neatly typed receipt to a British record company from one of its artists recording in Los Angeles: $936- Food, gifts, entertainment, liquor; $1,275 – Cocaine.

In 1975, an internal audit at CBS resulted in the firing of David Wynshaw, head of Artist Relations. CBS claimed that Wynshaw and label chief Clive Davis had conspired together to siphon off company funds for personal use. It seemed strange to those in the industry that Davis, who was doing extremely well for CBS, should be fired for allegedly embezzling sums of money for expenses like his son's Barmitzvah, for which he could easily have afforded to pay out of his own huge salary.

Digging deeper, it seems that Davis may have gone because Wynshaw was linked to a mobster named Pat Falcone, indicted in February 1973 for heroin dealing. In turn, Falcone had been involved with a number of CBS acts like Sly Stone and O.C. Smith, offering protection for Smith under a death threat for non-payment of gambling debts. Falcone had a New York base in the office of Frank Camparia, an ex-promotions man for a CBS subsidiary label, Epic Records. From here he performed security services for Jeff Beck, an Epic artist. All this was happening at a time when the Nixon administration was under threat from Watergate. Woodward and Bernstein's paper the *Washington Post* owned a Florida TV station and the FCC challenged its licence. With the industry worried about the FCC guidelines on song lyric content, the Senate payola hearings and CBS's own extensive investment in broadcasting outlets, the company was anxious to present a squeaky-clean image. In such circumstances, Davis was sacrificed. Wynshaw was to testify to the Senate that between 1971-3 $500,000 had been charged to CBS's promotions budget for payola payments.

Inevitably the wheel turned full circle and another 'drugola' scandal broke in 1986. NBC's *Nightly News* reporter Brian Ross ran a TV exposé. Only one DJ was willing to be interviewed on camera, Don Cox from Miami, who said it was quite common to be offered cocaine in return for pushing a particular record. However, his information soon dried up after he claimed he was beaten up and his family threatened with violence unless he stopped talking. Officially, the major companies knew nothing about payola. Yet as soon as the story broke, many of the main promoters suddenly found their contacts in the companies were 'in meetings' when they called. Many companies insist on 'no payola' clauses in their contracts with independent promoters. Warner Brothers actually stopped using 'indies' in 1981; sales started to fall, so the arrangements were reinstituted. Early in 1986, the RIAA launched an investigation into corrupt practices in independent promotion, but at a special meeting, CBS and one other label apparently vetoed the idea and it was dropped. However, after the NBC revelations, RIAA records of that meeting were subpoenaed by a Federal grand jury to see if there was a case for instigating criminal proceedings.

The NBC story focused on a group of about thirty top promoters dubbed 'the Network', the prominent members being Joe Isgro and Fred Disipio, men with alleged links to the Carlo Gambino Mafia family in New York. Speculation had been rife for many years about the involvement of the Mafia and other elements of organized crime in the music business. Senate hearings in 1973 established a link between the Mafia and Morris Levy's Roulette Records and judging by the treatment meted out to some of its artists, the same may well have been true in the late sixties of the subsidiary of a major US company.

William Knoedelseder's book *Stiffed* was a detailed investigation of the alleged links between MCA Records and organised crime in the early 1980s. The main focus of the book was Salvatore Pisello, a reputed member of the Gambino family and suspected drug trafficker, who had an office inside MCA from 1983-85. The book also covered both the links between Morris Levy and organised crime and the trial of Joe Isgro.

The media took intense interest in the Isgro trial, playing up the 'sex and drugs' angle, although as Knoedelseder comments, 'the prostitution angle had long disappeared from the government's case and the quantity of cocaine involved amounted to less than was consumed in a single day at the record industry's annual NARM convention'. Even so, Isgro's judgement as to who to entrust his professional affairs did not look too sound; his tax lawyer Dennis DiRicco had been convicted for laundering hundreds of thousands of dollars for a Colombian drug cartel. But it was DiRicco who eventually scuppered the government case, because he gave totally contradictory testimonies at his own trial and then before the Grand Jury in the Isgro trial. The contradictory nature of these accounts was witheld by the prosecution who believed that DiRicco was their best bet to nail Isgro. But the judge was not impressed and threw the case out. Isgro walked free from a fifty one count indictment on payola, racketeering, drug trafficking and tax fraud charges.

Organised crime has more tangential, but equally significant holds on the industry. These include stadium food and souvenir concessions, concert staging and lighting, work permit applications (through the Musicians Union), the passage of equipment through ports of entry (courtesy of the Teamsters and the Longshoremen) and trucking. It is said that nobody does a major US tour without various pay-offs being made. Failure to co-operate at the very least ensures that your equipment is mysteriously stranded in the Nevada Desert while you're in New York or perhaps the stage crew don't turn up. And of course, organised crime is a major supplier of drugs. About 70% of the heroin coming into America is Mafia-controlled and other non-Italian criminal families largely control the cocaine trade from South America through Florida, the main access point into the States.

Some of the world's top bands have, in the past, carried such large quantities of drugs with them for their own use, that drug enforcement agents have become convinced that they were involved in transporting drugs for sale on the US mainland. FBI agents were quoted as saying:

> We were told by insiders, that Presley's group had the same connections that the Rolling Stones had ... we were told on numerous occasions that members of the Stones provided drugs to the scene in some of the biggest and fanciest disco clubs in New York. However after watching them for months and months, we decided that the opposite was true, that if the Stones were doing drugs, which our sources said was positive and which they did little to hide, connections within the clubs were providing them with narcotics and not the other way round.[4]

Notwithstanding there is evidence to suggest that the high-powered, high-financed worlds of rock and drug-smuggling do support one another on occasion. In 1981, a convicted smuggler, Harold Oldham, testified to a Senate sub-committee on international narcotics trafficking. One of his main activities had been the importation of North African hashish:

> While I was in Morocco, I met a rock star with a major rock group. Through my contact with him I came into constant contact with many of the major rock and pop groups in the United States and Great Britain. My association with these groups led me to the formation of Startrans, a company I set up for the purpose of renting luxury buses to these groups while they were on tour. Startrans was a legitimate US company and business, though it had been capitalized by significant amounts of narcotics money which had been laundered through the Caymans.[5]

Payments in kind to DJs and road crews have established drugs as not only the social grease of the business, but also its currency. In recent years, however, as bands have ventured into new territories, this has taken on an altogether different dimension, evolving along the lines of the long-standing legitimate practice in international commerce of supplying goods for services rather than cash. The major precondition for 'sweeping', as it is generally known, is that the buying country is without an exchangeable currency in terms of international finance – such countries would include those in Eastern Europe and South America. Supposing a company supplies a power station to Romania or a fleet of trucks to Paraguay. The supplier does not want payment in Romanian lei or Paraguayan guarani. These countries and others like them might be able to pay in US dollars, but more likely they will offer a commodity of their own in exchange – in the case of Romania it could be oil. However, a tanker-load of oil is no good to the supplier as it stands – he needs the money. Therefore he will go to a dealer who specialises in selling off 'swops' and receives the proceeds of the sale. Naturally, this dealer plus any other intermediaries will charge a commission, so the value of any swop has to exceed the price of the original goods to cover this 'creaming off'.

Pop artists touring in Eastern Europe have come to similar arrangements, receiving, for example, cut timber or even forests in lieu of currency for concerts or royalty payments. For the touring band in South America there is one local product which is actually worth more than money as it travels round the world – cocaine. The trade in cocaine represents South America's biggest dollar-earner abroad; however shaky the political and economic base of the main producer countries like Bolivia and Colombia, without cocaine both countries would be seriously destabilised.

Where bands have taken cocaine in payment for tours and royalties in South America, the principle is the same as in legitimate business, but the practical arrangements are very different. Obviously, if any rock manager is going to get involved with South American cocaine dealers he had better know what he's doing; the dealers negotiate with guns, not over brandies in smart restaurants. The band might opt for cocaine to be supplied to them over a period equivalent to the monies owed, or they might opt to take the whole lot with them, which could run into several kilos, in which case a smuggling operation would be set up to get the drugs home.

Alternatively, the drugs might be sold on behalf of the band and the proceeds laundered through off-shore banking accounts, to reappear a few months later in an account of the management's choice. Either way, elaborate and expensive precautions have to be taken every step of the way to ensure that the band doesn't get ripped off or busted. Such a payment system would be out of reach for all but the world's top bands.

* * * * *

At the other end of the drug-supply continuum is the medical profession. Doctors are not immune, particularly the younger ones, from the attractions of being associated with the rich and powerful world of rock music. Commenting on 'hangers-on' in the business, Little Richard's bass player, Eddie Fletcher, said it wasn't just female groupies who wanted to be around the legendary rock 'n' roller. 'I've heard doctors say "I don't think I'll go in this week. I'll just travel back east with y'all." And the management just couldn't get rid of them.'[6]

Primarily, however, it has been in pursuit of profit that doctors have been more than happy to supply the drug needs of musicians, whatever the health cost. Without wishing in any way to understate the potential harm done by those who traffic in illegal drugs, they at least make no pretence of acting in the best interests of their clients nor are they bound by a code of professional ethics. Doctors are, and it makes the activities of those who recklessly prescribe drugs for gain all the more reprehensible.

In American law, it has never been accepted that to prescribe opiates like morphine and heroin to help maintain somebody's habit is legitimate medical practice. British law takes a very different view: up to 1968 it was perfectly legal for a doctor to prescribe these opiates and cocaine to addicts, most of whom would have become dependent through original prescriptions for chronic pain. But as the sixties progressed, increasing numbers of younger people, including several jazz musicians, began using doctors as a ready source of pure heroin to feed habits derived from recreational rather than therapeutic drug use.

Few doctors were willing to see such people, because of the problems they caused for the staff in the surgery. Those who were prepared to treat addicts often prescribed heroin in vast quantities. During the course of one year, one particular doctor, Lady Isobel Frankau, wrote out prescriptions for heroin totalling six kilos. Some of the world's most famous jazzmen would land in London, for example *en route* to Paris, just to pick up heroin prescriptions from her ladyship.

Some of these doctors genuinely believed that prescribing on demand kept their patients out of the black market and ensured a relatively stable lifestyle free from fears of police harassment, the degradations of street life and so on. Unfortunately, these doctors were unable to provide the kind of support needed to encourage their patients to become drug-free after a stable period. And in fact the black market in London was actually created by this over-prescribing on the grand scale. Invariably a user would ask for (and get) prescriptions in excess of his personal requirements and then sell the surplus. British jazz musicians who sold heroin around the clubs of Soho were usually selling their own surplus drugs in order to finance the purchase of their next doctor's prescription. And there were some doctors who could not even be credited with genuine if misguided beliefs; they saw no further than their bank balance.

After 1968 it became an offence for any doctor to prescribe heroin or cocaine to someone he knew would be using these drugs to support a habit. Only those with special licences could prescribe in the old way and these were granted only to doctors working in the drug clinics set up at the same time. There was one loophole: doctors could still prescribe these drugs to relieve symptoms of organic illness such as pain, so a doctor could supply drugs pretending it was for pain, or having been conned into thinking it was. However the Home Office Drugs Inspectorate, who check pharmacists' records, would eventually become suspicious if one doctor was prescribing in this way on a regular basis. Of more significance is the range of powerful opiates still available to the doctor to prescribe to anyone, such as dihydrocodeine (DF-118) and dextromoramide (Palfium).

But whatever the rules and regulations applicable to opiate drugs, people with wallets to match their reputations and a pressing need for discretion have always found ostensibly reputable doctors willing to oblige. As well as secret trips to Harley Street, it is common practice for bands and solo artists to have a doctor travelling with them. In his Senate Testimony, smuggler Harold Oldham said that these doctors 'would liberally distribute pills – controlled substances to anyone in the troupe who wished them. It became a common sight on the chartered flights taken by these groups and elsewhere for the physician to set up shop. As soon as the plane took off, members of the troupe would literally line up at his shop for pills.'

John Lennon immortalized these Dr Feelgoods in 'Dr Robert' (on *Revolver*), the same guy who gave hot shots to Warhol and friends from the Factory. A notorious example of cash before care was the doctor who supplied jars full of tranquillisers, barbiturates and methaqualone (Mandrax and Quaaludes) to Paul Kossoff. It was these drugs, according to Free manager John Glover, that caused most of Kossoff's problems, but despite pleas by Kossoff's father directly to the doctor and to the profession's watchdog committee, the General Medical Council, the doctor continued to supply drugs to the ailing guitarist. Kossoff died in March 1976; the doctor was still in practice.

Perhaps the most famous rock doctor was Dr George 'Nick' Nichopoulos, personal physician to Elvis Presley and other members of the entourage. Opinions differed about Dr Nick. Some said he tried to keep Elvis away from even worse drugs than the ones he was taking and that he substituted placebos where he could get away with it. Others dismissed him as a disgrace to his profession, who profited handsomely from Presley's famed generosity and who was largely responsible for his death.

It is possible that Presley was the biggest drug hog in the history of rock. He used the large Merck prescribing manual for doctors like a mail-order catalogue and the list of drugs he consumed in cocktails of unknown quantities included Placidyl, Valmid, Dalmane, Valium, Mandrax and various barbiturates (all sedatives, hypnotics or tranquillizers); Hycomine, Codeine, Darvon, Dilaudid, Demerol and Meperidine (all painkillers); Dexadrine, Dexamill, Eskotrol, Ritalin and amphetamine (all stimulants). Ironically, he was virulently anti-heroin and even planned to have a local dealer 'eliminated' in *Death Wish* style. But because all his drugs were on prescription, he never made the connection between heroin and the drugs he consumed so voraciously.

Dr. Nick was a classic rock 'n' roll doctor, on call day and night to tend the needs of his much-valued patient. On the day before he died, Presley took delivery of 150 Percodan and Dilaudid painkillers, 262 Amytals and Methaqualone and 278 Dexadrine and Biphetamine stimulants. How many of these he consumed is unknown, as is the exact cause of his death. Dr Nick's prescribing habits came under close scrutiny when computer records revealed that during the last seven months of Presley's life, Nichopoulos had prescribed no less than 5,000 pills for him. A chemical soup had been swirling round Presley's system for years. Apart from an occasional yoghurt crash diet, Presley ate nothing but junk food and suffered from an alarming list of ailments mainly of a respiratory and circulatory nature. Several drugs were prescribed for these, others (in combination with the mountains of ice cream and hot dogs) probably caused them. In the event, perhaps not surprisingly, the medical profession looked after its own: Nichopoulos was reprimanded, suspended for three months and put on probation for three years.

17 ... AND COPING

'Rock 'n' roll is here to stay/Better to burn out/Than to fade away.'

Neil Young

'I've got a friend named Greenspan that says, "I need a little cocaine to give me energy. I need a little liquor to give me courage. And I need a little pot to give me inspiration." I believe this to be the case for many musicians... I tend to stay slightly fucked up all the time.'

Michael Bloomfield, 1944-81

It is clear that drugs of all descriptions, both legal and illegal, are available in any quantity to those working in the music business who want them and who have enough money and the right contacts. But why should they want them in the first place?

Most musicians don't get into problems with drugs; they are able to control their use in the same way as they (and people generally) control their drinking. Obviously some (and it may well be an increasing number) abstain altogether. Nevertheless, there is a high incidence of drug use throughout the industry and a correspondingly high occupational casualty rate. So what is it about musicians and the music business?

An attempt has been made earlier in the book (particularly in chapter six) to examine some of the attendant issues, like the adolescent aspects of musician psychology. However, such a complicated subject needs a lot of space and is more appropriately dealt with in a single chapter, both by way of a conclusion and in the light of the recent and more candidly documented era of pop and rock. In looking for patterns of behaviour, there is always the danger of forgetting that we are all individuals, that no two sets of motivating forces or personal circumstances are the same. The 'addictive personality' has yet to be identified. But the fact of individuality aside, what we are trying to make sense of here is a twisted skein of circumstance and psychology set against a background of easy access. And possibly the best way of getting a general feel for what goes on is to tease out some of the main threads of motivation for the use of drugs by musicians The fairly arbitrary labels I would attach to these threads would be practical, recreational, symbolic and emotional. It should be emphasised, however, that it is impossible to identify which factors are more significant than others, as they vary between individuals.

Undoubtedly rock 'n' roll attracts some seriously unbalanced and deranged people, damaged and unstable. Some of them have business acumen and 'do lunch'; others are creative and 'do music'. But it is worth bearing in mind that many musicians who are or were chronic drug users were not driven to bad habits by the vissitudes of the business, but were actually drug users first who decided to become musicians, the New York Dolls being one example and Dee Dee Ramone another, who worked out all his hate and self-loathing in the Ramones and in the process helped thousands of other kids work out theirs. As he said in his autobiography, 'I think the Ramones saved me, got me off the street'. Aerosmith were another set of musicians who were drug hogs well before they had the money to do it seriously. Singer Steve Tyler was a hyperactive kid, always getting into scrapes, truanting, drinking heavily as a teenager to deal with bullying, and like the rest of the band, hanging around Greenwich Village doing dope and acid. 'Our best friends were drug dealers,' said Joe Perry. 'We identified with them because we felt like outcasts, outlaws, menaces to society. We all liked drugs, so it seemed natural to gravitate to the dealers.[1]

By any definition, being a professional musician can be a crazy way to make a living. Whether you are scuffling round Britain in a beat-up Transit van held together by string and God's munificence or criss-crossing the globe in a Lear jet on eighteen-month world tours, the principles are the same. It's just a question of degree.

In this world, you work while everyone else is at play and while the audience is at work, you're asleep. But that sleep may have to be taken when you are not tired, because of the travel itinerary, the show times, the press calls, the interviews, the sound check, the airport strike or whatever. The same goes with waking up. If you're lucky you might eat. And however awful you feel when the lights go up, you have to be some demonic superbeing for two hours or Joe Cool for as long as it takes to give that very important interview promoting the new album. Musicians cannot ring in sick, take days off (unless it is in the schedule), or turn up a week later with a sick note from the doctor. All sorts of horse dope has been pumped into people so that the show can go on. And in between these bursts of hyperactivity can be periods of cataclysmic boredom: hours spent in endless airport lounges, hotel rooms, dressing rooms, recording studios, trains, planes, buses and cars, each looking the same as the last.

In such a working environment, which cannot be fully appreciated by anyone who hasn't actually done it, it is very easy to jump on to a chemical carousel of drugs (including alcohol, of course) in order to go to sleep and wake up on demand, get you through the day, calm nerves, boost confidence and escape from boredom. It takes a special effort to avoid this potentially hazardous rollercoaster. One musician noted, 'My motto was to make sure I ate and slept because you get so caught up with the drugs and the frantic lifestyle that you actually forget to do those things and you can get very unhealthy and very sick on the road. So I always ate and slept properly, but I also took a lot of drugs. It was just normal.' Guitarist Johnny Winter highlighted the tedium of touring as the starting point of his journey towards drug dependency: 'As the road got harder and I've got tired of playing the same songs over and over again, we took a little bit more. And then it was a little more until everybody in the band except Rick Derringer was in pretty bad shape.'[2]

Life can quickly descend into chaos, as Al Bloomfield found out when trying to manage N-Joi, one of the top live dance acts of the mid 1990s;

> It's a hard schedule. If you've just finished off a remix, you're in the studio and the tour manager is coming to pick you up at 6 p.m. to fly to Zurich. You know you are not going to finish until 10, but you also know that 6 is the deadline. So in those situations, I've seen people do loads more coke or speed just to rush and get it done. Then the tour manager comes and you're not ready so there's an argument. An hour goes by and now you are in danger of missing the plane – so the tour manager has to negotiate with the airline to get another flight. Then you are on the plane and it's free drinks. We were coming back from New York once and I was really knackered, needing some sleep. It wasn't very busy, so we were able to use up some of the middle row seats as beds. It was a night flight and the band were really pissed, charged up and kept slapping me round the head. In the end I got so pissed off I punched one of them and he went down the aisle, hit the seat, cut his head and we had to get the medics in. And the police met us at the other end'.

Al Kooper captured some of the essential truths of the rock life on the road in his book Backstage Passes:

> It's 1966 and we play in your college town gym… You've arrived in the afternoon to your Holiday or Ramada Inn where the staff let you know you are most assuredly not welcome. You rush out to do a sound check where a skeleton crew is totally unprepared for you and the simplest matters wind up taking hours. You've maybe enough time to return to the hotel and shower (lunch, dinner – forget it – they wouldn't serve you in the restaurant even if you had time to eat), and then race back to the gym. Then it's wait around while the first act goes on late and plays twice as long as it's supposed to and the audience is real irritable just in time for you to go on.
>
> Your big hour. Now that was *golden*. It was, for sure, the only enjoyment in the entire schedule. God forbid you played a lousy show; then suicide seemed like the only alternative to the boredom, frustration and futility. After a quick perusal of the premises for a smiling female (nope!), it's back to the hotel where the kitchen is (you've guessed it) closed…
>
> So practically all of us got high a lot. I'm surprised we weren't junkies… Mostly we smoked hash, grass, opium and took some occasional mescalin. Imagine being revered on stage for that golden hour and then rushed back to your hotel cell. You felt like some talented animal in a zoo on temporary leave.[3]

And the next day, you do it all over again, and again and again and again. Drugs here were used to blot out the grind of being on the road, but Al Kooper also talked about the 'golden hour' on stage, and there is a great temptation after a gig to keep pumping the tremendous adrenalin surge that comes with a good performance. Musicians talk of an arrested orgasm when the show is over, and a few lines of cocaine in the dressing room keeps the whole experience on the boil, because whatever drugs you are using there is nothing like the high of playing a gig in front of a receptive audience when everything is cooking. And of course, if the concert is a disaster you may reach for something just as quickly. What musicians find particularly perplexing is the unpredictability of audiences. Al Kooper again:

> This was one of the major weirdnesses of being on the road. Sometimes you could play the best music you'd ever played and they'd just sit there on their hands, no encore, no nothing. And then … you shovel an hour's worth of dinosaur shit on 'em and get standing ovations and twenty encores. This usually helped to temper your respect for the people you played for.[4]

Eric Clapton has been quoted as saying with some bitterness that he could walk on with paper and comb and still get an ovation. Between themselves musicians are not happy to 'get away' with a bad gig, often contemptuous of an undiscerning, adoring audience. But then again, who wants to be booed off?

While on the road, a musician's leisure time is dramatically telescoped in comparison with that available to other working people. The working day is concentrated into, say, three hours instead of the normal seven or eight and these few hours are at the end of the day rather than at the beginning, after or during what for most people is leisure time. This means that a working musician's leisure or recreational time is quite limited both in the number of hours which can be devoted to it and by the advanced knowledge that another gig, which could be 500 miles away, has to be done tomorrow. Recreational time is thus robbed of reality to a certain extent and accrues an eerie, dislocated feel. Some musicians accept this and keep partying down to a minimum. Others chase the phantom and use drugs as a short cut to the party mood knowing that night will give way all too quickly to day and the sound of the tour manager hammering on the door. The physical constitution of musicians is legendary, as are the stories of after-hours excess – sex, drugs and rock 'n' roll in all its grim fascination. Few outsiders can stand this kind of pace – neither the lifestyle itself nor the chemicals needed to keep up with it – although many try. Some bands had a particularly fearsome reputation on the road – for drugs, damage and deviancy. Led Zeppelin was one, the Stones another. Robert Greenfield in his account of the Stones' two-month tour of the States in 1972 relates the story of Bob Gibson, partner in a rock PR firm who had the Stones as one of their clients. Gibson decided to join the band for their whole tour. He lasted one week.

Paradoxically, despite all the aggravations of life on the road, many musicians start climbing the walls within a very short time of finishing a tour. This was graphically illustrated by Barbara Charone in her biography of Keith Richard. When he wasn't playing he did nothing but get wasted and watch TV. 'I can't live without being on the road … every minute spent off the road, I either turn into an alcoholic or a junkie' 'cause I've got nothing else to do.'[5] For Keith Richard heroin was itself a means to combat the withdrawal effects of not being on tour.

Many metaphors have been used to describe the music business – perhaps one of the more apposite is the feudal hierarchy. In this association, promoters, producers and company men are the lords of the manor, the musicians are knights, and the managers and public relations people are their retainers. Dancing attendance on the knights are the squires and peasants i.e. the roadies and 'go-fers'. The stage is the tournament arena where the band pleases the crowd or wins over the audience with a display of axe (or guitar) skills. But this imagery can be pushed beyond purely structural concerns to encompass the principles of heraldic protocol as a metaphor for the symbolic function that drugs can play in a musician's life. By virtue of their talent and the demands of their unconventional lifestyle, musicians of whatever genre often consider themselves as outsiders, running off at a tangent from the normal constraints put upon everyday behaviour. This outlaw status is very appealing to fans and from this derives adoration and hero worship. The musician becomes a blank slate on which the fans project their own desires, hopes, frustrations and unfulfilled pleasures. The knights of old who rode out to tackle the monsters on behalf of the people, were handsomely rewarded, should they survive, while their heroic deeds passed into legend and glory. A similar idea is abroad in the music business.

The beast takes on many forms; in the sixties, it was often the music business itself, and musicians would tilt at the corporate windmill in the name of artistic freedom. But this many-headed hydra snapped back and few survived intact; some, like Hendrix, soared into rock immortality. Lessons have been learnt, the lambs lie down with the lions and the artists are nowadays just as anxious about their 'product' and turning up for accountants' meetings as the bosses who run the show. But still musicians do things that many wish *they* had the money and the nerve to do, and it has oft been expressed by musicians that they take the risks for ordinary people, they provide the vicarious thrills – in a very literal sense, they go out and 'chase the dragon'.

Recalling the time in 1986, when Steve Tyler of Aerosmith was faced with tackling his drug problem or losing the band and possibly dying as well, he initially resented the idea that all the band's problems were because of his drug use, 'Because I'm the lead singer, the focus of attention, the fuckin' guy who gets paid to be crazy onstage. I'm the guy that has to climb the fuckin' trees!... I'm a tree climber, living out on a limb because how else are you supposed to pick the fruit?... and what the fuck did they think would happen to my talent, to my ability to be Steven Tyler, when my life and personality were smoothed out by rehab and therapy? Didn't they realize I was nothing without my drugs?'[6]

But the battles can be private as well as public: part of musician mythology is 'payin' your dues' and earning your spurs. Some musicians have regarded their drug experiences very much in this light, as a test, as a rite of passage like any Knight of the Round Table sent out on his quest. To quote Eric Clapton, 'There was definitely a heroic aspect to it. I was trying to prove I could do it and come out alive.'

Soldiers on a crusade or musicians on the road develop a tight camaraderie and, within a band, drugs can be a very significant social cement which binds some or all of the members together. One sociologist has identified drug use and its associated rituals of preparation as one of any band's shared experiences. 'The sequential relationship of drugs before playing provides a sacrament which symbolizes the edge between onstage and offstage.'[7] This is fine, so long as all the members are involved in the same drugs with equal commitment, which is rarely the case. Where one or more persons are into heroin, the others will find it virtually impossible to communicate with them. Cocaine caused any amount of trouble in the Police because of the aggression it generated, while one member of the late Lynyrd Skynyrd was heavily into LSD, which tended to isolate him from the others. Eventually the social cement can crumble. One player described the demise of his band's bass player in a group of regular marijuana smokers: '... you'd start hearing these mistakes in the bass, it was really ragged ... just sorta falling apart. The thing is Mike was getting hung up on speed. First he was just popping and finally he was shooting up every morning. And he just looked like shit warmed over. Finally we just had to get rid of him, he was bringing the whole band down.'[8] The other side of the coin is peer pressure; one roadie remarked, 'A new member of a band I was with did come under a lot of pressure and ended up freebasing cocaine in a big way.' Tony Sanchez, Keith Richard's supplier, said in his memoirs of life with the Stones: 'Working in the rock world and refusing to use cocaine is like joining a rugby club and preaching total abstinence. If you don't accept an occasional snort and proffer one in return, you are an instant outcast.'[9]

In tandem with camaraderie on the road comes a very deliberate policy of not only excluding outsiders, but making those who do try and get close feel very uncomfortable. Drugs are a prime instrument to achieve this, as illustrated by this tour manager:

> A lot of musicians are quite nasty to people who are visiting them now and again, especially women. Suppose you wanted to pull somebody, say a girl out of the audience. If she visited the band or one of the crew and she didn't want to take the drugs, then they'd pressurize her, call her chicken, etc. When you are on a tour, you are like a family and you're totally enclosed with everybody else. Whoever visits is an outsider ... you all know what's going on because you're on the inside, so it's, 'Oh, let's try and shock them and do a lot of drugs in front of them,' especially journalists. You get them to do it as well. And it was very nice being part of the in-group.

A group like the Stones, who drew people to them like a magnet, often used drugs to stay one jump ahead of the hangers-on to emphasize the value of elitism as a chic commodity. As described by Robert Greenfield, on tour with the band in 1972, it was the year of the 'lude' (Mandrax) – 'great for falling down, fucking people you might not otherwise speak to and forgetting your name'. This was for the audience; backstage, the rock parasites were trying to impress the Stones with the quality of the heroin they bore as gifts like the Magi to Bethlehem. However, the Stones don't impress easily; the in-chemicals on that tour were coke, Kaluha and cream and tequila with grenadine, to which the Stones added amyl nitrite. This drug, chemically related to nitrous oxide (laughing gas), was used for the treatment of angina as it opens up the vessels carrying blood to the heart. On the street at the time, it was available in small glass capsules which pop when crushed (hence the slang name 'poppers') and the nitrite is then inhaled. The effect is a bit like being hit in the face with a brick, especially if you are caught unawares. Open season was declared on smack carriers and the sport was to sneak up on somebody and snap a popper under his nose.

Drugs are also 'a reward' in their own right: access to limitless quantities of illegal drugs is one of the rewards for being a rock hero – they symbolise success. If you can afford to be cavalier with expensive commodities, be it drugs or cars, you must be doing well. The same principle applies to smashing up hotel rooms; you can indulge your adolescent fantasies and then get the accountant to write a cheque afterwards. Money gives you the freedom to be contemptuous of what most people would cherish, like a valuable car. It reinforces the 'rebel' image and the notion that as a big star you can do what you like, whether it's line after line of cocaine, driving a Rolls-Royce into a swimming pool or copulating with anything that moves. This is the instant gratification demanded by children – 'gimme it all – I want it now'. Speaking as someone who has had to minister to these demands, one personal manager says most musicians are like 'overgrown children – every whim seen to'. The music industry is like Never-Never Land, nobody wants to grow up, even relatively level-headed stars like Mick Jagger. In 1965 he told Ian Whitcomb, then enjoying brief glory as a pop star. 'You don't think I want to be singing "Satisfaction" when I'm forty do you? Christ on a bicycle, I'd rather be dead!'[10] Musicians in the public eye face many pressures and it seems painfully true that the desire to succeed in the music business burns brightest in those whose frailties that same business is particularly adept at exposing.

Unlike the writer, the painter or the sculptor, the musician (among other performing artists) cannot reach the pinnacles of artistic fulfilment in private. This can only be achieved in the recording studio surrounded by other musicians and technicians or standing on a concert stage in front of thousands. And for that to happen, musicians have to sail the shark-infested waters of the music business. Through long-term contracts, advances against royalties and the universal truth that 'he who pays the piper calls the tune', the record companies generally hold their musicians in thrall: 'No, sorry, the tour's off … you'll have to wait another six weeks to record … No, we don't think you should go to New York and play with – we'd ask for too much money anyway … No, we can't really let you record this – where's the hit single?' And it isn't only the companies; at every turn somebody is waiting to screw you – managers, agents, promoters and music publishers. This is a war the public never sees, surfacing by implication when label changes are announced or litigation erupts. Musicians (especially black musicians) have been systematically cheated out of millions of pounds in royalties, while bands and solo artists have been destroyed by law suits which have kept them off the road until the public have forgotten who they are. Not surprisingly, this causes much resentment and anguish in private, where some musicians give vent to their personal view that these games constitute a cynical process of manipulation. As we have seen, drugs can play a part in this process, while becoming a chemical crutch when life turns sour. As a performing artist, the musician can get trapped between an audience whom he often regards as lacking understanding and critical judgement, and the industry with which he has to work but which has entirely different goals. The fans never want an artist to 'sell out', but the company demands a more commercial approach. On the other hand, neither the company nor the fans want progression. The audiences wanted to see Hendrix smash his guitar and both the company and the management saw this as the way to sell records and put bums on seats. Hendrix backed himself into a room full of mirrors from which he couldn't get out.

For the international rock star there is plenty to run away from – the press, the fans, the conmen, the hustlers and the whole rock circus. Everyone wants a piece of the star, everyone thinks they have a right to something because they bought an album or a concert ticket, or just because the person is famous and therefore public property. There is a proto-audience that lurks on the edges desperate to be part of the scene trying to gain acceptance by bringing in drugs and in turn believing that if a musician gets smashed on your drugs, then what he does subsequently has something to do with you. As Barbara Charone noted, 'characters would go to great lengths suffering personal humiliation just to please the Stones'.[11] But probably the most invidious elements are those closest to the star, the personal entourage, something which John Lennon for one became all too aware of:

> I was used to a situation where the newspaper was there for me to read and after I'd read it, somebody else could have it... I think that's what kills people like Presley and others of that ilk ... The King is always killed by his courtiers, not his enemies. The King is overfed, overdrugged, overindulged, anything to keep the King tied to his throne. Most people in that position never wake up. They either die mentally or physically or both ... and that's how the Beatles ended. Not because Yoko split the Beatles, but because she showed me what it was like to be Elvis Beatle and be surrounded by sycophants and slaves who were only interested in keeping the situation as it was. And that's a kind of death.[12]

In the midst of all this vested self-interest, a star may find there is nobody he can really trust, and so retreats into drugs in order to feel secure. Mike Bloomfield, who died in 1981 of a drug overdose, had an illustrious career as a brilliant blues/rock guitarist with Bob Dylan, Paul Butterfield, Electric Flag, Muddy Waters, John Hammond and Sleepy John Estes, together with a string of solo albums: 'People may think this or that about me. People may want this or that of me. I may want this or that of me. But I know if I take a particular chemical, I'll attain a state that I can rely on. So in this way, I think drugs make a musicians's life a little more dealable.'[13]

Eric Clapton has likened heroin dependency to being wrapped up in a large ball of cottonwool, totally insulated from the world. Clapton appeared to take up heroin, both as his piece of artistic dues-paying and as his 'permission' to step out of the limelight after some personal loss and critical failures.

From the 'safety' of drugs, too, one can create an illusion of independence of *not* being tied to the throne, in control, even though what seems like an act of rebellion is in fact very conservative and ritualistic. And again from this vantage point, another illusion – that drugs are actually necessary to play better. This was part of the mythology of Charlie Parker and infected many musicians well into the sixties and seventies, particularly those who crossed over from jazz to rock. The belief has some validity, but only in the initial stages when a loosening of inhibitions may well be a stimulus to experimentation and progression. Saxophonist Dick Heckstall-Smith, who made the transition with Alexis Korner, Graham Bond, John Mayall and Jon Hiseman puts it like this: 'My time with alcohol and speed, especially at the beginning, actually improved my playing. I thought of things I wouldn't otherwise have thought of.' How does this come about?

> Well, in a sense, music is not made by the fully rational, fully conscious human being; part of a musician's training is to 'get out of the way' and let the music flow through. The perfect artist is one whose individual human characteristics are as good as wiped off – the nearer to 'not there' they are, the more music can take command. Alcohol and drugs are a short cut to

removing many of the properties of consciousness. Alcohol enabled me to concentrate, but my tolerance soon went up and the amount I needed to get me to the right level was also enough to physically slow me down. There was more work, more pressure, so I decided I needed something to speed me up. I had warnings when my head knew what I wanted to do, but my fingers couldn't do it. After five years came the real diminishing returns.[14]

Those who are successful or who are on the verge of success can be suddenly panicked by it all, craving stardom while being afraid of it and sometimes paranoid of being exposed as a talentless fraud. After leaving Television, guitarist Richard Lloyd looked set for a successful solo career with the launch of Alchemy in 1979: 'The big business aspect of chew-you-up-and-spit-you-out corporate behaviour terrified me and the "we're gonna make you a star" machinery had me running hard and scared. Frankly I showed up at some very important business meetings three sheets to the wind and the corporate people just threw me in the toilet.' It took five years for Lloyd to sort out his drink and drug problem; he finally made it back with *Field of Fire*, a solo album released in 1986.

But fear of success is more than matched by fear of declining popularity. However hard it may be to claw your way to the top – it seems much harder to stay there. Brian Jones was desperate for stardom, but the harder he tried, the harder life became. Like so many before and since, he fell into the fatal trap of believing he had to be larger than life, off stage as well as on. He could never keep any perspective or distance about being a Rolling Stone – it consumed him constantly, plaguing him with insecurities and anxieties. For Brian, it was showtime all the time; he won the battles that were no use to him as a trendsetter and a drug-hog. He drowned in a swimming pool, dosed into oblivion by alcohol and sedatives, but his love affair with LSD was his real downfall. He slipped into a twilight world of unreality, unable to do the one thing that might have saved his life – play music.

Janis Joplin was a classic overdriven soul wanting to grab as many life experiences as possible and stuff them in her mouth all at once. Her physical constitution was frightening; she deliberately embarked on the toughest gig schedules, indulging in endless partying, consuming on the way vast quantities of drugs and alcohol in exotic combinations. She said to a reporter not long before she died: 'I wanted to smoke dope, take dope, lick dope, suck dope and fuck dope.' But her mental frailty could not match her physical appetites. She was very dependent on people, terrified of loneliness, yet sometimes impossibly demanding and overbearing. She begged and pleaded for love and attention and fell into the depths of despair if she felt rejected or used. Any signs of fading popularity in rock polls she took especially hard. For her, the band she fronted was never enough – like Art Pepper, she was most at home with her drug-using friends who hung around the fringes of the business. They demanded the least of her, treated her like royalty and understood her relationship with drugs, a relationship nobody else could fathom.

Drugs have claimed the lives of many rock, pop and jazz musicians, black and white, spanning all the decades of post-war modern music, but although the actual circumstances of their deaths were very different, several of them happened during periods of transition, readjustment to a new situation or a career decline – all associated with great apprehension or despair.

Frankie Lymon was one of the more extreme examples of too much, too soon.

Fronting a vocal group, the Teenagers, Frankie Lymon had a number one hit at the age of thirteen in 1956 with 'Why Do Fools Fall In Love?' It remained in the Hot Hundred for five months and sold two million copies worldwide. Earning $5,000 a week, Lymon was smoking eight-inch cigars, causing mayhem in hotel rooms and sleeping with a procession of much older women. Within three years, it was all over; no further recordings were anything like as successful, he split with the Teenagers and was eventually dropped by his label.

Lymon came from a harsh Puerto Rican environment in Washington Heights and stumbled back there as a chronic heroin user while still in his teens. In 1961 he was rescued by two managers who put him through a drug cure at Manhattan General Hospital and generally tried to revitalize his career. He released two singles, both ignored, and found himself tied to the small print of a Columbia recording contract for five years. In 1964 he was back in the news, but only because he was convicted on a heroin charge. In January 1967 the black magazine *Ebony* ran an optimistic interview with Lymon as he struggled once more to find his feet: 'I have been born again,' Frankie proclaimed – I'm not ashamed to let the public know I took the cure. Maybe my story will keep some other kid from going wrong ... I was lucky, God must have been watching over me ... nobody ever sold me a bad fix.' A year later, his luck ran out. On 28 February 1968, aged twenty-six, he was found dead on the bathroom floor of his grandmother's apartment. Tragically, like his brother, he had succumbed to an overdose of heroin.

Although something of a pill-popper as a teenager, Free guitarist Paul Kossoff had no real problems with drugs until the band broke up. Free were formed in 1969 and by 1970 had three albums under their belt. Their single 'All Right Now', taken from their third album, pushed them into the big league. It could have been a recipe for disaster: they were a young band (Andy Fraser, the bass player, was only fifteen when they started out) and they had found fame and fortune very quickly. However, according to manager John Glover, there were no destructive habits in the band and they formed a very tight self-contained unit which successfully absorbed all the pressures of the business. When the follow-up album and single failed to chart, however, the fortress crumbled, with singer Paul Rodgers and Andy Fraser, who together wrote all the songs, quarrelling bitterly. Yet so self-contained were Free, that when Andy anounced that the band was finished, it came as a great shock to everyone, including the management.

Drummer Simon Kirke was very upset, but managed to cope; Paul Kossoff was devastated. He was an exceptionally gifted guitarist with a unique feel and sound and also a very sensitive person. Free meant everything to him and without it he was lost. Fraser and Rodgers tried bands of their own which failed. Simon Kirke got Paul involved in a studio band which released one album, *Kossoff, Kirke, Tetsu and Rabbit*, and Kossoff also did some Island studio sessions for Robert Palmer and Jim Capaldi. But the collapse of Free had turned Kossoff to drugs 'Pills were really his problem,' says John Glover, 'Valium, Librium, Mandrax, Tuinal – you name it, he'd take it. He had the most astounding resilience – he just took them by the handful.' Kossoff was spending much of his time in the company of other drug-using friends like Uriah Heep's bass player, Gary Thain. (In 1974, Thain survived electrocution on stage in Dallas, but quit Uriah Heep soon after saying they were insensitive to his injuries. A heroin user, he died of an overdose February 1976. Paul Kossoff survived him by one month.)

With all the splinter bands failing, John Glover persuaded Free to reform for a farewell tour and then see what happened. Free II limped on from January to July 1972, when Andy Fraser quit again; their US tour had been badly hampered by Kossoff's non-appearance at several gigs. He was out of the band by October, replaced by Wendell Richardson from Osibisa who remained until Free broke up for the last time in July 1973. John Glover takes up the story:

> Despite all the problems, I agreed to manage him [Kossoff] as a solo artist and Back Street Crawler was formed in 1975. We had to use three Americans because it was extremely difficult to get any British musicians who would work with Paul.
>
> At that time, strenuous efforts were being made to persuade the doctor involved to stop handing out these drugs like sweets. But we couldn't get it stopped. He stayed with me and my wife for a while, so I know what he was like and he really wanted to get out of this drugs thing. But I'm convinced that all these drugs together severely affects his mind – part of him wanted to be straight, the other part staying wrecked.
>
> I told Paul that I was going to hire somebody to be with him all the time, and everywhere they played I insisted the promoter provide police backstage to discourage people from giving him drugs. I just couldn't understand it – you'd tell people, his friends, 'Please don't give him any, they're killing him, you've seen him on stage, he can't play.' But it made no difference.
>
> Whatever I did, he'd find a way. We were recording once at Olympic Studios. He went to the toilet, climbed out of the window, got his car, drove off and we lost him. He went to a dealer, picked up a load of pills, took them all and then wrecked four cars in the Portobello Road, plus his own. He abandoned the car and went back to his flat where we found him eight hours later. The following day he was full of remorse. The smallest thing would send him off on a bender, like if somebody said anything about a solo he'd played. That day, as it happened, it wasn't so small: he'd just got back from a doctor who told him he was going deaf.
>
> Paul couldn't do anything about it in the sense that all he wanted to do was to play music. So if you took him out of the environment where music was, he'd be very unhappy. Trouble was, that's where the drugs were as well. While Back Street Crawler was being established, he was reasonably straight, but once we started touring, he went completely over the top and that's when he was admitted to hospital. [This was in August 1975. The UK tour to promote the debut album was cancelled. Paul Kossoff was allegedly clinically dead for several minutes when his heart stopped.] In January 1976, we went to America to do the second album and a tour. Paul started on the pills again and the band were getting very angry. I went to his hotel room and had this furious row with him. He came at me with a bottle of Scotch; I pushed him and as he fell, he broke his little finger, his playing hand, would you believe, so he couldn't play anyway. After his finger healed, we did the tour, finishing with four dates in Los Angeles. There were a couple of girls around throughout that tour who obviously fancied Paul like mad. One of them was serious bad news and I had to

keep throwing them out. We went to get the overnight plane to New York which left at 10 p.m. I was going to stay in New York to do the tour accounts while the band flew back to London. Before we left, Paul had been with this girl and she gave him a whole load of stuff – God knows what. We got the plane which was due in at 9 a.m. They called out to fasten safety belts, but Paul was not where he should have been – in the seat next to me. He was found dead in the toilet. His heart had stopped, but he must have been doing something.'

This was on 19 March 1976. Six days earlier, *Melody Maker* ran an article by Chris Welch called 'Save Our Stars', coming (as the headline pointed out) in the wake of Gary Thain's death and that of former Supremes star Florence Ballard, who was subsisting on welfare and whose death may also have been indirectly drug-related. Welch argued that the rock industry should act to try and prevent the waste of life and talent in the business:

> The singers, songwriters and musicians know the risks … yet it is not always possible for people to be cold, calculating and rational … [however] … this is not to suggest that rock musicians are wholly innocents abroad. Talk to Jimmy McCulloch, the young lead guitarist with Wings, who has been playing professionally since he was fifteen, and he says firmly on the subject of pitfalls and exploitation: 'I'm no mug.'

On 28 September 1979 Jimmy McCulloch was found dead, apparently from the effects of drugs.

For fourteen years, bass player and lead vocalist Phil Lynott was the inspiration and driving force of Thin Lizzy, one of the finest bands ever to come out of Ireland. Throughout their career they were an exciting dynamic band, their image set by Lynott's cool, hard, machismo stance. Thin Lizzy had a stormy, unsettled history but enjoyed massive hits like the albums *Jailbreak, Johnny the Fox* and *Live and Dangerous* and chart singles 'The Boys are Back in Town' and 'Don't Believe a Word'. But despite pulling a large and loving crowd wherever they played, in 1983 it all went stale and sour and they called it a day. Lynott admitted to *Melody Maker* that he was the most reluctant of the band to split up; hardly surprising, as he had led Thin Lizzy for nearly all his professional life. He was never known for being exactly abstemious and had more than his share of drug convictions. But once Lizzy collapsed, his drug habit got worse, fuelled by the army of low-lifes that trailed after him. His solo career never took off and his marriage failed. An ex-girlfriend told a reporter; 'Sadly he could never face the fact that his days with Thin Lizzy were over. He had a jukebox in his house and every song was a Thin Lizzy record.' Drugs eventually destroyed his health and on 30 December 1985 he was admitted to Salisbury Infirmary with a serious kidney and liver infection. He died shortly afterwards.

Nico, too found it hard not to be in the limelight. The twilight of her career is grimly told in James Young's superlative account of his days as Nico's keyboard player in the 1980s and the sordid degradations of the band's hopeless excursions into music. The prologue outlines the sorry pass that Nico had reached – heroin was the insulation against everything that had faded, from her beauty to her fame. She now inhabited that dimly-lit corner of the rock business peopled by the has-beens and the never-weres, the fringers and the hangers on – grubby, banal and soul-destroying, flopping from one ghastly hovel to another, 'We never, for an instant' observed Young, 'thought of ourselves as part of the Music Business. We were just there when it didn't happen'. There was nothing to ground Nico in her life – heroin just increased her air of dreamy detachment from reality. After Andy Warhol had quite literally delivered to Nico her fifteen minutes in the sun, she spent the rest of days into lonely middle age simply trying to blot out the memory of what had and what hadn't happened since. She wasn't even allowed to go out in a blaze of junkie glory – she simply fell off her bike one day and died.

The litany of problems faced by musicians in their encounters with drugs have continued unabated. Steve Tyler and Joe Perry of Aerosmith were once known as 'The Toxic Twins'. Tyler said that 'we did a lot of albums fucked up'. Perry started taking heroin in 1976 during the recording of the album *Rocks*. His chief recollection of recording 'Draw The Line' was 'this huge bottle of Tuinals which I hid under the sink'. On some nights, Aerosmith would play the same song twice because they had forgotten that they had already played it. Tyler and Perry actually fought on stage over drugs. It got the point where 'we never really left the States because we were afraid to go through Customs'. As a whole, the band were doing such quantities of drugs that 'hiding the shit under band aids and inside backstage passes wasn't workin' any more. Our managers knew what sorta state we were in, so what was the percentage for them in going to Europe when they figured they'd end up having to bail us out' (*Q Mag* November 1989). The truth was that America was a big enough market for the band and however messed up they were, the audiences kept coming and the records kept selling.

Eventually though, the whole edifice collapsed and the band were put through a lengthy period of drug rehabilitation. The hiatus lasted four years, after which they re-formed to score a top ten hit at the end of 1986 with Run DMC and 'Walk This Way'.

Despite Axl Rose's disdain for those journalists who compared Guns 'n' Roses to the rock bands of an earlier period like Led Zeppelin, G 'n' R were no less strangers to chemical excess than any of their mentors. Indeed, it was something that the band were proud of, 'we brought back that whole element of danger ... which was severely lacking'. This was in the pre-grunge early eighties when the new American underground with bands like Black Flag and the Meat Puppets were very anti rock 'n' roll. Except when it came to drugs. Perry Farrell of Jane's Addiction said he was 'exploring chaos' and rapidly slipped into heroin addiction. David Gahan of Depeche Mode was a heroin addict for most of the nineties with two failed attempts at coming off, overdoses, arrests and a suicide attempt.

Eventually N-Joi, for all their chart success, hit a brick wall as their manager recalls, 'They were hard work since Day One, but things got progressively worse as time went on. If you have a hit single, you are continually looking for the next one, so you constantly have to stay on the case of what's happening, going to clubs and so on - you've got to be out there, up all night, doing studio work. And that's when the spiral starts. They ran out of ideas, the money wasn't coming in, overdrawn at the bank. And the money that was coming in, say, from selling a sample, was never re-invested. They'd just go out on a binge for three days. It got to the crisis point; I was working really hard and not getting paid, living in a house we couldn't afford because the record company wouldn't give us any more money. The band broke up, fell out, don't talk. You can give your life to something, produce great music, then it can't be repeated, everything falls apart and you're back living with your mum'.

But probably the saddest story of all is that of Kurt Cobain. He had a history of drug and alcohol abuse, but seemed to make a conscious decision to become a heroin addict, possibly to deal with the chronic, but undiagnosed stomach pain which he said plagued his life. More likely, his path to self-destruction was through a lack of self-esteem even more debilitating than his stomach pain. After his parents split up, he grew to hate himself and once Nirvana took off, being hailed as the messiah of a new generation, being told he could do no wrong, that he was a genius, only served to compound his misery. He couldn't handle fame, couldn't face the feeling that he had cheated on the music.

In his obituary, Nick Kent wrote, 'even the sketchy details of his final days currently available scream volumes to anyone conversant with the way heroin addiction first breaks its victim's spirit, exiles him from his nearest and dearest, drives him crazy and then casually snuffs him out, after yet another night of soul-sucking moral conflicts and the black funk of hopelessness even the most numbing high can't obliterate ... Cobain's denial of his drug addiction had sent him off on the lam from a drug clinic, had apparently destroyed both his group and his marriage and finally caused him to deny his own life". (*Q Mag* June 1994)

The clear message is that only those who are really ready to be cured can actually succeed, whatever facilities are available. So what is available for the musician who wants to become drug-free? When a musician (or anyone else for that matter) decides that the reasons for stopping drugs outweigh those for carrying on, how does he or she get help to achieve a drug-free life?

In America during the fifties, an era of regular incarceration for jazz musicians on drugs charges, several found their way to the prison treatment centres at Lexington and Fort Worth. For a brief time, too, there was a jazz musicians' clinic in New York. In the sixties, therapeutic communities like Phoenix House and Synanon provided a drug-free environment, while on the street outpatient methadone regimes were (and still are) widely favoured by the authorities in both America and Britain. Britain, too, has therapeutic communities following the American example, including private clinics operating a style of psychotherapy known as the Minnesota Model, also imported from America.

Not surprisingly, well-heeled musicians seeking treatment normally book themselves into private clinics which offer detoxification and counselling programmes. At one time, the much-publicized Betty Ford Addiction Clinic in the States was the in-place to be drying out. Other musicians have sought out less conventional therapies.

There was a time when the keyboard skills of Nicky Hopkins graced the records of many famous bands, most notably the Rolling Stones. Then drugs took their toll and he disappeared from view, occasionally sighted in odd places, for example slumped over a piano in a dude ranch owned by a mobster. The brainchild of L. Ron Hubbard, Scientology has attracted converts from the music business such as Stanley Clarke and Chick Corea. The Scientologists also run a drug rehabilitation programme called Narconon. Hopkins went through the Narconon programme and was quoted in a somewhat chilling manner in Scientology publicity literature:

> L . Ron Hubbard is a pioneer in the truest sense of the word. He spent a
> lifetime researching and developing the only workable technology ever to

enable man to become free.

It was this technology that literally saved my life a few years ago when I was totally caught up in the trap of drugs and had only a short time left to live. Not only was that problem terminally handled, but my awareness as a spiritual being and my artistic creativity have increased beyond measure.

I can never adequately express the love, admiration, respect and gratitude that I have for this superb being, who is surely the greatest friend Mankind ever had.

Thank you Ron, for so very, very, much.

Nicky Hopkins, musician and composer.

Nicky Hopkins died in 1994 of that mysterious Cobain-like stomach complaint that similarly plagued his life.

Probably the treatment most associated with rock stars was neuro-electric therapy, better known as the black box treatment, developed by Dr Meg Patterson. The treatment was discovered by chance in 1972 when Dr Patterson was working with a Dr Wen in the Tung Wah Hospital, Hong Kong. Dr Wen was experimenting with electro-acupuncture, sending an electric current through acupuncture needles as a form of anaesthesia during surgery. On an island with a substantial addict population, many of his patients were addicts and in hospital they were obviously deprived of supplies. To their surprise, the doctors were getting reports from their addict patients that as well as being an effective anaesthetic, the electro-acupuncture was also relieving withdrawal symptoms on a scale which ruled out coincidence.

Back in England, the technique was adapted into a small box which generated an electric current through electrodes attached to the ears. Exactly why withdrawal symptoms are alleviated is still unclear. The most popular theory is associated with the discovery that the brain has its own natural opiates called endorphins. During a period of heroin dependency, the artificial painkiller replaces those found naturally in the brain. When heroin is stopped, the natural opiates do not rush back immediately to fill the space left by the heroin, and so the person suffers withdrawal symptoms. What the black box was supposed to do was to stimulate the natural opiates or endorphins quickly to occupy the space left by the heroin and so head off the misery of withdrawal.

In the very early days of her treatment, Dr Patterson had Paul Kossoff as one of her patients, but it was her treatment of Eric Clapton that earned her international publicity. The names of Clapton, Pete Townshend, Jack Bruce and George Harrison became associated with Dr Patterson as sponsors of a charity set up to fund a clinic at Broadhurst Manor in Sussex. Money came from the Robert Stigwood Organisation and other commercial interests. The clinic opened in 1976 amid much ballyhoo and it was these other funders who began cynically to market the Black Box as a 'cure' for heroin addiction, a claim which Dr Patterson never made. In 1981, the funding ran out and, unable to attract government assistance, Dr Patterson and her husband George moved to California, where they were sought out by Pete Townshend for help with his own drink and drug problems. They later returned to the UK to take on another famous patient, Boy George, although he actually came off heroin through more conventional means and in later comments (e.g. *Observer* 28th February 1987) was none too complimentary about the black box.

So was it effective? Those who underwent the treatment say it was, while critics in the medical profession claimed that nothing more was at work than a placebo effect.

Research carried out in Britain failed to demonstrate that neuro-electric therapy was any more effective in relieving withdrawal symptoms than methadone, let alone being any sort of cure. What is interesting is that when interviewed about their treatment, Meg Patterson's star patients went on at some length about how wonderful she was, but said little about the efficacy of the treatment itself. What may have been more important than gadgets was the comfortable, non-challenging environment provided by the Pattersons in contrast to the regimentation and confrontation of the hospital or rehabilitation clinic. Jerry Lee Lewis stormed out of the Betty Ford Clinic claiming he wasn't getting the star treatment he thought he deserved and many of the latter day addict musicians haven't done too well in conventional treatment environments. Kurt Cobain, for all the help he needed, lasted two days in the Los Angeles-based Exodus Program before he discharged himself. Two days later he was dead.

What the Pattersons provided as much as anything was space and time out of the glare of publicity for re-thinking and taking stock. At best, the black box may have aided detoxification, but whatever the method, coming off drugs is nothing like as hard as staying off them. No black box prevented Eric Clapton sliding into very destructive post-heroin drinking which brought him much closer to death than snorting heroin ever did.

Neuro-electric therapy slid out of the news and there was little interest in the drug problems of the music business for the best part of ten years until very recently. Then in 1995, Jerry Garcia died from complications arising out of heroin addiction, Blind Melon's Shannon Hoon died of a cocaine overdose, to be followed by Sublime lead singer Bradley Nowell and Jonathan Melvoin from the Smashing Pumpkins. Both David Gahan and Stone Temple Pilot's singer Scott Weiland were arrested on drug charges. All this fed into the US political debate about 'heroin chic' in the entertainment and fashion business and suddenly drug taking by musicians was back in the news.

However behind the scenes and for some while, attempts were being made to increase the help available to musicians. Buddy Arnold, a jazz musician who hung out with Charlie Parker and Billie Holiday and kicked a thirty year heroin habit, set up the Musician's Assistance Program (MAP) based in Los Angeles in 1992. Advisory Board members include Natalie Cole, Dr John, Quincey Jones, Bonnie Raitt, Steve Earle and Eric Clapton who himself is now heavily involved in drug counselling and has funded a rehab facility in Antigua with subsidised places for locals.

In 1993 MAP received a $50,000 grant from the National Academy of Recording Arts & Sciences (NARAS). But none of this came to public attention until 1995. NARAS president Mike Greene had been close to Shannon Hoon; when Hoon died, Greene experienced a personal epiphany and decided more high profile action was required. He announced a call to arms for the music industry, set up several meetings of industry bosses and added a drug treatment programme similar to MAP to NARAS' own MusiCares Foundation. However, he upset many in the industry by accusing those who wouldn't attend his meetings as being 'in denial' about the problem and has had to fend off counter-accusations that he was simply jumping on a bandwagon for the purposes of self-publicity.

But industry in-fighting aside, the recent deaths of a new era of musicians through drugs, has again underlined the fact that whatever the music, whatever you call it and whoever is playing it, the old mythologies are a long time dying – not least the Charlie Parker death wish.

APPENDIX A: – A TOUCH TOO MUCH

The highway to pop immortality is littered with the wrecks of smashed cars and planes, while in the toilets and motel rooms lie the bodies of those who've had a touch too much.

A number of factors contribute to an acute toxic reaction or overdose. Where heroin is concerned, those who resume injecting after a period of abstinence are especially at risk; too often they make the mistake of picking up at the dosage level where they stopped. In the interim, the tolerance has fallen and cannot cope with what has now become too powerful a dose. Janis Joplin had been off for six months prior to her death, although her passing was a classic drug death where all was not as it seemed.

Certainly her period of abstinence played an important role, but she might have lived through it had she not been drinking. Alcohol is implicated in many so-called heroin deaths: both drugs depress the nervous system and in combination, one will exacerbate the action of the other to the point where the respiratory system may pack up.

Deaths are also caused by the impurities contained in street drugs; paying over the odds for your supplies, as most famous musicians do, is no guarantee of quality. To die from an overdose of relatively pure heroin can take anything from one to twelve hours, starting with lethargy and progressing to prolonged coma during which time effective treatment can be administered. However, users have been found dead with the needle still sticking in a vein and research in America has identified quinine as the contaminant capable of causing sudden death.

Then again, users have succumbed to the 'hot shot'. The story goes that being accustomed to a New York heroin purity of no more than 5%, Sid Vicious's metabolism was unprepared for the 30% plus powder thoughtfully brought over from England.

Should those who inject their drugs survive the hazards of a shot too pure or too impure, or the dangers of using drugs in combination, there are other perils to avoid. In 1939, an epidemic of malaria broke out among New York addicts caused by using contaminated needles. The same unwise practice of sharing 'works' has also been responsible for the spread of hepatitis and AIDS.

But even those who snort their drugs are not immune from the uncertainties inherent in using illegal drugs of unknown constituency. At least two musicians have died through mistaking heroin for cocaine. Folk artist Tim Buckley was one, but the most celebrated case involved Robbie McIntosh, drummer with the Average White Band. On 23 September 1974, the band were at a party hosted by record company executive Kenneth Moss. McIntosh collapsed after snorting what he thought was cocaine but in fact turned out to be heroin laced with strychnine. Panic stricken at what he had done, Moss persuaded McIntosh's wife that everything would be all right if she took the drummer back to his North Hollywood hotel room instead of going to hospital. She took the advice and McIntosh died. Guitarist Alan Gorrie was very nearly another victim of the same batch, but he was saved by singer Cher who kept him walking about packed with ice to prevent him losing consciousness. Moss pleaded guilty to involuntary manslaughter and served four months with four years probation.

Overdosing is a shorthand description for a very complicated clinical phenomenon, but in the face of research conducted in 1984 it becomes almost inexplicable. It was already known that ex-users often exhibit the symptoms of withdrawal without going near any drugs, just by walking in the vicinity of an old drug-using haunt. It now seems that these Pavlovian-type responses may also be a factor in who survives an overdose and who doesn't. Out of an admittedly small sample of ten survivors of drug overdoses interviewed, seven had overdosed in circumstances unusual for their own drug use. For example a regular heroin user who usually injected alone was the sole overdoser in the company of others using a common supply. If this theory is correct, drug-using musicians are particularly at risk, as they are often away from home in strange places and in the company of people they don't know.[1] According to the memoirs of Peggy Caserta, a lover of Janis Joplin, the singer invariably shot up with her friends, but when she took her last fix she was alone.[2]

A verdict of death from overdosing can be a handy let-out for a coroner when no other impelling evidence presents itself like suicide, violence or obvious natural causes. Did Elvis die from one last handful of uppers or downers or did his heart just give out after years of drugs and junk food, i.e. natural causes? For a family and a business anxious for reputations to remain unsullied, the latter is much preferred

Thus for all these reasons, determining the cause of death where drugs are implicated, is hardly an exact science. What follows is a list of those whose deaths appear directly or indirectly to have been attributable the misuse of drugs.

Those Who Reportedly Died from the Direct Toxic Effects of Drugs
Deaths due entirely to alcohol have been excluded

SONNY BERMAN 16 January 1947
Star trumpeter with Woody Herman who overdosed on heroin aged twenty-three
HANK WILLIAMS 1 January 1953
Combination of alcohol and amphetamines
CARL PERKINS 17 March 1958
Pianist with Art Pepper and other West Coast Jazz musicians
DINAH WASHINGTON 14 December 1963
Combination of alcohol and amphetamine – like diet pills, although some reports quoted barbiturates as the cause of death
RUDY LEWIS 1964
Replaced Ben E. King in the Drifters, but died of a drug overdose the morning they were due to record 'Under the Boardwalk'
BRIAN EPSTEIN 27 August 1967
Died from an overdose of a bromide-based sleeping pill called Carbitrol
FRANKIE LYMON 28 February 1968
Heroin overdose
AL WILSON 3 September 1970
Guitarist with Canned Heat who was nearly blind and suffered from depression, died of a barbiturate overdose
JIMI HENDRIX 18 September 1970
Babiturate overdose.
JANIS JOPLIN 4 October 1970
Overdose of heroin, alcohol and Valium in combination
JIM MORRISON 3 July 1970
Some reports say heart attack, others suggest a heroin overdose. His widow Pamela

died of a heroin overdose on 25 April 1974

BRIAN COLE 2 August 1972

The bass player and vocalist with the Association died of a heroin overdose

RORY STORM 27 September 1972

Leader of Rory Storm and the Hurricanes, a popular Mersey band who boasted Ringo Starr on drums before he joined the Beatles. Storm took an overdose of sleeping pills in a suicide pact with his mother

PHIL SEAMAN 13 October 1972

Long time heroin user and one of the greats of British jazz drumming. He died of a heroin overdose

BILLY MURCIA 6 November 1972

Drummer with the New York Dolls overdosed on alcohol and pills

DANNY WHITTEN 18 October 1972

Guitarist with Neil Young's Crazy Horse, died of a heroin overdose. Bruce Berry, a roadie in the band went the same way

MISS CHRISTINE 18 October 1972

One of Girls Together Outrageous (GTO), a groupie collective who recorded an album in 1969 on Frank Zappa's Straight label. She died of a heroin overdose

GRAM PARSONS 19 September 1973

A major pioneer of country rock. Actual cause of death inconclusive but possibly due to a combination of heroin, cocaine, alcohol and amphetamine. His manager stole the coffin *en route* to the funeral and burned the body in the desert, apparently in accordance with Parsons wishes

VINNIE TAYLOR 17 April 1974

Guitarist with Sha Na Na, died of a heroin overdose

ROBBIE McINTOSH 23 September 1974

Drummer with the Average White Band died of a heroin overdose thinking it was cocaine

NICK DRAKE 23 October 1974

British folk artist who died of an overdose of Tryptizol, a trycyclic anti depressant

TIM BUCKLEY 29 June 1975

Heroin overdose. A case of mistaken identity – for cocaine

GARY THAIN February 1976

Formerly bass player with Uriah Heep, Thain was found floating in his bath dead from a heroin overdose. He was a very good friend of Paul Kossoff; the *Rolling Stone Encyclopaedia of Rock & Roll* cites their deaths as occurring on the same day, 19 March 1976. Eerie, if true, but in fact Thain died about six weeks earlier.

PAUL KOSSOFF 19 March 1976

Died *en route* home from a US tour with Back Street Crawler. Had a history of heart trouble, but was known to have been involved in heavy sedative drug-taking prior to his death

TOMMY BOLIN 4 December 1976

Star guitarist with a later permutation of Deep Purple. Died of a heroin overdose

ELVIS PRESLEY 16 August 1977

The great mystery (or one of them at any rate). Presley had so disturbed his metabolism with horrendous quantities of drugs, anything could have happened but the deathly hush from official sources suggests an overdose. Few people believed 'cardiac arrhythmia'

GREG HERBERT 31 January 1978

Saxophonist with Blood, Sweat and Tears. Died of a drug overdose on tour with the band in Holland

PETER MEADEN 5 August 1978

First manager of the Who, who committed suicide with pills

KEITH MOON 7 September 1978

Just one month later and by the cruellest of ironies, Keith Moon overdosed on Heminevrin, the drug he was taking to help control his drinking

SID VICIOUS 2 February 1979.

Heroin overdose

JIMMY McCULLOCH 29 September 1979

Former Wings guitarist died of an unspecified drugs overdose

MALCOLM OWEN 14 July 1980

Lead singer with British New Wave band, the Ruts. Owen died of a heroin overdose

TIM HARDIN 29 December 1980

Many long-term heroin users 'mature out' of their dependency by their mid-thirties. Sadly, Hardin didn't and died of a heroin overdose aged thirty-nine

STEVE TOOK and DAVE BIDWELL

Took was formerly with Marc Bolan in Tyrannosaurus Rex, Dave Bidwell played drums with the British blues band Chicken Shack. Took was sacked by Bolan because of his drugs problem. He finally teamed up with Bidwell in a band called Shagrat, which played only one gig, the principals reportedly being stoned throughout. Both Took and Bidwell died through overdoses as did both Took's girlfriend and Bidwell's wife

MIKE BLOOMFIELD 15 February 1981

A stellar blues guitarist and committed drug user, found in his car having apparently overdosed on heroin

JOHN BELUSHI 5 March 1982

Not strictly a musician, despite the Blues Brothers movie, but a drug hog of the first order. Died of a drug overdose – a mixture of heroin and cocaine known as a speedball. Had the same minders who tried to keep Eagles guitarist Joe Walsh away from dangerous substances, but it didn't save him

LESTER BANGS 30 April 1982

One of the great names of rock journalism found dead in his New York apartment of a heart attack precipitated by stimulants

JAMES HONEYMAN SCOTT 16 June 1982

Guitarist with the Pretenders who succumbed to a cocktail of alcohol and cocaine

PETE FARNDON 16 April 1983

Former bass player with the Pretenders and another 'speedball victim

WELLS KELLY 20 October 1984

Drummer with Meatloaf and another victim of the heroin/cocaine combo

GARY HOLTON 25 October 1985

Vocalist with the Heavy Metal Kids, a mid-seventies British band. And later TV star who died of a heroin overdose.

SHANNON HOON 20 October 1995

Lead singer of Blind Melon died from a cocaine overdose

BRADLEY NOVELL July 1996

Lead singer of Sublime died of a heroin overdose

JONATHAN MELVOIN July 1996

Tour keyboard player with The Smashing Pumpkins died of a heroin overdose. Drummer Jimmy Chamberlin who was in the hotel room when Melvoin died was fired shortly afterwards.

ROBIN MACLENNAN April 1997

Former manager of The Pogues was found dead with a mixture of heroin, cocaine and alcohol in his blood after celebrating his 44th birthday.

Those Whose Deaths were Drug-Related

NB Most of these people were also heavy smokers; but the role of tobacco in musician mortality cannot be properly ascertained.

FATS NAVARRO 7 July 1950

His death was officially listed as tuberculosis complicated by narcotics addiction. Other sources say a heroin overdose

CHARLIE PARKER 12 March 1955

Death was officially attributed to stomach ulcers and pneumonia with a contributing condition of advanced cirrhosis and heart disease. Parker was thirty-five when he died; to the doctor he looked twenty years older

BILLIE HOLIDAY 17 July 1959

On admittance to hospital the diagnosis changed from non lethal dose of heroin to a liver complaint complicated by heart failure and then changed again to a serious kidney condition. Alcohol was probably the real culprit, although years of heroin use would have done nothing for her digestive system.

BRIAN JONES 3 July 1969

Drowning associated with alcohol, amphetamine and 'sleeping pills'

CLYDE McPHATTER 13 June 1972

Lead vocalist with the Drifters, he had a long history of drug and alcohol problems and died from complications arising out of heart, liver and kidney disease

LOWELL GEORGE 29 June 1979

One of the finest slide guitar players of all time, George led the awesome Little Feat. His drug problems, however, pushed him to the sidelines towards the end and he died of a heart attack related both to drugs and obesity

CARL RADLE 30 May 1980

Eric Clapton's first-choice bass player for nearly a decade, Radle had serious heroin problems and died of a chronic liver complaint

ALEX HARVEY 3 February 1982

Harvey was forty-nine when he died, ostensibly of a heart attack, although it was said this was brought about by the large amount of speed being pushed at him to maintain a punishing schedule

ART PEPPER 25 May 1985

He was on methadone at the time of his death. It seems as if after years of drug and alcohol abuse, his body just said 'enough'

PHIL LYNOTT 30 December 1985

Died in hospital from severe kidney and liver infection

Those Who Had a Long History of Drug Misuse but Died of Unrelated Causes

WARDELL GRAY 25 May 1955

The tenor sax player was found with a broken neck in the Nevada Desert probably killed by gangsters because of gambling debts. An official report said he was a drug addict, but no autopsy was performed

GRAHAM BOND 8 May 1974

One of the unsung heroes of British jazz-rock and r & b and a legend in the music business. Bond had a serious drug habit for many years, mainly heroin and opiate-based cough medicine, but in practice anything would do. A couple of months after being discharged from mental hospital, he died under a London underground train.

MAMA CASS ELLIOTT 29 July 1974

Allegedly she died after choking on a sandwich in a London flat. It may have been fate that she died so close to Graham Bond in time and location. Bond and Mama Cass had something of a fling when he was in the States in the late sixties, sharing intimacies and syringes

DENNIS WILSON 29 December 1983

Beach Boys' drummer who drowned in the sea while swimming: the autopsy revealed alcohol, cocaine and Valium in his system

KURT COBAIN 8 April 1994

Committed suicide after a long and unsuccessful battle against heroin addiction

MICHAEL HUTCHENCE 22 November 1997

Committed suicide with a mixture of cocaine, alcohol, Prozac and several other prescription drugs in his blood – and after many years of drug misuse.

AND FINALLY ...

OTIS REDDING 10 December 1967 and **RICK NELSON** 31 December 1985

The stuff that rock rumours are made of. Both came down in planes, but...one story that circulated after Redding's death was that he was out of his head on cocaine on the evening of the flight and that rescuers pulled him from the pilot's seat when it ditched in a Wisconsin lake. First reports of Rick Nelson's death were that the plane caught fire after a cocaine freebasing session. However, further investigation suggests that as usual the press took 2 and 2 and made 137. The only basis for the story was that all the bodies had contained recently ingested cocaine or alcohol. From this, knowing a little of the freebasing process, some hack made the quantum leap and came up with the freebase fire story.

NOTES

(Where the full reference is cited in the bibliography,
only the first named author is cited here)

Introduction
1. Narcotics Control Digest, 21 August 1985, p. 5
2. Bakalar, p. 68
3. Catholic Institute for International Relations, *Caught in the crossfire: developing countries, the UNDCP and the war on drugs*, 1998.

PART ONE
Chapter One
1. Latimer, p. 40
2. Berridge, p. 66
3. McNamara (*Step Right Up*) p. 27
4. ibid., p. 65
5. Epstein, p. 35
6. McNeal, p. 77
7. Cook, p. 119
8. Toll, pp. 221-2
9 White (Charles), p. 31

Chapter Two
1. Carroll, p. 238
2. ibid., p. 307
3. Luc Sante *Low Life: lures and snares of old New York*. London: Granta, 1991, p. 143.
4. ibid., p. 147
5. Toll, pp. 65-6
6. ibid., p. 97

Chapter Three
1. Mezzrow, p. 98
2. ibid., p. 4
3. ibid., p. 18
4. Ostransky, p. 2
5. Sidran, p 44
6. Before he switched to clarinet, Mezzrow wanted to be a saxophonist
7. Mezzrow, p. 55
8. ibid., p . 59
9. Morris, p. 22
10. ibid. , p. 25
11. Mezzrow s p . 72
12. ibid., pp. 79-80
13. Leonard, pp. 60-1
14. Mezzrow, p. 99
15. ibid., p. l01
16. ibid., p. 115
17. ibid., p. 210
18. Robert Palmer. *Deep Blues* London: Macmillan, 1982, p. 31
19. Mezzrow, p. 216
20. ibid., pp. 345-6
21. ibid., p. 275

Chapter Five
1. Ehrenberg, p. 83
2. ibid., p. 84
3. Leonard, p. 37
4. ibid. , p. 38
5. Bonnie, p. 34
6. Jones, p. 113
7. Sloman, p. 42
8. Anslinger, p. 8
9. Anslinger private papers
10. ibid.
11. ibid.
12. *Variety*, 26 November 1969
13. Anslinger private papers

Chapter Six
1. Hawes, p. 9
2. This is not to suggest that bebop was 'born' in Kansas City, but that its political set-up in the thirties made Kansas a particularly fertile breeding ground for the development of new music.
3. Hentoff, p. 87
4. Taylor, p. 180
5. Mailer, pp. 2-3
6. Hentoff, p. 87
7. Hawes, p. 96
8. ibid., p. 86
9. Pepper, p. 5
10. Charles, pp. 110-11
11. Russell, p. 232
12. Reisner, p. 80
13. Hawes, p. l3
14 ibid., p. 45
15. Pepper, p. 226
16. Taylor, p. l56
17. Pepper, p. 97
    Two researchers, Zinberg and Lewis, quote the case of an American jazz musician (unnamed) who was admitted to hospital a second time with hepatitis. Since he used junkie slang in his speech, it was suspected he might be an addict. He admitted ashamedly that he had tried heroin twice and hadn't enjoyed it either time. He begged his doctors not to tell his wife or family since he would lose the status of being hooked. He was so psychologically dependent on the experience of being a heroin user (he obviously wasn't dependent on the drug), that the only way the hospital could get him to abide by the treatment regime for treating hepatitis was to play up the fact that having the disease was a sure sign of being an addict and so preserve his own self-image and esteem (Laurie. pp. 52-3)
18. Hentoff, pp. 84-5
19. Pepper, p. 41
20. *Downbeat,* 20 February 1958
21. Hawes, p. 32
22. Shaw, p. 310
23. Reisner, p. l9
24. ibid., p. 52

Chapter Seven
1. O'Day, p. 137

2. ibid., p. 145
3. ibid., p. 227
4. Holiday, p. 132
5. Anslinger, p. 199
6. O'Day, p. 268

PART TWO
Introduction
1. However, jazz was not entirely *passé* to young people; trad jazz remained part of the European dance scene to 1962

Chapter Eight
1. Kerouac, p. 114
2. Fong-Torres, p. 450
3. Lyle, *British Journal of Addiction*, 1953, 50 p. 52
4. Spear, *British Journal of Addiction*, 1969, 64 p. 254
5. Brown, p. 38
6. Burchill (*Damaged Gods*), p 34
7. Like the Krays and the Richardsons, the Nash gang was one of London's major criminal organisations of the sixties
8. Wilson, C.W.M. (ed): *The Pharmacological and Epidemiological Aspects of Adolescent Drug Dependence* (Oxford: Pergamon, 1968), p. 266
9. Interview with author
10. Clarke (Steve), p. 32
11. ibid., p. 24
12. Marsh, p. 122
13. ibid. , p. 140
14. Pidgeon, John: *Facing the Music. History of Rock*, 1982, 4, p. 808
15. Stein, p. 295
16. ibid., p. 266
17. Bockris, p. 31
18. *Melody Maker*, 1 March 1986
19. Gay and Elsenbaumer, p. 197
20. *High Times*, March 1984
21. Aerosmith and Davis, p. 221
22. Ramone p. 56
23. *New Musical Express*, 11 December 1976

Chapter Nine
1. Hofmann, Albert: *LSD: My Problem Child* (New York: McGraw-Hill, 1980), p. 15
2. Lee, p. 57
3. ibid., p. 71
4. Robinson, p. 135
5. Chapple, p. 305
6. ibid., p. 20
7. Jackson, p. 45
8. DMT is a synthetic hallucinogen similar to that found naturally in psilocybin mushrooms. The confusion of initials which represents the pharmacological shorthand of hallucinogens was captured in The Alphabet Song (1968), an unashamedly pro-drug anthem by David Peel and the Lower East Side.

> A-B-C-D-E-F-G-LSD and DMT, P. O. T. and L-S-D
> D-M-T & amphetamine
> P-O-T and L-S-D, L-M-D and D-M-T S-T-P
> D-M-T L-S-D got hold of me

Smoke pot, Smoke pot, everybody smoke pot.
Smoke pot, Smoke pot, everybody smoke pot.
Smoke pot, Smoke pot, everybody smoke pot.
ABCD P-O-T, L-S-D and amphetamine
D-M-T S-T-P heroin and C-O-P, L-S-D, P-O-T C-O-P
A-B-C L-S-D
Help! I'm stoned
Help! I'm stoned
Help! I'm stoned
L-S-D P-O-T, D-M-T S-T-P C-O-P & amphetamine
Here comes the cat with heroin

9. Metzner, p. 304
10. Gray, p. 119
11. ibid., p. 192
12. 'Yellow Submarine' has often been thought of as referring to barbiturates or amphetamines. This suggests it was probably an oblique reference to LSD
13. Other acid-pop singles included 'San Francisco Nights' (Eric Burdon); 'I Can Hear the Grass Grow' (The Move); 'Whiter Shade of Pale' (Procol Harum) and 'Mellow Yellow' (Donovan). One of the earliest mentions of LSD on record was a single released by the Gamblers in 1962
14. Chapple, p. 108
15. Radio Caroline survived by moving into international waters

Chapter Ten

1. The FBI later claimed that they set McCartney up. His luggage was screened as he boarded the plane in America and the marijuana was detected. But instead of arresting him, the FBI informed Japanese customs, quoted in: Greenshaw, Wayne: *Flying High: Inside Big-time Drug Smuggling* (New York: Dodd Mead, 1984), p. 91
2. Comment to author
3. Wiener, p. 81
4. ibid., p. 225
5. Under the Misuse of Drugs Act 1971, this regulation only applies to opium and marijuana and has been a quirk of British drugs legislation since 1920
6. Brown, p. 282
7. *Musician*, August 1985, p. 110
8. *Macon Telegraph*, 20 August 1979
9. ibid.
10. *Macon Telegraph*, 29 May 1976
11. *Macon Telegraph*, 20 August 1979
12. Although Davison was caught with a pound of cocaine, he was only charged with half that amount. The rest 'disappeared'. Nowadays, with the high-profile crackdown on drug dealing, for possession of half a pound of cocaine with intent to supply the convicted person probably would be sentenced to at least five years in jail.
13. Cornwell, p. 27

Chapter Eleven

1. Epstein, p. 41
2. ibid., p. 43
3. The study was conducted jointly by the Association of the Bar of the City of New York and the Drug Abuse Council
4. CBS Records ran a slogan in the late sixties 'The Man Can't Bust Our Music'. More recently, Yves St Laurent came up with some seductive marketing images for a perfume called Opium. Another fragrance on the market is Addiction.

5. *Variety*, 23 September 1970
6. Epstein, p. 170
7. ibid., p. 171
8. *Billboard*, 24 October 1970
9. ibid., 21 November 1970.
10. ibid., 14 November 1970
11. *Rolling Stone*, 15 April 1971
12. ibid.
13. *Billboard*, 27 October 1973
14. For example, Schwartz (1972); Douse (1973); Robinson (1976)
15. Stillman, Deane and Weiner, Rex: *The Woodstock Generation* (New York: Viking Press, 1979)
16. Schwartz 1972
17. Bearing in mind that most of the overtly drug-oriented songs tend to be anti-drug, an interesting variation on the theme of drug lyrics and youthful experimentation with drugs was demonstrated by Arlene Marks in a study entitled 'Adolescents Discuss Themselves and Drugs through Drugs', *Journal of Substance Abuse Treatment*, 1986. 3. pp. 243-9. In this study, Marks used the lyrics of drug-related rock songs as a starting point for discussion about alcohol and drugs with a group of juvenile offenders. The aim was that through a medium young people could relate to, they could come to a better understanding of what drug dependency was all about.
18. The furore in America about the allegedly malevolent influence of rock on young people stimulated a discussion in Canada in June 1986 hosted by the Addiction Research Foundation of Ontario (ARF). The public debate was entitled 'Rock's Role in Drug Use: Myth or Reality?' The platform panel included female heavy-metal artist Lee Aaron and other members of the Canadian music business. Not surprisingly, the panel decision was in favour of 'myth'. This sparked off a lively debate with dissenting voices through the letters page of the *ARF Journal*.
19. When commentators wish to point to a recent example of how rock glorifies drug use, 'Cocaine', written by J.J. Cale, but popularised by Eric Clapton, is often quoted. It is alleged that Clapton sings: 'She's all right/she's all right/she's all right/cocaine'. After many careful listenings to J.J. Cale's original version on the album *Troubadour* (1976), I must conclude that what he actually sings is, 'She don't lie/she don't lie/she don't lie/cocaine'. This is an altogether different sentiment, expressing the notion that cocaine will provide the effect the user is looking for, but being non-committal as to whether this is ultimately good or bad. To my ears, however, Clapton does sing the offending lyric on the album *Slowhand* (1977). For some season it seems he changed the lyric. Interviewed in *Musician* (November 1986) Clapton was asked specifically about the association young people might make between a guitar hero and a very infectious, popular song about cocaine. 'Thank God,' said Eric, 'J.J. wrote a very ambivalent song there... I mean he's written a song that is so two-way. I can sing that song now and be anti-cocaine. And I actually think it's more anti- than pro-. But most people don't recognise that.'

Chapter Twelve

1. Dr Lambos Comitas in an interview with *High Times*. 1978, 32, p. 33
2. Henman, p. 45
3. ibid   p. 85
4. Davis (*Reggae Bloodlines*)
5. Pryce, p. 152
6. Davis (*Bob Marley*) p. 135
7. ibid., pp. 145-6
8. *High Times*, September 1976, p. 89
9. *Home Grown*, 1979. 1 (5) p. 13
10. Pryce, p. 156

11. Hebdige, p. 63

Chapter 13
1. Thornton, S.
2. Ritz, p. 114
3. *Dark Star* 1978, 3(6) p. 15
4. *Rolling Stone* 4th December 1982
5. *Musician* January 1990
6. Aerosmith/Davis p. 253
7. *Musician* November 1990
8. Ritz, p. 139
9. Ritz p. 121
10. *Rolling Stone* 1985.
11. *Q Mag* July 1996
12. Adam Sexton ed. *Rap on Rap*
13. Lawrence Stanley, *Rap: the lyrics*. Penguin 1992 (intro)
14. Williams, p. 20
15. Fernando, p. 96

Chapter 14
1. Reynolds, p. 414
2. ibid., p. xvii
3. ibid., p. 131
4. Kohn, p. 131
5. Stone p. 111
6. ibid., p. 177
7. Ashenhurst, A. (1996). The ecstasy subculture: beyond the rave. *British Medical Anthropological Review,* 3(2), p. 22-27.
8. Middles, p. 24
9. ibid., p. 29
10. ibid., p. 71
11. Hutton p. 96
12. Robb p. 27
13. Saunders p. 18
14. Reynolds p. 14

Chapter 15
1. Keeler, C. *Scandal.* Xanadu, 1989, p. 79.
2. ibid., p. 85.
3. Irving, C. et al. *Scandal '63.* Heinemann, p. 75
4. Fabian, R. *London After Dark.* Naldrett Press, p. 38.
5. Shapiro, H. What's in a sausage: the roots of cannabis prohibition. *Druglink* 13 (4), p. 10-13.
6. Bestic, A. *Turn Me On Man.* Library 33 Ltd, 1966, p. 127.
7. Abrams, S. The Hashish Fudge: *The Times* advertisement and the Wootton Report, 1993.
8. ibid.

Chapter 16
1. Dannen, p. 171
2. Young p. 66
3. *Dark Star* 1978, 3, (6), p. 15.
4. Greenshaw, p. 91-92
5. *See* Bibliography, Official sources, item 3
6. White (Charles) p. 168

Chapter 17
1. Aerosmith/Davis p. 119
2. Cable, p. 180
3. Kooper, p. 103
4. ibid., p. 99
5. Charone, Barbara: *Keith Richards* (London: Futura, 1979), p. 10
6. Aerosmith/Davis p. 10
7. Bennett, p. 77
8. ibid., p. 33
9. Sanchez, p. 212
10. Whitcomb, p. 195
11. Charone, op. cit. . p. l2
12. *Newsweek*, October 1980
13. *High Times* June 1983, p. 42
14. Author interview

Appendix
1. Siegel, Shepard: 'Pavlovian Conditioning and Heroin Overdose: Reports by overdose victims', *Bulletin of the Psychonomic Society*, 1984, 22 (5), p. 428-30
2. After Otis Redding's death in 1967, rock managers began taking out insurance policies on the lives of their valuable stars. Following Janis Joplin's death an unsavoury court case was heard because the insurance company refused to pay out. Suicide was not part of the policy and the company claimed that a self-inflicted overdose was tantamount to suicide. It took four years for Joplin's manager Albert Grossman to obtain a decision in his favour.

BIBLIOGRAPHY

Official Sources

Harry J. Anslinger Collection, Pennsylvania State University

Hashish Smuggling and Passport Fraud: The Brotherhood of Eternal Love. US Senate Committee on the Judiciary. 3 October 1973 (Washington: USGPO, 1973)

International Narcotics Trafficking. Senate Committee on Governmental Affairs, 10-18 November 1981 (Washington: USGPO, 1981)

International Study Missions. Senate Select Committee on Narcotics Abuse and Control (Summary Report 1984)

The Role of the Entertainment Industry in Deglamorizing Drug Use. US Senate Committee on Governmental Affairs. 20 March 1985 (Washington: USGPO, 1985)

US Narcotics Control Programs Overseas: An Assessment. Congress Committee on Foreign Affairs. 29 February 1985 (Washington: USPGO. 1985)

Articles

Allsop, Kenneth: 'Jazz and Narcotics', *Encounter*. June 1961. pp. 54-7

Ashley, Richard: 'Patent Medicines', *High Times*. November 1979, pp. 59-63, 97

Bakalar, James and Grinspoon. Lester: 'Why Drug Policy is So Harsh', *Hastings Centre Report*. August 1983, pp. 34-9

Baumeister, Roy: 'Acid Rock: A Critical Reappraisal and Psychological Commentary', *Journal of Psychoactive Drugs*, 1984. 16 (4), pp 339-45

Beckley, Robert and Chalfant, H. Paul: 'Contrasting Images of Alcohol and Drug Use in Country and Rock Music', *Journal of Alcohol and Drug Education*, 1979, 25 (1). pp. 44- 51

Benson, Richard. 'Rave New World'. *The Guardian*, 21st May 1996

Berger, Monroe: 'Jazz Resistance to the Diffusion of a Culture Pattern', *Journal of Negro History*. 1947, 23, pp. 461-94

Brecher, Edward: 'The "Heroin Overdose" Mystery and Other Occupational hazards of Addiction'. Chapter in: Brecher, E (ed.), *Licit and Illicit Drugs: The Consumers' Union Report,* Boston, Mass.: Little, Brown 1972

Catholic Commission for Racial Justice: 'Rastafarians in Jamaica and Britain', Notes and Reports No. 10. January 1982

Corzine, Jay and Sherwood. Janis: 'The Occupational Orientations of Jazz Musicians: Some Recent Findings and a Re-examination of the Evidence', *Sociological Spectrum*, 1983, 3, pp. 317-37

Curry, Andrew: 'Drugs in Jazz and Rock Music', *Clinical Toxicology*, 1968, 1 (2), pp. 235-44

Dickson, Donald: 'Bureaucracy and Morality: an Organizational Perspective on a Moral Crusade', *Social Problems*, 1968, 16 (2), pp. 143-56

Douse, Mike: 'Contemporary Music, Drug Attitudes and Drug Behaviour, *Australian Journal of Social Issues*, 1973, 8 (1), pp. 74-80

Farren, Mick: 'Sex, Drugs and Rock 'n' Roll' *Home Grown*, Summer 1979, 1 (5), pp. 16-18, 39

Federal Communications Committee: 'Licensee Responsiblity to Review Records Before Their Broadcast', in: Coombs, Robert H. , Fry, Lincoln J, *et al* (eds) *Socialization in Drug Abuse* (Cambridge Mass. : Schenkman, 1976)

Gannon, Frank: 'Pot, Pop and Acid', *New Society*, 21 September 1967

Garon, Paul: 'If Blues was Reefers', *Living Blues*, Autumn 1970, 3, pp. 13-18

Gay, George, Elsenbaumer, Robbie et al: 'A Dash of M*A*S*H – the Zep and the Dead: Head to Head', *Journal of Psychedelic* Drugs, 1972, 5 (2), pp. 193-203

Gay, George: 'You've Come a Long Way, Baby! Coke Time for the New American Lady of the Eighties', *Journal of Psychoactive Drugs*, 1981, 3 (4), pp 297-313

Hall, Stuart: The Hippies: an American Moment', Sub and Popular Culture Series Occasional Paper No. 16, Birmingham University, 1968

Hamid, Ansley, 'The decline of crack use in New York City: drug policy or natural controls?'. *International Journal of Drug Policy* 2, (5), p. 26-28

Hebdige, Dick: 'The Style of the Mods', Sub and Popular Culture Series Occasional Paper No. 20, Birmingham University, 1974

Hopkins, Jerry: 'Cocaine: a Flash in the Pan, a Pain in the Nose', *Rolling Stone*, 29 April 1971, pp. 1-6

Hopkins, Jerry: 'Cocaine Consciousness: the Gourmet Trip', *Journal of Popular Culture*, 1975. 9 (2), pp. 305-14

Kane, Joe: 'Dope Lyrics – the Secret Language of Rock', *High Times*

Lauderdale, Pat and Inverarity, James: 'Regulation of Opiates', *Journal of Drug Issues*, Summer 1984, pp. 567-77

Leech, Kenneth: 'Amphetamine Abuse', Evidence to the Advisory Committee on Drug Dependence, 1969 (unpublished)

Lyle, George: 'Dangerous Drug Traffic in London', *British Journal of Addiction*, 1953, 50, pp. 47-55

MacNamara, Brooks: The Medicine Show Log: Reconstructing a Traditional American Entertainment', *Drama Review*, Fall 1984, 28 (3)

Malyon, Tim: 'Just Another Cash Crop? The Cannabis Market Present and Future,' *Ecologist,* 1980, 10 (8/9), pp. 293-9

Margolis, Norman: 'A Theory on the Psychology of Jazz', *American Imago*, 1954, *11*, pp. 264-91

Melly, George: 'A Jazzman's View of Dope', *Home Grown*, 1979, 1 (5), pp. 20-2

Merriam, A. P. and Mack, R. W: 'The Jazz Community', *Social Forces*, 1960, 25, pp. 211-22

Newcombe, R.
  Monitoring and surveillance of Quadrant Park nightclub, September to November 1991. Report to Spencer Leisure.
  Raving and Dance Drugs: House music clubs and parties in North-West England 1991

Pharchem Newsletter: 'The Nation's Toughest Drug Law: Evaluating the New York Experience', *Pharchem Newsletter*, 1978, 7 (10) pp. 1-3. 7-9

Post, William and McGrath, James: 'Potents and Potions – Precursors to Modern Drug Use and Abuse', *Journal of Drug Issues*, 1972, 2. pp. 50-6

Preble, Edward and Casey, John: 'Taking Care of Business – the Heroin User's Life on the Street'. *International Journal of the Addictions*, 1969, 4 (1), pp. 1-24

Robinson, John and Pilskaln, Robert *et al* 'Protest Rock and Drugs', *Journal of Communications*, 1976, 26 (4), pp. 125-36

Schwartz, Elaine and Feinglass, S.J. *et al*: 'Popular Music and Drug Lyrics: Analysis of a Scapegoat'. in: *US National Commission on Marijuana and Drug Abuse*. Vol. II (Washington: USGPO. 1973) pp. 718-46

Seymour, Richard: 'The Chemical Muse'. *Street Pharmacologist*, 1982, 5 (6) pp. 5-7, 14-17

Shapiro, Harry: 'Singin' the Blues on Reds', *Home Grown*, 1980,1(8) pp. 29-33

Siegel, Shepard: 'Pavlovian conditioning and Heroin Overdose: Reports by Overdose Victims', *Bulletin of the Psychonomic Society*, 1984, 22 (5). pp. 428-30

Sluman, Larry: 'Copping – Stories from a lifetime of Getting High on the Road by Michael Bloomfield as Told to Larry Sloman', *High Times*, June 1983, pp. 42-5, 66-7, 93

Smith, David and Luce, John *et al*: 'The Health of Haight Ashbury'. *TransAction*, 1970, 7 (6), pp. 35-45

Smith, Roger: 'Status Politics and the Image of the Addict', Issues in *Criminology*, 1966, 2 (2), pp. 157-75

Spear, H.B. : 'The Growth of Heroin Addiction in the United Kingdom', *British Journal of Addiction*, 1969, 64, pp. 245-55

Spencer, Neil: 'The Ja Connection', *New Musical Express*, 16 October 1976

Sutter, Alan: 'The World of the Righteous Dope Fiend', Issues in *Criminology* 1966, 2 (2) pp. 77-222

Swenson, John: 'Peter Tosh Captured: Dread or Alive', *High Times*, November 1981, p. 9

Taqi, S. : 'Approbation of Drug Usage in Rock and Roll Music', *Bulletin on Narcotics*, 1969, 21 (4) pp. 29-35

Tosh, Peter: 'Rasta, Reggae and Ganja', *Home Grown*, Summer 1979, *1* (5)

Winick, Charles: 'How High the Moon – Jazz and Drugs', *Antioch Review*, Spring 1961, pp. 53-68

Winick, Charles and Nyswander, Marie: 'Psychotherapy of Successful Musicians Who are Drug Addicts', *American Journal of Orthopsychiatry*, 1961, *31*, pp. 622-36

Winick, Charles: 'The Use of Drugs by Jazz Musicians'. *Social Problems*, 1959, 7, pp. 240-53

Books

Abel, Ernest L. : *Marijuana – the First Twelve Thousand Years* (New York: Plenum Press, 1980)

Aerosmith with Davis, Stephen: *Walk This Way: the autobiography of Aerosmith* (New York: Avon Books, 1997)

Albertson, Chris: *Bessie* (London: Barrie & Jenkins, 1972)

Algren, Nelson: *The Man with the Golden Arm* (New York: Doubleday, 1949)

Allsop, Kenneth: *The Bootleggers: The Story of Chicago's Prohibition Era* (London: Hutchinson, 1961)

Anslinger, Harry J. and Ousler, Will: *The Murderers: The Story of The Narcotics Gangs* (New York: Farrar, Strauss and Cudady, 1961)

Ashley, Richard: *Cocaine: Its History, Use and Effects* (New York: St . Martins Press, 1975)

Auld, John: *Marijuana and Social Control* (London: Academic Press, 1981)

Austin, Gregory (ed.): *Perspectives on the History of Psychoactive Drug Use* (Rockville, Md: National Institute on Drug Abuse, 1978)

Bakalar, James and Grinspoon, Lester: *Drug Control in a Free Society*, (Cambridge: Cambridge University Press. 1984}

Becker, Howard: *The Outsiders: Studies in the Sociology of Deviance* (New York: Free Press, 1963)

Bennett, H. Stith: *On Becoming a Rock Musician* (Amherst, Mass: University of Massachusetts Press, 1980)

Benson, Richard ed: *Night Fever: Club Writing in The Face 1980-1997* (London: Boxtree, 1997)

Berridge, Virginia and Edwards, G: *Opium and the People Opiate Use in 19th-century England* (London: Allen Lane, 1981)

Block, A.A. and Chambliss,W.J. : *Organizing Crime* (NewYork: Elsevier,1981)

Blum, Richard: *Society and Drugs* (San Francisco: Mosey Bass, 1969)

Bockris, Victor and Malanga Gerard: *Up-tight: The Velvet Underground Story* (London: Omnibus, 1983)

Bonnie, Richard J and Whitehead, Charles H. *The Marijuana Conviction: A History of Marijuana Prohibition in the United States* (Charlottesville, Va. : University Press of Virginia, 1974)

Boot, Adrian and Thomas, Michel: *Jamaica: Babylon on a Thin Wire* (London: Thames & Hudson, 1976)

Boot, Adrian and Goldman, Vivian: *Bob Marley: Soul Rebel – Natural Mystic* (London: Eel Pie, 1981)

Brake, Michael: *Comparative Youth Culture* (London: Paul, 1985) .

Brown, Peter and Gaines, Steven: *The Love You Make: An Insider's Story of the Beatles* (London: Pan, 1984)

Buerkle, Jack V. and Barker, Danny: *Bourbon Street Black: The New Orleans Black Jazz Man* (Oxford: Oxford University Press, 1973)

Burchill, Julie and Parsons, Tony: *The Boy Looked at Johnny: The Obituary of Rock and Roll* (London: Pluto Press, 1978)

Burchill, Julie: *Damaged Gods* (London: Century, 1986)

Cable, Michael: *The Pop Industry Inside Out* (London: W.H. Allen, 1977)

Campbell, Horace: *Rasta and Resistance: from Marcus Garvey to Walter Rodney* (London: Hansrib. 1985)

Card, Richard and Ward, Richard: *The Criminal Justice and Public Order Act 1994.* (London: Jordans, 1994)

Carr, Ian: *Miles Davis: A Critical Biography* (London: Quartet, 1982)

Carroll, Peter and Noble, David: *The Free and the Unfree: A New History of the United States* (Harmondsworth: Penguin, 1977)

Caserta, Peggy and Knapp, Dan: *Going Down with Janis* (New Jersey: Lyle Stuart, 1973)

Cash, Johnny: *The Man in Black* (London: Hodder and Stoughton, 1975)

Cashmore, Ernest: *Rastaman: The Rastafarian Movement in England* (London: Unwin, 1983)

Chambers, Ian: *Urban Rhythms: Pop Music and Popular Culture* (London: Macmillan, 1985)

Chapple, Steve and Garofalo, Reebee: *Rock n Roll is Here to Pay* (Chicago: Nelson-Hall, 1977)

Charles, Ray and Ritz, David: *Brother Ray: Ray Charles' Own Story* (London: Macdonald & Jane, 1978)

Charters, Sam: *The Legacy of the Blues* (London: Calder & Boyars 1975)

Chilton, John: *Billie's Blues: The True Story of the Immortal Billie Holiday* (London Quartet, 1975)

Clarke, Sebastian: *Jah Music: The Evolution of the Popular Jamaican Song* (London: Heinemann, 1980)

Clarke, Steve (Comp.): *The Who in Their Own Words* (London: Omnibus,1979)

Cohn, Nik: *Pop from the Beginning* (London: Weidenfeld & Nicolson, 1969)

Coleman; Ray: *Survivor The Authorized Biography of Eric Clapton* (London: Sidgwick & Jackson, 1985)

Collin, Matthew: *Altered State: the Story of Ecstasy Culture and Acid House.* (London: Serpent's Tail, 1997)

Cook, Bruce: *Listen to the Blues* (London: Robson Books, 1975)

Cornwell, Hugh: *Inside Information* (London: Stranglers Information Service, 1980)

Courtwright, David: *Dark Paradise: Opiate Addiction in America Before 1940* (Cambridge, Mass. : Harvard University Press, 1982)

Cox, Barry and Shirley, John et al: *The Fall of Scotland Yard* (Harmondsworth: Penguin, 1977)

Davis, Clive and Willwerth, J. *Clive: Inside the Record Business* (New York: William Morrow, 1975)

Davis, Stephen: *Bob Marley* (London: Arthur Barker, 1983)

Davis, Stephen and Simon, Peter: *Reggae Bloodlines: In Search of the Music and Culture of Jamaica* (London: Heinemann, 1979)

Dowley, Tim and Dunnage, Barry: *Bob Dylan: from a Hard Rain to a Slow Train* (Midas, 1982)

Epstein, Edward Jay: *Agency of Fear: Opiates and Political Power in America* (New York: Putnam, 1977)

Erenberg, Lewis A: *Steppin' Out: New York Nightlife and the Transformation of American Culture 1890-1930* (Chicago: University of Chicago Press, 1981)

Fernando, S.H. *The New Beats: Exploring the Music Cultures and Attitudes of Hip-Hop* (Edinburgh: Payback Press, 1994)

Fong-Torres, Ben (ed.): *The Rolling Stone Rock 'n' Roll Reader* (New York: Bantam, 1974)

Freemantle, Brian: *The Fix* (London: Michael Joseph 1985)

Friedman, Myra: *Buried Alive: The Biography of Janis Joplin* (New York: Bantam, 1974)

Gillespie, Dizzy and Fraser, Al: *Dizzy To Be or Not to Bop* (London: W.H. Allen, 1980)

Gleason, Ralph: *The Jefferson Airplane and the San Francisco Sound* (New York: Ballantine, 1969)

Goldman, Albert: *Elvis* (Harmondsworth: Penguin, 1982)

Goldman, Albert: *Grass Roots: Marijuana in America Today* (New York: Harper & Row, 1979)

Gorman, Clem: *Backstage Rock* (London: Pan, 1978)

Gray, Michael: *The Art of Bob Dylan* (London: Hamlyn, 1981)

Green, Shirley: *Rachman* (London: Michael Joseph, 1969)

Greenfield, Robert: *A Journey Through America with the Rolling Stones* (London: Panther, 1975)

Grime, Kitty: *Jazz Voices* (London: Quartet, 1983)

Harrison, Hank: *The Grateful Dead* (Star Books, 1973)

Hawes, Hampton and Asher, Don: *Raise Up Off Me: A Portrait of Hampton Hawes* (New York: Da Capo, 1979)

Hebdige, Dick: *Subculture: The Meaning of Style* (London: Methuen, 1979)

Helmer, John: *Drugs and Minority Oppression* (New York: Seabury Press, 1975)

Henman, Anthony *et al Big Deal: The Politics of the Illicit Drugs Business* (London: Pluto Press, 1985)

Hentoff, Nat: *The Jazz Life* (London: Peter Davies, 1962)

Herman, Gary: *Rock n Roll Babylon* (London: Plexus 1982)

Himmelstein, Jerome L. *The Strange Career of Marijuana: Politics and Ideology of Drug Control in America* (London: Greenwood Press, 1983)

Holiday, Billie and Dufty, William: *Lady Sings the Blues* (New York: Doubleday, 1956)

Hollingshead, Michael: *The Men Who Turned on the World* (London: Blond & Briggs, 1973)

Hopkins, Jerry: *Elvis: The Final Years* (London: Omnibus, 1981)

Hunter, Ian: *Diary of a Rock n Roll Star* (London: Panther, 1975)

Inglis. Brian: *The Forbidden Game: A Social History of Drugs* (London: Hodder & Stoughton, 1975)

Jackson, Blair: *Grateful Dead: The Music Never Stopped* (London: Plexus, 1983)

Jones, Max and Chilton, John: *Louis: The Louis Armstrong Story 1900-1971* (London: Studio Vista 1971)

Joynson, Vernon: *The Acid Trip: A Complete Guide to Psychedelic Music* (Todmorden, Lancs: Babylon Books, 1984)

Kaplan, John: *Marijuana: The New Prohibition* (New York: The World Publishing Company, 1970)

Kelleher, Maureen et al: *Drugs and Society: A Critical Reader* (Dubuque, Iowa: Kendall/Hunt, 1983)

Kennedy, Joseph: *Coca Exotica: The Illustrated History of Cocaine* (New York: Cornwall, 1985)

Kerouac, Jack: *On the Road* (Harmondsworth: Penguin. 1976)

King, Rufus: *The Drug Hang-up: America's Fifty-year Folly* (New York-W. W. Norton, 1972)

Knoedelseder, William: *Stiffed: A True Story of MCA, The Music Business and the Mafia.* (New York: Harper/Perennial, 1994)

Kohn, Marek: *Dope Girls.* (London: Lawrence and Wishart, 1992)

Kooper, Al and Edmonds, Ben: *Backstage Passes Rock n Roll Life in the Sixties* (New York: Stem & Day, 1977)

Lacker, Marty *et al*: *Elvis: Portrait of a Friend* (New York: Bantam, 1980)

Latimer, Dean and Goldberg, Jeff: *Flowers in the Blood: The Story of Opium* (New York: Franklin Watts, 1981)

Laurie, Peter: *Drugs: Medical Psychological and Social Facts* (Harmondsworh: Penguin, 1974)

Lee, Martin, and Schlain, Bruce: *Acid Dreams* (New York: Grove Press, 1985)

Leech, Kenneth: *Keep the Faith Baby* (London: SPCK, 1973)

Leonard, Neil: *Jazz and the White Americans: The Acceptance of a New Art Form* Chicago: University of Chicago Press. 1962)

Levine, L.W.: *Black Culture and Black Consciousness* (Oxford: Oxford University Press, 1977)

Lomax, Alan: *Mister Jelly Roll*, 2nd ed. (Berkeley: University of California Press, 1973)

Lusane, Clarence: *Pipe Dream Blues: racism and the war on drugs.* (Boston, Mass: South End Press, 1991)

McKnight, Cathy and Tobler, John: *Bob Marley: The Roots of Reggae* (London: Star, 1977)

McNamara, Brooks: *Step Right up* (New York: Doubleday, 1976)

McNeal, Violet: *Four White Horses and a Brass Band* (New York: Doubleday, 1947)

McNicoll, Andre: *Drug Trafficking: A North-South Perspective* (Ottawa: North-South Institute, 1983)

Mailer, Norman: *The White Negro* (San Francisco: City Lights Books, 1970)

Marsh, Dave: *Before I Get Old: The Story of the Who* (London: Plexus, 1983)

Mezzrow, Milton and Wolfe, Bernard: *Really the Blues* (New York: Random House, 1946)

Middles, Mick:
    Shaun Ryder. (London: Independent Music Press, 1997)
    *From Joy Division to New Order: The Factory Story (*London: Virgin, 1996)

Mingus, Charles: *Beneath the Underdog* (Harmondsworth: Penguin, 1975)

Morris, Ronald L.: *Wait Until Dark: Jazz and the Underworld 1880-1940* (Bowling Green, Ohio: Bowling Green University Popular Press, 1980)

Musto, David: *The American Disease: The Origins of Narcotic Control* (New Jersey: Yale University Press, 1973)

Napier-Bell, Simon: *You Don't Have to Say You Love Me* (London: New English Library, 1982)

Nelli, Humbert, S.: *The Business of Crime: Italian and Syndicate Crime in the United States* (Oxford: Oxford University Press, 1976)

Neville, Richard: *Playpower* (London: Paladin, 1971)

Norman, Philip: *The Stones* (London: Elm Tree, 1984)

Nuttall, Jeff: *Bomb Culture* (MacGibbon & Kee, 1968)

O'Day, Anita and Eells, George: *High Times, Hard Times* (London: Corgi, 1983)

Oliver, Paul: *Songsters and Saints* (Cambridge: Cambridge University Press, 1984)

Ostransky, Leroy: *Jazz City: The Impact of Our Cities on the Development of Jazz* (New Jersey: Prentice-Hall, 1978)

Palmer, Tony: *All You Need is Love* (London Futura, 1977)

Parssinen, Terry: *Secret Passions, Secret Remedies: Narcotic Drugs in British Society 1820-1930* (Manchester: Manchester University Press, 1933)

Peebles, Andy: *The Lennon Tapes* (London BBC, 1981)

Peele, Stanton and Brodsky, Archie: *Love and Addiction* (New York Taplinger, 1975)

Peele, Stanton: *The Meaning of Addiction: Compulsive Experience and Its Interpretation* (Lexington, Mass: Lexington Books, 1985)

Penman, Ian: *Vital signs: music, movies and other manias.* (London: Serpents Tail, 1998)

Pepper, Art and Pepper, Laurie: *Straight Life* (London: Collier Macmillan, 1979)

Phillips, Joel and Wynne, Ronald: *Cocaine: The Mystique and the Reality* (New York: Avon Books, 1980)

Pichaske, David: *A Generation in Motion: Popular Music and Culture in the Sixties* (London Macmillan 1979)

Pryce, Ken: *Endless Pressure: A Study of West Indian Lifestyles in Bristol* (Harmondsworth: Penguin, 1979)

Ramone, Dee Dee: *Poison Heart: Surviving The Ramones* (London: Firefly, 1997)

Reinarman, Craig and Levine, Harry eds: *Crack in America: demon drugs and social justice.* (Berkeley, University of California Press, 1997)

Reisner, Robert: *Bird: The Legend of Charlie Parker* (London: Quartet, 1974)

Reynolds, Simon: *Energy Flash: A Journey Through Rave Music and Dance Culture* (London: Picador, 1998)

Ritz, David: *Divided Soul: The Life of Marvin Gaye* (London: Michael Joseph,1985)

Robb, John: *The Stone Roses and the Resurrection of British Pop* (London: Ebury Press, 1997)

Rolling Stone: Rock Almanac: The Chronicles of Rock Music (London: Macmillan, 1983)

Rosenbaum, Marsha: *Women on Heroin* (New Brunswick, NJ: Rutgers University Press, 1981)

Rubin, Vera and Comitas, Lambros: *Ganja in Jamaica* (Amsterdam: Mouton, 1975)

Russell, Ross *Bird Lives!* (London: Quartet, 1973)

Sanchez, Tony: *Up and Down with the Rolling Stones* (New York William Morrow, 1979)

Sander, Ellen: *Trips: Rock Life in the Sixties* (New York: Scribner, 1973)

Saunders, Nicholas: *Ecstasy and the Dance Culture* revised as *Ecstasy Reconsidered* (London: Nicholas Saunders 1995/97)

Scaduto, Anthony: *Bob Dylan* (London Abacus, 1972)

Scullatti, Gene and Seay, Davin *San Francisco Nights: The Psychedelic Music Trip* (London: Sidgwick and Jackson, 1985)

Shapiro, Harry: *Just a Crazy Dream: The Life of Graham Bond* (London: Guinness)

Shapiro, Harry: *Slowhand The Story of Eric Clapton* (London: Proteus, 1984)

Shaw, Arnold: *52nd Street: The Street of Jazz* (New York Da Capo, 1971)

Sidran, Ben: *Black Talk* (New York: Da Capo, 1971)

Silver, Gary (ed.): *The Dope Chronicles 1850-1950* (San Francisco Harper & Row, 1979)

Sloman, Larry: *Reefer Madness: The History of Marihuana in America* (New York: Bobbs-

Mernil, 1979)

Small, Geoff: *Ruthless: The Global Rise of the Yardies* (London: Warner Books, 1995)

Stallings, Penny: *Rock 'n' Roll Confidential* (London Vermillion. 1984)

Starks, Michael: *Cocaine Fiends and Reefer Madness: An Illustrated History of Drugs in the Movies* (New York: Cornwall Books, 1982)

Stein, Jean Edie: *The Life and Times of Andy Warhol's Superstar* (London Panther, 1984)

Taylor, Arthur: *Notes and Tones: Musician-to-Musician Interviews* (London: Quartet, 1983)

Tendler, Steward and May, David: *The Brotherhood of Eternal Love* (London: Panther, 1984)

Titon, Jeff: *Early Downhome Blues* (University of Illinois Press, 1977)

Toll, Robert C: *Blacking up: The Minstrel Show in Nineteenth-century America* (New York: Oxford University Press, 1974)

Tosches, Nick: *Hellfire: The Jerry Lee Lewis Story* (London: Plexus, 1982)

Trebach, Arnold: *The Heroin Solution* (New Haven: Yale University Press, 1982)

Turner, Steve: *Conversations with Eric Clapton* (London: Abacus, 1976)

Tyler, Andrew: *Street Drugs* (London: New English Library, 1986)

Wailer, Maurice and Calabrese, Anthony: *Fats Waller* (London: Cassell, 1977)

Whitcomb, Ian: *After the Ball* (London: Allen Lane, 1972)

White, Armond: *Rebel for the Hell of It: the Life of Tupac Shakur.* (London: Quartet Books, 1997)

White, Charles: *The Life and Times of Little Richard* (London Pan, 1984)

White, Timothy: *Catch a Fire: The Life of Bob Marley* (London: Elm Tree, 1983)

Whitney, Malika and Hussey, Dermott: *Bob Marley: Reggae King of the Word* (London: Plexus 1984)

Williams, Terry

   The Cocaine Kids. (Reading, Mass, Addison-Wesley, 1989)

   *Crackhouse:notes from the end of the line. (*Reading, Mass, Addison-Wesley, 1992)

Winstanley, Russ and Nowell, David: *Soul Survivors: the Wigan Casino Story* (London: Robson Books, 1996)

Wolfe, Tom: *The Electric Kool-aid Acid Test* (London: Weidenfeld & Nicolson,

Young, James: *The Toadstool Millionaires: A Social History of Patent Medicines in America before Federal Regulation* (Princeton, NJ: Princeton University Press, 1961)

Young, James: *Nico: Songs They Never Play on the Radio* (London: Arrow, 1994)

INDEX

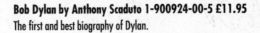

Available From Helter Skelter Publishing

Bob Dylan by Anthony Scaduto 1-900924-00-5 £11.95
The first and best biography of Dylan.

"Scaduto's 1971 book was the pioneering portrait of this legendarily elusive artist. Now in a welcome reprint it's a real treat to read the still-classic Bobography". **Paul Du Noyer, Q*****

"Superb on the Greenwich Village scene, insightful on the meaning of John Wesley Harding ... it's still perhaps the best book ever written on Dylan".
Peter Doggett, *Record Collector*

XTC - The Exclusive Authorised Story Behind the Music
by XTC and Neville Farmer
ISBN: 1 900924 03 X   306 pages (illustrated). UK £12.00
Co-written by one of the most popular - and usually reclusive - cult bands of all time, this book is timed to coincide with their long-awaited new album.
"A cheerful celebration of the minutiae surrounding XTC's music with the band's musical passion intact. It's essentially a band-driven project for the fans, high in setting-the-record-straight anecdotes. The personality of Partridge dominates this book as it does XTC's music. Superbright, funny, commanding." **MOJO**

Back To The Beach - A Brian Wilson and the Beach Boys Reader
edited by Kingley Abbott 1-900924-02-1 £12.99
A collection of the best articles about Brian and the band, together with a number of previously unpublished pieces and some specially commissioned work. Features Nick Kent, David Leaf, Timothy White and others with a foreword by Brian.
"A detailed study and comprehensive overview of the BB's lives and music. Most impressively Abbott manages to appeal to both die-hard fans and rather less obsessive newcomers." **Time Out**
"Rivetting!" **** **Q Magazine**

Born In The USA - Bruce Springsteen and the American Tradition
by Jim Cullen 1-900924-05-6 £9.99

The first major study of Bruce Springsteen's that looks at his music in the context of his blue collar roots, and his place in American culture

"Cullen has written an excellent treatise expressing exactly how and why Springsteen translated his uneducated hicktown American-ness into music and stories that touched hearts and souls all around the world." **Q*****
"This is a provocative look at one of America's cultural icons." **Newsweek**

Available From Helter Skelter Publishing

Like The Night -
Bob Dylan and the Road to the Manchester Free Trade Hall.
ISBN: 1 900924 07 2   192 pages (illustrated). UK £12.00
The full history and background to the show that would become Bob Dylan's latest album, the most famous bootleg in history, now The Bootleg Series vols 4 and 5.
"When Dylan went electric, he both alienated the audience that had championed him and changed the face of rock music.
Lee's enjoyable and atmospheric reconstruction of this phase of Dylan's career is essential reading." **Uncut Magazine**
"CP Lee was there, but the point is that he can put you there too". **Greil Marcus**

GET BACK: The Beatles' Let It Be Disaster
by Doug Sulphy and Ray Schweighhardt
ISBN: 1 900924 12 9   256 pages   UK £12.99
A detailed document of the group's breakdown seen through the prism of the Get Back recording sessions. Instead of making the planned new album, the greatest band in the world were falling apart.

"One of the most poignant Beatles books ever." **Patrick Humphries, MOJO**
"Monumental... Fascinating and revealing" **Goldmine**

Solo: A Biography of Sandy Denny by Pamela Winters
Due in August. 256 pages,   ISBN 1 900924 11 0   Price: £12.99
Sandy Denny became famous as the distinctive singer Fairport Convention, and later with Fotheringay, as well as releasing four highly acclaimed solo albums. Melody Maker voted her best female singer in 1970 and 1971. But like many of the great musical artists of the seventies, she took refuge in drink and drugs. Sandy Denny died 20 years ago in mysterious circumstances, and this is the first ever Biography. US music journalist Pam Winters has had unprecedented access to Sandy's personal papers. She has interviewed at length all those who were close to her, to produce an illuminating portrait of one of the great English singers.

A Journey Through America With The Rolling Stones
by Robert Greenfield   1-900924-01-3   £12.00
Definitive insider's account of the Stones' legendary 1972 US tour.

"Greenfield is afforded extraordinary access to the band... drugs... groupies. In all, it's a graphic if headache inducing document of strange days indeed".
Tom Doyle, Q**

"Sure, I was completely mad. I go crazy."
Mick Jagger

Available From Firefly Publishing

an association between Helter Skelter and SAF Publishing

**Poison Heart - Surviving The Ramones by Dee Dee Ramone
and Veronica Kofman**   ISBN: 0946 719 19 5
192 pages (illustrated). UK £11.95
A crushingly honest account of his life as a junkie and a Ramone.
*"One of THE great rock and roll books...this is the true, awesome voice of The
Ramones".* **Q magazine** *****
*"His story - knee deep in sex, drugs and rock and roll - is too incedent packed to
be anything less than gripping".* **Mojo**
"A powerful work that is both confessional and exorcising" **Time Out.**

Minstrels In The Gallery - A History of Jethro Tull by David Rees
ISBN: 0 946719 22 5   224 pages (illustrated) - UK £12.99
At Last! To coincide with their 30th anniversary, a full history of one of the most
popular and inventive bands of the past three decades. Born out of the British
blues boom, Jethro Tull sped to worldwide success and superstardom - the band
were one of the biggest grossing acts of the seventies. With LPs like
Aqualung,Thick As A Brick and *Passion Play*, Anderson mutated from the wild-eyed
tramp through flute wielding minstrel to the country squire of rock n' roll.
*"Rees has interviewed all the key players and told the Tull tale with zest and
candour. A fine read for Tull fans and non-believers alike."* **MOJO**

**DANCEMUSICSEXROMANCE - Prince: The First Decade
by Per Nilsen**   ISBN: 0946 719 23 3
256 pages approx (illustrated). UK £12.99
For many years Per Nilsen has been a foremost authority on Prince. In this
in-depth study of the man and his music, he assesses the years prior to the change
of name to a symbol - a period which many consider to be the most productive
and musically satisfying. Through interview material with many ex-band members
and friends Nilsen paints a portrait of Prince's reign as the most exciting black
performer to emerge since James Brown. In this behind the scenes documentary
we get to the heart and soul of a funk maestro.

Coming Soon from Firefly:

Soul Survivor - A History of Santana by Simon Lang -192 pages, ISBN 0946719 29 2, UK Price £12.99
The first full biography of the band who first incorporated Latin rythms into rock, led by guitar legend Carlos Santana.

Opening The Musical Box - A History of Genesis by Alan Hewitt - 192 pages, ISBN 0946719 ** *,
Price £12.99, A complete illustrated biography of Genesis - includes all current and ex-band members & discography.

Manic Street Preachers biography by Ben Roberts - due early next year!

All Helter Skelter titles can be ordered direct from the world famous Helter Skelter music bookstore which is situated at:
Helter Skelter, 4 Denmark Street, London WC2H 8LL
Tel: +44 (0) 171 836 1151   Fax: +44 (0) 171 240 9880.
Consult our website at: http://www.skelter.demon.co.uk
This store has the largest collection of music books anywhere in the world and can supply any in-print title by mail to
any part of the globe. For a mail order catalogue or for wholesaling enquiries, please contact us.